£17·50

C000204122

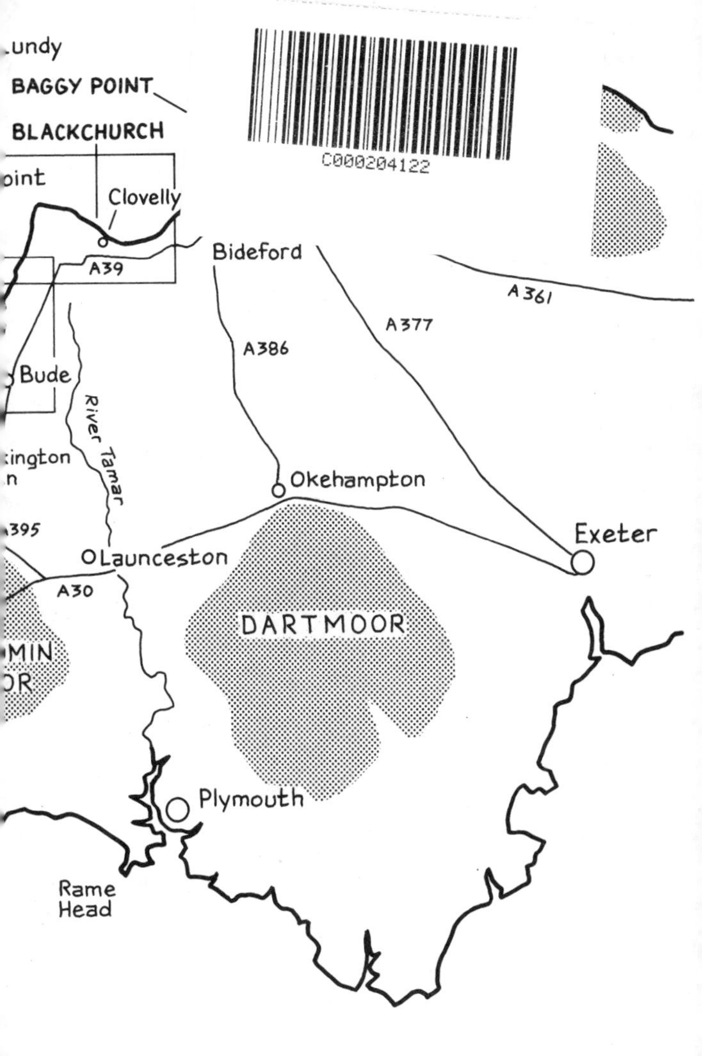

Emma Smith

07746 948536

BREW
2000

Climbers' Club Guides

Edited by John Willson

North Devon and Cornwall

by

David Hope (Baggy Point and The Atlantic Coast)

and

Brian Wilkinson (The Culm Coast)

Artwork by **Don Sargeant**

Front Cover: Dave Turnbull on the first ascent of *Bugsy* (E5), Maer Cliff
Photo: Chris Rees

Rear Cover: David Hope and James Cornwell on *Turk* (E2) at Pentire
Photo: Ian Parnell

Frontispiece: Cow and Calf
Drawing: Brian Wilkinson

Reverse Frontispiece: Stormy Seas in Backways Cove
Photo: Dave Turnbull

Published by The Climbers' Club

Rock Climbing in Devonshire (RNMC 1966)
by Bob Moulton

Climbing in Cornwall (1973)
by Toni Carver, Pete Stanier, and Pat Littlejohn

Devon Rock Climbs (RN&RMMC 1978)
by Bob Moulton

North Cornwall – Interim Guide (CC 1982)
by Pete O'Sullivan

North Devon and Cornwall – First Edition (The Climbers' Club 1988)
by Iain Peters

North Devon and Cornwall – Second Edition (The Climbers' Club 2000)
by David Hope and Brian Wilkinson

Hope, David Wilkinson, Brian North Devon and Cornwall
(Climbers' Club Guides)

British Library Cataloguing in Publication Data

A catalogue record for this book is available from the British Library

796.552

ISBN 0-901-601-62-4

Typeset by the editor
Produced by The Ernest Press, Glasgow G46 6AQ
Distributed by Cordee, 3a de Montfort Street, Leicester LE1 7HD

Contents

Maps and Diagrams

Climbers' Club Guides

The Climbers' Club

The publisher of this guidebook is The Climbers' Club, which was founded in 1898 from origins in Snowdonia and is now one of the foremost mountaineering clubs in Great Britain. Its objects are to encourage mountaineering and rock-climbing, and to promote the general interest of mountaineers and the mountain environment.

It is a truly national club with widespread membership, and currently owns huts in Cornwall, Pembrokeshire, Derbyshire, and Snowdonia. Besides managing six huts, The Climbers' Club produces an annual Journal and runs a full programme of climbing meets, dinners, and social events. Club members may also use the huts of other clubs through reciprocal arrangements. The Club publishes climbing guidebooks (currently 18 in number) to cover most of Wales and Southern England. The Club is a founder-member of, and is affiliated to, the British Mountaineering Council; it makes annual contributions to the BMC's Access Fund, as well as to volunteer cliff and mountain rescue organizations. In 1999, the Climbers' Club Colin Kirkus Guidebook Fund was established as a means of distributing some of the profits earned from guidebooks to assist climbing-related projects that are in keeping with the aims of the Club, though they need not be confined to the Club's guidebook areas.

Membership fluctuates around 1,000, and at present there are no limits on growth. Members of two years' standing may propose a competent candidate for membership and, provided that adequate support is obtained from other members, the Committee may elect him or her to full membership; there is no probationary period.

Climbing Style

The following policy statement on climbing style was agreed in principle at The Climbers' Club Annual General Meeting on 25th February 1990:

The Climbers' Club supports the tradition of using natural protection and is opposed to actions which are against the best interest of climbers and users of the crags. This applies particularly to irreversible acts which could affect the crags and their environs.

Such acts could include: the placing of bolts on mountain and natural crags; retrospective placing of bolts; chiselling, hammering, or altering the rock appearance or structure; excessive removal of vegetation and interference with trees, flowers, and fauna.

The Climbers' Club policy is that guidebooks are written to reflect the best style matched to the ethos and traditions of British Climbing.

Guidebook Disclaimer

This guide attempts to provide a definitive record of all existing climbs and is compiled from information from a variety of sources. The inclusion of any route does not imply that it remains in the condition described. Climbs can change unpredictably: rock can deteriorate and the existence and condition of *in-situ* protection can alter. All climbers must rely on their own ability and experience to gauge the difficulty and seriousness of any climb. Climbing is an inherently dangerous activity.

Neither The Climbers' Club nor the authors and editor of this guidebook accept any liability whatsoever for any injury or damage caused to climbers, third parties, or property arising from the use of it. Whilst the content of the guide is believed to be accurate, no responsibility is accepted for any error, omission, or mis-statement. Users must rely on their own judgement and are recommended to insure against injury to person and property and third party risks.

The inclusion in this guidebook of a crag or routes upon it does not mean that any member of the public has a right of access to the crag or the right to climb upon it. Before climbing on any crag in this guidebook, please read the access notes on page 15.

Information

The definitive guidebooks published by the main climbing clubs are compiled and processed almost entirely by voluntary effort. In order to lighten the tasks just a little when they come round and to ensure greater accuracy and completeness of the result, as well as to disseminate information in the meantime, The Climbers' Club has recently taken a number of initiatives:

- Dave Viggers is the Club's co-ordinator for new-route information in South Wales and South-West England. Please send such information to him at Windale, 64 Park Grove, Henleaze, Bristol BS9 4LQ. Please ensure that the descriptions are as clear and complete as possible and that all the statistics are supplied.
- Jointly with the BMC SW&S Area, the Club last year published *Climb South West 1999*. This contained up-to-date crag access information for the whole South West, details of all the region's bolt policies, a selection of new routes, and addresses of various BMC and Club contacts. It is hoped that this will be the first of a probably biennial series.
- The Club's *Guidebook Authors' Manual* was rewritten in 1998 and sets out fully the tasks and levels of commitment involved, not only for authors but also for anyone interested in helping with research, artwork, proof-reading, etc. Copies are free to Club members; others are asked to contribute £2 towards the cost of printing and postage.

Editor's Note & Acknowledgements

The coastline between Ilfracombe and St Ives Bay must, with the possible exception of some of the remotest Scottish Highlands and Islands, be one of the most difficult areas in Britain for which to produce a rock-climbing guidebook. Fortunate indeed, therefore, that its early explorers included such diligent, articulate, and objective chroniclers as Pat Littlejohn, Toni Carver, Alan Baker, and Pete O'Sullivan. Equally important, and of even greater significance for the wider climbing community, Bob Moulton began in 1966, with *Rock Climbing in Devonshire*, an intense involvement in guidebook production – as author, editor, and administrator, not to mention friend and fount of wisdom to those who aspire to follow – that after more than a third of a century must be and be likely to remain unparallelled.

Later, along came Iain Peters. Introduced to climbing while still in short trousers by his grandfather, Admiral Keith Lawder, the undoubted *doyen* of Devon climbing (the records show that he was involved in the most significant early ascents on the North Coast and The Dewerstone, as well as on Lundy), Peters was steeped in the area's ethos and folklore as no one else could be. Although he generously opined that, had Keith Darbyshire not been tragically killed in 1975, the latter would have been the obvious choice to write the first comprehensive guide to this coastline, it is difficult to believe that the 1988 guide could have been bettered – indeed, it is probable that only someone with Peters's inimitable sense of humour could have completed the Herculean task of drawing together all the disparate strands. Perhaps the greatest compliment to his achievement is the difficulty which the current authors have had in abandoning much of his original text (somewhat to my irritation at first, until I came to tidy up some of the ancillary sections and underwent the same experience).

The editor of that 1988 guide was David Hope, who subsequently found himself not unwillingly embroiled in collecting all new information in order to write the next edition himself. As the development of the Culm Coast took off in the early 90s, local climber Brian Wilkinson was drafted in to look after that section. Their mammoth efforts in checking and collating the quantities of sometimes unreliable and incomplete route-descriptions in locations often inhospitable and difficult of access must be accorded the highest praise.

The section on bouldering at Northcott Mouth was written and illustrated by Simon Young.

For information, encouragement, and help in a variety of forms, the authors themselves would like to thank: Rick Abbott, Clark Alston, James Cornwell, Martin Corbett, Martin Crocker, Mick Fowler, Andy Grieve, Nick Hancock, Sean Hawken, Dave Henderson, Ed Heslam, David Hillebrandt, Graham Hoey, Howard Lancashire, Pat Littlejohn, David Scott-Maxwell, Ian Parnell,

Tony Penning, Frank Ramsay, Derek Ryden, Pete O'Sullivan, Dave Turnbull, and Dave Viggers.

The editor would like especially to thank Nigel Coe, Martin Crocker, Bob Moulton, and Ian Parnell for reading all or very substantial sections of the script at various stages and providing much missing information and valuable comment; and Mike Vetterlein for his incomparably perceptive check of the typeset proofs.

Yet again, Don Sargeant has been responsible for providing to order maps, drawings, and photodiagrams of the highest quality. Some of the original drawing and photography was done for the 1988 guide, and Peters's tribute then is unsurpassable: '...the sight of a lonely figure in a canoe bobbing dangerously up and down in the teeth of an Atlantic gale, desperately trying to stay afloat, compose his pictures, and vomit – all at the same time.' However, all has been revised and up-dated, and the contribution of the authors in providing fresh photo-references and advising on the lines to be drawn must also be acknowledged.

We are very grateful to all who have submitted action photographs, especially: Rick Abbott, Graham Butler, Alan Cook, Martin Corbett, Steve Davies, Martin Doyle, Mick Fowler, Andy Grieve, Nick Hancock, David Hillebrandt, Mark Lee, Brian Lessware, Rich Mayfield, Tim Noble, Ian Parnell, Carl Ryan, Dave Turnbull, Simon Young.

Despite the huge increase in numbers of routes since 1988, this book appears little larger than its predecessor. There will, therefore, doubtless be those who complain that (amongst other things!) there are no lists of campsites, cafés, and local climbing walls; that the Coast's colourful history is less expansive than accounts in weightier tomes; and that the print-size of the First Ascents list is too small to read. They will be missing the point, or rather two points: first, that as this is an adventure climbing area *par excellence* the provision of too much incidental information would create unfounded illusions of comfort and security; and, second, that the book will have to be carried on the majority of the (mostly demanding) climbs – and the descents or approaches to them – herein.

However, the size has been contained mainly by the omission of three sections that were included in the 1988 book: the Exmoor Coast is to be documented fully in a separate guide by Martin Crocker and Terry Cheek to be published by the Club in 2001 or 2002; the South Cornish Coast from Mounts Bay (Penzance) to The Lizard will be included in the forthcoming double-volume guide to West Penwith (also Climbers' Club); while the remainder of Cornwall has been well covered in *Cheesewring and South-East Cornwall* by Sean Hawken (St Ives 1998).

JW Spring 2000

Introduction

This guidebook covers the North Devon and Cornwall coastline between Ilfracombe and St Ives Bay – a length of a hundred miles as the gull flies, but a lot more when you allow for every creek and zawn. With the exception of limestone, of which there is a surfeit elsewhere in South-West Britain, virtually every type of climbable rock can be found; though 'climbable' is used here subjectively, and certainly in its loosest sense.

The scenery is outstanding almost everywhere and ranges from the quiet wooded slopes bordering the Bristol Channel at Clovelly to the towering vertical cliffs overlooking the wild ocean breakers of the Atlantic Coast. The cliff-tops are traversed by the most impressive, absorbing, and demanding section of the South-West Coast Path, and are well-endowed with sites of considerable local historical interest and significance. Many of the crags rise directly from tidal boulder-beaches, constitute the dark walls of sea-filled zawns, or appear stranded in the middle of vast vegetated slopes; but conventional seaside attractions from sandy bathing-beaches to international surfing venues, not to mention pubs and cream-tea cafés, are never too far away.

Using any road atlas in combination with the front endpaper map and the area maps in this guide, out-of-county visitors will find it simple to work out the appropriate link roads to the coast from the A30 west of Exeter. However, those coming south on the M5 and making for the North Devon crags from Baggy Point to the Hartland area can take the A39 'scenic' north coast route to Barnstaple from junction 24 or the slightly more direct A361 from junction 27. Parking-places and approach paths are described under the crag introductions. Although the aim has been to make the guidebook largely self-sufficient, those who wish to visit some of the minor crags or explore in greater detail will find the following 1:50,000 Ordnance Survey Landranger maps useful:

- for Baggy Point, sheet 180;
- for the whole of the Culm and for the Atlantic Coast as far as Rocky Valley Zawn, sheet 190;
- for the Atlantic Coast from Bossiney Haven to The Miners' Cliff, sheet 200;
- for Cligga Head, sheet 204;
- for Carn Gowla and on down to Hell's Mouth, sheet 203.

For the specialist, the new Explorer series of 1:25,000 maps will be the choice, but a complete set would be inordinately expensive. However, the Ordnance Survey also publish a series of trail guides to the South West Coast Path. The first volume, sub-titled 'Minehead to Padstow', covers Baggy Point, the Culm Coast, and the Atlantic coast as far as Pentire (as well as, initially, the Exmoor Coast). The second volume, 'Padstow to Falmouth', continues south-west from Stepper Point and takes in the whole of West Penwith and The Lizard. These books contain 'key' maps for the link roads, and snippets of the 1:25,000 maps for the whole coastline, which show most of the cliffs and their approach paths. They are also ideal for rest days and family walks as well as providing much interesting and valuable local information

The seriousness of climbing on many of these crags cannot be over-stressed. Factors that must be taken account of include: the difficulties of approach and escape, lack of perspective from top or bottom, the tides, the extreme unpredictability of the rock, proneness of some areas to vegetation growth, and the deterioration of *in-situ* gear. An additional factor, but also *a result* of all the foregoing, is that the guide *cannot* be as accurate, detailed, and up-to-date as one to an area where the foot of every route can be easily walked to and/or the line abseiled down or top-roped at more or less any time, and where a good proportion of the routes have regular ascents, providing a fount of information for writers to draw upon. Many of the climbs herein, new and old, have not had a second ascent and even those that have may not have attracted a consensus of opinion. Thus, although the authors have made every effort to check and present clearly as much of the information as they can, its accuracy in all detail cannot be guaranteed. At least, some of the more extreme and seemingly wilful obfuscations of the 1988 guide have been clarified.

Grades

The standard system is used. But heed the warning that many routes have had few or no repeat ascents, and so not only the assessments of first ascensionists but also the absence of affecting factors since have to be relied upon. A few of the routes on the more esoteric rock-types defy rational assessment of an adjectival grade, and sometimes an E-number is abandoned in favour of the non-specific 'Extremely Severe' (without distinction between the 'Hard' and 'Mild' qualifications) – it is advisable always to assume that this approximates to a high rather than low E-number relative to the technical grades.

Stars

Here, too, the usual system is used, though stars in this area are as likely to relate to situation and exhilaration as to rock-quality, purity of line, or mere technical interest. An innovation is to print as hollow symbols the star-ratings allotted by first ascensionists on routes that have not been repeated. The principle of this is that authors make no attempt to moderate the assessment as a result of visual impression or the climber's reputation.

Conventions

Throughout the book the crags and the routes upon them are described from left to right, even where the normal or only approach is in the opposite direction. The terms 'left' and 'right' always apply as you face the crag unless the opposite is explicitly stated.

- The dagger symbol † shows that the route is not known to have had a second (on-lead) ascent.
- A double dagger †† indicates that the route is believed to have been affected by a rockfall to the extent that the grade and description given may no longer be accurate. The word 'rockfall' is here taken to mean anything from the loss of a hold to the collapse of an entire cliff (not an unknown occurrence on this coast!).
- Climbs affected by vegetation regrowth to a point that they may not be climbable at the given grade are given a ‡ symbol. This may indicate merely a recommendation to some prior cleaning or it may mean that the route is a lost cause. The star-ratings for routes so marked must be considered as potential only.
- Routes affected by a seasonal bird-nesting restriction are shown by [R].

Tides

Where cliffs are tidal, this is stated, and an indication of the extent to which the routes or approaches are affected is given. Greater precision is often not possible owing to two factors: the very high tidal range in the Bristol Channel (one of the greatest in the world) and the overwhelming effect of the Atlantic swell and breakers. It is advisable to purchase tide-tables (available at most local booksellers and printed in local newspapers), but these must be used in sensible combination with weather forecasts and visual assessment of the state of the sea.

In-Situ Gear

The vulnerability of pegs to salt corrosion is well known, and so all *in-situ* pegs should be regarded with suspicion and backed-up wherever possible. Many pegs have been removed by first-ascent parties, presumably because it was felt pointless to leave them to rot; others *have* rotted or gone missing for a variety of reasons. Where a peg has been reported or found missing, it is marked 'removed'; where not so marked it is believed to be still in place. Many of the original placements have been made redundant by the invention of newer cams and wedges; but, in general, where pegs are mentioned in the description (especially as necessary for main belays) it will be worth considering whether either to carry a hammer and selection of pegs or to abseil first and place whatever is necessary. The fact that the authors have recommended the carrying of pegs on certain climbs and crags is not an indication that that they would not be needed elsewhere.

The BMC South-West and Southern Area Committee decided at meetings in 1993 and 1995 that the whole of this coastline should be a no-bolt area, and this has been reaffirmed on occasions since. Four bolts remain from earlier days, though they are neither necessary to their climbs nor, probably, any longer safe to use.

Access

There are remarkably few restrictions at present, though many of these wild and lonely cliffs possess a varied and, on occasion, unique flora and fauna, which owing to their relative inaccessibility have remained undisturbed. However, this delicate balance could be upset by a substantial increase in the numbers of climbers or, more especially, the exercise of indiscriminate gardening or other insensitive environmental practice.

As access restrictions come and go more frequently than guidebook editions are published, it is important to respect any new signs that may be found, at least until they can be checked with the BMC. The BMC publishes annually a leaflet listing all bird-nesting restrictions nationwide, and future editions of *Climb South West* (see page 9) will list all crag access information in the region.

Baggy Point

Currently, only routes at Baggy Point from Scrattling Zawn to *Pink Void* are affected by a bird-nesting restriction, which runs from 15th March to 31st July. The area is delineated by large marker-posts; the restriction may be lifted early if the birds fail to nest.

Tintagel Head

Permission to climb should be sought well in advance (enclosing a stamped addressed envelope will expedite matters) from English Heritage, Room 225, 25 Saville Row, London W1X 2BT. All members of the party will need to sign the disclaimers sent.

Penhale Camp

The land (see map page 269) is owned by the Ministry of Defence. Cars should be parked at The National Trust car-park at Holywell Bay. Climbers must approach the crag via the coast path and not through the military camp.

Devon and Cornwall in the 21st Century

Owing largely to its swiftly-acquired reputation for some stunning photographs of little-known crags and Peters's unique blend of light and dark humour with a derring-do narration of heroic exploits, the 1988 guide sold at a rate beyond the publishers' wildest expectations. Nevertheless, an impression has persisted in many quarters (and some of the foregoing remarks in this Introduction may have reinforced it) that actual *climbing* in the region (Baggy Point excepted) is strictly for Celtic throwbacks and a handful of itinerant loose-rock freaks. True, success and satisfaction on many of the cliffs will come only to those with initiative and commitment, and with a sense of adventure balanced by a sound judgement; but the rewards to be thus reaped are both prodigious and profound. Nor is movement confined to the higher technical grades: those prepared to take the time and care will experience many glorious days on routes with real, old-fashioned hand and footholds.

As for further development, the last decade has produced over four hundred new routes, several of a quality to match the very best of the earlier legacy, and there is undoubtedly scope for the quest to continue.

Marsland and Gull Rock Photo: Brian Wilkinson

Historical

First Probings 1898-1950

Tom Longstaff's ascent of *Scrattling Crack* at Baggy Point in 1898 was one of the earliest rock-climbs of any significance on a British sea-cliff; it predates A W Andrews's first tentative probes on Wicca Pillar in West Penwith by five years and the more substantial *Ledge Climb* on Bosigran's Main Face by seven. However, *Scrattling Crack* was an isolated event, soon forgotten as the emphasis gradually shifted to the granite of the far South West, where Andrews entertained an increasing number of visitors from the traditional mountain area of North Wales. Horizontal sea-level excursions opened up stretches of sound, eminently climbable rock, but the less friendly terrain of the North Coast was ignored. A few minor scrambles were made by Noel Odell (later of Everest fame) in the early years of the century, though these were probably motivated mainly by his professional interest in geology.

Prior to the Second World War Rennie Bere prospected along the Culm Coast, climbing many of the characteristic foreshore pinnacles and stacks as well as the more solid of the promontory ridges. He doubtless relished the contrast between the exploration of these strange little sea-cliffs and his exploits in such diverse locations as Clogwyn d'ur Arddu, Scafell, and the Ruwenzori.

On the outbreak of war R M Hazleton, a teacher, found himself in Bude along with his evacuated school and put his spare time to good use. Few records remain, though a tantalizing reference to 'a very hard climb up the third slab from the sea' at Compass Point might indicate a prior ascent of *Tydomin* or even *Crimtyphon;* either would have been a notable achievement.

The post-war years saw little activity, and this neglect continued throughout most of the 50s, when the Biven brothers and the Cliff Assault Wing Commandos were making their dramatic contributions in West Penwith. However, while the granite understandably made all the headlines as the decade progressed, two colourful and enterprising climbers were undertaking, independently, explorations which were to play a major part in future developments.

Coasteering 1955-61

C H Archer, living close to the North Devon coast, became interested in the idea of traversing the entire foreshore between the Somerset and Cornwall borders. Having completed most of the eastern section, including the now legendary Exmoor Sea Traverse, he reached an impasse at Baggy Point and needed to elicit the support of a technically more proficient climber. He contacted Admiral Keith Lawder, who had taken up climbing on his retirement from the Navy and was currently engaged, along with the indefatigable Ted Pyatt, in a far-ranging reconnaissance of potential areas of interest throughout the region. Lawder, despite the seeming handicap of what others might define as advancing years, possessed all the ability Archer required to overcome this last major obstacle of his grand traverse.

Together, they successfully negotiated *Scrattling Crack*, unaware of Longstaff's earlier ascent, and the potentially serious section past Concrete Wall and The Long Rock. However, an incoming tide prevented further progress around the point. Rather than take the easy option offered by the gentle grass slopes above, they decided to investigate a narrow passage which appeared to offer a sporting through-route to the other side of the headland. Lawder's grandson, Iain Peters, was present as a somewhat over-awed 11-year-old and, when the two senior members of the party were prevented by reason of girth from progressing along the cave, he was ordered to continue. Feeling like Kingsley's chimney-sweep, he was thrust into a narrow opening which led, after many contortions, out into the back of one of the rotten zawns on the southern side of The Promontory Slab. Sometime later, a very lonely small boy was relieved to see the others descending towards him. After one further diversion to rescue a crag-bound sheep from another cave, the boy having been lowered by his ankles to capture the recalcitrant creature while Archer fumed impatiently, the traverse was duly completed. Such an apprenticeship must have been an invaluable preparation for the equally daunting role Peters was to play some twenty years later as the area's first definitive guidebook author.

The Big Slab Pioneers 1957-62

Lawder's contribution to climbing on the North Coast cannot be measured merely in terms of technical achievement or the number of routes, but rather in his ability to appreciate that beneath the unpromising surface-appearance of many of these impressive crags lay the potential for rock-climbs of the highest quality, and he became adept at the art of on-sight shale slab climbing, with its characteristic flaky holds and frightening earth and boulder cornices. Pyatt faithfully documented their explorations, compiling a dossier of information that he later expanded in his book *A Climber in the West Country*, which was to provide the members of a new generation with the basis for their own extremely productive quest for routes.

In 1959, Tom Patey was posted as a junior surgeon lieutenant to Devon and Cornwall and, after typically audacious forays on the then ivy-festooned Chudleigh and Dewerstone, he was introduced by Lawder to the Culm Coast, where even richer fields for his unique talents lay waiting.

Wreckers' Slab at Cornakey is the largest single slab on the Devon and Cornwall mainland, and the team that now gathered for its first ascent, Patey, Zeke Deacon, and Lawder, had all the necessary qualifications for success: experience on loose rock, technical ability, and a robust, individualistic, almost buccaneering approach to climbing in the finest nautical tradition. Copious vegetation and a dismal lack of protection merely added spice and variety to the occasion. With Patey and Deacon sharing the long leads, they climbed the slab, not by its present wandering line which seeks out the more solid rock, but directly up a central groove of flakes and spikes loosely embedded in grass and mud, with a piton or two driven into expanding cracks to lend an air of respectability to the proceedings. Not content with this *tour de force*, the irrepressible trio climbed its even more repellent neighbour, *Smugglers' Slab*.

Patey so enjoyed the experience that he returned alone to reclimb *Wreckers' Slab* and, in due deference to the senior-ranking officer of the original team, wrote to the Admiral apologizing for having unavoidably removed a number of the crucial holds!

In 1961, Bob Lewis and D Findlayson climbed *Barely Possible* at Bear Rock and three routes at Brownspear Point, including *Mainsail*, a line of genuine technical interest on good rock but with an unprotected crux.

Mainsail and *Wreckers' Slab* were the key to the opening-up of the Culm, but with the emphasis still very much on Devon limestone and Cornish granite it was to be nearly ten years before the undoubted potential was exploited.

Serious Discoveries 1968-72

In the mid 60s, a group of enterprising boys from Truro School, led by Toni Carver and Peter Stanier, cut their teeth on the granite of Cheesewring Quarry on Bodmin Moor, and in 1968 turned their attention to the industrial wasteland of Cligga Head, north of St Agnes, an area of granite and killas, much of which is of indifferent construction. The routes they found were mostly in the lower grades and, although these did not represent a radical departure from the climbs in adjoining West Penwith, they at least indicated that further investigation of this totally unknown coast might be productive, a proposition borne out two years later when another local climber, Tony Newberry, discovered the complex of much more impressive cliffs only a few miles south at Carn Gowla.

Given the length of the coastline, the variety of the terrain, the lack of readily available information, and the general air of *terra incognita* prevailing at the time, it is hardly surprising that only these random small outbursts of exploration occurred in the region in the late 60s. With no ground-rules and little tradition, the situation was eminently suitable for exploitation.

In 1969, Pat Littlejohn climbed *Resurrection* at Baggy Point but, with great expectations waiting to be fulfilled elsewhere, chose to ignore or simply missed the obvious challenge of the main slabs. Thus when Tony Willmott, Dave Johnson, Ben Wintringham, Alan Baker, and other members of the North London MC arrived in the autumn of that year, they were able to initiate an unprecedented and colourful blitzkrieg. With so many capable leaders, competition became an important feature, resulting in much frantic activity and division of loyalties. Willmott, in his ceaseless search for the ultimate climbing experience, narrowly escaped just that when he had to be extricated from the depths of Baggy Hole: as he prusiked up, the thin rope dropped by his friends from above slowly shredded on the razor-sharp edges. Ben Wintringham, with more practical ambitions, concentrated on the slabs, and his series of superb open routes justifiably resulted in Baggy's becoming the most popular crag in the region. *Lost Horizon, Twinkletoes, Midnight Cowboy,* and *Sexilegs* are all routes for the connoisseur and in their time were the prime examples of an exuberant approach that brought a breath of fresh air to the introverted if not moribund climbing scene.

A few months earlier, Bill Chevrest and Ian Duckworth had disappeared into the deep woods near Clovelly Court to emerge at Blackchurch. Intimidated as much by the stygian gloom of this, Devon's most sombre crag, as by the copious plant life and the abominable rock, they were forced to employ aid tactics on their on-sight ascent of *Loose Woman*, although this has since become the most amenable route on the crag. A year later, Littlejohn paid a visit to climb the striking line of *Archtempter* – a grim struggle for survival on sharp loose flakes and in the face of that ubiquitous feature of climbing folklore, a snowstorm.

In February 1971, Keith Darbyshire opened up Lower Sharpnose, and again Littlejohn followed, that April, to provide its first important route, *The Smile*. The same month, he made one of his most historic and momentous discoveries, *Eroica* at Pentire, and exactly a year later capped it with Tintagel's *Il Duce*. Except for the area around Hartland Point, all the major crags on the North Devon and Cornwall coastline were now identified, and the scene was set for one of the most exciting periods of intense exploitation in the history of South West climbing.

The Classical Era 1971-75

Over these five years Littlejohn, with a small clique of local climbers, succeeded in establishing some of the country's finest sea-cliff routes, which were to reinforce his reputation as the leading exponent of this special aspect of British climbing. His name appears with an almost monotonous frequency in the First Ascents list, though the routes themselves, as may be inferred from their names, are far from monotonous: *The Almighty, Savage God, Earth Rim Roamer, Mascon, Uphill,* the incomparable *Il Duce, Eroica, Darkinbad the Brightdayler* (perhaps the most outstanding quality route in the region), *America, Mercury,* and many more – a powerful collection by any standards, and an achievement rendered quite outstanding by the variety of effort and commitment required to reach and then climb them. Tintagel, for example, falls steeply and directly into a turbulent sea, is impossible to view from above or below, and induces an overpowering sense of isolation despite the tourist hordes in the castle ruins. On the first ascent of *Il Duce*, having established himself beneath the overhangs that bar entry to the main groove-line, Littlejohn launched up and out, the difficulty increasing as his minimal protection receded. Darbyshire, seconding, parted company with the rock and swung wildly out over the void, pulling his leader tight onto marginal belays. A rapid prusik restored a vestige of normality to the proceedings but two less experienced climbers might easily have suffered disaster. Ed Hart and David Hope on the second ascent experienced much the same trauma on this pitch, and Ed Cleasby, the Lakeland climber well known for his ability on new hard rock, summed it up when he wrote, 'Forget *T Rex* – *Il Duce* is much more the Great Dictator.'

Though Littlejohn was the spearhead of the North Coast campaign through the early 70s, the nature of the routes demanded that seconds were hardly less talented. Steve Jones, Gus Morton, and Keith Darbyshire were all very fine climbers in their own right, and Darbyshire, in particular, soon was making his own significant contributions.

These years were very much a cross-roads in British climbing ethics. The norm had always been an on-sight ascent, with any essential peg-placing or gardening being effected on lead. But then, the (very) recent invention of the figure-of-eight descendeur and the sit-harness, together with expanding views of what constituted climbable (and accessible!) rock, led to the general practice of abseil cleaning and preplacement of pegs. From here it was but a short step to the visual and then manual assessment of holds (and nut placements), and so to outright rehearsing of moves or whole sequences – generally surreptitious at first, though within ten years or so openly acknowledged and widely accepted as legitimate.

The more remarkable, therefore, that this small group set out to avoid abseil inspections or approaches wherever possible, thus creating, in Littlejohn's words, 'the means by which these routes can transcend their outcrop (sic!) status.' The original ultra-serious traverse to the base of the America Buttress is a prime example of this attitude. Another device was Darbyshire's cleaning of routes for Littlejohn to lead, offering the additional advantage of allowing the latter time to scour the coast for yet more lines and crags with potential for development. On occasions, of course, such avoidance was not possible, and defeat on the first attempts on both big routes on Pentire's Great Wall necessitated the preplacement of pegs – a radical solution at the time, but now universal – as well as some use of aid. At Blackchurch and other Culm crags the wisdom of removing most of the surface debris prior to an ascent soon became obvious.

Darbyshire also developed the smaller cliffs on the Culm such as Compass Point. After a day's work as a thatcher he would grab a companion, drive the 30 miles to the coast at breakneck speed, clean a line feverishly, and then proceed to make a rapid and powerful ascent. The delightful *Crimtyphon* is one such route. Darbyshire's seconds tended to come from outside the small group who had followed Littlejohn since his Chudleigh and Torbay days. Hugh Clarke, Paul Buttrick, Angus Clark, and Dave Garner had, too, to be more than mere rope-holders and, on the odd occasion when his enthusiasm outweighed the quality of the rock, they performed that function efficiently.

Nineteen-seventy-five started well: in February, Darbyshire was filmed for local television making a customary fast and effortless ascent of *The Entertainer* at Compass Point. Peters, his unwilling second and still a relative novice at the art of high-standard shale climbing, relates how after two hours he emerged at the top in a shell-shocked state, having fallen off or pulled off virtually every hold, to find the cameras long gone and Darbyshire and Littlejohn smiling amiably, belayed to a pile of empty beer cans thoughtfully provided by the BBC.

But only two weeks later this most productive and exciting period in the development of the region was over: whilst exploring cliffs on Cornwall's south coast, Darbyshire was killed. In a short space of time he had become the central figure in the small group of active local climbers, not merely as a result of his ability but also through his enthusiasm and gregariousness. In the aftermath, Littlejohn moved via Bristol to Cardiff and Steve Jones overseas, leaving behind a vacuum which those who stayed could not adequately fill.

A Period of Consolidation 1975-77

The more amenable routes at Baggy Point continued to gain in popularity; and, as word got out that there really were challenging climbs between Torbay and The Great Zawn, visiting parties arrived to investigate. Unsurprisingly, stories of epic failures added to the coast's reputation. Ed Hart, whose penchant for making second ascents (usually with his sister Anne, Mick Haffner, or David Hope) of the hardest and boldest (read Littlejohn's! – at least as far as the South West was concerned) routes of the day was legendary, travelled widely and productively. Pete Livesey, on his way to notable efforts at Bosigran at Easter 1975, stopped off at Pentire for long enough to free-climb *Eroica*, reduce the aid on *Darkinbad the Brightdayler* to one point, and make two powerful additions of his own on the Great Wall: *Cobra* and *Last Leviathan*. The following year, Ron Fawcett succeeded in removing the last offending aid point on *Darkinbad...* to render it one of the best and hardest routes in the West Country.

Other exceptions to this general trend of concentration on repeat ascents were Wintringham's very thin slab pitch at Baggy, *Soft Touch*, Littlejohn's serious *Terrapin*, and a long-overdue free ascent of Willmott's aid extravaganza *Heart of the Sun* by Arnis Strapcans and Chris King after a prodigious cleaning effort. Littlejohn was unable to resist the occasional foray back on the North Coast, despite the magnetic attraction of miles of steep unclimbed limestone on the other side of the Bristol Channel, and returned to Carn Gowla in 1977 with Peters in tow to complete a line attempted some years before on the wall right of *Mercury*: *Andromeda Strain*, with its appalling protection and serious situation. Later the same day the pair added *Lotus* on the comparatively pleasant Doyden Point as light relief.

In 1978 Bob Moulton's excellent Devon guide, covering both Baggy Point and the Culm Coast, appeared, complementing Carver's earlier documentation of the Atlantic Coast, and summing up nearly a decade of extraordinary achievement that could not have been foreseen at its start and establishing the area as, if not exactly 'mainstream', certainly of major importance and in parts worthy of widespread interest.

Towards the Eighties

Emergence from the recession was unspectacular at first, but proved well-founded. Rowland Edwards moved to Sennen and, before the saturation concept had gained the degree of acceptance that was to provide him with unlimited potential literally on his doorstep, focused his attention on the still wide empty spaces on Carn Gowla. Concentrating on the wall left of *Mercury*, a sector previously rendered unsavoury by the sewage pipe that had now been rerouted well to the north, he was able to produce such typical Gowla climbs as *Silver Dollar* and *Crystal Voyage*, steep and bold, but with generally good holds. Three locals were also busy on the crag: Roland Perriment, Simon Harry, and Andrew Tobin were beginning to justify predictions of its importance with a series of fine discoveries. Perriment added climbs at regular intervals, many of which have a distinct lateral component, *Journey to Ixtlan*, the superb *Tomb*, and *Aprez-Vous* being good examples. These were all high-level excursions, and perhaps the fact that Perriment was a non-swimmer with an understandable distrust of the ocean had some bearing on the choice of line. Tobin and Harry for their part were responsible for a trio of hard and very serious routes in the vicinity of the notorious 'anchor' for abseil into the Heliport – a glorified lavatory chain and bolt inserted some years before by Darbyshire but now sadly (according to some!) defunct.

At the opposite end of the coast, Blackchurch was subjected to a reappraisal by Mick Fowler. This representative of the next generation of North London climbers was soon to become famous for his ability to cope with any type of rock, snow, or ice, and even extreme combinations of all three in mountain situations. Having enjoyed a few practice runs on some of the less respectable areas of Baggy, he found its big and serious near neighbour ideally suited to the exploitation of his talents. Eschewing prior cleaning, he headed straight for its darker corners, revelling in the experience of such rarely-to-be-repeated classics as *The Heathen* and *Summerhouse*. On one occasion, an enthusiastic Roger Lanchbury and a sceptical David Hope spent many arduous, dirty, and dangerous hours removing vast quantities of organic and inorganic matter from a line only to discover subsequently, much to their chagrin, that Fowler had already climbed it *au naturel*. He rose rapidly through the sparse ranks of slate and shale devotees to reach his unchallenged position as high priest of their black arts. A pilgrim's progress along the coast over the next six or seven years resulted in some of the most spectacular and dangerous climbs in the country. Routes such as the incredible *Breakaway* at Henna and *Private World* at Bukator defy rational description and meaningful grading (as well, somehow, as gravity). Not surprisingly, objective opinions as to their merits were not readily available, and such a typical Fowler accolade for a route as having 'excellent DP' (death potential) is still received with little enthusiasm.

However, with his ascents of *King's Arête* and *Vagabond* at Tintagel, he demonstrated his ability on more conventional rock, though their comparative air of permanence must to him have seemed somewhat tedious. Luckily, *Headbanger* at Brownspear Point redressed the balance in spectacular fashion, being one of the few routes in the country to have fallen down while in the process of being climbed.

A common characteristic of most of those involved in the development of North Coast climbing had been a marked individuality of approach, and in 1978 another in this tradition appeared on the scene. Pete O'Sullivan had acquired a taste for shale on the secluded sylvan cliffs of the Tamar Valley. He opened his account on the coast with a series of short but comparatively solid routes at Baggy, but soon began to display all the symptoms of an addiction identified by Ken Wilson, that notorious and acerbic diagnostician and analyst of climbers' motives and foibles, as 'peninsulitis'. Such an epithet may have been intended as pejorative but, in the light of O'Sullivan's 250-odd routes in the South West, not to mention his guidebook work, it warrants a more charitable interpretation.

At Baggy, Steve Bell pointed the way to future development on the crag with *Slip It In Quick*, a line of possibility rather than weakness, while local activists, Brian Wilkinson and Andy Gallagher, spotted the rather more obvious *Slip Sliding Away*. Gary Gibson's new-route odyssey was at this time little advanced upon the planning stages, but after a mere handful of climbs at Baggy and a minor excursion to Blackchurch he decided that, for the South West, Lundy granite and the more access-friendly limestone of the Wye Valley and Pembroke offered better returns (to many retrospective sighs of relief down south!).

Peters and Buttrick, the remaining links with the great age of exploration, chanced upon the impressive but densely vegetated Oldwalls Point. Marathon gardening sessions revealed two excellent crack-systems, of which *Matchless* has become one of the undoubted middle-grade classics of the Culm. At the same time, O'Sullivan found Lawder's dismissal (in a 1960 article) of the Cow and Calf as 'of little interest' to be unfounded by climbing the fine *Tsunami*.

The Discovery of Exmansworthy

Exploding the myths surrounding the achievements of Littlejohn and Darbyshire proved an arduous task, and early forays onto some of their bolder creations served only to reinforce the reputation for seriousness and difficulty. There was a tacit assumption that the area was worked out as far as the major lines were concerned, and so miles of unexplored cliffs were completely ignored. The discovery of Exmansworthy in 1979 was the first indication that Littlejohn might have missed the odd crag or two. Erstwhile rivals Peters and O'Sullivan had temporarily joined forces to search for a large cliff rumoured to exist west of Blackchurch. A strenuous boulder-hop from Shipload Bay confirmed the speculation, and the pair were astounded that a crag of such obvious potential could have been overlooked. An incoming tide forced a luckily straightforward *Tactical Retreat* and a traumatic jungle-bash on top, but they soon returned suitably prepared to hack out a more amenable mode of access from above, and got to work cleaning. O'Sullivan chose to investigate the long concave seaward face, while Peters, later joined by Buttrick, began excavating a compelling crackline on the inset wall to its right that was destined to became *Cat Burglar*. Success on the immaculate *Shadow Walker* so fired O'Sullivan's enthusiasm that he was unable to comply with the agreement that they would respect each other's lines, and the by-now pristine crack was duly stolen, the name serving only to rub salt into the wound. Peters retired from the scene in a fit of pique, leaving the arch villain a free hand to create a series of superb crack and face climbs. It was left to gravity to administer retribution more than a decade later.

The news filtered up the Bristol Channel and inspired Andy Brazier and Martin Corbett to take some leave from the bustle of Avon. Brazier was prised away from his cameras long enough to lead the bold *Danzig*, and Corbett provided *Cat Burglar* with an equally fine companion, *The Outlaw*. Fowler continued his individualistic explorations at Crackington Haven and Bossiney, and Pete Whillance, another inveterate long-distance traveller, made a number of brief but productive raids resulting in such fine and demanding routes as *Dreadlock Holiday* at Compass Point, *Godspell* at Blackchurch, and, above all, *Culm Dancing* to the left of *Shadow Walker*, now sadly also razed. Nor was Pentire's Great Wall forgotten in this flurry of activity further north, as two more Bristolians, Steve Findlay and Andy Grondowski, succeeded in breaching the lower wall between *Eroica* and *Darkinbad...* with *Pulses Unreal* and *Dislocation Dance*.

In May 1982 Littlejohn raided the South West once again. Dismayed to learn of the cataclysmic collapse of his *Earth Rim Roamer* at Dyer's Lookout, he returned with a vengeance to climb *Earth Rim Roamer II* up the soaring crack and arête to the right of the vague outline of the first edition, remarking drily that he was not much looking forward to *Earth Rim Roamer III*. (Against all the odds, the call has not yet come!) Then, after searching his inexhaustible memory banks, he moved on with Hugh Clarke to the scene of previous epics, the America Buttress at Carn Gowla. An action-packed encounter eventually yielded success on the region's most difficult and serious route of its day, *Guernica*, and set a standard which for some time was only approached by Nipper Harrison's daring lead of *Siren Cry* to the right of *Darkinbad...* at Pentire. Many of these recent activities were recorded by Pete O'Sullivan in a New Climbs Supplement for North Devon in 1980 and a North Cornwall Interim Guide in 1982.

Light but Local Relief

However, it was not always necessary to climb in the rarefied atmosphere of the upper E grades, for fine routes were being discovered at surprisingly amenable standards. Renny Croft's delightful *Steppin' Razor* at Smoothlands was a prime example – an exciting expedition in unusual surroundings requiring only a finely-tuned sense of equilibrium and a good head for heights. Nick Hancock's equally good *Two Pints to Capel* on Upton Slabs was another. Paradoxically, in contrast to more popular areas where climbing-wall-developed skills and strength were fast becoming obligatory for anyone with new-route aspirations, here imagination and a sense of adventure were of greater importance. And these qualities were nowhere more apparent than in David Hillebrandt, a local GP fired with a Patey-like enthusiasm for the unusual, who opened up the Penhale Cliffs and other far-flung and forgotten reaches of the Atlantic Coast with a series of middle-grade routes in the most unlikely surroundings. Unperturbed by the complexities of approaching his chosen lines, he thought nothing of making long, desperate abseils down tottering walls to reach likely-looking slabs lost in the depths of sea-filled zawns, or of exploring rotting green recesses close to sewage outfalls.

Lower Sharpnose in the Eighties

Lower Sharpnose was the last of the big cliffs to be given the 80s treatment. Little interest had been shown since the Littlejohn routes of the early 70s except for the fine *Out of the Blue* by Keith Marsden and Andy March, more Bristol marauders, in 1980. However, Chris Nicholson, after psyching himself up at Maer Cliff, started a five-year campaign in 1982 to put things right, ably supported by Nick White. His *Bolder Boulder, Diamond Smiles*, and a substantial attempt at the line to become *Break On Through* were all notable efforts, the latter thwarted only by his second's inability to maintain a satisfactory belaying technique whilst treading water. In April 1986, Bell and O'Sullivan seized the much-coveted *Spoils of War*, but any complacency locals may have felt over their contributions were rudely shattered a few days later when Littlejohn, irrepressible and audacious as ever, decided the time had come to round things off by completing *Break On Through* and a month later bagging *Fay, Pacemaker,* and *Twilight Zone*. Thus, in the space of a few weeks this unlikely crag had knocked Exmansworthy into second place in the hierarchy of the Culm Coast.

Galvanized by this, Steve Monks and John Wilkinson arrived the following spring to add a further three major routes, including *Coronary Country*. Initially graded E7, it attracted a lot of attention and a number of repeats, including an on-sight flash by Martin Crocker. It settled at E6, but was still the Culm's first. Over the next two years, a younger generation of West Country talent was to make these standards look almost commonplace: Nick White climbed *Culm to Mother* (still unrepeated) and *Azrael*; Frank Ramsay almost managed a flashed ascent of *Hearts and Minds*; and Crispin Waddy found several gaps to fill with quality E5s. Finally, the last year of the decade saw a staggering leap of two grades (to E8 6c) when Mark Edwards, with his father Rowland, created *The Monks' Satanic Verses*; this challenge, too, with its exceedingly thin crux above suspect protection has been shunned since.

Eighties Roundup

O'Sullivan had not been inactive elsewhere, despite the distraction of writing a complete guide to *West Penwith* (CC 1984). After finally passing his driving test he beetled furiously around the region: one weekend it would be *Pressure Drop* at Speke's Mill Mouth or *Easter Risings* at Compass Point, the next *Capital Offence* at Penhale. The offence in question was the placement of a bolt, following two used by the Edwardses at Carn Gowla earlier in 1985. Mercifully, the North Devon and Cornwall Coast was spared any further such improprieties and the resulting controversies that were soon to tear climbing communities apart, not least in neighbouring West Penwith.

In early 1986 Peters, now supposed to be at work on the new guide but studiously ignoring passing deadlines and an impatient editor, rediscovered Kellan Head with fellow veteran Ken Hosie, climbed the unusual *Endgame*, and clocked up valuable flight time on the very steep *Zugzwang*. That harassed editor retaliated by finally enticing Tony Penning, recently emerged from one of numerous mid-life crises, south-west to climb the hanging groove left of *Darkinbad the Brightdayler* – *Through the Looking-Glass*. At the same time Hope inspected the line that was to become *Black Magic*, but it was left until another day because 'no one else is going to be interested'. A year later, the complete Gloucester–Worcester Goonshow arrived for the first of many trips to Pentire and Gowla (as well as further on to Bosigran's Great Zawn and neighbouring Penwith crags). Led mainly by Penning, who at a time most are hanging up their boots was going from strength to strength, David Hope, Pete Cresswell, and Roger Lanchbury not only teamed up to make several powerful and quality ascents but ensured the continuity in Cornish climbing of the buccaneering spirit of humour and adventure – exemplified most notably by *A Sackful of Clowns* and *How the West Was Won*, the latter a delightful sea-stack expedition with a swim to start and a Tyrolean to finish – that new trends and darker forces elsewhere looked to be in danger of eclipsing permanently. Sadly, a series of personal tragedies curtailed the act, but their legacy shines bright.

If Lower Sharpnose was the Culm's main attraction at the cutting edge at this time, so Pentire's Great Wall remained the Atlantic Coast's. In 1987, after *Coronary Country*, Monks and Wilkinson moved straight on west to confound Hope and produce the very fine *Black Magic*, and two months later Nipper Harrison matched this with *Urco's Revenge*, while Waddy's contribution the next year was the bleak *Your Funeral, My Trial*.

Pastures New 1989-91

The 1988 guide eventually arrived, and it rapidly became apparent that there was still so much to go for – major unclimbed lines on established cliffs, impressive unclimbed areas of known crags, and even whole unclimbed crags. Many soon discovered or rediscovered the delights of the amenable Baggy Point; others began to look for a little adventure in quieter areas such as Screda Point and Compass Point, with their easy access, good-quality climbing, and yet still that sense of isolation missing from Stanage or Pembrokeshire on a bank holiday. Starting in the autumn of that year, Dave Viggers and Damian Carroll spent nine months filling some unexpected gaps at Baggy Point and roaming the more northerly Culm crags very profitably.

It was at one of those crags, Dyer's Lookout, that a momentous day's events took place in July 1989 with a visit from White and fellow south coaster Dave Thomas. The tenuous E6 test-piece of *The Culmination* was Thomas's lead and was felt to be 'at the limit of what is possible on this rock'. White, though, was not to be outdone and promptly made a stupendous lead of *The Earthsea Trilogy Part I*, another E6, taking the thin crack and outrageous arête which *Earth Rim Roamer II* understandably avoids. (Parts II and III of The Trilogy are to be found on Lundy granite and South Devon limestone respectively.)

The next month saw the Plymouth-based group of Nick Hancock, Andy Grieve, Chris Rees, Ken Palmer, and Dave Turnbull explode onto the scene. Although the first three of those names had appeared at regular intervals in the old guide's First Ascents list from as early as 1982, and Grieve, in particular, was famed for his detailed knowledge of the Culm Coast and his exceptional strength (also, believing that his limit was around E4 when it was actually at least two grades higher, for his propensity for under-grading), the Torbay team's successes at Dyer's Lookout were a challenge they could not ignore. At nearby Smoothlands, a thin discontinuous crack in the steep and apparently otherwise holdless Great Slab gave Palmer *Creeping Flesh*. Destined to become a classic in its own right, it more significantly inspired him to return the next spring along with Grieve in an attack on the centre of The Great Slab, *Hellbound*. Another year on, Grieve added his own improbable line, *Slave to the Rhythm*, crossing the crack of *Creeping Flesh* to make its way into the middle of the slab. The day before *Hellbound*, Dave Turnbull, with Andy Donson, made his first foray onto the Atlantic Coast to climb, by mistake (for *Private World*), the deadly serious *Where There's a Will*; and a few weeks later he discovered the impressive box zawn at Backways Cove to reveal *The* (equally bold) *Strangest Secret*.

Meanwhile, Ed Heslam filled gaps at Kellan Head that O'Sullivan and Peters had left, and then visited Nabor Point with Brian Wilkinson in a storm. Despite this, the pair saw enough to compel a return visit, when they climbed the coveted *Lifeline*. Their next trip ended disastrously with Heslam falling 60 feet onto jagged rocks from a failed abseil anchor, and a dramatic helicopter rescue in the darkness ensued. Wilkinson, undaunted by these events, went on over the next few years to develop middle-grade routes on the remote and often isolated cliffs that appealed to his sense of adventure – Hole Rock, Nabor Point, Bude Pillars, Hippa Rock, Vicarage Cliff, Menachurch Point, Lynstone, Maer Cliff and Damehole Point – some forty-odd routes in all. David Hillebrandt continued to explore closely every bay and hidden zawn over much of the Culm and parts of the Atlantic Coast, searching out delights such as

Rectory Tearooms and *Romping Robert*. His specialty was finding obscure and esoteric hidden cliffs, doing one route, then producing dozens of typewritten descriptions promising execrable experiences to those who ventured onto them. (Instances of good-natured retaliation inflicted by his victims will be found scattered throughout this guidebook, starting in the next paragraph.)

Further up the coast, Hillebrandt persuaded Ben Rowe and Martin Corbett to commence proceedings with two new routes on the previously unclimbed 'little big crag' of Upright Cliff. Meanwhile, on the nearby Cow and Calf, Corbett and Greg Forward began what was to be a total transformation with *Bulldyke* and *Dr Bollox*. A further eight routes followed in quick succession by Corbett and Forward, with the arête of *Elisa Johanna* and the snaking crackline of *Over the Moon* being the cream. The last, and hardest, addition of this period, however, was *Howling at the Moon*, the work of Julian Matthias. Also at this time, Frank Ramsay and Doug Smith climbed the bold and technical arête right of *Archtempter* at Blackchurch: *Lord Bafta*, which received another powerful companion on the same impressive piece of rock the following summer. Originally called *Lady Emmy*, now renamed *The Naked God*, this too was a serious lead with minimal protection: while others had abandoned Blackchurch to the return of myth and vegetation, Ramsay had shown that there was still life left in the old girl yet.

After successfully editing the 1988 guide, Hope accepted responsibility for collecting the region's new information and, naturally enough, set about making some of the news himself. Under the constraints of a seven-day working week and a lack of partners with enthusiasm for on-sight epics on loose and unprotected rock, he dragged along one of his school pupils, James Cornwell, to discover The Black Zawn at Pentire, and established an ongoing routine of calling in to pick off a couple of lines here and there before heading further south, usually to Carn Gowla. It proved a prosperous arrangement for several years until Hope was able to start lining up his daughters on his rope!

In the summer of 91, Dave Turnbull visited the softer Culm measures around Bude and on successive days produced two outstanding though very different routes, the first of which would influence the whole development of this southern area. No one can have failed to be impressed by the huge black wall at the southern end of Northcott Mouth, and its apparent lack of opportunity for natural protection. Six years earlier, O'Sullivan had sampled its horrors on the still unrepeated *Ground Fall*, and the experience had not encouraged him to return. Turnbull, however, went straight for the central buttress, and *Bugsy* was yet another serious lead with poorly-protected 6a climbing. *Abandon Hope*... on the nearby Menachurch Point the following day took a 60-foot crack in the low ceiling of a cave, thereby climbing the longest roof on the Culm. A combination of hand-jams, fist-jams, arm-jams, leg-jams, and body bars were welded together by desperate thrutching. Deciding upon the name (no reference to the Atlantic Coast author!) was apparently a comparable effort.

Fins, Slabs, and Pinnacles of Culm

In 1993 Wilkinson and Margaret Grapes discovered the friendly Lynstone fins, a miniature version of Lower Sharpnose. Grieve went *Full Tilt* up the impending back wall of Compass Point, and hurt both fingers and toes climbing the desperate little crack of *Both Ends Burning* at the seaward end of Brownspear. Wilkinson, in the meantime, had a mysterious premonition concerning the supposedly imminent publication of this guide to the coast when he rounded off a batch of routes at Maer with *Millennium*!

The next year saw the first long slab route at Cornakey since Darbyshire had ploughed his own furrow up its esoteric fields of rock and vegetation twenty-two years earlier. *Heaven and Hell* was an 'impulse climb' by Sean Hawken and Lee Earnshaw, navigating the narrow slab immediately left of *Wreckers' Slab* in three long and exciting pitches, all climbed on sight in true north coast tradition. Dave Hillebrandt continued his development of the Knaps Longpeak areas of slabs with *Shaken Not Stirred* and, while there, rationalized and reinforced the abseil points for the nearby Foxhold Slabs. This caretaker role, which he has exercised all along the coast has largely gone unrecognized and unrewarded.

Unsurprisingly, the magnet of the unclimbed and inaccessible pinnacle of Chapman Rock was to have the greatest draw on Hillebrandt, the arch mountaineering romantic. It, too, was an arch, similar to Blackchurch Rock; it was not quite so steep, but required a low spring-tide even to approach it. Late June saw Hillebrandt, in company with Ians Ross and Maddock and Murphy the dog, negotiate the long convoluted descent and boulder-hop for Ross to lead the obvious line up the seaward slab. The dog almost pegged out with the effort of the approach and eventually had to be carried up Gawlish Cliff on the return journey. As Hillebrandt ruefully noted, 'He was not a small dog...' While there, Hillebrandt tried the other obvious but harder direct line left of *Murphy's Nightmare* (as the first route was dubbed) but retreated. It was left for Mark Kemball four years later to ask *Who's Chapman?*

The last unclimbed pinnacle on the coast to submit was an altogether different affair - a dramatic and shapely arrowhead raking the sky at the Culm's most southerly point. The young Hawken teamed up with old hand Grieve the following February to climb the obvious crack on its south face: *Mine's a Point*. The challenge for one person to climb all the free-standing Culm Coast pinnacles still remains.

The Ex-Man Cometh 1990-93

Although he had been visiting for several years and had achieved a number of significant early repeats, belatedly but inevitably Crocker joined the first-ascents scene. Of all the prodigious personal tallies of new routes, Crocker's must be the most consistent in terms of both quality and difficulty, and it is hard to think of anyone, present or past, other than Littlejohn, Joe Brown, and perhaps Fowler who has spent so long at or very close to the cutting edge of British rock-climbing. This has been achieved by a family man with a career job unrelated to climbing, who wrote single-handed (and is now rewriting) the double-volume *Avon & Cheddar* guide, as well as contributing to other guides both directly and – by virtue of the fact that his meticulous and vivid new-route descriptions usually defy amendment by author or editor, and because his unrivalled knowledge of so many crags and especially their harder routes proves absolutely indispensable to them – indirectly.

A visit, in the late summer of 1990, found him standing amidst the ruins of Shadow Walker Slab at Exmansworthy, the 'perfect rock' of which had recently suffered a cataclysmic collapse. Undaunted, he climbed the only patch that was (and still is) standing to create the evocatively-named *Haunted by Hoodoos* at what was then (with the exception of the unconfirmed Edwards E8 at Lower Sharpnose) still the coast's top grade of E6 6b. This, together with a less nerve-racking route at Lower Sharpnose three weeks earlier, sufficed for the year.

The following August he found his way to the Atlantic Coast, clutching a copy of new-route development notes, and immediately rendered any review out of date. The prime target was the connection between *Eroica* and the upper hanging grooves of *Through the Looking-Glass* and *Reflections* at Pentire. The result was *A Groove Full of Mirrors*, dramatically bold and thin, with minimal protection in the true tradition of the area. Crocker remarked that, it was '...the most emotionally demanding piece of climbing' he had ever done. *Another Nervous Breakdown* and *Beneath Black Waters* completed a trio of very hard climbs all ideally befitting the stature of The Great Wall.

Tintagel was on the hit list for spring 1992, and here a very intense period of development saw established three worthy companions to *Il Duce* that modernized High Cliff: *Faschisti, Isle of Avalon,* and *Ocean Colour Dream*. On the first two of these, Pete O'Sullivan, tempted out of retirement, followed some wild, hanging pitches more out of contact with the rock than in and, bemoaning the fact, exclaimed later, 'I'd like to know who gave him my phone number!'

Carn Gowla, the last of the big five, was next on the agenda, and in the summer of the same year Crocker, with method born of passion, set about eliminating the remaining faint weaknesses in the ramparts of that formidable cliff. On America Buttress he celebrated the quincentenary of *1492*, a typically searing portrait of exposure, seriousness, and commitment on the same canvas as *Guernica;* on the Red Walls he discovered *Barren Lands;* and on The Baptist Cliff it was *Welcome to the Human Race*. For the latter two, as on so many of his serious exploits around the country, he was partnered by the ever dependable John Harwood. For several others, he joined forces with Ramsay, a formidably strong pairing.

Crocker and Harwood also paid a visit to Cow and Calf, their interest no doubt aroused by news of the Corbett/Forward team's activities. To their amazement the towering black wall that rose out of the narrow zawn behind the cliff remained unclimbed: an inescapable challenge to someone of Crocker's ambition and temperament. The flashed ascent of *Kalahari Black*'s rippled surface on spaced gear was a bold, committing undertaking which set it apart as one of the really big leads on the Culm. Back there the following weekend they found high seas running to compound the head-games. The hauntingly serious *Mind-Melt* on the bald grey wall right of *Tsunami*, with its deck-out potential start, added yet another dimension to the climbing on this rapidly maturing cliff. Soaked from the hostile waves, the pair dried out by rushing off across the boulders to the not-so nearby Smoothlands for Crocker to record his own distinctive contribution to The Great Slab: *Smoothtalkin'* sweeps across the slab using disjointed cracks beneath *Hellbound* and eventually climbs directly up it with minimal protection. In October, he visited Baggy Point and succeeded where others had failed on the very bold and run-out *Last Testament*, still the only E6 on the crag. Early the following year, Crocker added the short peg-protected, technical test-piece *The Ghost of Bell Aire*, his last new route on the Culm before his serious accident the following month, and his last contribution there for three years.

Ragamuffin

A self-styling, this first-new-route name? Having the misfortune to hail from the only county in south-west Britain unable to boast even a man-made hole in the ground worth climbing, let alone mile upon mile of natural coastal or at least river-gorge rock, a young Swindon journalist with less than the legendary arm-span of a Crocker or muscle-bulk of a Grieve might have been expected to gravitate towards the new state-of-the-art climbing walls in the region. Not so Ian Parnell. Spurning the advocacy of bolting in West Penwith by some of his contemporaries as well as its practice by most of the others in less contentious areas, Parnell devoted himself solely to the 'adventure experience'; and where better was this to be found than the Devon and Cornwall northern coastline? Although *Ragamuffin* (1992) is a lowly 70-foot E2, its pithy description 'no protection; poor rock at the top' hinted at what was to come. Not that Parnell was to seek out bad rock, or technical difficulty for that matter, for its own sake: his philosophy was to go for the lines and situations that appealed to him aesthetically and to take in his stride, with the minimum of fuss and encumbrance, whatever obstacles or hazards they presented.

Although it was another two years before his full potential was realized, his impact then became second only to Crocker's. For not only did every subsequent year see notable achievement on the new-route scene, but his many audacious repeats, on a number of occasions solo, testify to his extraordinary commitment, as does the fact that he is still alive, to his judgement and skill.

Dyer Straits (E8) Dyer's Lookout
Climber: Ian Vickers Photo: Carl Ryan

Mrs Pepper Pot (E5 ~ first ascent) – Butter Hole
Climber: Dave Turnbull and Crag Jones – Photo: Mark Carnall

The Summer of 94

Dave Henderson added two new lines on the South Face of the Middle Fin, one of which, *Heart By-Pass*, took such an obvious diagonal crackline on superb rock that one was left wondering whether too much training had induced partial myopia among Henderson's 'culmtemporaries'. Ramsay was still able to spot a good line though, even on the unfashionable Blackchurch, with the spectacularly exposed arête of *The Big Sheep*.

Another great find came about when Grieve paid a visit to the friendly crag of Marsland, where the narrow Baywatch Wall is covered in bulging ripples or load-cast formations often found on this part of the coast, and instantly realized the potential for what was far from a *Booby Prize*, in fact a sustained and technical pitch which should become a high-standard classic.

Mostly with Jim Cheshire, Parnell climbed several routes at Baggy Point, showing, especially with the brilliant *Dark Angel*, that the crag was by no means played out. In mid July he teamed up, on equal terms, with a miraculously back-to-form Crocker for a momentous weekend. Together, they produced six outstanding routes at Carn Gowla and another three at Tintagel's High Cliff that gave tallies of stars and E-points unrivalled in any three-day period in the development of this coastline; in fact, quite possibly by any pair anywhere.

The next weekend Parnell joined up with Paul Twomey, a climbing-school instructor in West Penwith, who had already gained a reputation for hard and bold ascents. To start, two new routes were climbed at Lower Sharpnose; the next day they redecorated The Black Wall of Maer Cliff with two more in the ultra-serious style of *Bugsy*: *Big Black* and the excellent and even harder *Fortune Faces the Brave*, both on fragile rock with spaced gear. Another three major climbs followed a couple of weeks later. Unfortunately, all the fixed gear here was removed, allegedly by the outdoor pursuits centre a short stroll from the cliff, and this will doubtless ensure that the routes receive few repeats: a shame!

To round off this extraordinary month, Crocker returned to Tintagel with Ramsay and others to work out virtually all remaining possibilities in another display of outstanding virtuosity.

The Golden Years 1995-98

The next spring it finally became the turn of Kellan Head and Doyden Point, with *Kellanesis* and *Kellan Arête* at Kellan and *Wilting* at Doyden, on all of which Crocker was partnered by Henderson. The latter was a not uncommon example on this coastline of a new route being climbed by mistake – 'it proved to be the most draining on-sight new route I had done'.

Although 1995 and subsequent years were rather quieter, they nevertheles yielded unsurpassed riches in terms of quality. Devotees such as Hillebrandt, Hope, Wilkinson, Cheshire and Derek Ryden continued to fill gaps and discover a number of esoteric gems, especially the routes by Ryden and Cheshire on The Black Walls at Carn Gowla. Perhaps most noteworthy was Hope's development of the many smaller cliffs at Pentire that had hitherto lain silent in the shadow of The Great Wall.

Baggy Point conceded yet another two notable routes, this time to Twomey and Clark Alston, the aptly-named *Death on a Stick* and, in complete contrast, its optional extension *Hawaiian Pipeline* – you have to travel all the way to Carn Gowla to find the next three-star E1! Another long distance, 'several thousand feet' (unroped above the sea) was that traversed by Hancock and Earnshaw *Through the Looking-Glass* from The Promontory to The Long Rock. Hancock also climbed three exhilarating routes, two of them bold solos, on good granite at forgotten Cligga Head.

Not to be eclipsed, Fowler reappeared on shale, this time at the Atlantic crag of Trewethet before heading back north to the Culm's Windbury Head. Three typical XSs resulted, providing climbing of an unexpected quality. David Scott-Maxwell and Turnbull climbed a very Fowleresque horror, *Jerusalem*, at the 300-foot Henna-like precipice north of Hartland Quay, with the obligatory paraphernalia of pegs, warthogs, helmets, etc., also given the dreaded XS grade. They must have felt like singing a hymn of thanksgiving on reaching 'the green and pleasant (and horizontal) land' above. (A year later, someone must have asked DSM, 'What greater love hath a man than this, that he spend his *Stag Night...?*'). The same pair went *Back to the Old Ways* (and others) at the scene of Turnbull's earlier discovery, the box zawn at Backways Cove, and Turnbull concluded his tally, relatively small in number but huge in terms of variety, audacity, and difficulty, with the first (and so far only) sortie into the awesome Pepper Hole.

At Easter 1996, Crocker returned to Exmansworthy with his trusty partner John Harwood to investigate the smooth and impressive wall, the upper part of which was only nibbled at by *Formation Flying*. The resulting ascent straight up the middle, *The Ex-man Cometh* at E7 6c, set a new standard for extreme and sustained intensity, and confirmed Crocker's suspicion of the golden opportunities remaining along this dark and mysterious coast.

The following day, they drove south to the friendly Damehole Point, where, unseconded (Harwood having burnt his hands in an abseiling mishap), Crocker proceeded to lace the long low headland with a network of new routes.

On days when he was unable to find a partner for his adventures, Crocker devised a 'trailing back-rope' soloing technique (clipping gear into a trailing rope to provide a modicum of security only in the opportunity to grab it if necessary) and was to use it time and again over the following weeks to increase his already prodigious tally of first ascents. Oldwalls, Vicarage,

Hippa, and Smoothlands all came under his intense scrutiny as further, often unexpected and unexpectedly fine, discoveries were unearthed, *More than a Match* (for the classic *Matchless*) at Oldwalls being an outstanding example. On this route he recalls having left his mobile phone on the boulders where he calculated he would end up if he fell so that he could then talk to his family!

In 1997 he was back only briefly with Parnell to conclude once and for all the development at Tintagel (and play with names on Bossiney Haven Buttress), while his sole offering in 1998, at Dyer's Lookout, was another typically committing lead, the seriousness of which 'is proportional to the size of the fallout zone's pebble/boulder material'.

Thus, in less than the decade, Crocker had largely single-handedly thrust the coastline into the modern era, pushing the standards higher than any before, continuously reassessing what was possible on this adventurous coast and proving that boldness, commitment, and adventure were not ideals of the past that current bolt-protected climbers only read about in guidebook histories.

And So to the Millennium

An obvious challenge up the centre of the massive slab/wall left of *Earthsea Trilogy* had been tried by a number of worthies including Andy Donson, Johnny Dawes, and Paul Riley, and a string of pegs marked their lack of progress. One summer weekend in 1998 saw a young superstar with an international reputation as a technically outstanding and broad-skilled climber, Ian Vickers, give it a half-hearted attempt. He came back a week later to practise the route on a top-rope and, feeling on form, decided to go for the lead. The complex sequences of tenuous moves he had 'wired' in his mind slowly and smoothly unravelled in real time to produce *Dyer Straits*, at E8 6b, a new challenger for status of the most continuously sustained piece of climbing on the Culm.

In the last year of the old millennium and the old guide, it was perhaps comforting to realize that it was still possible for the Culm to throw up also a new crag, a new approach, and even a new material from which to forge fresh adventures.

The new crag was Sloo Slabs at Peppercombe, tucked away beyond Clovelly, which was 'discovered' by Hillebrandt on his perambulations along his beloved coast. The offset slabs were quickly developed by him in association with Ben Rowe, Adrian Moore, and Andrew Partington and are a useful addition for those wanting really 'to get away from it all'.

The new approach was Simon Young's controversial decision to place eleven pegs to protect four miniature desperates on the diminutive Unshore Rock, which rises from the sands of the popular Northcott Mouth beach. While pegs have always been accepted as part of the north-coast tradition for sections of longer routes where the rock does not run to natural placements, and while no one can dispute the difficulty or quality of the lines, some have felt that he may here have over-stepped the limits of acceptability: time will tell! However, his bouldering developments in the same area have received greater welcome, and he has brought the very highest technical standards to the Culm.

The new material for climbing on was also the product of Young's boundless enthusiasm – rolled steel! *The Incredible Hulk* was not to be found on the tottering cliffs of Hartland Point but up the rusting steel hull of the wreck of the *Johanna* lying among the boulders below.

It may be no coincidence that the last climb on the Culm in this new guide was the work of one also involved in the last of the previous guide, namely the Exeter-based north coast adventure enthusiast Clark Alston, and both routes are on Lower Sharpnose. There have been some dramatic spurts of development, and high levels of achievement have been reached by locals and raiders from all parts of the country, but throughout the 90s there have always been those, like Alston, for whom just climbing on this mysterious coast is reward enough and, 'if you can snatch a new line from under everyone's nose, then so much the better'. Long may it remain so – it is a sentiment to which Crocker, Parnell, Penning, et al. would all reply 'Amen!'

On the Atlantic Coast, too, Hillebrandt continued to prove a most persistent explorer, having the advantage of living on the doorstep. Scarnor Point, Penhale, and many others are all worth a visit, if only to initiate the unsuspecting into 'North Coast Atmosphere'. At Shag Crag, an abseil in the vicinity of a sewage outfall resulted in the comment, 'You can catch some interesting diseases on this coast', but did not inspire in his companions the same sense of adventure. His contributions over the years have been many and varied, providing a range of enjoyable middle-grade routes as well as some hideous rock. His habit of taking unsuspecting newcomers to a cliff and departing rapidly once they were ensconced on some mangy horror is a characteristic that his closest friends long remember. Penning and James Boosey ended up on one of these at Butter Hole, the horrific *The Mind Field*, which turned out to be E4 5b after Penning had remarked at the bottom while looking up at an apparently easy-angled and solid crack, 'James, I think we've got a classic VS here.' They might have done better to recall that Iain Peters and Roland Perriment had had a similar experience on the wall to the right in 1982: in the words of Peters, 'We had one *Friend* in an expanding crack after 150 feet of 5a climbing in which every hold was replaceable. We were out of our trolleys on that one. When we got to the top we were so thankful we didn't dare write it up!' Nevertheless, Hillebrandt set an exemplary standard of meticulous record-keeping and he has been responsible for identifying and correcting many of the errors in the 1988 guide.

The Crusade

Just before [i.e., long after – *Ed*] guidebook deadlines ran out, became extended, and ran out again, Hope tempted Penning back to Pentire with tales of the bristling overhangs and magnificent black rock of the little-developed

Shield Cliffs. Penning, irrepressible as ever, was not disappointed and in a late flurry he climbed the excellent *Easy Prey* with Boosey, while Hope and Hillebrandt accompanied by Theresa Dunn added an excellent traverse-line, *Our Stars, Our Sky*, taking the steep black wall above the line of overhangs. The best routes were still to come: Penning and Hope broke through the overhangs to traverse the amazing line of *Pounding Heart*, and then added the even harder *Black Hunter*.

Finally, with unerring timing, and the perfect choice of a name that not only described his own five-year campaign upon the route in question but summed up the very essence of half a century of almost unique adventurous exploration, Parnell achieved success on his coveted line up the centre of The Shield itself, *The Crusade*.

The Sceptred Race (first ascent) Cow and Calf Photo: Don Sargeant

Baggy Point

OS Ref 419 406

Baggy Point [photo p.64a.] is by far the most popular area in this guide, owing mainly to its series of sun-trapping, south-facing slabs and all the accompanying delights of the seaside fleshpots of Croyde and Woolacombe.

The headland is owned by The National Trust, which maintains a car-park at the end of the narrow road leading past the beach at Croyde Bay. From it, the track continues past several hotels and houses, eventually becoming a footpath contouring gently along the coast through gorse-covered slopes for three-quarters of a mile, until the grassy, flat-topped spur above the unmistakable white expanse of slab, resplendent with warning notices, is reached. The spur is a perfect viewpoint for identifying the main areas of interest and for enjoying the antics of those unfortunate enough to have misjudged the tide or the height of the waves on Promontory Slab and The Long Rock.

Unfortunately for geographers, locals, and Coastguard, the original climbing development here led to a **swapping** of the names, **The Promontory** and **The Long Rock**; and all succeeding guides have sustained this error. **This guide is taking the opportunity to correct the situation**.

Immediately north of The Promontory is Slab Cove, ringed by high cliffs of steep grass, loose corners, and tottering walls, except for one area of relative stability – the tall, slender slab of *Pink Void*. Beyond Slab Cove, The Long Rock, with its two striking groove-lines, extends seawards from the enormous Baggy Hole, the repellent interior of which is emphasized by the weird striations and flutings of The Central Wall. Northwards again, the parallel, angled slabs of Scrattling Zawn can be seen. The steeper section of cliff to the south of Scrattling Zawn is split into two areas, Cheesegrater Cliff and Concrete Wall. The rock here is generally less secure, making the routes more serious propositions than climbs of the same grades on other cliffs. However, recent development on this section has opened up a new arena for adventure that should not be shunned by the ambitious.

On the slabs the situations are usually superb, protection is at worst adequate, and the rock is normally solid, though the finishes of some routes are somewhat over-vegetated. The excellent friction combines with the amenable angle, and the emphasis on footwork rather than the arms is welcome news for the old, weak, infirm, and those suffering surfeits of Peak District limestone. The sea, as always, enlivens proceedings, as the tidal variation can be more than 30 feet, though imagination and a flexible approach in the choice of climb can usually overcome any problems so caused.

Please refer to page 15. The [R] symbol shows that climbing on routes so marked is forbidden from 15th March to 31st July unless there are notices to the contrary.

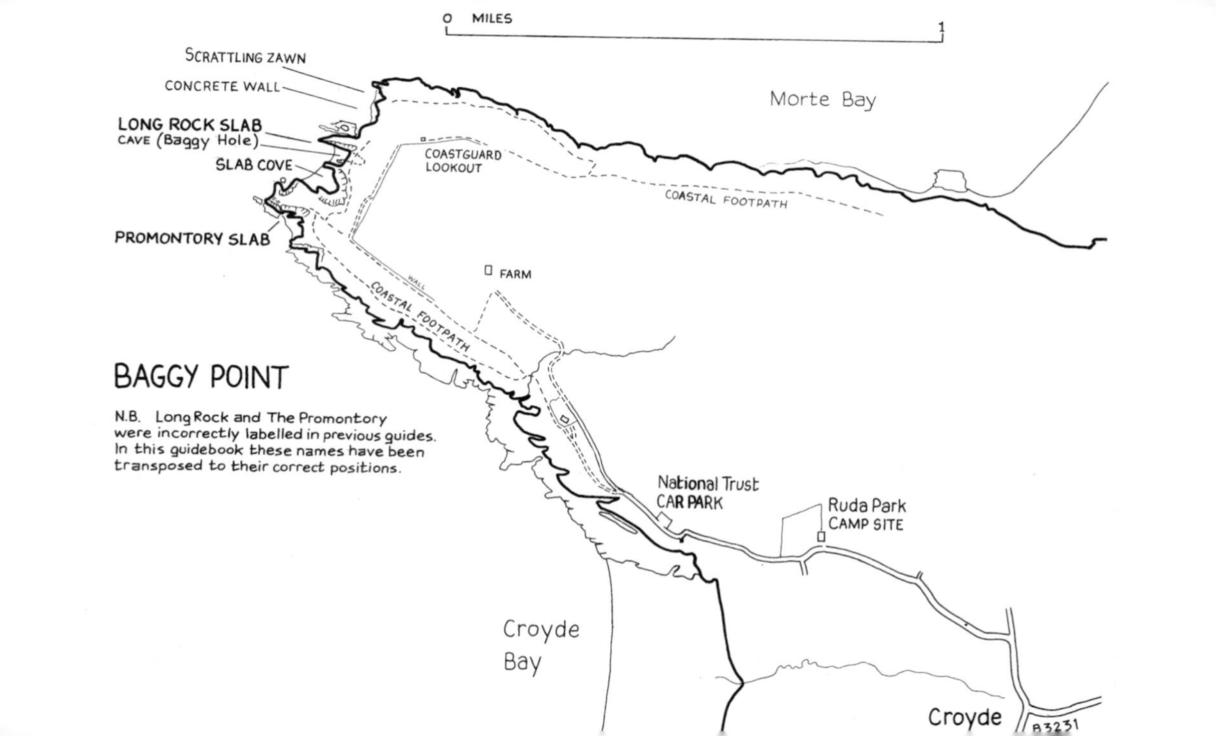
0 MILES 1
SCRATTLING ZAWN
CONCRETE WALL
LONG ROCK SLAB
CAVE (Baggy Hole)
SLAB COVE
PROMONTORY SLAB
Morte Bay
COASTGUARD LOOKOUT
COASTAL FOOTPATH
FARM
WALL
COASTAL FOOTPATH
BAGGY POINT
N.B. Long Rock and The Promontory
were incorrectly labelled in previous guides.
In this guidebook these names have been
transposed to their correct positions.
National Trust
CAR PARK
Ruda Park
CAMP SITE
Croyde
Bay
Croyde
B3231

The northern-most routes at Baggy are found in a narrow, brooding zawn on the reverse side of the *Scrattling Crack* slab, which has a steep, dark wall.

Last of the Big Nuts 70 feet E1 4c † (1.6.85)
Climb the crack that is the backside of *Scrattling Crack*. The rock is suspect.

Chouinard's Back Yard 60 feet Very Severe 4c † (1986)
Start directly behind *Chouinard's Yard*, at a ledge level with low-water. Climb up into a corner and finish between it and the arête.

Scrattling Zawn

This is the zawn to the right of the conspicuous slanting slabs. The approach to all the routes in this area is by descending the corner-crack in the landward of the two slabs, the line of *Moonshot*.

Chouinard's Yard 2 100 feet Very Severe 4c (10.4.71)
The seaward of the two slabs has two parallel lines of weakness (geologically known as kink bands) left of the corner of *Scrattling Crack*. Gain the left-hand line from the right and follow it to the top.

★**Chouinard's Yard 1** 100 feet Hard Very Severe 5a (10.4.71)
Climb the right-hand line, which is more central on the slab. Poor protection.

The Go Between 100 feet Hard Very Severe 5a (3.9.77)
An eliminate line. Climb the slab directly between the preceding route and *Scrattling Crack*.

★★**Scrattling Crack** 120 feet Very Difficult (1898)
Climb the obvious corner-crack in the seaward slab. Perhaps the first ever sea-cliff classic.

Smile 130 feet Severe 4a (1.11.69)
Climb the thin crack in the centre of the landward slab.

Moonshot 130 feet Difficult (1968)
The corner-crack of the landward slab is not a great climb but is a very useful and convenient descent.

To the right of the slabs is a narrow zawn with two chimney/cracklines.

Egg 170 feet E1 (28.3.70)
This takes the left-hand chimney. A serious route.
1 80 feet 4c. Climb the chimney near its outside edge to a stance. Poorly protected.
2 30 feet 4b. Continue up the loose chimney to a good stance.
3 60 feet 4c. Continue to the final impending corner and traverse right to a loose finish. Peg belay on the edge.
3a 60 feet 5b. Climb the chimney direct (peg on the overhanging section).

Baggy Point
Scrattling Zawn Area

	Route	Grade
1	Chouinard's Yard 2	VS
2	Chouinard's Yard 1	HVS
3	Scrattling Crack	VD
4	Smile	S
5	Moonshot	D
6	Rindstone	E1
7	The Concrete Rose	HVS

Cheesegrater Cliff

Concrete Wall

The Blacksmith 150 feet Hard Very Severe [R] (23.6.79)
The black slabby wall to the right of *Egg*. Start at the foot of a very thin crack 15 feet left of the right-hand crack (the line of *Satisfaction*).
1 70 feet 5a. Pull over the bulge and climb straight up for 20 feet to gain the foot of a ramp leading up left. Follow the ramp to a stance on the edge of the chimney of *Egg*.
2 80 feet 5a. Move back right and climb the centre of the slab to a ledge beneath the short overhanging corner of *Egg*, and finish as for that route.

Satisfaction 150 feet E1 5a [R] (28.3.70)
Climb the black bulging crack to the right of *The Blacksmith*. Move left just below the top to the ledge and final corner of *Egg*, and finish as for *Egg*. Peculiar and loose rock throughout, often wet.

White Noise 100 feet Very Severe [R] (2.11.69)
Loose and not recommended. It takes the blunt rib opposite the *Scrattling* slabs. Approachable at half tide or below. Start 20 feet right of *Satisfaction* at the right-hand side of the arête, on top of a block.
1 70 feet. Climb up, trending left to the rib; then move up and right to a stance.
2 30 feet. Go up easy but loose rock and grass to the top.

Around the corner from the rib of *White Noise* is a large flat slab in a recess. There is an impressive corner at the back of this bay, which is taken by *Resurrection*. The next route climbs the black wall to the left of the corner.

☆**Reborn Man** 90 feet E3 5b † [R] (29.7.95)
A good, mostly solid adventure. Start under the obvious crack in the black wall left of *Resurrection*. Climb the crack to the ledge. Move right to the square-cut groove and go up this; then follow a rightward-trending line to the top to finish just left of *Resurrection*.

Resurrection 90 feet Hard Very Severe 4c [R] (20.4.69)
Precarious climbing with a distinct lack of protection: large nuts needed! Accessible from half tide or below. Start below the corner (peg belay). Climb up a ramp to gain the corner, which is followed to the top. Poor peg belay on the exit ledge or a stake 20 feet higher.

Cornflake Crack 90 feet Hard Very Severe 5a [R] (10.80)
The wall to the right of *Resurrection* has a distinctive crinkly appearance. Follow the obvious flake-line.

Emmental Arête 70 feet E4 5c † [R] (1.7.94)
The short leaning arête right of *Cornflake Crack*. Start on its right-hand side and climb to a hanging pod (crucial *Friends* 3 and 2½). Crimp up the left side to better holds, and exit diagonally rightwards to an easy slab. Peg and abseil-rope belay.

Cheesegrater Cliff

To the right of *Emmental Arête* is a steep, arched, serrated face. Low-to-mid tide is necessary for the scrambling approach from Scrattling Zawn.

☆☆☆**Dark Angel** 110 feet E5 6a † [R] (15.7.94)
'A contender for the finest single-pitch adventure route in the South West', taking the offwidth crack-and-groove-line 20 feet right of *Emmental Arête*. Take a full set of *Friends*. Climb the crack.

Rindstone 150 feet E1 [R] (20.8.77)
An interesting route on reasonable rock. At the right-hand end of the face, and 10 feet right of *Dark Angel*, is a deep chimney. Start at a thinner and more attractive crack just left of the chimney.
1 90 feet 5a. Climb the crack; then move right at its top to take a stance above the main part of the chimney.
2 60 feet 5a. Climb the shallow and exposed chimney to the top.

Death on a Stick 65 feet E5 6a † [R] (6.8.95)
Poor rock, poor protection, and a high crux make this a serious lead. Start on a ledge to the right of *Rindstone* and 20 feet above the sea, and climb the innocuous-looking groove above. Finish, with heart in mouth, directly above the amazing pancake.

☆☆☆**Hawaiian Pipeline** 90 feet E1 5a † [R] (6.8.95)
A potential North Coast classic – low on technicality, high on adventure. From the belay at the top of *Death on a Stick*, follow the leftward-rising traverse-line on bucket holds, with a brief upward excursion in the groove, to finish on the large ramp above *Emmental Arête*.

Concrete Wall

This is the section of cliff between Cheesegrater Cliff and The Long Rock. The best approach is from Scrattling Zawn at low-to-mid tide: heavy seas would make this exciting but unwise. Most of the rock is decidedly loose but recent exploration has shown that there is scope for adventure.

To the left of the obvious ramp-line of *The Concrete Rose* is a smooth golden wall with a high ramp at its base, approached by scrambling easily up a spur used by nesting gulls. The routes accepting this challenge are well protected and non-tidal. The left-hand side of the wall is marked by a flaky corner-system.

Bird's Nest Crack 80 feet Extremely Severe 5a † [R] (3.2.96)
Thoroughly traditional. Climb the corner to a ledge (belay possible). Gain the overhang above by climbing up to its left-hand side; then surmount it on its right (peg removed) to finish up cracks in the slab above.

Two Birds, One Stone 80 feet E3 5c † [R] (2.94)
Start at the top of the ramp at a series of deep flake cracks. Go up and rightwards onto a wall to the diagonal break. Climb straight up a thin crack to reach a traverse-line, which is followed to the right to the obvious hanging corner at the right-hand side of the golden wall. Finish more easily but on loose rock.

Fafnir 80 feet E2 5b † [R] (2.94)
Climb *Two Birds, One Stone* onto the wall; then traverse right to the diagonal break. Continue up and right to the bottom of the hanging corner. Finish more easily but up looser rock.

Concrete Karma 150 feet E3 5b † [R] (14.3.99)
The route is based on the left arête of *The Concrete Rose*. Start a few feet left of *The Concrete Rose*, at a corner. Climb the corner to the overhang, traverse left to the arête, and continue to a ledge. Step right onto the slab and climb its left edge to the overhang. Step down and left to join the hanging corner of *Fafnir* and finish up this.

The Concrete Rose 220 feet Hard Very Severe [R] (12.10.69)
Although the climbing is technically straightforward, this is a serious lead on very doubtful rock. It takes the impressive ramp containing two large roofs just right of an easy-angled subsidiary buttress. Start between two caves.
1 80 feet. Follow the ramp to the first roof. Small stance and peg belays (removed).
2 140 feet 4c. Traverse right; then climb a steep wall to reach the second ramp, which is climbed to the second roof (peg removed). Move left around the arête and climb up and across the wall to a small ledge and a spike runner. Continue up, then right to a shallow groove, which is followed easily to the top. Stake belay 10 feet back (may not be in place).

New Boots and Panties 215 feet Extremely Severe [R] (12.7.83)
Start on the opposite side of the cave to *The Concrete Rose*.
1 60 feet. Start on a boulder and climb a crack leading to slabs below the obvious corner.
2 45 feet 5b. Climb the corner to a stance on the right.
3 90 feet 5b. Step left and climb the steep wall (peg) to a ledge. Move up to an overhang and traverse left across dubious flakes to an obvious left-trending groove. Climb the groove for 20 feet to a stance.
4 20 feet 5a. Continue in the same line to the top.

The Arête 300 feet Very Difficult [R] (23.6.79)
The prominent sharp arête between Concrete Wall and The Long Rock is gained from the right and followed throughout. Steep grass to finish.

The next three routes are on the right wall of the arête and can be approached from Scrattling Zawn at low-to-mid tide, or by scrambling down the steep grass as for The Long Rock. A 200-foot abseil down further steep grass and rubbish leads into the zawn on the north side of The Long Rock.

Subsultus 60 feet Very Severe 4c [R] (13.11.83)
Start beneath the thin vertical crack approximately a third of the way along the wall. Climb the crack to reach and follow the shallow groove next to an overlap, and make a final delicate move to gain *The Arête*. Peg belay.

★**Slipstream II** 70 feet E1 5b [R] (13.11.83)
Start just right of *Subsultus*. Climb a thin crack to the overlap, move right over this, and continue along the horizontal break. Mantelshelf over the break and climb the 'blank' wall to a second break. Finish direct up a short, shallow groove to nut belays on *The Arête*.

Fowl Play Fowler 70 feet Very Severe 4b [R] (13.11.83)
To the right of the preceding routes are three prominent crack/chimney lines. Start at the shallow left-facing corner-groove right of the first chimney. Climb the groove to a sloping ledge leading left into a wide finishing-crack. Nut belays on *The Arête*.

The Long Rock

Previously known as **The Promontory**.

Though not as high as The Promontory, The Long Rock slab is a degree or two steeper and mostly much cleaner, and the climbs follow generally more independent lines. The two prominent grooves/corners taken by *Doors of Perception* and *Urizen* are useful identification features. Half-way between these two is the shallower, vertical overlap of *Undercracker*. At the left-hand (seaward) side of the slab is a well-defined horizontal overlap, and further parallel horizontal breaks are found between *Doors of Perception* and *Urizen*. The higher slab to the right of *Urizen* contains a number of vegetated straight cracks in its upper half before it is swallowed up by the cavernous mouth of Baggy Hole.

At low tide The Long Rock can be gained by boulder-hopping from Slab Cove (see page 53). The routes right of *Urizen* actually start from the beach so this approach suits them. At other times it is possible to descend the steep grassy slope leading directly to the crest of The Long Rock. The proximity of Baggy Hole on one side and the unattractive alternative on the north side make a fixed rope from the *in-situ* stake a sensible precaution. Abseil anchors are located above the corner of *Urizen*. At its base is the start of a ledge-system giving access to most of the foot of the slab except when wave-washed at high tide.

Come Back Canute 70 feet Very Severe 4c [R] (1978)
The first feature right of the seaward edge of the slab is a ramp leading to a corner. This is the line of the route.

Don't Bring Harry 70 feet Very Severe 4c [R] (8.7.80)
Start 30 feet left of the end of the ledges, as close to the sea as your second will tolerate, below some thin cracks. Climb these direct past a scoop to the top.

Drift 70 feet E1 5b [R] (8.7.80)
Start just right of the preceding route and climb straight up the slabs to the overlap. Surmount this via a painful crack to reach a smooth scoop. Finish direct.

Culm-de-sac 85 feet Very Severe 4c [R] (6.76)
Start 15 feet left of the seaward end of the ledges. Climb to a small hold, and then break left to a larger one. Move up to ledges below the overlap and finish directly over this on large holds and up the crack above.

Sting 75 feet Very Severe 4c [R] (27.3.70)
Start at the left-hand end of the ledges, beneath a diagonal crack, which is climbed to a thin vertical crack. Follow this crack to the overlap at a protruding block and surmount it on good holds to finish up the crack above. Alternatively, continue left for 15 feet beneath the overlap to a crack leading through it to a crusty wall and the top.

★Dream Lover 90 feet Hard Very Severe 5b [R] (21.1.79)
An interesting route taking a direct line above the start of *Sting*. Climb the thin crack above the left-hand edge of the ledges to a right-angled break in the overlap. Surmount the overlap via the break and follow the thin crack to the top.

★★Pickpocket 130 feet Hard Very Severe 5b [R] (23.11.69)
An excellent route, the hard moves of which are very well protected. Start 20 feet to the left of the obvious groove of *Doors of Perception*, at a short corner. Climb the corner to the overhang and step right beneath this to a rib. A precarious step up right enables a pocket to be reached. Then move right to a much larger pocket. Step up and move up and left to a small ledge, and follow the obvious diagonal line to the top.

Coast of Triumphs 75 feet Hard Very Severe 5a [R] (26.4.80)
Start 10 feet left of *Doors of Perception*, below a lone, thin, hanging groove, which is climbed as far as the overhang. Step left into the top of the *Pickpocket* groove and climb over the overlap on the left to two thin parallel cracks, which lead to a good ledge. Move left to finish.

★Ye Olde Scrote 120 feet E3 5c [R] (6.10.79)
A sustained route giving technical climbing. Start at a thin crack a few feet left of the base of *Doors of Perception*. Climb the crack to the overlap, and then move leftwards (peg) up the diagonal overlap to join *Pickpocket*. Move back right and climb the thin cracks (peg removed) in the slab to the top.

Baggy Point
The Long Rock

No.	Route	Grade
1	Sting	VS
2	Dream Lover	HVS
3	Pickpocket	HVS
4	Coast of Triumphs	HVS
5	Ye Olde Scrote	E3
6	Doors of Perception	E1
7	Speed and Distance	E3
8	Twinkletoes	VS
9	Inferno	E5
10	No Sweat	E1
11	Undercracker	HVS
12	Ghecko Blaster	E4
13	Slip It In Quick	E3
14	Terrapin	E3
15	Soft Touch	E4
16	Lost Horizon	VS
17	Urizen	VS
18	Shangri-La	S
19	Wee Beastie	VS
20	Blowin' Free	HVS
21	The Great Gig in the Sky	VS
22	The Great Beast	E1

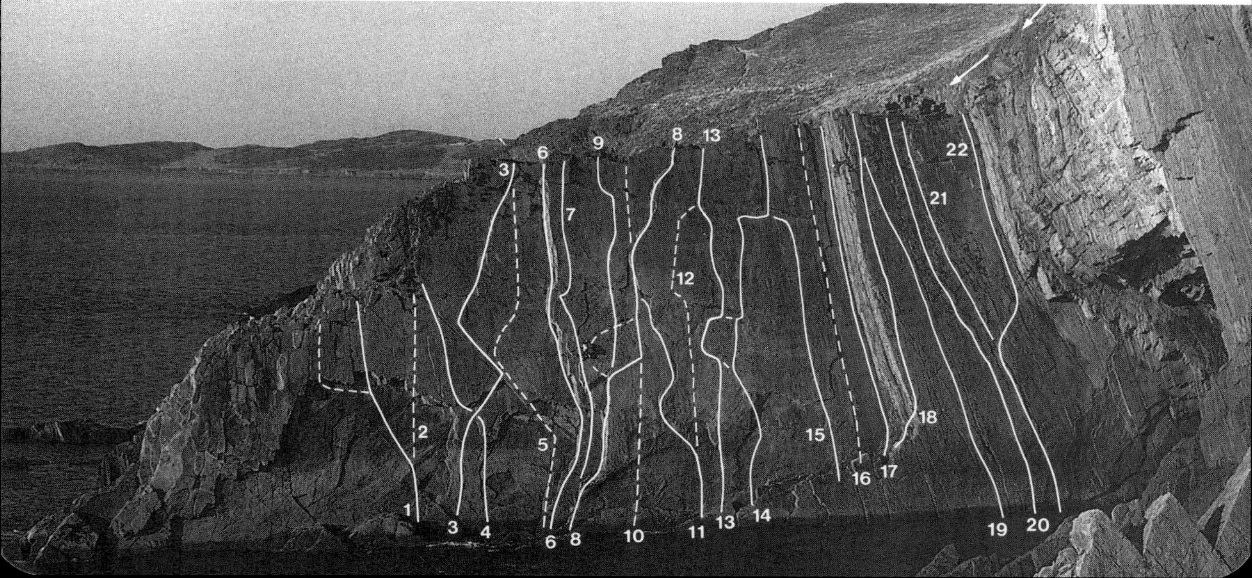

★★Doors of Perception 120 feet E1 5b [R] (15.3.70)
The obvious left-facing groove – an excellent route. Climb the groove to the overlap and then continue with more difficulty to the roof in the main groove above. (The original line traversed in left from *Twinkletoes* to reach this point.) Move left and up to reach a ledge. Follow the groove to the top.

★Speed and Distance 130 feet E3 5c [R] (8.7.80)
The right arête of the groove of *Doors of Perception*, a bold and fine climb, though contrived. Climb up the slab just right of the initial groove of *Doors of Perception* to a good ledge. Go up to gain a thin curving crack in the arête, which is climbed to the ledge in the main groove. Step right and sprint up the bald arête to the top.

★Twinkletoes 130 feet Very Severe 4c [R] (18.10.69)
A good open climb trending diagonally right to finish up the V-groove of *Undercracker*. Start as for *Speed and Distance*. Climb up and right to the foot of a short blank corner, and climb it. Then, either move right to a crack leading past a horizontal break to the slanting overlap; or move left to the arête, step up, and traverse right before climbing up to the same point. Continue rightwards into the inverted V; then follow the right-slanting ramp to the top.

★★Inferno 130 feet E5 6a [R] (1985)
A very sustained and technical route up the centre of the blank slab above the *Twinkletoes* traverse. Start as for *Twinkletoes*, and move up and right to the short blank corner. Continue direct to the overlap (peg 6 feet above). Climb past the peg by a series of very thin moves to reach a good finger-slot. Further difficult climbing leads up and right to a good peg in a short diagonal crack. Over to the right is a fingerhold in another diagonal crack and, above this, a welcome jug in a horizontal break. Traverse 8 feet left to good finishing-holds.

☆☆Embers 130 feet E5 6b [R] (5.9.86)
Bald and bold – a more sustained companion route to *Inferno*. Start as for *Twinkletoes* or *No Sweat* and climb as far as the slanting overlap below and left of the inverted V. Pull over onto the slab, and go up hairline cracks on microscopic holds until it is possible to move left and join *Inferno* at its top peg. Finish up *Inferno*.

★No Sweat 120 feet E1 5c [R] (1979)
To the right of *Twinkletoes* a thin crack splits the slab, eventually joining *Twinkletoes* at the inverted-V-groove. Above and to the left is a very thin crack (not to be confused with the hairline cracks of *Embers* further left), which is climbed with difficulty to the top.

★Undercracker 140 feet Hard Very Severe 5a [R] (20.3.74)
Between the two main groove-systems is a series of shallow corners ending at a prominent inverted V, giving a fine open climb with well-spaced protection. Start below a short groove topped by a block overhang some 30 feet right of *Doors of Perception*. Climb up to and pass the overhang on

its left to reach good holds. Traverse left along a crystalline break; then go up onto a small sloping ramp. Follow the ramp and the more difficult blank groove to the foot of the left-slanting overlaps leading to the inverted V. Climb these and move right to finish up the obvious ramp.

Right of the *Undercracker* corners, the slab becomes blanker and has few features other than a series of parallel horizontal breaks and, in the centre, a shallow depression formed by a vague arched overlap.

★**Ghecko Blaster** 130 feet E4 5c [R] (1.8.85)
One of the independent eliminates common to this section of the slab, giving excellent sustained climbing. Start as for *Undercracker* and climb to the short roof-capped groove, which is climbed to the ledge at 20 feet. Continue straight up to reach a horizontal break a few feet left of the obvious arched overlap. Make two moves left to a thin crack in the otherwise very blank slab. Bold climbing up the crack leads to the next break. The thin crack above is difficult for the short. At its top, move left to finish, or step right and climb the final crack of *Slip It In Quick*.

★**Slip It In Quick** 140 feet E3 5c [R] (18.11.79)
Again, something of an eliminate but the climbing is of fine quality throughout. Start at a thin crack midway between the initial groove of *Undercracker* and the right-slanting overlap of *Terrapin*. Climb the crack direct to the open slab, on which you are forced rightwards to good holds (on *Terrapin*) below the arched overlap. Traverse left for a few feet; then go up right to a horizontal break and climb the left-hand side of the arched overlap to reach large pockets in the slab on the left. Climb the very thin cracks above, and then move left until it is possible to step right to a short final crack which leads to the top.

★★**Terrapin** 140 feet E3 5b [R] (16.5.76)
Though technically reasonable, this very fine climb is a bold undertaking as protection is well spaced and some of the flakes creak like old door-hinges. Start 25 feet left of *Urizen*, at a thin crack leading to a right-slanting overlap. Climb the crack and step left into the overlap, which is used to reach the narrow ledge above. Follow the diagonal crack up to the left to a horizontal break, and step right to a series of vibrating flakes (treat with appropriate care – others have to climb this route after you) that lead to another horizontal break. (This point can be reached by traversing left from the lower break, then moving up and back to the right – much less worrying than the flake experience.) Above and to the right of the shallow arching corner are more thin flakes, which are climbed past a peg to a thinner horizontal break. Step left to a pocket, move up, and then traverse right along a crack for 15 feet past a shallow blind corner to a narrow ledge. Finish up the thin face-crack above.

★★**Slipstream I** 140 feet E5 6a [R] (9.82)
Highly technical and sustained climbing, similar to *Soft Touch* but harder.

Start at a very thin crack in the slab right of the slanting overlap of *Terrapin*, and climb it to the first horizontal break. Continue with increasing difficulty to the next break, which is reached just right of a downward-pointing flake. Move up and slightly left to a very narrow foot-ledge; then climb diagonally right to a third and thinner break. Step left onto *Terrapin* at the peg and follow a diagonal line rightwards on thin flakes to the final horizontal break. Move left below the final crack of *Soft Touch* and finish via a diminutive hanging corner on the left.

★★**Last Testament** 100 feet E6 6b [R] (4.10.92)
An intensely run-out, super-direct but natural line between *Slipstream I* and *Soft Touch*. None of the difficulties is next to gear and a preparedness to stay cool and attached, rather than to panic and detach, is vital. Start 8 feet right of the initial vertical crack of *Terrapin*.
Take fingernail edges to a break at 10 feet. Swing left and then bear thinly rightwards to a good undercut at the overlap. Pull over rightwards and step left to the first main horizontal break (awkward gear – *Friend 1½* and *Rock 6* essential). Go straight up the slab above, with no gear and thinner and thinner moves, to reach the second main horizontal break just to the right of a fragile downward-pointing flake. Continue direct up the next blank section until a decisive long reach from a left-hand layaway gains the third main horizontal break (peg). Move up again (direct and immediately left of *Soft Touch*) to better holds (on *Slipstream I*) and the final horizontal break. Finish as for *Slipstream I* by bearing leftwards to a tiny right-facing corner.

★★★**Soft Touch** 130 feet E4 6a [R] (5.9.76)
The original hard route on The Long Rock still demands respect. Start 10 feet left of *Urizen* (as for *Lost Horizon*). Move left immediately and climb up and over a right-angled overlap on very small holds. Continue to a short horizontal crack at its right-hand edge. Step up and left to a thin crack (peg), above which a series of very delicate moves leads to good holds in a horizontal break. Easier climbing past a peg gains a higher break. Step right to an obvious hold; then go straight up to a small ledge on the uppermost break. Finish up the thin crack above.

Touch and Go 130 feet E5 6a † [R] (1.10.88)
The climbing is more independent than it looks. Bold and thin with several dubious but crucial flakes. As for *Soft Touch*, climb up to the overlap and over it to reach the break. Clip the upper peg on *Soft Touch* (sensible); then climb the right edge of the slab to the next break. Above, the right edge is out of bounds since *Lost Horizon* uses it, so continue up the eliminate line, passing a peg on the left of the right edge (crux).

★★★**Lost Horizon** 130 feet Very Severe 5a [R] (31.1.70)
[Photo p.64a.] An enjoyable, interesting, and very safe route. One of the best 5a pitches anywhere. Climb the obvious continuous crack-system in the slab 10 feet left of *Urizen*.

★Urizen 130 feet Very Severe 4c [R] (8.10.69)
The striking right-hand corner, climbed by using a repetitive sequence of movements with your left foot on delicate friction and your right foot following a parallel line in the corner or on its right wall. Protection is superb.

Keep Left 150 feet Very Severe 4c †† [R]
Climb the right arête of *Urizen* starting from the beach at low tide. Artificial and rather pointless; poor-quality climbing. (The start may have been affected by a recent rockfall.)

★★★Shangri-La 130 feet Severe 4a [R] (1.3.70)
The best climb of its grade at Baggy and probably on the North Coast. At high tide (especially in heavy seas, when care should be taken to belay), the situations are magnificent and only the first few moves are tricky. Start at the foot of *Urizen* and step up and around the arête to gain a deep crack, which is followed on excellent holds, taking the easiest natural line to the top. (The start has been affected by a recent rockfall, but the route has been climbed since and remains within the grade.)

The slab right of *Shangri-La* is split by a series of cracks but is more vegetated. It ends at the corner formed by its junction with Baggy Hole. All the climbs start at low tide from the beach, but a traverse can be made from *Urizen* if necessary.

Wee Beastie 160 feet Very Severe ‡ [R] (23.10.75)
Good climbing in its lower half, but spoiled by vegetation higher up. Start at a crack 15 feet right of and below *Urizen*.
1 120 feet 4c. The crack is smooth and awkward to start but better holds soon arrive. Belay on some small ledges.
2 40 feet. Continue up the line, heading for *Shangri-La*.

Blowin' Free 150 feet Hard Very Severe 5a ‡ [R] (3.9.77)
Another good line spoilt by the hanging gardens. Start in the centre of the slab, below a leftward-leaning ramp. Climb up the ramp with difficulty to reach the crack, which was clean once but alas is no longer. Follow this to the top, where loose rock adds seriousness to the route.

The Great Gig in the Sky 160 feet Very Severe ‡ [R] (5.9.76)
The top pitch is loose and vegetated. Start at a black crack directly beneath the corner at the right-hand end of the slab.
1 70 feet 4a. Climb the crack, which soon eases, to another, diagonal crack leading towards the edge of the roof and a small stance. Peg belays removed.
2 90 feet 4c. To the left are slanting cracks, which are followed leftwards to finish at the left end of the overlaps.

The Great Beast 160 feet E1 [R] (27.3.70/18.9.77)
An atmospheric route, on slightly worrying rock, with the black depths of Baggy Hole to its right, where unseen horrors are said to lurk. Start directly

beneath the edge of the roof.
1 70 feet 5b. Climb rightwards up a series of steps to a thin crack, which is climbed passing a small overlap to its right to a stance.
2 90 feet 5a. Continue up to the corner, past a rock scar, and bridge up to the first overlap (peg). Continue up the corner past further overlaps to a difficult finish.

The Long Rock Traverses

★★**Fools Rush In** 300 feet E1 [R] (28.3.70)
A fine left-to-right girdle of The Long Rock, following a natural line of weakness at half-height. Start at a notch in the crest of the ridge, level with the large ledge on *Doors of Perception*, approached by scrambling down the crest of the ridge
1 70 feet 4c. Traverse right to a ledge on *Pickpocket;* then, at a white scar, step down to the right and then up to the right. Continue into the groove of *Doors of Perception*. Move up to a ledge and nut belays.
2 140 feet 5b. Move out right onto the arête and follow the overlap across *Twinkletoes* and into the shallow, slanting groove of *Undercracker*. Descend this to a horizontal break, which is followed to a shallow niche. Step down, and continue traversing until forced to move up to a higher break (at *Soft Touch*) and continue to a small ledge in the corner of *Lost Horizon*. Difficult moves on small holds allow easier ground on *Urizen* to be reached. Swing across the right retaining wall on large creaking holds and take a stance in the crack of *Shangri-La*.
3 90 feet. Follow *Shangri-La* to the top.
(Originally the traverse continued across *Wee Beastie* etc. to finish up *The Great Beast*. The return of copious plant life makes this rather unattractive now.)

Fallen Angel 250 feet E3 [R] (16.6.85)
A low-level girdle, which is contrived though not without technical interest. Start at lowish tide, at the seaward end of The Long Rock.
1 120 feet 5c. Climb up to the obvious horizontal band of overhangs and traverse right beneath these to *Pickpocket*. Follow this route for a few feet to a junction with *Ye Olde Scrote*. Reverse the latter's crux down to the peg – pleasant for the leader but very exciting for the second. Traverse right to belay below the initial roof of *Doors of Perception*.
2 130 feet 5c. Traverse right into *Twinkletoes;* then follow a thin crack leading to the traverse of *Undercracker*. Continue up to a ledge on the right; then go diagonally across the open slab as for *Slip It In Quick* and join *Terrapin*. Descend slightly and follow a thin crack all the way to *Urizen*. Finish up or down.

Floodland 210 feet E1 5b † [R] (6.10.91)
A rising traverse from bottom right to top left of The Long Rock. Probably the most 'useful' of The Long Rock traverses, since it starts from the bottom ledge yet is accessible at high tide, when it is especially atmospheric.

1 80 feet 5b. Follow the obvious rising traverse from the foot of *Soft Touch* into the initial groove of *Terrapin*. Continue in the same line to gain the first peg of *Undercracker*. Belay on this and the peg above.
2 130 feet 5b. From the top peg, make a long move left to gain the flake traverse of *Twinkletoes* (lower option) and follow it to a bent peg on the arête of *Speed and Distance*. Step round into *Doors of Perception* below the bulge and follow the obvious traverse-line leftwards until it reaches the top of *Dream Lover*. The wise will top out here as the last 15 feet are lichenous. The adventurous and doom-laden will continue.

The Oldest Swingers in Town 150 feet E3 † [R] (2.10.88)
This follows a traverse-line above the main pitch of *Fools Rush In*. Start two-thirds of the way up *Urizen* from a hanging stance, level with the line.
1 100 feet 6a. A hard move left gains *Lost Horizon* and the main break. Continue along the break past the second peg on *Soft Touch*. The moves from here to the arête are the crux. Belay on the ledge at the base of the *Undercracker* ramp.
2 50 feet 5c. Climb the thin crack above to the break below the top. A strenuous traverse left leads to the arête, and this is followed to the top.

The Central Walls

Immediately right of Baggy Hole is an impressive fluted wall containing a number of futuristic possibilities. Beyond, the rock disintegrates dramatically. There are two unsavoury routes. **Multiplator** (320 feet Extremely Severe [R] 29.3.70) starts up a steep groove to the right of a yellow slab and follows the main ridge to a mass of grass-covered bulges before trending left to a reasonable ledge below an overhanging block. Finish rightwards on bad rock and up a final short wall. Belay as for the top of *Pink Void*. An alternative start, **Mini Moose's Turnip Poem** (Extremely Severe †† [R] 10.91), starts half-way up a striking 45-degree ramp to the right of Baggy Hole and climbs broken grassy rock diagonally rightwards to gain the main ridge.

Slab Cove

There are three North Coast once-classics in the cove, and five other lines that might, with a stretch of the imagination, be called rock-climbs. Even the former group now show much vegetation and are climbed increasingly rarely. A steep path leads down the grassy north side of The Promontory to the boulder-beach at half tide or lower. Scramble over this to the base of the *Pink Void* slab. Left of the main slab is a long, grey, slanting groove.

Astrodyne 290 feet Extremely Severe † (12.7.81)
1 140 feet 5b. Climb the grey groove past an old peg at 60 feet. Place a peg where the groove becomes smooth and difficult and continue to a stance on the left at the top.
2 70 feet 5a. Overcome the bulge on its left side (peg) to gain a grassy groove leading to a stance below the remains of the prominent chimney of

Astronomy Domine.
3 80 feet 4b. Climb the dangerous, disintegrating chimney above with no protection. The first ascensionists made it to the top.

★Set the Controls 270 feet E5 †† (22.4.89)
Contrived but good technical climbing left of *Heart of the Sun*. There may be some holds missing on pitch 3.
1 70 feet 5c. *Heart of the Sun* pitch 1.
2 60 feet 6a/b. Move right onto the horizontal break leading across the open slab, and go easily up and to the right to a thin vertical crack (as for *Heart of the Sun*). From here, step left and move up to clip a high peg (possibly missing). Traverse left keeping low, and then move up to a peg and a good hold. Reach two pockets up left, and go up right to good flake holds. Ignore easy ground to the left, and step right past a peg to a thin crack which leads to narrow ledges. Multiple nut belays just right of *Pink Void*.
3 140 feet 6a. Step right from the stance to a thin diagonal seam. Follow this seam, passing to the right of a peg, to reach ledges; then climb up a thin ramp to the big diagonal overhang. Pull over via a thin ragged crack and make a long step right to a small foothold. Traverse back left above the overhang with increasing difficulty to the rib of *Pink Void*. Finish up *Pink Void*.

★Heart of the Sun 300 feet E2 †† (19.10.69/2.77)
Once considered a superb route, its second pitch takes the fine crack in the centre of the open wall to the right of *Pink Void*. The upper section of this pitch is now suffering increasing instability, thus much reducing the enjoyment. The shallow groove-system of *Pink Void* curves rightwards near its base. Start left of this, near the left-hand edge of the slab, below a small serrated roof and 20 feet right of *Astrodyne*.
1 70 feet 5c. A fine pitch. Climb the overhang and continue more easily up the thin crack before bearing right to a break below a bulging section. Step left and make a series of steeper moves using the thin crack in the bulge. Continue up the crack above to a small stance and peg and nut belays in the groove of *Pink Void*.
2 80 feet 5b. Move right onto the horizontal break leading across the open slab and go easily up and to the right to a thin vertical crack, which is climbed with increasing difficulty past a peg to a hanging stance in slings at a horizontal break. Peg and nut belays.
3 150 feet 5b. Follow the thin crack diagonally right, heading for the overlap. Cross this and ascend the rotten corner until it is possible to move left into a thin crack leading to the final section of *Pink Void*.
Variation
3a 70 feet 5a. An easier and cleaner finish, avoiding the unpleasant corner, can be made by climbing the thin diagonal crack to gain a faint break, which leads delicately up and across to the left to the final stance of *Pink Void*.

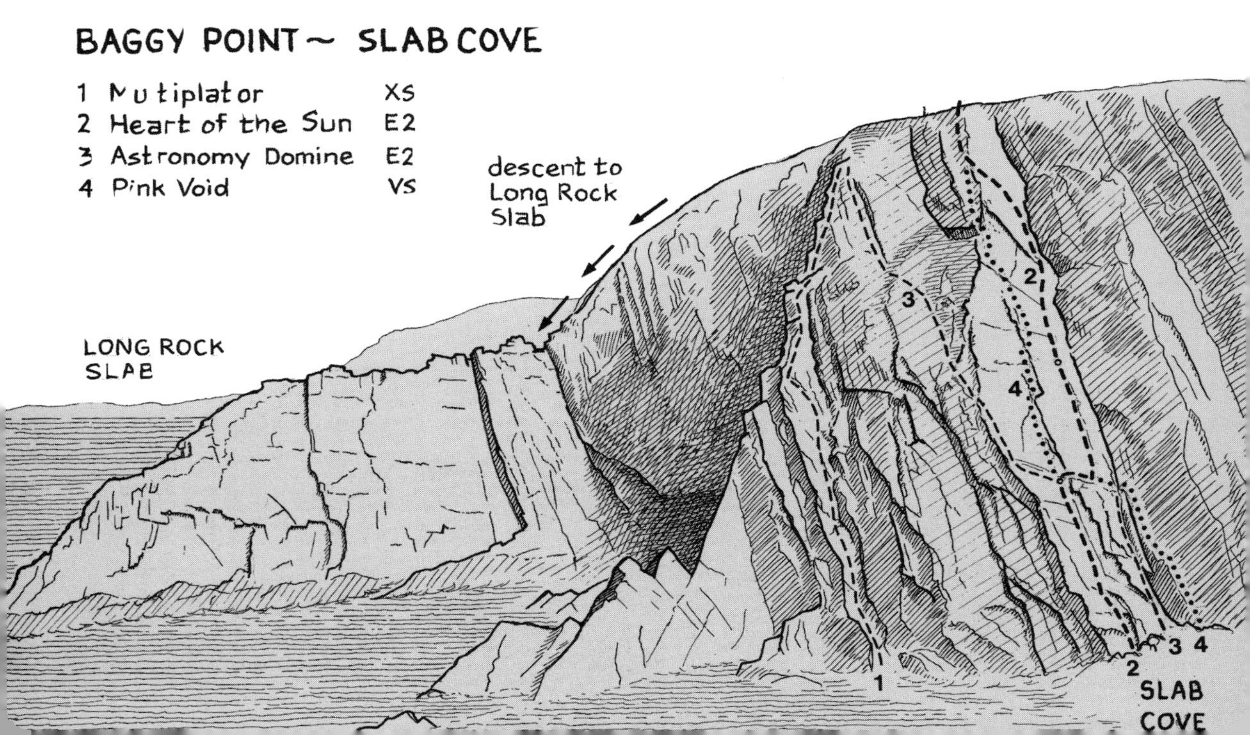

BAGGY POINT ~ SLAB COVE

1 Mutiplator XS
2 Heart of the Sun E2
3 Astronomy Domine E2
4 Pink Void VS

descent to Long Rock Slab

LONG ROCK SLAB

1 2 3 4

SLAB COVE

Astronomy Domine 370 feet E2 †† (11.9.70)
The independent climbing on this route is horrific. Start at the foot of the loose red corner.
1 50 feet 5a. Totter up the loose red corner to a large stance and knife-blade peg belays (not in place).
2 50 feet 4c. Traverse left on the obvious line as for *Pink Void* and go up to the small stance and peg belay in the groove.
3 70 feet 5a. Now things really start to deteriorate! Continue traversing left for 20 feet across the grey slab. Go up a crack; then tremble left again to a stance on the edge (of sanity).
4 120 feet 4c. Climb the groove above for about 30 feet; then cross a grassy gully on the left and climb a broken wall to the foot of the obvious corner.
5 80 feet 5a. A dangerous pitch – the second should be belayed well to one side (preferably on *Scrattling Crack*!) Shake up the terminally loose chimney, with no protection, to triumph at the top.

★Pink Void 340 feet Very Severe †† (13.10.69)
Owing to a number of rockfalls over the years, this is not the great sea-cliff classic that it once was. Nevertheless, it is still a grand expedition. Start just left of the loose corner bounding the right edge of the slab.
1 130 feet 4c. Climb the cracked slab for 30 feet; then move left over poised blocks to a ledge in the corner (peg). Continue across the break in the main slab to gain the main groove-line. Continue up the groove to a stance and peg belays.
2 100 feet 4b. Continue up the groove above for about 30 feet to a peg. Move up right, then back left to regain the groove, which is followed to its end. Climb up and right for 10 feet and then go straight up on good holds to a sloping ledge beneath the final rib. Step round to the left to a stance and peg belays.
3 110 feet 4a. Follow the line of the rib above on good but increasingly earthy holds to stake belays. This pitch has suffered recent rockfall and is in an unstable state.

The cliff on the landward side of *Pink Void* consists of a mixture of tottering grooves, unstable cracks, and vertiginous grass. There are three routes for those bored with safe climbs and solid rock.

Bike 320 feet Hard Very Severe (2.11.69)
A line of discontinuous grooves at the left-hand side of the headwall. Start 40 feet right of *Pink Void*, at an easy-angled groove leading up to a grass patch – The Green Spider.
1 140 feet. Climb the groove with no difficulty and less protection to a ledge just left of an overhung niche at the top of The Green Spider.
2 90 feet. Traverse right (The Traverse of the Sods) to a second grass patch, possibly passing a decaying bicycle frame, to reach a peg belay below an overhang.
3 90 feet 4c. The Exit Creaks. Climb the wide corner on the left on good

grass and bad rock to reach a grass ledge. Continue more easily to the top.
Variations

Bike Direct 300 feet Hard Very Severe (1980)
Bypass the first two pitches of *Bike* by climbing a prominent groove-system that runs up the rib on the left of that route's main groove.

Tandem 300 feet Extremely Severe (1980)
Climb *Bike* to where it veers right; then continue up the wide crack in the slab on the left to a large ledge. Step right and continue as for *Bike Direct* (peg); then finish up the easier-angled groove. Most seconds would say no to this ride!

At the seaward end of The Promontory is a large through-cave which forms a zawn on its southern side. Scramble down the ridge overlooking the zawn to the base of the slab on its seaward side There is a series of cracks on the slab – these provide the main lines. Accessible only at low tide.

Margin 75 feet Hard Very Severe 4c † (9.12.85)
Climb the left-hand crack in the slab. Go up to reach the arête.

☆**Feint** 80 feet Hard Very Severe 5a/b † (9.12.85)
A delicate route. Climb the crack to the right of the preceding route to a quartz break, and continue with more difficulty to the main slanting fault. Follow the curving crack above, climbing the overhang on its left-hand side.

Ruled 80 feet Hard Very Severe 5a/b (9.12.85)
The crack to the right of *Feint* is followed to gain that route's curving crack and overhang.

The Last Lap 90 feet E2 5b † (9.9.86)
To the right again is a wider crack, which is climbed to a niche in the overlap. Pull across this and continue rightwards below a thin overlap towards the overhanging wall. Step up left onto the slab and climb it delicately leftwards, in an exposed position, to the top.

Clipper 80 feet E1 5b † (9.9.86)
To the right of the preceding route is the base of a ramp. Start up the crack from here to reach the niche in the overlap but, instead of moving right as for *The Last Lap*, continue direct to join that route for its last few feet.

The Promenade 80 feet Difficult (4.9.86)
Climb the ramp-line leading up to the left from the bottom right-hand end of the cliff.

★**Contraband** 75 feet Hard Very Severe 4c (9.9.86)
A pleasantly sustained route. Follow *The Promenade* for a few feet and then move up to the overlap at a short crack. Follow the overlap leftwards to the top.

The following routes are on the area of rock just seaward of a cave before the main through-cave is reached. They can be identified from the extreme left end of Left-Hand Slab and can be reached only by abseiling down the very narrow slab, the lower of two slabs which reach the top. All these routes are equally unattractive.

The Scythe 120 feet Very Severe 4c (14.3.70)
The top appears dangerously loose. Climb the arête to the overhangs. Take slabby rock on the left between them to finish up a short wall.

The Pox 120 feet Hard Very Severe 4c (29.3.70)
Probably contagious and definitely unsavoury, so wear rubber gloves. Climb the shallow grooves right of the arête to finish up the narrow slabs of the abseil.

Spare Rib Very Difficult (11.4.71)
Climb the clean slabby rib left of the disintegrating wall in the zawn on the north side. The approach appears to be lethal.

The Promontory

Previously known as **The Long Rock.**

The seaward end is marked by some sea-caves.

Bird Ban 120 feet E4 5c (12.6.91)
This is a serious and demanding pitch up the wall between the sea-caves at the seaward end of The Promontory. Belay on the rib between the caves, reached by abseil or by a traverse in at low tide. Go up the rib to a large flake/block; then traverse left below the leaning wall (right on the lip of the big sea-cave). Move up on a dubious flake to a square-cut roof (crux). Move right, then up past a block to a wide crack. Finish up the obvious V-groove. Belay stake missing.

Candyman 90 feet Hard Very Severe 5a † (5.91)
Climb *Bird Ban* to the large flake/block. Climb diagonally right to finish up a short corner.

The main slab is about 200 feet high and 300 feet wide, and is broken just below half height by a chain of stepped overhangs. The rock beneath these is clean and seamed with thin cracks, and offers excellent friction. Above the overhangs the vegetation becomes more intrusive, and the upper pitches of most of the routes lack the merit and interest of the lower pitches. At the left-hand side, the slab is bordered by an eroded muddy slope above a deep narrow zawn, with a blunt rocky rib to its left containing a conspicuous jammed boulder-bridge. Left of this is the smaller left-hand slab. To the right of the main slab is the striking right-angled corner of *Grand Vizier's Garden Party*, beyond which there is a further scruffy area of slab finally merging into the steep, grassy landward slope above another small zawn.

Baggy Point
The Promontory

No.	Route	Grade
1	Freddie	HS
2	Ben	S
3	Marion	HS
4	In Her Eyes	S
5	The Bridge of Khazad-Dum	VD
6	The Ridge of Khazad-Dum	M
7	Blind Faith	VS
8	Kinkyboots	VS
9	Cirrus Minor	VS
10	Midnight Cowboy	HVS
11	Long Rock Eliminate	HVS
12	Right-Hand Eliminate	HVS
13	Sexilegs	HVS
14	Hot, Sweet, and Sticky	E2
15	Gladiator	E1
16	The Straight and Narrow	E1
17	The Narrow Way	E1
18	Slip Sliding Away	E2
19	Grand Vizier's Garden Party	HVS
20	Permafrost	HVS
21	Renata	HVS
22	Svenja	VS
23	Peeping Tom	E1
24	Goats	S
25	Yellow Submarine	VS
26	Shortera	HS
27	Titmould Incorporated	HVS

At low or half tide, the simplest descent is down the muddy slope and easy rib separating the two slabs. However, routes at the right-hand end can be gained by going down steep grass until a move around a small bluff leads to a rib which angles down beneath a conspicuous corner. At high tide, the first pitch of *Kinkyboots* provides an atmospheric entry to the main slab.

Through the Looking-Glass (Several thousand feet) E3 5c (5.9.96)
A sea-level traverse from The Promontory to The Long Rock. An exciting expedition through amazing rock architecture. Start shortly before low tide and with calmish seas.
From the foot of *Double Overhang* (see below), traverse leftwards around the point to an impressive zawn. Climb into this and make a difficult swing down to gain small ledges. From here, a very short swim leads to the far side (it is possible to throw boots and chalk bag across). Continue around the next promontory to a cave leading inwards. Enter this with increasing difficulty to join another cave crossing at right angles. Head left (north) through a hole to reach easier climbing leading into Slab Cove. Cross the boulder-beach to Baggy Hole; then climb diagonally up leftwards below *Shangri La* (crux, and serious) to finish on the big ledge below *Urizen*.

Left-Hand Slab

This is the smaller slab, which has three slanting cracks to the left of the boulder-bridge. Just below the boulder-bridge is a deep gully/chimney which leads easily down to the wave-washed platform at the base of the slab. It is possible to wander at will up this slab, and many variations on the main lines of weakness have been claimed over the years. The routes described are a mixture of the original, the tried, and the tested, and offer excellent introductions to the art of Baggy slab climbing. They are also very popular, as the eroded condition of the finishing-slopes testifies. Climbers are asked to stick to the repaired areas and paths and not to wander at will over the summit slopes. To the left of the seaward arête of the slab is a large slanting roof.

Double Overhang 70 feet Severe (1.11.69)
Climb the obvious groove just left of the seaward arête over two small overhangs, and take a thin crack in the slab to a short corner, which leads easily to the top.

Affluence of Incahol 70 feet E2 5c (1983)
Climb the evident overhanging crack and niche to finish up the crack in the roof.

Nudy Rudy 75 feet Very Difficult (3.8.70)
Climb the slab just to the right of the seaward arête for 25 feet; then cross the rib and traverse left beneath the roof to gain a crack, which leads to the top. A slightly harder direct start can be made by climbing the crack below the left-hand end of the roof.

Freddie 100 feet Hard Severe 4b (15.9.76)
Climb the left-hand edge of the slab.

★**Ben** 130 feet Severe 4a (14.2.70)
[Photos p.64b.] Climb the left-hand of the three distinctive slanting cracks.

Sleepy Toes 125 feet Very Severe 4c (1978)
Climb the thin crack between *Ben* and *Marion*.

★**Marion** 120 feet Hard Severe 4b (14.2.70)
The central cracks are climbed with interesting moves in the upper section. Perhaps the best of the trio.

A recent rockfall may have affected the next four routes.

In Marion's Eyes 110 feet Very Severe 5a ††
An example of the variations possible. Climb the thin crack to the right of *Marion*, and join *Marion* for the final 20 feet.

In Her Eyes 100 feet Severe 4a †† (19.10.69)
Follow the right-hand crack to a delicate move near the top, or move right at a horizontal crack to a belay just above the boulder-bridge. There is a direct start up the thin crack to the right at Very Severe 4c.

The thin crack leading to the boulder-bridge has been climbed at Severe.

The Bridge of Khazad-Dum 50 feet Very Difficult †† (19.10.69)
Start as for *In Her Eyes*. Ascend the boundary rib of the left side of the triangular buttress which lies between Left-Hand Slab and The Main Slab. Belay on the boulder-bridge.

★**Sheet Whitening** 180 feet Very Severe †† (14.10.79)
An enjoyable right-to-left girdle of the slab. Start at the foot of the descent gully.
1 60 feet 5a. Climb a thin crack to the quartzy break. Traverse left to another thin crack and move up to a horizontal break, which leads into *In Her Eyes*. Continue left to *Marion* and belay slightly lower.
2 120 feet 5a. Traverse horizontally left along a bulge, passing an undercut flake at foot-level, to the left-hand crack. Proceed to a larger undercut flake; then go left to the arête and finish up it.

The Ridge of Khazad-Dum 100 feet Moderate
Follow the crest of the ridge from sea-level. A pleasant scramble, open to considerable variation.

The Main Slab

Where the descent route of the muddy slope meets the narrow zawn, a thin crack splits the overhang on the opposite side.

Blind Faith 160 feet Very Severe (12.9.70)
Start on the grass slope, just left of where the overhang fades.
1 40 feet 4c. Step right onto the slab and traverse to the crack, which is then followed to the right of a large flake to a small stance and peg belay (removed).
2 120 feet 4a. Carry on rightwards in the same line.

★**Kinkyboots** 200 feet Very Severe (19.10.69)
Falling over at the start of a route is normally taken as a sign of incompetence, inebriation, or both. On this climb it is both inevitable and essential. Start (usually with the words, 'You've got to be joking!') on some ledges 30 feet above the base of the narrow zawn.
1 60 feet 4c. Estimate the distance to an obvious handhold on the opposite side and fall across the zawn. Small climbers may well miss! – those who make it should then transfer their feet. Comfortable holds allow a traverse right past an overlap to a peg beneath the large overlap. Swing right to a good handhold and proceed rightwards without further excitement for 20 feet to peg and nut belays on a small ledge.
2 140 feet 4b. Reverse the traverse and go straight up to a detached flake. Continue up slightly leftwards on the line of least vegetation to the top. This pitch can be split at 90 feet.
Original Start
1a 60 feet 4c. Slightly harder, but quite entertaining. From the peg on pitch 1, descend the narrow slab to the right for 15 feet (awkward) to a good hold on the arête on the right. Swing over this and continue up to the stance.

Cirrus Minor 180 feet Very Severe (11.9.71)
This takes the narrow inset slab in the right wall of the zawn. Start at a crack curving up under overhangs.
1 60 feet 4c. Move up to the crack, which is followed via an easy ramp to the peg on the first pitch of *Kinkyboots*. Climb over the overlap to a small stance on the left. Peg belay.
2 120 feet 4a. Climb diagonally left to an obvious flake, and traverse left to a pocket (peg). Continue straight up until a line of holds trends right to the top past two pegs.

The shallow groove just right of the arête leading to the first stance of *Kinkyboots* has been climbed at Severe but lacks the character of the starts described.

★★**Midnight Cowboy** 240 feet Hard Very Severe (15.11.69)
A very good route taking the strongest natural line on the main slab, the diagonal stepped overlaps. At high tide the *Kinkyboots* entry can be used,

which much improves the route. Start at a large sea-washed boulder 15 feet right of the left edge of the slab.
1 60 feet 4c. Climb up diagonally left to reach thin cracks, which are followed until some moves horizontally right lead to a small stance beneath a reddish bulge at the left-hand side of the overlap.
2 90 feet 5a. Move diagonally right onto the slab above the overlap, step down a thin crack with difficulty to a hidden hold beneath the overlap, and traverse right to a small flake foothold. (This point can also be reached by hand-traversing the horizontal thin quartz break above.) Step up and follow the line of the overlap for 30 feet until it merges into a shallow corner. Stance on footholds 10 feet above – good nut placements.
3 90 feet 4b. Climb straight up to the top – clean rock lasts for only a few feet. Stake belays.

The next six routes have delightful first pitches on clean rough rock, above which vegetation takes over.

★Long Rock Eliminate 200 feet Hard Very Severe (11.4.71)
A pleasantly delicate route, though the second pitch is poorly protected. Start right of the large boulder, below a prominent inverted-V overlap.
1 60 feet 5a. Climb up to thin cracks, which are followed to the overlap; then go up the thin cracks above and step left to the stance of *Midnight Cowboy*.
2 140 feet 4c. Move up over the overlap and go up to the next. Climb the shallow scoop above to a small ledge (stance possible). Take the right-hand of two cracks and finish up vegetated ledges.

★Right-Hand Eliminate 210 feet Hard Very Severe (4.72)
A sustained first pitch. Start at a prominent pointed boulder below a small diagonal ramp.
1 120 feet 5a. Climb the ramp past two thin cracks to a third, which leads to a short smooth groove. Climb this and the crack above to the second overlap. Carry on up the crack above to a small stance and peg belays (removed).
2 90 feet. Above is a large, loose, and earthy overhang. Avoid it on its right and follow the easiest line to the top.

★Sexilegs 220 feet Hard Very Severe (26.10.69)
Another enjoyable first pitch. Start at the prominent pointed boulder.
1 120 feet 5a. Climb the short ramp to the second and main crack, which is climbed to a quartz break. Traverse left into a short smooth groove and go up to an undercut flake. Traverse left to a hole, and then move up a flake and step left to the overlap. Cross this by a thin move and continue to a horizontal quartz break, which is followed to a grass ledge on the left.
2 100 feet 4b. Climb up and left to grass; then bear slightly right to finish above the stance.

★Hot, Sweet, and Sticky 180 feet E2 (8.85)
An interesting but more difficult variation finish to *Sexilegs*.
1 90 feet 5c. Follow *Sexilegs* as far as the first horizontal break; then climb the very thin continuation crack directly above to the first overlap (on *Peeping Tom*). Either step left and go up to the bigger overlap on *Midnight Cowboy* or, better, move right to reach a semi-detached section of the overlap. Make a series of hard moves on tiny flakes and pockets to regain *Midnight Cowboy* just below its second stance.
2 90 feet 4b. *Midnight Cowboy* pitch 3.

★Gladiator 200 feet E1 (12.5.79/22.9.79)
Although this is an eliminate line, the climbing is of great technical interest. Start as for *Sexilegs* at the pointed boulder.
1 100 feet 5b. Follow the first very thin crack rightwards to ledges left of the first stance of *The Narrow Way*. Climb direct, crossing *The Narrow Way*, to an overlap just below the level of the belay on *Midnight Cowboy*. Traverse left to that belay.
2 100 feet 5b. Step left and climb the slab left of *Midnight Cowboy*, first slightly leftwards and then rightwards to an overlap. Surmount this on the right and finish direct.

The Narrow Way 280 feet E1 (26.10.69)
Start beneath the slanting rib and subsidiary corner 15 feet right of the pointed boulder.
1 40 feet 5b. Climb the reddish corner to the roof and make a difficult move onto the slab above. Follow the crack more easily to peg and nut belays.
2 100 feet 4b. Follow the obvious line, which leads diagonally up left to the overlap on *Midnight Cowboy*. Go up the short corner; then move left onto the slab and follow the break leftwards to a small stance and peg and nut belays.
3 140 feet 4b. Continue diagonally left; then choose the cleanest line back to the right and finish up turf. The final pitch of *Midnight Cowboy* is marginally better.

The Straight and Narrow 170 feet E1 (1.2.70)
Hardly an accurate name, but a better route than *The Narrow Way*.
1 40 feet 5b. *The Narrow Way* pitch 1.
2 100 feet 5a. Step right from the stance and climb the thin crack above; continue to a grass ledge at 80 feet. Traverse right into the corner of *Grand Vizier's Garden Party* (peg belays).
3 30 feet 4c. *Grand Vizier's Garden Party* pitch 2.

★Slip Sliding Away 180 feet E2 (26.9.79)
A fine, varied route, which initially takes the conspicuous right-facing corner left of the longer corner of *Grand Vizier's Garden Party*.
1 50 feet 5c. Climb awkwardly to a ledge left of the corner. Make a long step right into the corner, and follow it until beneath the long capping roof.

Aerial View of Baggy Point   Photo: Brian Lessware

Lost Horizon (VS)   Baggy Point
Climber: Kerry Smith   Photo: Alan Cook

Ben (S) Baggy Point
Climber: Stephanie Craddock Photo: David Hope

Make a hard move left onto a ledge (peg belays on *The Narrow Way*).
2 100 feet 4c. Traverse right beneath the second tier of overhangs for 20 feet to a crack. Follow this, moving left at a bulge, to a grass ledge leading to the peg belay of *Grand Vizier's Garden Party*.
3 30 feet 4c. *Grand Vizier's Garden Party* pitch 2.

Arterial Bypass 80 feet E3 6a † (12.7.92)
Start midway between *Slip Sliding Away* and *Grand Vizier's Garden Party*. Hard moves over an overhang are followed by more hard moves past a peg to a big roof. Swing over on a good jug to reach the traverse of *Slip Sliding Away*. Step left and follow a faint crack until it merges with the other routes. A good pitch.

Grand Vizier's Garden Party 160 feet Hard Very Severe (30.11.69)
The compelling corner at the right-hand end of the slab. A fine line spoiled by vegetation above and brittle rock below. Start beneath the corner in the dark trench.
1 130 feet 5a. Climb the corner awkwardly over bulges to the roof (peg). Traverse left and climb up into the continuation corner, which is followed to a stance above a small square-cut overhang. Peg belays.
2 30 feet 4c. Climb the fragile corner above.

★**Permafrost** 150 feet Hard Very Severe 5a (14.10.79)
The impressive right arête of the *Grand Vizier's Garden Party*. Start just right of the arête and right of an overhang in its lower section. Surmount the overhang to reach a flake 5 feet right of the arête and follow the flake to a clean ledge. Step left to a foothold on the lip of the overhang beneath the arête. Climb the crack above to a good ledge and follow the arête to a sloping ledge (peg belay). Scramble to finish.

Renata 130 feet Hard Very Severe 5a (28.2.70)
A route up the continuation slab to the right of *Grand Vizier's Garden Party*. Start above some boulders in the gully bed, at a diagonal crack, which is followed to a grass ledge on the left. From the left end of the ledge, step up to a smooth groove and to a doubtful jammed block, and use this to gain flakes above. Step right and go straight up before moving left onto the arête near the top.

Svenja 130 feet Very Severe 4b (28.3.70)
A loose, vegetated, and thoroughly unattractive climb up the grass-filled crack in the continuation slab.

There are two girdle traverses of the slab. The higher, **G-String** (380 feet Very Severe 1.11.69), follows an unprepossessing line across the top of the Left-Hand Slab and then continues across the fields of the Main Slab. More interesting to the adventurous botanist than to the dedicated rock jock.

The lower of the traverses contains some of the best climbing on the slab.

★★**Peeping Tom** 240 feet E1 (28.2.70)
A low-level girdle on perfect rock. The situations, particularly at high tide, are splendid. Start as for *Kinkyboots*.
1 70 feet 4c. Fall across the gap and traverse right to reach the peg beneath the larger overlap, as for *Kinkyboots*. Then traverse right to the first stance of *Midnight Cowboy* beneath the area of reddish bulging rock.
2 80 feet 5b. Descend the obvious undercut flake and hand-traverse its base into the groove formed by its right-hand edge (on *Sexilegs*). Climb the groove to the next overlap and traverse right to its end before continuing diagonally down and right to the first stance of *The Narrow Way*. (As an alternative to following the flake to its base, traverse with difficulty about 5 feet higher to the groove of *Sexilegs* – E2 5c.)
3 90 feet 5a. Step right into an exposed short corner above the roof and climb the thin crack through the overlap until it is possible to traverse right into the corner of *Grand Vizier's Garden Party* at the level of the large overhangs on its first pitch. Reverse the moves under the roof past a peg; then pull steeply across the right retaining wall to good holds and a grass-filled crack leading down and right to the base of the slab.

The rib taken by the lower section of the right-hand descent to the main slab has a small steep face on its southern side. Low tide is necessary to reach the base of this face.

Goats 50 feet Severe 4a (4.82)
Start at a faint buttress below and to the left of a light-coloured scoop and left of an overhang. Climb a thin, left-slanting crack.

Yellow Submarine 50 feet Very Severe 4b (4.82)
Start at the same point as for *Goats* and climb direct up a crackline with a small, left-facing corner at half-height.

Shortera 70 feet Hard Severe 4b (4.72)
Start as for the preceding routes and climb a series of scoops and bulges to the base of the large scoop. Go up and diagonally right to finish.

Titmould Incorporated 90 feet Hard Very Severe 5a (20.7.81)
Start directly beneath a light-coloured circular scoop and a roof. Make a series of bold moves to surmount the roof and reach the small incut ledge just left of the large scoop. Go right into the scoop and gain a ledge above. Continue steeply left, then back right to a short corner. After a few feet, a difficult swing right leads to the top.

Southern Slabs

A hundred yards south of The Promontory col, the path crosses close to the top of a steep, rippled, concave slab, bordered on its right by a cavernous, tottering groove. Owing to the nature of the terrain, the routes here fail to provide the single most important ingredient of Baggy climbing – enjoyment!

The approach for these routes requires low tide and can be made from The Promontory to the north or by descending steep grass and mixed slopes well to the south. Past the ridge forming the southern side of The Promontory cove, the first major feature is a long grey slab, the upper half of which is covered in scabrous platelets of loose shale. Near its right-hand side is a prominent corner, curving at its base to form an overlap.

Multiple Fractures 120 feet E1 4c (14.4.81)
Start beneath the corner and climb up to the overlap. Pull over it direct and move left into the corner, which is followed on increasingly loose rock and with little protection.

Beyond the slab is an area of mixed ground and recent avalanches leading to a zawn, the left side of which consists of the impressive *Loosera* slab, broken at its centre by a right-angled groove terminating in a grass and earth ramp. Immediately above is the rippled concave slab.

Loosera 230 feet Hard Very Severe (18.10.75)
The right-angled groove in the slab – an impressive line with little else to recommend it. Start in a gully above a cave and rock-pool.
1 150 feet 5a. Climb the corner to an overlap (good peg removed). Go over this and continue up the groove to the grassy ramp at its top. Poor peg belays.
2 80 feet. Above and to the right the rock has a nightmarish quality. This is the finish; though the following route provides an alternative.
Variation
Pinch of Salt E3 (12.4.80)
2a 120 feet 5b. A bold line up the steep rippled slab. Traverse left across the slab to gain a thin crack, which leads with increasing difficulty past a peg.

Sundance 150 feet Hard Very Severe 4c (16.4.81)
Right of the groove of *Loosera* is a subsidiary slab with a thin crack running up the centre. Follow *Loosera* to the overlap; then swing right onto the slab and move right to the crack, which leads, via two further overlaps, to a junction with *Loosera* near the top.

Bags' Corner 180 feet Severe (1979)
Climb the huge corner at the back of the *Loosera* zawn. Easy but dangerous.

The following routes are situated on a hidden area of slabs reached by descending steep grass and gently-angled slabs some 200 yards south of The Promontory. Easy scrambling back towards The Promontory gains a steepening slab with a large corner on its right. Left of this is a subsidiary slab/corner, accessible at most states of the tide.

Interalp's Yard 90 feet Severe (7.82)
Climb the open face of the subsidiary slab past an overlap near the bottom, following a line just left of an obvious vegetated crack.

Gumbo 90 feet Very Difficult (7.82)
Climb the corner of the subsidiary slab to a nut belay at its top. Dangerous rock above suggests that an abseil descent is the best escape.

Short Rock Eliminate 170 feet Hard Very Severe (3.7.82)
1 110 feet. Climb a line of criss-cross cracks in the middle of the main slab to reach a narrow grass ledge. Move right to some small flakes and go up to another grass ledge. Belay at the left-hand and wider edge of the ledge.
2 60 feet 5a. Move up and slightly left for 15 feet; then step right onto another grass ledge beneath an obvious flake overlap. Ascend this with difficulty near its left-hand side and continue to the top. Stake belay removed.

Shark's Fin Soup 180 feet Severe (4.82)
Climb the corner of the main slab with three prominent zigzags in two pitches to a loose exit. Stake belays removed.

Blackchurch Rock Photo: John Willson

The Culm Coast

The Culm Coast is a unique and fascinating area of the north coast, straddling the Devon/Cornwall border and stretching for some twenty miles from east of the quaint harbour of Clovelly to the broad sandy beach of Widemouth.

Culm, the local collective name for the stratified rock found along this coast, is composed of alternating bands of sandstone and shale. Needless to say, most routes are found on the solid sandstone left after erosion of the softer shale has taken place. Although the basic structure of Culm is uniform, variations in the thickness and quality of the material originally deposited, together with the colossal pressures the sediments have subsequently endured, provide the cliffs and climbs with a surprising variety from area to area. Slabs, walls, cracks, and arêtes abound. Impending walls and overhangs are rarer, but shapely pinnacles crop up at regular intervals along the coast for those interested in bagging 'summits'.

Culm cliffs easily approached by vehicle do exist, but for the most part this is not an area for the crag rats who like their climbs by the roadside: climbing on isolated cliffs in a wild environment forms an integral part of the Culm Coast atmosphere. That said, no really long walks are necessary to reach any of the crags in this section of the guide. Narrow country roads leading off the main A39 (which runs parallel to the coast) allow access to parking-spots along the coast. More often, an easy stroll along the coast path or the foreshore will lead to the climbs.

The sea is an important factor in Culm Coast climbing as access to some of the best areas is severely affected by the state of the tide. It is not always enough just to consult the tide-tables and arrive at the right time: in some areas it is also important to keep a weather eye on the incoming waters as you climb to avoid being cut off from the easy access – this is especially true of remote areas such as Nabor Point and Smoothlands.

Sloo Slabs

OS Ref 374 240

The most easterly Culm crag, located below Sloo Woods west of Peppercombe.

Approach from Horns Cross on the A39. Walk down either side of Peppercombe Valley to the beach and then west for half a mile (at any state of the tide) to two 100-foot north-facing slabs (30 minutes walk from Horns Cross). The slabs steepen as height is gained and are topped by steep vegetation leading to dense woods.

There are four routes on the left-hand slab.

Ik Heb 100 feet Hard Very Severe 5a † (15.6.99)
Start 10 feet left of the vertical grass strip that runs the full height of the slab. Climb easily for 40 feet, then more delicately via two pockets to a thin ledge and runners at 75 feet. Very delicate moves lead up to a thin cleaned crack, which is followed to better holds and a peg belay just below the earthy headwall. Abseil from the peg.

Witch's Slide 100 feet Severe 4a † (15.6.99)
Climb the slab immediately left of the grass strip to the right-hand side of the thin ledge at 75 feet. Follow the wide, cleaned cracks to the earthy headwall, and step left to the belay peg above *Ik Heb*. Abseil from the peg.

Kirsten's Last Climb 100 feet Very Severe 4c † (3.7.99)
Climb the slab immediately right of the grass strip to delicate moves (micro-wires) leading into a cleaned crack at 70 feet. Climb the crack to a two-peg belay. Abseil from the pegs.

Bent Sixpence 100 feet Very Severe 4b † (27.5.99)
Start 6 feet left of the arête defining the right-hand side of the slab. Climb direct to a good nut runner at 70 feet. Continue up the cleaned crack above to the earthy headwall and the two-peg belay of *Kirsten's Last Climb*. Abseil from the pegs.

The next route climbs the right-hand, triangular slab to its apex.

The Coffins Wait for Betty Trembelow 110 feet E3 5b † (10.1.99)
A very serious route, from which the dubious peg protection has been removed – easily! Start just right of the left edge of the slab. Climb with relative ease to place micro-wires in two fine cracks. Make thin moves up and slightly right, and place a blade peg at 30 feet. Further thin moves lead up until a thin blade peg is placed to give dubious protection for easier moves up and then right to a grassy ledge below the very brittle rock that forms the apex of the slab. A tied-off thin blade peg here gives psychological protection for moves rightwards, on crumbling rock and grass, to reach the final vegetated blocky 'headwall'. This is climbed, using levitation techniques to avoid a potential groundfall, to reach welcome heather and, beyond, the more reassuring gnarled dead-tree belay. Abseil from here.

Blackchurch OS Ref 299 267

This big brooding cliff, with its impressive array of steep slabs, ribs, and grooves has not received the attention it rightly deserves. The reasons are fairly

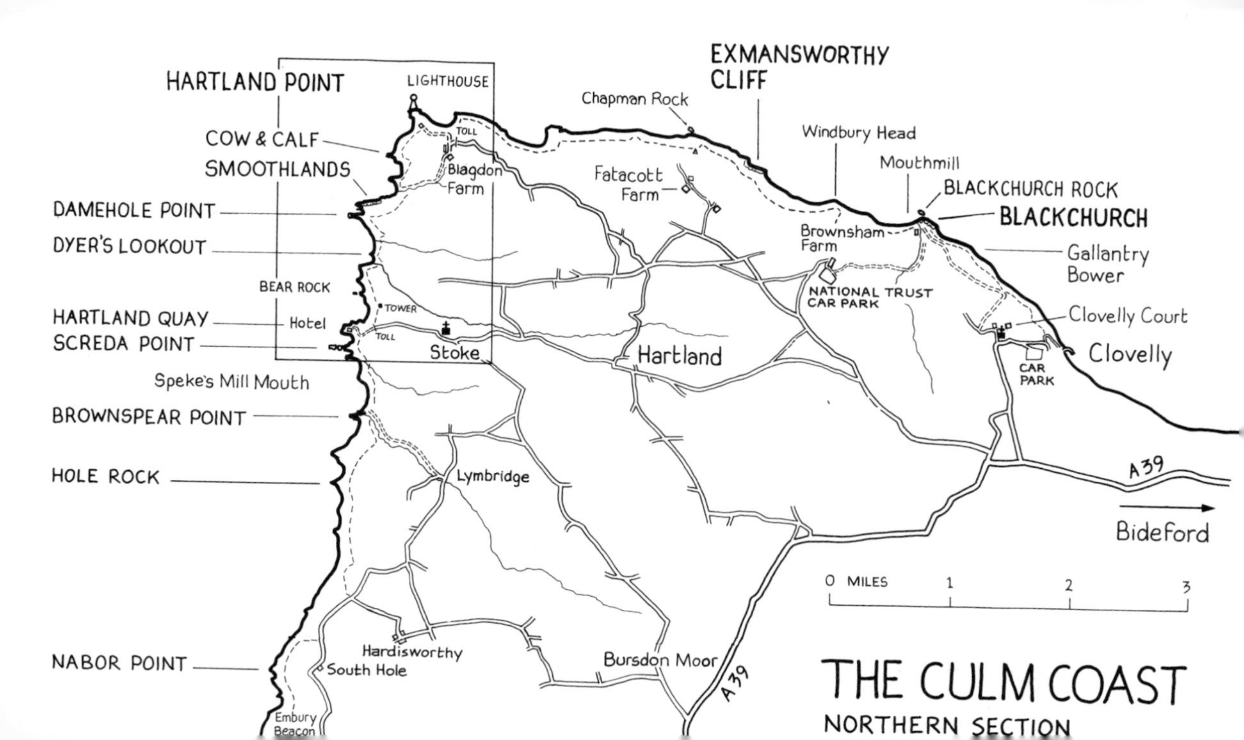
THE CULM COAST
NORTHERN SECTION
HARTLAND POINT
LIGHTHOUSE
TOLL
COW & CALF
SMOOTHLANDS
Blagdon Farm
DAMEHOLE POINT
DYER'S LOOKOUT
BEAR ROCK
TOWER
HARTLAND QUAY
Hotel
SCREDA POINT
TOLL
Stoke
Speke's Mill Mouth
BROWNSPEAR POINT
HOLE ROCK
Lymbridge
NABOR POINT
Hardisworthy
South Hole
Embury Beacon
Bursdon Moor
A39
Chapman Rock
EXMANSWORTHY CLIFF
Fatacott Farm
Hartland
Windbury Head
Mouthmill
BLACKCHURCH ROCK
BLACKCHURCH
Brownsham Farm
NATIONAL TRUST CAR PARK
Gallantry Bower
Clovelly Court
Clovelly
CAR PARK
A39
Bideford
0 MILES 1 2 3

apparent. Not only are the routes intimidating, but on first acquaintance the rock seems uninviting and the crag as a whole appears vegetated and, in places, structurally unstable. However, once the actual climbing is sampled first impressions are soon modified. The Main Cliff routes have an impressive grandeur, and the sense of adventure and satisfaction gained from having completed one of them more than compensates for any initial worries and reservations. Nevertheless, climbing here requires care and some experience, and this is not therefore the ideal first venue for a novice leader straight from the climbing wall!

The isolated stack of Blackchurch Rock, with its smooth, seaward slab of solid rock, is the very antithesis of The Main Cliff, and provides a collection of delicate routes needing balance, strong calves, and a bundle of small wires.

The cliff is approached from The National Trust car-park at Brownsham Farm (OS Ref 286 259). The bridleway sign, hidden among the collection of farm buildings, points the way to a wide track leading downhill through the trees. After half a mile take the right fork, and at the next junction in the track after 100 yards turn left (following the bridleway signs). After a further 150 yards the bridleway is signposted off the track to the right. Ignore this and continue along the track, round a right-hand bend, and take the left-hand fork at the next junction and head down to Mouth Mill (1½ miles, 30 minutes walk). Alternatively, the cliff can be approached from Clovelly via the coastal footpath or a tortuous stumble along the boulder-beach at dead low tide beneath the impressive Gallantry Bower (1½ miles, 40 minutes walk).

The unmistakable stack of Blackchurch Rock is seen on the foreshore, and The Main Cliff is further east.

At the right-hand end of The Main Cliff are the two obvious grooves of *The Sexton* and *The Archtempter*, left of which are the clean-cut cracks of *Loose Woman* above a central scree and grass cone. Left again is the striking groove of *Savage God* with its smooth, green, left-retaining wall. Further to the left, at half height, is the pinnacle that provides the belay above the first pitch of *The Almighty*.

Routes on the seaward face of Blackchurch Rock can be approached two hours either side of low spring-tide. Access to routes on The Main Cliff, except those at the extreme left-hand end, is unaffected by the tide.

The Main Cliff

Descent from The Main Cliff is by a long winding path that eventually leads down, past a ruined summerhouse, to the west of the crag.

☆**The Shrine** 230 feet Extremely Severe † (29.4.80)
This takes the big prominent groove at the left-hand end of the cliff. Start just left of the undercut base of the groove.

Blackchurch
The Main Cliff

	Route	Grade
1	The Shrine	XS
2	Rude Nude	E3
3	The Almighty	E1
4	Pilgrim	XS
5	The Big Sheep	E3
6	Savage God	E4
7	Blunderbuss	E3
8	The Heathen	XS
9	Antichrist	E3
10	Summerhouse	E3
11	The Verger	E1
12	Machineries of Joy	E2
13	Crucial Bunny	E2
14	Prayermat	E1
15	Loose Woman	E1
16	Barabbas	E1
17	Stopford	E1
18	The Sexton	E3
19	The Archtempter	E3
20	Godspell	E4
21	Making Plans for Nigel	XS

1 70 feet 4b. Climb black, shallow, slanting grooves until it is possible to step right onto the easy-angled slab of the left wall of the main groove. Climb this to a peg belay where it steepens.
2 80 feet 4c. Climb the groove above, still on the left wall, and move right to an excellent stance on the arête when the angle eases. Peg belays.
3 80 feet 5c. Step right and climb the slab to the overhangs (peg). Traverse right for 10 feet between the overhangs and gain a depression beneath a large roof (peg). Climb around the right-hand end of the roof (crux) and follow the left-slanting line above to the top.

★★Rude Nude 240 feet E3 (2.4.83)
This climbs the impressive wall of narrow vertical bedding-planes to the right of the groove of pitch 1 of *The Shrine* and shares the latter's top pitch. Pegs need to be carried (E4 without).
1 160 feet 5b. Climb up the wall, trending left, and then the left-hand of two weaknesses before stepping right into the prominent left-trending groove which starts at 40 feet. Follow this to its end (peg removed) and continue up the wall to an obvious slim groove. Climb a parallel groove on the left (peg removed); then swing right and climb the main groove to reach the arête stance on *The Shrine*.
2 80 feet 5c. *The Shrine* pitch 3.

★The Almighty 250 feet E1 ‡ (11.6.71)
The first pitch suffered a major rockfall in the late 80s. The description is for the reclimbed version. Start at the stepped and grassy groove 20 feet left of the obvious smooth green groove of *Savage God*.
1 100 feet 5a. Climb the overgrown groove for 40 feet over two awkward steps and follow a left-trending crackline to reach the base of the crack leading up the right-hand side of the pinnacle. Climb the crack, and belay by looping the rope over the pinnacle's summit.
2 60 feet 4b. Step from the pinnacle onto the broad rib, and climb this to a small overhung corner (peg). Traverse around the rib on the right to a small foot-ledge to reach nut and cam belays on the left wall of the corner.
3 90 feet 4c. Traverse across the corner and make an awkward move onto the rib. Climb just right of the rib; then move left above the overhang and climb the slab above on small positive holds to the top. Exposed and on good rock.

Pilgrim 260 feet Extremely Severe † ‡ (21.10.78)
The groove-line to the left of the smooth groove of *Savage God*. Pitch 1 is very overgrown and pitch 2 is unstable!. Start as for *The Almighty*.
1 100 feet 4c. Climb the groove over two awkward steps (and a lot of grass) and continue direct to a stance and peg belay on the right.
2 60 feet 5b. Continue up the steep groove above to a junction with *The Almighty*. Move right to the latter's foot-ledge stance (nut and cam belays).
3 100 feet 5b. Climb straight up the narrow slab above the stance to the overhangs. Traverse right across the steep wall to gain the final slab of *The Almighty*, which is taken to the top.

☆**The Big Sheep** 250 feet E3 † (31.7.94)
An excellent main pitch.
1 50 feet 5b. *Savage God* pitch 1.
2 110 feet 5c. Gain the left arête of the *Savage God* groove and climb this (several pegs) to the stance on *The Almighty*.
3 90 feet 4c. *The Almighty* pitch 3.

★★**Savage God** 240 feet E4 (9.73)
[Photo p.80a.] A demanding route that can leave one a little stunned. But it is still an excellent climb. Take pegs for belays and a helmet for the second man.
1 50 feet 5b. Start up the conspicuous steep groove with a smooth left wall. Belay at a small cramped stance where the angle relents below the upper, green groove.
2 100 feet 5c. Climb up just right of the groove for 30 feet past some loose rock until it is possible to move left into the groove. Climb the groove to capping overhangs; then go diagonally right to a stance and peg belays beneath the arête.
3 90 feet 5a. Follow the arête to a grassy finish.
Variation
Savage God Direct E4 6a † (6.93). Follow the original route to the capping overhangs of the main groove; then climb the continuation groove through the overhangs to *The Almighty* stance to finish as for that route. Not as fine as the original.

★**Blunderbuss** 260 feet E3 (1.10.78)
A good route taking the next open groove right of *Savage God*. Right of the main groove is a subsidiary groove ending in a bottomless chimney at 20 feet. Start beneath this.
1 110 feet 5b. Gain the subsidiary groove, which is followed to the overhangs. Swing left into the main groove and follow it (peg removed) to a good stance and peg belays (removed).
2 60 feet 5b. Continue up the groove for 45 feet to grass; then traverse left and round the arête to the second stance of *Savage God*.
3 90 feet 5a. *Savage God* pitch 3.

The Heathen 300 feet Extremely Severe ‡ (7.1.78)
A powerful line spoilt by a grassy second pitch. The deep groove to the right of *Blunderbuss* has a set of overhangs at three-quarters height on its right wall.
1 100 feet 5a. The lower section of the groove splits into two; follow the cleaner, left-hand groove (two pegs) to a belay on a grassy ledge.
2 80 feet 4c. Steep grass and a little rock leads to a ledge, where the groove becomes very smooth. Two pegs.
3 70 feet 5b. Climb the groove, mainly on the left (two pegs), to gain the shallow continuation groove. Follow this to a traverse-line leading right to a good ledge just left of the arête. Peg belays.
4 50 feet 5b. Move left back into the groove and climb it to more grass. Avoid this on its left to finish up the left arête.

Antichrist 300 feet E3 (26.10.75)
Rarely climbed and loose in places, it for the most part follows a line of corners and grooves left of the more open slab left of *The Verger*. Start below the first groove.
1 100 feet 5a. Climb easily to the groove and follow it to exit left on chossy ledges. Peg belays.
2 150 feet 5b. Go up for 10 feet to a spike; then move right and climb steeper rock to a groove-line right of the prominent fin. Climb the groove to a ramp; then take a further series of (three) grooves leading to a holly bush. Struggle through the holly and continue up a wide crack in the edge of the slab to a ledge. Peg belays on the left.
3 50 feet 4c. Climb the slab near its left edge to the top.

Summerhouse 270 feet E3 (8.10.77)
The deep groove between *Antichrist* and *The Verger*. Jungle-bashing through brambles and ants' nests on the third pitch.
1 85 feet 4c. Climb the groove to the left-hand side of the ledge-system.
2 115 feet 5b. Move left into the main groove and follow it (peg, removed, where the angle relents) to a difficult grassy exit and a tree belay.
3 70 feet 4a. Tree and grass climbing leads to belays on the railings.

★★**The Verger** 270 feet E1 (14.8.74)
A superb natural line up the exposed central section of the cliff, unfortunately marred by a very loose second pitch. Protection is sparse and the top pitch is a long and lonely lead, despite the lack of any great technical difficulty. Start left of the rubble cone, at a crack which widens ominously higher up.
1 85 feet 4c. Gain the crack from the right and follow it to a ledge beneath the obvious rib. Block and *Friend 3* belays.
2 45 feet 4c. The corner above, full of vegetation and loose flakes, is avoided by rounding a subsidiary rib on the left. Climb the cracked corner above until overhanging rock suggests a swing to the right on large but creaking holds. Continue up and to the right to a secluded stance beside the main rib, usually complete with the necessary pegs to belay.
3 140 feet 5a. Traverse right and around an arête to a friendly crack, which is followed steeply to a small ledge. Continue for 15 feet until a line of small incuts leads back left above the roofs to gain the arête. Climb the arête in an exhilarating position. Belay on the railings.

Machineries of Joy 270 feet E2 † (31.5.84)
Start at the base of the narrow groove immediately right of the first pitch of *The Verger*. Note the length of the first pitch!
1 200 feet 5b. Climb the groove to gain the narrow foot-ledge on pitch 1 of *Crucial Bunny*. Traverse right; then climb the steep wall above (hanging belay possible). Step right and climb a corner leading to a series of loose and vegetated ledges, which are followed up and right to a tree belay in the far corner.

2 70 feet 5c. Move back left and climb a series of leftward-slanting overlaps to finish up the centre of a final exposed slab.

Crucial Bunny 270 feet E2 † (11.83)
A serious route, which in its upper reaches shares *The Verger*'s open situations. Start at the foot of the slab right of the narrow groove of *Machineries of Joy*.
1 130 feet 4c. Climb up the slab to a peg at 40 feet; then move left and continue to the belay ledge of *The Verger* (stance possible). Move back right and gain a long narrow ledge. Climb the crack at its right-hand end to a peg. Follow flakes diagonally left to belays in the crack on *The Verger*'s third pitch.
2 140 feet 5a. Follow *The Verger* for 30 feet until a line of holds leads right towards the middle of the slab. Climb up to gain a crack. At its top, move right and climb the line of weakness in the final slab past a peg.

Prayermat 170 feet E1 (8.74)
Above the central scree and grass cone is the conspicuous straight crack of *Loose Woman;* to its left is a wide, slanting crack.
1 70 feet 4c. Enter the wide crack and follow it past some precariously wedged blocks until it is possible to move left onto a large ledge (peg belays).
2 60 feet 4c. Go up the grassy ramp, passing a steep section just right of the corner, and continue up to a stance on the right on *Loose Woman*.
3 40 feet. Step left and climb the grassy slab to the top.

★★**Loose Woman** 170 feet E1 (4.69/1974)
The name applies only to the last, easy pitch. An enjoyable route, which is low in the grade; the crux is short and well protected. Start at the base of the conspicuous crack above the central scree and grass cone.
1 70 feet 4c. Climb the crack to a belay on the left.
2 60 feet 5b. Climb up into the corner on the right and continue to the roof. Steep moves past this gain better holds and a stance.
3 40 feet. Climb the line of least resistance up the loose slab above.

Barabbas 160 feet E1 (1974)
A bold and powerful line. Large nuts are required. Start towards the right-hand side of the rubble cone at the base of a prominent wide crack.
1 70 feet 5a. Climb the crack to a stance on the slight tower.
2 90 feet 4c. Continue up the crack, bearing left past a bush to finish as for *Loose Woman*.

Stopford 220 feet E1 † (30.9.77)
Another route where the grade is a reflection of conditions other than technical difficulty. Left of the parallel arching grooves of *The Sexton* and *The Archtempter* is a steep red corner. Start at the foot of the buttress below the corner.

1 100 feet 4b. Climb the groove, then its right arête to a shallower groove. Climb this for a few feet; then traverse left to a stance and flake belay just right of a large pinnacle.
2 120 feet 4c. On the right, a grassy ramp leads to the foot of the red corner. Climb the right edge of the ramp to gain the corner, which is followed to a grassy groove leading to the top.

★★**The Sexton** 200 feet E3 (20.5.74)
A serious and powerful line up the left-hand of the two arching grooves. Start at a shallow groove in the slab below the main offwidth crack.
1 75 feet 5a. Climb the groove (peg); then go up the slab to better holds leading to a stance and belay on a pedestal.
2 125 feet 5c. Climb the crack, passing an awkwardly placed, rounded, jammed chockstone. Above an overhang, easier climbing leads almost to the top. A flaky slab on the right is climbed to finish.

★★**The Archtempter** 150 feet E3 (30.3.70)
A superb route up the soaring groove-and-corner-line just left of the huge blank wall near the right-hand end of the cliff. The situations are dramatic and a selection of large nuts and cams will come in useful. Start with a grassy scramble from the left up a ramp and chimney to a ledge beneath the main groove.
1 80 feet 5b. Climb the groove to a bulge (peg), pull steeply round it, and continue for 30 feet (past two pegs). Then, with increasing difficulty, progress on more dubious rock to a small sloping stance.
2 70 feet 5a. Climb the towering corner-crack above, with exciting moves to pass the overhang (large nut). Continue up the corner, which eases near the top.

☆☆**Lord Bafta** 150 feet E5 † (3.11.90)
The arête to the right of *The Archtempter* is technical, sustained, and bold. Start as for *The Archtempter*.
1 80 feet 6a. Climb the arête for a few feet, and then a short crack. Continue for 15 feet in a direct line slightly rightwards to a prominent but poor blade peg. Traverse left to the arête and climb past a peg to a junction with *Godspell*. Continue on up the arête to a sloping ledge. Swing left to the stance of *The Archtempter*.
2 70 feet 5c/6a. Climb back onto the arête and continue straight up to a good peg after 30 feet. Move back left to the arête above an overhang and climb the arête direct past a peg.

★★**Godspell** 150 feet E4 (9.8.78)
[Photo p.80b.] The wall right of *The Archtempter* gives another impressive climb, which has been led in one pitch. Start as for *The Archtempter*.
1 90 feet 6a. Climb the arête for a few feet, and then a short crack. Cross the wall diagonally right to reach an obvious scar (peg). Climb up and left to another (silver) peg, from where difficult moves left gain the

arête. Follow the arête for 25 feet (without protection) to a sloping ledge, and swing left onto the stance of *The Archtempter*.
2 60 feet 5c. Climb back to the arête and go rightwards across the wall to a thin crack. Follow this; then step left into a wider crack, which leads more easily to the top.

★★**The Naked God** 150 feet E6 6a (7.91)
This powerful climb tackles the smooth expanse of rock right of *Godspell*. Start as for *The Archtempter*. Step right onto the wall and climb direct to the rock-scar (very bold – skyhook runner, peg). Move up left as for *Godspell* to its second (silver) peg; then step up to clip a poor knife-blade. Climb slightly rightwards up the wall for 25 feet (bold) to another peg, and continue in the same line to finish at the top of *Making Plans for Nigel*.

Making Plans for Nigel 100 feet Extremely Severe 5b † (5.5.84)
Towards the right-hand side of the *Godspell* wall is a conspicuous slanting overlap. Climb thin cracks to the overlap, which is followed to the top (peg at 80 feet).

Fifty yards right of the main climbing area is a small outcrop of steep, smooth rock with a knife-edged fin at the right-hand end. A vertical line of pegs up the middle of the impending wall is an unidentified 'project' which finishes at the same point as the following route.

★★**The Ghost of Belle Aire** 60 feet E6 6b/c (25.4.93)
An exquisite amalgamation of moves, some technical, some powerful, some bizarre. The pitch takes the obvious right-to-left-rising flake-line and overlap in the impending wall left of *Eraser Blade*. Follow the very sustained flake-line past a crux at half height and five pegs (essential *Rock 2* placement at 12 feet). Multiple-peg lower-off.

The knife-edge further right gives a short but airy climb, **Eraser Blade** (60 feet E1 5a 30.6.83). The short slab much further right across the beach provides a number of pleasant problems, all at around 4b.

Blackchurch Rock

[Photo p.68.] All routes but the first are situated on the fine steep and open seaward face. The base of the slab can be approached two hours either side of low spring-tide. Descent from the summit is by scrambling down the landward side.

Moluscicide 75 feet E2 5b † (2.3.96)
The sidewall, left of the arête of *Noir et Blanc*, is split by two cracks. Climb the left-hand crack until near the top, where steeper rock forces an escape rightwards to the arête. Finish up this.

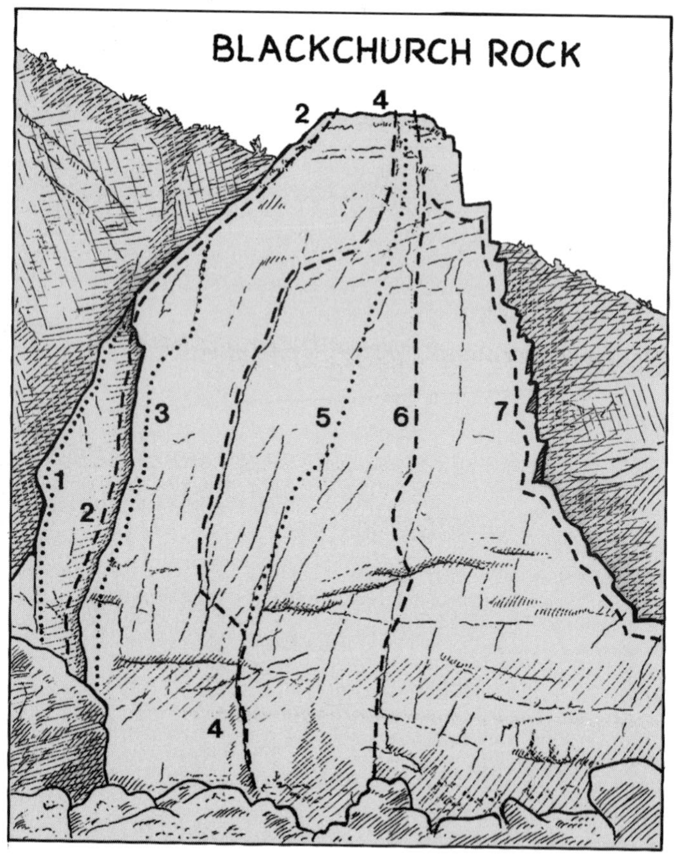

1	Noir et Blanc	HVS
2	Rite of Spring	VS
3	Les Invalides	E2
4	Sacré Cœur	E2
5	Dance on a Volcano	E3
6	Jamaican Dub	E3
7	Notre Dame	VS

Savage God (E4) Blackchurch
Climbers: Bruce Woodley and Tony Morley Photo: Brian Wilkinson

Godspell (E4) Blackchurch
Climber: Unknown Photo: Steve Davies

Over the Moon (E4 ~ first ascent) Cow and Calf
Climber: Martin Corbett Photo: Corbett coll.

The Incredible Hulk (E5) Hartland Point
Climber: Simon Young Photo: Young coll.

Noir et Blanc 95 feet Hard Very Severe 5a (27.4.80)
Start as for *Rite of Spring*, at the foot of the obvious corner. Climb up until above the barnacle line; then traverse left to the arête, which is followed delicately to the top.

★Rite of Spring 90 feet Very Severe 4c (8.2.70)
A pleasant route up the conspicuous corner at the left end of the main slab.

Les Invalides 100 feet E2 5c (22.7.79)
Climb the slab just to the right of the left arête of the main slab for 70 feet to reach a short crack. Climb the crack to the arête, step left into a gully, and scramble up this to the top.

★★Sacré Cœur 110 feet E2 5b/c (20.5.74)
An immaculate pitch, sustained, on good rock, and with excellent protection. Near the left end of the slab is an obvious thin crack, right of which is a deep slot at 20 feet. Climb directly to the slot; then make a thin move left to the main crack. Follow the crack, and move slightly right when it peters out to gain vague cracks leading to the top. A fine direct finish avoiding the move right has been climbed (E3 5c 27.11.88).

★Dance on a Volcano 100 feet E3 5c (11.10.82)
A sustained route up the centre of the slab. Climb up to the deep slot on *Sacré Cœur* and move up and right to a small ledge. Trend rightwards for 15 feet before climbing direct to a short curved crack leading to the top.

★★Jamaican Dub 100 feet E3 6a (11.7.81/29.9.90)
Another fine sustained pitch giving intricate climbing. Described with the better, direct start. Start at a thin crack 15 feet right of *Sacré Cœur*. Climb up the crack to the bulge, which is surmounted using the obvious flared slot. Follow the line of thin cracks above for 25 feet; then step right to a better crack which leads to the top few moves of *Notre Dame*.
The original route started just right of *Sacré Cœur* and climbed to good flakes before traversing right 10 feet to gain the flared slot.

☆Rant 150 feet E3 6a † (12.7.87)
A right-to-left girdle of the slab at one-third height, giving thin, technical climbing. Start below the right arête of the slab and climb boldly to reach the arête, which is followed to a point level with a slight bulge at 40 feet. Move left and surmount the bulge at a thin crack (on *Jamaican Dub*). Continue horizontally left on very thin holds, passing a narrow crack to reach *Sacré Cœur* at the slot. Move out to the arête, swing left into the corner of *Rite of Spring*, and follow it to the top.

★Notre Dame 130 feet Very Severe 4b (1974)
The right arête of the seaward face gives a pleasant, well-situated climb with an air of seriousness. Start at a line of weakness well to the left of the arête and climb up to an airy ledge 15 feet below the top. Climb the crack on the left or continue up the arête (harder and better) to finish.

Windbury Head

OS Ref 287 268

Three-quarters of a mile further west is the formidable-looking Windbury Head, upon which is the following route taking the obvious faultline leading to the highest point of the crag.

☆**Forces of Nature** 240 feet Extremely Severe † (17.9.95)
Fine, serious climbing. Start beneath a rockfall scar where a rising line of weakness leads up right to the main faultline.
1 100 feet 5b. Move up right and climb through loose overhangs to gain the main faultline. Follow this to a stance behind the prominent pinnacle.
2 40 feet 5b. Descend slightly and traverse 10 feet left. Continue up the obvious line above to belay 15 feet below an overhang.
3 70 feet 5b. Climb up to and surmount the overhang. Continue up to a large overhang blocking the faultline and crawl 10 feet up left on a narrow ramp to belay.
4 30 feet 5a. Traverse back right above the overhang to regain the fault, which is followed to the top.

Three hundred yards east of Exmansworthy is a crag situated in the shallow valley running down to Beckland Bay beach (OS Ref 282 267). It is best approached from below by following the river bed from the beach.

Raiders of the Lost Bark 240 feet E1 4c (17.9.95)
A unique climb.
1 120 feet 4a. Follow the shallow scoop at the right-hand end of the crag until a delicate traverse left to a ledge can be made. Tree belay.
2 120 feet 4c. Move back right into the scoop and follow it with increasing difficulty until a series of moves up oak trees on the right can be made to reach the top.

Exmansworthy

OS Ref 277 272

This once proud crag, a jewel in the Culm Coast crown, has suffered a number of cataclysmic rockfalls which have wiped out the original abseil entry and affected whole sections of the cliff, leaving them in a dangerous condition. A huge avalanche of debris has fallen over the top of the Shadow Walker Slab and Cat Burglar Wall. This has destabilized the rock and stripped or flattened all the *in-situ* gear (and probably most of the holds), as well as raising the beach level. In spite of this, it may still be possible to reascend some of the routes on these faces, albeit at a different grade and always with the likelihood of disturbing the precariously poised rubble now lying at the tops of the routes.

A decision has been taken to include abbreviated and unstarred descriptions of the routes on these walls until a more considered view of their worth (or even existence) can be made. *The Ex-man Cometh* and routes to its right appear unaffected by the rockfall.

As before, the crag can be approached at low tide by means of a long and time-consuming boulder-hop along the beach from Blackchurch to the east or Shipload Bay to the west. Exit from the crag must then be made by climbing *Hand Job* and taking the tortuous trek back through the undergrowth above to the coast path, as the tide will not allow a retreat along the shore.

An approach can also be made from Fatacott Farm (OS Ref 268 269) once permission has been sought from the farmer to park and to walk north across his land to join the coast path. From a trig point, continue east for half a mile, crossing four stiles, until a prominent white-topped boulder can be seen in the sea below. Seventy-five yards past the last stile it should be possible to breach the thorn hedge and descend through the dense undergrowth until a joined-rope abseil can be made to the sloping grassy terrace at the top of *Iron Fist*, from which a further abseil lands you on the beach.

At the eastern (left-hand) end of the cliff is the smooth Shadow Walker Slab. Right of this, beyond a right-to-left-sloping ramp, is the inset Cat Burglar Wall. Right again, the cliff is defined by a series of steep grooves and walls.

Warning: it must be pointed out that climbing at this very remote crag is now **even more serious**.

Shadow Walker Slab

Tactical Retreat 150 feet Very Severe 4c †† (7.9.79)
From the left-hand arête, traverse right to reach the base of a diagonal quartz intrusion, which is followed to the rib. Move right and climb a steep crack.

Culm Dancing 150 feet E3 †† (1982)
The left-hand crack in the headwall.
1 80 feet 5c. Climb direct to a large pocket at the base of the crack.
2 70 feet 5c. Climb the widening crack.

Shadow Walker 170 feet E3 †† (18.10.79/1980)
The right-hand crack in the headwall.
1 90 feet 5c. Climb a thin crack to a peg (gone), traverse left to another crack, and climb this to the second pocket above.
2 80 feet 6a. Climb to the next pocket, and up and left to another. Step right to the crack and follow it and its continuation to the top.
Superdirect Start E2 5b/c (1982).

Sheepdog Trials in Babylon 140 feet E2 5c †† (29.4.80)
Climb the obvious ragged crack to its close. Move right and climb up and right with difficulty.

The next two cracks are **Ratcatcher** (85 feet Hard Severe 4b †† 3.5.80) and **Nasty Little Bags of Poison** (70 feet Hard Very Severe 5b †† 3.5.80).

The following route was climbed after the rockfall.

☆**Haunted by Hoodoos** 60 feet E6 6b † (1.9.90)
'Sure the route is short but if it were longer the groundfall potential would be less great!' In the main, marginal *RP* gear helps little to ease the anguish. Start below a vague line of weakness in the black slab 25 feet right of the right-hand diagonal crack of *Nasty Little Bags of Poison*. Step off a small boulder and follow reasonably positive holds to a narrow foot-ledge. A committing stretch gains small ledges at a break – complete with bombproof *Rock 6* placement. Go straight up the shallow scoop above, finishing with a highly taxing move on tiny edges – the overwhelming probability of an on-sight plummet from this would be reduced to acceptable proportions by a little top-rope practice!

Rasta Collie (270 feet E2 5c 5b 4c †† 12.7.81) was a low-level girdle climbing across the slab at 40 feet.

Cat Burglar Wall

Dog Burglar 120 feet E4 6a †† (12.5.84)
The left-hand of three cracks in the wall.

Cat Burglar 130 feet E3 5c †† (6.1.80)
The central crack.

The Outlaw 140 feet E4 6a †† (7.8.81)
The right-hand crack.

Decadent Days 150 feet E3 5b †† (9.5.81)
The loose corner and crack right of *The Outlaw* above.

Right-Hand Walls

Right of the wreckage of Cat Burglar Wall, in the centre of the crag are two long arching grooves. Rockfall may have affected the finishes of the following three routes.

Second Sight 200 feet E1 †† (9.9.79)
An impressive line up the left-hand groove. Start on a huge block abutting the base of the grooves.
1 130 feet 4c. Climb up into the groove and follow it to a sloping ledge beneath the roof.

2 70 feet 5a. Continue up the groove, move left at the roof (thread), and follow the crack above, which widens to a chimney. Belay on a large ledge.

Dresden 200 feet E2 †† (5.1.80)
The right-hand groove. There is 'hostile' rock on the second pitch. Start on a huge boulder.
1 110 feet 4c. Climb up a series of short walls and grassy ledges to reach the main groove, which is followed to nut belays below the roof.
2 90 feet 5a. Go up to the roof and make a series of strenuous moves left and up into the corner above. Climb this and move left to a good foothold (peg removed). Traverse left to grassy ledges.

Choreographic Variant 130 feet E2 †† (1.8.81)
A better alternative to the first pitch of *Dresden*. Start below a grey wall with three vertical cracks in it.
1 60 feet 5b. Climb the central crack to exit on grass. Scramble up to a belay below the obvious crack.
2 70 feet 5b. Climb the crack with increasing difficulty, and traverse left at the top to the stance on *Dresden*.

Right of *Dresden* is an impressive wall taken by the crag's most powerful line, a contender for status of the most intense and sustained route on the coast.

☆☆☆**The Ex-man Cometh** 150 feet E7 6c † (6.4.96)
An immense lead which provides a rope's length of marginal, nail-bitingly steep face-edging with only one rest and well-spaced (but reliable) gear. 'A successful ascent will be cause for some celebration.' Start from a flake of unquestionable instability 15 feet above the bottom left-hand corner of the wall; poor belays (an abseil rope back-up would be excusable given what lies above).
Step right from the flake (short knife-blade removed) and scratch thinly – first crux – up and right to a circular hole containing a good hold (*RP2*). Step up into the hole (*RP4*) and climb more or less direct on increasingly diminutive edges (moderate tied-off knife-blade and poor tied-off short knife-blade 3 feet above both removed) until an especially bold piece of footwork leads right to a horizontal crack (good peg and *Rock 3* placement). Move up past the peg – second crux – then left below another (good angle removed) – third crux – to a welcome finger-slot (*Rock 4*). Bear left to a superb rest at the overlap (bomber gear: *Friend 1½*, *Rock 8*, and *Rock 3*). Climb the wall above on reasonable edges to a small slot (*Rock 4*). Balance moves right lead to a jug below the second overlap – fourth crux (good thin blade removed). Gain a foot-ledge above the overlap (*RP1*) – fifth crux; then continue expectantly (very poor tied-off short knife-blade, then good long knife-blade 3 feet above both removed) to the third overlap. Sprint up the delightful finger-crack above to the finishing-line.

Formation Flying 220 feet E3 (4.5.80)
Carry pegs for the first belay. Start at the foot of the groove bounding the wall of *The Ex-man Cometh* on its right.
1 100 feet 5c. Climb the groove, awkward and serious, to an exit on grass ledges. Move right and go up to a horizontal crack. Peg belays (removed).
2 120 feet 5b. Climb to a thin crack below the overhangs (peg) and traverse left to an exposed crack which splits the upper wall and leads to grass slopes. Peg belay in place in a small bluff of rock 30 feet up and to the left.

The next major feature to the right of the groove of *Formation Flying* is a remarkably smooth wall split by a deep crack-system.

★★**Hand Job** 140 feet E1 5b (12.3.80)
Star-rated and graded for an ascent in its unvegetated state (last cleaned summer 1997), this is an excellent, well-protected route up a gradually widening crack which periodically suffers from severe attacks of 'retrograssing'. Start at the base of the crack and follow it awkwardly to a move right onto a narrow shelf (peg in poor condition). Climb the obvious wider crack, hard at first and offwidth at the top, to finish on a small grassy ledge. Peg belay. Escape by taking the easiest line up the mixed slopes above – depressingly long and tiresome. (It is worthwhile staying roped up for the early part of the escape.)

★★**Iron Fist** 120 feet E3 5c (8.3.85)
A superb variation finish to *Hand Job*, climbing the obvious thin crack, which is gained by breaking right where the original route moves slightly left. Sustained. Also cleaned summer 1997.

Umbra Crack 140 feet E3 5c (6.80)
The upper section is worthwhile. Start at the right-hand edge of the smooth wall to the right of *Hand Job*. Climb dangerous grass slopes to reach the obvious crack on the left, which is followed to a bulge. Move left and surmount the bulge to finish up the crack above.

The next route climbs the arête of the conspicuous curving slab with a deep corner to its left.

Nomad 220 feet Hard Very Severe † (17.10.79)
1 130 feet 4c. Climb the left arête of the slab until an overhang necessitates a move right onto the slab itself (peg). Climb the slab for 20 feet (peg removed) to regain the arête. Belay at a good crack beside a large block.
2 90 feet. Go up rock and other material to a small bluff.

Danzig 200 feet E1 † (12.4.80)
A serious line up the flaky slab. Pegs should be carried for belay and

runners on the first pitch – assuming placements can be found.
1 130 feet 5a. Climb the slab, keeping towards its right-hand side (pegs whenever appropriate – one, at least, at 80 feet). Peg belays.
2 70 feet 4b. Continue up the slab, moving left towards the arête.

The next climbing that can be reached from the beach is on an isolated slab 400 yards west of the crag.

Cul-de-sac 100 feet Severe † (4.5.80)
Climb the obvious crack in the steepening slab to a bulge. Surmount this and continue to the top on friable rock. Belay on the shoulder. Abseil descent.

To the right of the main climbing area is a series of slanting stratified walls and ridges. The next two routes take lines up the top sections of these ridges and should be approached from above. From the trig-point on the coast path at OS Ref 268 274, reached from Exmansworthy Farm, follow the path eastwards over four stiles. Continue past the last stile for a few yards; then struggle through a gap in the hedge. Descend 'through rainforest to more open savannah' leading down a spur on the west side of the upper ridge, which at this point consists of a large slab. Both the following routes have become overgrown and would need cleaning before an ascent.

★**Chase the Dragon** 90 feet E3 5c ‡ (5.7.87)
The thin crack just left of the first pitch of *Reefer Madness*. A sustained pitch of high quality. Climb the crack until a long reach gains a small pocket. Continue on flakes left of the crack to reach better footholds. Follow the crack as it curves right until it peters out; then launch boldly out left to gain the terrace. Scramble off right to the grass slopes or climb pitch 2 of *Reefer Madness*.

☆**Reefer Madness** 200 feet E1 † ‡ (20.4.84)
The reward for the long and arduous approach. Start beneath the right-hand of the obvious cracks in the centre of the buttress.
1 90 feet 5b. Climb the thin crack until a move left gains a wider crack. Continue past a pocket to an earthy ledge, which should be treated with care. Nut belay in the upper wall.
2 110 feet 5a. Climb the crack above until a thinner crack on the right can be used to reach a ledge-system. Traverse 10 feet right; then move up delicately to a wider crack leading to the top. Belays well back.

Chapman Rock OS Ref 267 277

For the maritime peak-bagging eccentric who likes to get away from it all, this more isolated version of Blackchurch Rock has a narrow, seaward-facing slab, which becomes accessible only around low spring-tide. An ascent is a collector's item. A smaller stack with a pointed summit lies just next to the main Rock.

Approach from The National Trust car-park at Exmansworthy Farm. Take the new path out to the coast path, which is followed to the west end of Fatacott Cliff (OS Ref 2315 2745). Descend a vegetated ridge, then across scree to the east, and continue on down to the beach. Access to a large block at the base of the seaward slab can be effected by an abseil from the top of the Rock, which is reached by scrambling up its landward side – very loose near the top.

☆**Who's Chapman?** 90 feet E1 5b † (28.2.98)
Fine sustained climbing, adequately protected by small wires. From the block at the bottom of the slab, climb directly up the middle of the slab.

Murphy's Nightmare 90 feet Very Severe 4b † (26.6.94)
Climb the prominent crack near the right-hand side of the slab until it joins the right arête at 60 feet. Move delicately left into the middle of the slab and climb direct to the top.

The smaller stack (Little Chap?) has a left-facing groove in its upper half leading to the summit. **Was Chapman a Fat Boy?** (60 feet Hard Severe † 28.2.98) climbs the central ramp to the left arête and follows cracks leading back right to the groove, which is followed to the summit. **Chapman's Sister** (60 feet Very Severe † 28.2.98) climbs the right arête to the same groove and finish.

Hartland Point

OS Ref 230 277

The car-park at Hartland Point is convenient for Blagdon Cliff Buttress and for the crags at Cow and Calf, Upright Cliff, Smoothlands and Damehole Point. There is a £1 (1999) charge to use the road leading down to the car-park.

Blagdon Cliff Buttress

A narrow buttress of reasonable rock 200 yards south of the point itself. Access to the boulder-beach below the buttress (half tide and below) is via the road (officially closed) from the car-park to the lighthouse and the old quay. The crack in the narrow seaward prow of the buttress is taken by **The Enchanted Cabbage Garden** (80 feet Hard Severe 4a 19.7.98). Abseil descent from two pegs.

The Johanna

On New Year's Eve 1982, the 960-ton Panamanian-registered vessel the *Johanna* went aground 300 yards north of Cow and Calf, and the national press of the time had a field day accusing local 'wreckers' of plundering her valuables within hours of the accident. These days, the rusting remains of the

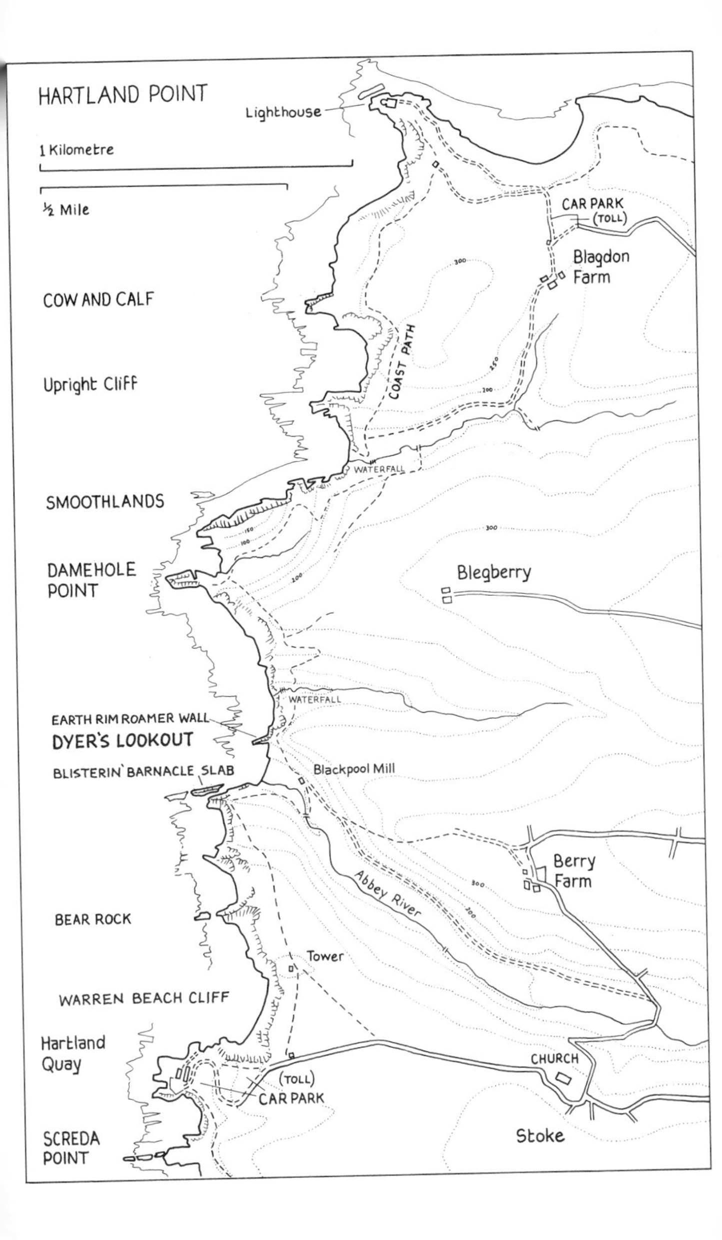
HARTLAND POINT
Lighthouse
1 Kilometre
½ Mile
CAR PARK
(TOLL)
Blagdon
Farm
300
COW AND CALF
COAST PATH
250
200
Upright Cliff
WATERFALL
SMOOTHLANDS
300
150
100
DAMEHOLE
POINT
200
Blegberry
WATERFALL
EARTH RIM ROAMER WALL
DYER'S LOOKOUT
Blackpool Mill
BLISTERIN' BARNACLE SLAB
Berry
Farm
300
Abbey River
200
BEAR ROCK
Tower
WARREN BEACH CLIFF
Hartland
Quay
CHURCH
(TOLL)
CAR PARK
SCREDA
POINT
Stoke

Johanna, formerly the *Elisa Johanna*, provide a metallic playground for many an adventurous soul. Most 'routes' on this 'crag' have rightly gone unrecorded but one line, up the disembodied prow of the wreck, provides a superb 'gritstone slab', which is worth seeking out if you happen to be in the area. It should be noted, though, that even a slight shifting of this relic during a winter storm could render the grade meaningless.

Approach as for Cow and Calf and head north along the boulder-beach for 300 yards to the most southerly section of the wreck. **The Incredible Hulk** (30 feet E5 6a 7.99) starts beneath two parallel ramp-lines at the right-hand side of the prow. Climb straight up to a good edge and a difficult move. Step right to better holds and make a long stretch for the top. [Photo p.80d.]

Cow and Calf

OS Ref 227 272

[Frontispiece drawing.] A fine cliff of light grey rock that now boasts a collection of sustained routes in all but the easiest grades. The climbs lie on the north face of the first promontory south of Hartland Point. Walk south along the coast path from Hartland Point for half a mile, until a view of the bay containing Upright Cliff opens out on the right. Follow a faint path seawards along the northern rim of the bay, now becoming slightly overgrown with gorse, until the path passes down between shattered rock walls to the beach on the northern side of the promontory (20 minutes walk).

The north face consists of a number of overlapping walls with the prominent *Kneewrecker Chimney* in the centre. The climbs at the seaward end of the promontory are affected by high water but the landward end is accessible at most states of the tide. Care is required on the brittle honeycombed rock of which the upper sections of many of the routes are composed.

The first route on the landward face is:

Jizz 30 feet E2 5c (25.11.90)
Climb the short, left-hand crack.

Boiling Mercury 60 feet E3 5c (22.10.90)
Climb the second, slanting crack past two pegs to finish at the top left-hand corner of the wall. Belay to rounded blocks above.

Pearl Necklace 70 feet E3 6a (22.10.90)
Climb the third crack from the left end of the wall past three pegs.

★**Bulldyke** 80 feet E2 5b (30.9.90)
Climb the slanting cleft in the centre of the landward wall and then the twin cracks above.

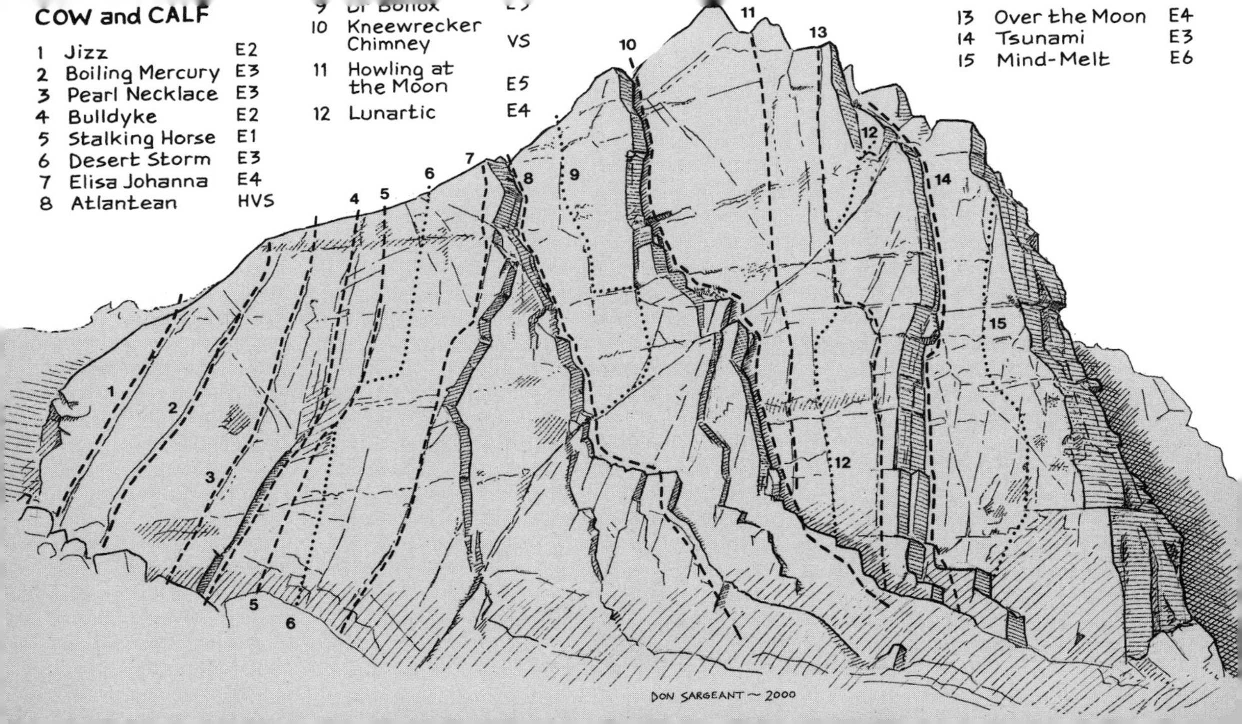
COW and CALF
1 Jizz E2
2 Boiling Mercury E3
3 Pearl Necklace E3
4 Bulldyke E2
5 Stalking Horse E1
6 Desert Storm E3
7 Elisa Johanna E4
8 Atlantean HVS
10 Kneewrecker Chimney VS
11 Howling at the Moon E5
12 Lunartic E4
13 Over the Moon E4
14 Tsunami E3
15 Mind-Melt E6
DON SARGEANT ~ 2000

★Stalking Horse 90 feet E1 5b (25.11.90)
Start just right of the slanting cleft of *Bulldyke* and climb steeply to the base of the twin cracks. Move right and follow the thin crack to the top.

★Desert Storm 90 feet E3 6a (13.1.91)
Climb the thin crack 10 feet right of the slanting cleft of *Bulldyke* for 25 feet. Climb the thin crack of *Stalking Horse* for 10 feet, traverse horizontally right to an area of pockets in the centre of the wall, and climb direct to the top.

★★★Elisa Johanna 100 feet E4 6a (24.10.90)
An excellent sustained route based on the seaward arête of the landward face. Serious. Start at a thin crack 10 feet left of the arête. Climb the thin crack to a notch on the arête. Climb the face to an area of finger-pockets before traversing up and right to rejoin the arête. Follow a thin crack to another notch on the arête and climb the face on the left to the top.

Atlantean 110 feet Hard Very Severe 5a (30.6.79)
Climb easily into the bottom of the left-slanting corner-crack and follow it to an overhanging section near the top. Layback over this with care.

★Dr Bollox 120 feet E3 6a (10.90)
The thin zigzag crack in the face right of *Atlantean*, although escapable, gives fine technical climbing. Climb the first 30 feet of *Atlantean* to a rightward-slanting ramp. Follow this (serious) to a crack in the wall leading to a niche. Hand-traverse left and climb a thin crack (crux) to finish up left via pockets.

Kneewrecker Chimney 120 feet Very Severe 4b (16.4.83)
The obvious cleft in the centre of the cliff gives a serious pitch.

★Howling at the Moon 120 feet E5 6a (20.10.90)
A great but serious pitch taking a direct line to the highest point of the cliff. Start at the foot of *Kneewrecker Chimney* and step right to climb the left-hand of two vertical cracks through the first bulge. Take a direct line to the top, finishing to the left of the summit pinnacle.

★Lunartic 120 feet E4 6a (4.5.91)
Start 10 feet right of *Kneewrecker Chimney* and climb the wall to the bulge. Climb the crack for 15 feet and traverse up right to the crack of *Over the Moon*. Climb directly up to a ramp, step right, and take a line up to a crack leading to the top right edge of the face.

★★Over the Moon 120 feet E4 6a (13.10.90)
[Photo p.80c.] A superb route taking the obvious snaking crack left of *Tsunami*. Start just left of the arête and climb the thin crack to where it kinks left. Traverse 10 feet left; then move up and slightly left to join the discontinuous crack in brittle rock, which leads vertically to the top.

★**Tsunami** 100 feet E3 5c (14.7.79)
A fine and well-protected route taking the big corner near the seaward end of the cliff. Climb the corner for 30 feet (peg). Make bold moves past the overhang (peg) into the groove, which is followed to the top.

Mind-Melt 90 feet E6 6b † (2.8.92)
The sheer wall right of *Tsunami* gives a serious lead with deck-out potential. From the right-hand end of the flat ledge below *Tsunami*, follow a line of crystalline holds up right (poor wire on the right) before climbing very boldly to the first peg at 35 feet. Using a side-hold on the left, go straight up to better holds above a blank section. Continue past a peg to rest at a horizontal break. Step right and climb on good pockets to the arête, which is followed (peg) to the top.

Carriatid 120 feet E2 5c (27.4.80)
Climb the overhanging crack of *The Sceptred Race*, step right, and continue up a brown groove to a roof (peg). Surmount this with difficulty and the one above to reach better holds and a ledge. Move left and climb an awkward crack to the top.

The Sceptred Race 140 feet Hard Very Severe 4c (30.6.79)
[Photo p.37.] The easiest line up the front face of the promontory. Start below an overhanging crack. Climb to the crack; then move right beneath it (E1 if the crack is climbed direct) and climb a groove to a slab. Step left and gain a large flake. Climb directly up pockets to a crack and follow this to a step right to a groove to finish.

☆☆**Kalahari Black** 110 feet E6 6b † (25.7.92)
This impressive route climbs the black rippled south face of the promontory, starting in the dark narrow cleft at its seaward end (best gained by abseil). Climb direct on good but spaced holds past a peg to a crucial small wire placement. Climb to the overlap above and make committing moves past this to reach a flake (good peg and poor wires). Extending climbing leads boldly up and slightly right to pockets and a fine jug handrail. From a slot (*Friend* 2) continue up the milder wall (small cams) to a break (peg). Climb direct up the final section of wall, exiting slightly to the left.

Ripple 90 feet Very Difficult (14.7.79)
The boot-wide crack in the slender buttress right of the cleft.

Further south, **Culming Apart** (Very Difficult 75 feet 3.7.94) climbs a crack in the seaward of three south-facing slabs between Cow and Calf and Upright Cliff. Loose.

Upright Cliff

OS Ref 227 268

A steep, north-facing cliff of a character very different from the majority of the Culm cliffs in that the climbing takes place on the joint faces of the rock layers rather than on the bedding-plane fins. The climbs are situated on the headland that makes up the north side of the bay that is dominated by Smoothlands on its south side. It offers short routes with a big feel.

Park just outside the entrance to the toll road to Hartland Point and approach by walking down through Blagdon Farm (footpath) to the bay. Alternatively, walk along the coast path from Hartland Point. At half-to-low tide, scramble round the northern headland of the bay direct to the cliff (30 minutes walk). If the tide is further in it is possible to scramble up easy-angled slabs that make up the south side of the headland and abseil in from the tops of the routes. The best belays are in cracks at the base of these slabs, and so an extra 120 feet of rope is needed to link them with the tops of the climbs. A third alternative is to cross the bay from Cow and Calf at low tide.

The cliff divides into four areas; from left to right these are: the tall landward buttress, the landward walls with an overhanging base, cave bay dominated by a large cave, and the seaward buttress. All the climbs are on the first two; the rest appear too loose for climbing.

Straightjacket 80 feet E4 6a † (12.5.96)
An engaging line that climbs the pink groove in the right-hand arête of the landward buttress; a steady lead is required. Pull into and easily ascend the broad, open yellow groove left of *Black Dog* to the ledge. Bridge up into the groove and follow it (*in-situ* thread), using some good holds on the left arête, to the left-hand end of the rock-ledge and terrace atop the landward walls. Place a good wire in the corner and walk rightwards along the ledge to belay.

Homo Erectus 80 feet E3 5c † (12.5.96)
The slim grey groove in the wall left of the corner of *Black Dog*: crisp. Follow *Black Dog* to the foot of the corner. From a pocket in the left wall (cams) swing left into the groove and climb it, bold at first, to finish up a tricky little groove. Place a good wire in the corner and walk rightwards along the ledge to belay.

Black Dog 80 feet Hard Very Severe 5a † (22.9.90)
Start at the base of the fourth groove from the left on the landward walls. Using an undercling on a layaway flake, make a wild move to reach jugs, and surmount the overhang by using a bum-wedge. Climb the groove to cross the broken terrace and take the continuation groove directly above. Traverse right across lighter rock at its top to gain the cliff-top.

Persistent Pup 85 feet Hard Very Severe 5a/b † (12.10.90)
Start just below the obvious jug hold on the lip of the overhang in the second groove from the right-hand end of the landward wall. Using the jug and the one above, and a little momentum, pull over the overhang into the groove and climb this to the horizontal break. Continue direct over it and make thin moves up the unprotected corner above (just left of the top groove of *Rockhound*) until better holds in horizontal pockets lead to the top.

Rockhound 85 feet E1 5b † (22.9.90)
Start below the first groove from the right-hand end of the landward walls. Climb up the groove to the break. Make a hard move to gain the next groove, which is followed easily to the arête at the right-hand end of the terrace of broken rock. Continue up the groove above, which steepens at its top.

Lazy Dawg 80 feet E1 5a † (7.10.90)
The groove to the right of *Rockhound*. Start at a groove in the back of the bay on the left-hand side, directly below the bottomless groove just right of the top section of *Rockhound*. Climb dynamically into the groove and go up it to the horizontal bands, where a tired leader can lay himself down to rest. Work up through the bands, trending slightly left to gain the crack that splits the main overhang. Using this, gain the cracks above and climb to the top.

Forthright 70 feet E3 5c † (12.5.96)
An exciting pitch up the grey, right-hand arête of the landward walls. Start 20 feet left of the chimney in the cave, beneath a crack just to the right of an orange corner. Grapple with the crack and reach the big ledge above. Cross the bands to an undercut slot in the roof. Pull straight up onto the grey wall left of the groove to gain good pockets (*Friend 1½*), move left to the arête, and follow it with some trepidation to the top.

Further right, **Dog Day Afternoon** (75 feet E1 5b †† 18.11.90) took a direct line up the back of the bay but a recent rockfall has removed the crucial central overhang, making the route unclimbable in its original form.

Smoothlands

OS Ref 226 266

A huge whaleback ridge, sliced along its length by the sea to reveal impressive sweeps of Culm, Smoothlands was once the home of just a handful of esoteric masterpieces. However, recent hard additions on The Great Slab have unlocked its potential to become one of the great crags on the coast.

Park just outside the entrance to the toll road to Hartland Point and approach by walking down through Blagdon Farm (footpath) to the beach, from where the concave formations of the lower part of the cliff can be clearly seen to seaward (30 minutes walk).

At the southern end of the beach, just beyond the stream, there is a non-tidal slab, which has the following two routes on it. Belay points at the top are poor and it is advisable to belay to a rope dropped from above and attached to a stake – not *in situ*.

Qui-3 60 feet E5 6a/b † (12.5.96)
The blank slab left of the prominent crack – a test of 'cool' and rubber! Start below the centre of the blankness. Connect misaligned pockets and scratch for a good break above. Place protection and go up to another shallow pocket (peg). Pursue a very direct line up the slab (hand-placed long knife-blade after 10 feet, and wire) to finish.

En Famille 70 feet E2 5b † (12.5.96)
The prominent crack. Start just to the left of a hollow and make thin moves to gain and climb the widening crack. At its close, traverse left and belay to a preplaced rope.

Further along the beach, on the way to the main crag, is a short, stubby stack close to the landward cliff with the following short routes on good rock.

Snuffelupagus 30 feet E2 5b (24.5.92)
The right-hand crack on the seaward face of the stack.

On the left-hand side of the landward face of the stack overlooking the through-passage are two steep and strenuous cracks, both solid and well protected: **Kermit** (30 feet E2 5b 17.5.92) is the left-hand crack and **Elmo** (30 feet E2 5b 24.5.92) the right-hand.

Opposite *Kermit* and *Elmo* and across the passage are two easier cracks: **Ernie** is the left-hand and **Bert** the right-hand crack, starting through a notch (both 30 feet Very Severe 4c 24.5.92).

A boulder-hop at half to low tide allows the through-cave to be identified – an alternative exit up grass slopes at the back of the cove to the left is worth noting in case the tide should bar exit along the beach on the return journey. On the curved slab forming the outside of the cave, **Dirty Dick** (100 feet Severe 7.7.84) climbs the wall and groove above a pool on the landward side of the slab. Other easy routes are possible (and indeed have been realized) on this slab. Escape from the top down the seaward ridge.

On the other side of the through-cave is the remains of an extremely thin fin on the left. **Swaying in the Wind** (70 feet E5 6a †† 21.4.96) took its north face and **Steppin' Razor** (90 feet Severe †† 4.81) the arête.

Hellbound (E6) Smoothlands
Climber: Andy Grieve Photo: Graham Butler

Hellbound (E6) Smoothlands
Climber: Andy Grieve Photo: Dave Turnbull

Immediately before The Great Slab is a ridge descending from the plateau to two pinnacles, where the following idiosyncratic (but wonderfully aesthetic) routes are to be found.

Surrealands 50 feet E1 5b † (11.5.96)
On the north face of the inner pinnacle is an elegant grooved arête. Climb the slim groove in the arête all the way to the top. Descend to the south or abseil from the summit.

Peardrop 50 feet E1 5b † (11.5.96)
The west face of the seaward pinnacle is split by a crack. Climb the crack and balance up onto a peculiar brown lump from the right. Step left to the arête and go up to the top. Descend by abseil.

A Scream Edgeways 50 feet E5 5c † (11.5.96)
Decisiveness is required. A wire at 25 feet is the only runner. Start below the left arête of the seaward pinnacle. From a raised ledge, climb the scalloped wall immediately right of the arête via long reaches to and from a good fingerhold to gain better holds on the arête. Continue easily up the arête.

The Great Slab

Further along, the cliff begins to tower above the beach and the unmistakable purple sweep of The Great Slab, with its arching overlaps low down, forms the left-hand side of the main crag. The base can be reached by abseil from the stakes above the slab if the tide is high. The slab is bounded on its left by a broken corner. Right of this, a thin cleaned crack (*Creeping Flesh*) is the only apparent line of weakness to stretch the full height of the slab.

★★**Slave to the Rhythm** 130 feet E5 6b (25.5.91)
A fine route that crosses *Creeping Flesh* and sweeps up the centre of the slab. Start at a rightward-diagonal crack reached by scrambling about 30 feet up the corner. Climb the crack to where it closes (peg) and follow the improbable line diagonally left and then direct, past another two pegs, to the top. Stake belay.

★★**Creeping Flesh** 130 feet E5 6a (8.89)
The original route on The Great Slab. Steep, sustained, and well protected. Start just right of the corner. Climb the steep wall to a good nut placement and make committing moves to reach a good edge (peg). A hard move up left is made to the crack, which is followed to another peg. Thin crux moves to another peg lead to better holds and the more amenable crack above. This is followed to the shattered headwall (peg) and the top. Stake belay above.

☆**Lowlife** 140 feet E6 † (21.4.96)
A fine companion route for *Hellbound*. Although technically less difficult it is bolder and more sustained. Numerous micro-wires and a short

1 Slave to the Rythm E5
2 Creeping Flesh E5
3 Lowlife E6
4 Hellbound E6
5 Smoothtalkin` E5
o peg
SMOOTHLANDS ~
THE GREAT SLAB
belay
D.J.S. ~ 2000

knife-blade are required. Start as for *Creeping Flesh*.
1 90 feet 6a. Follow *Creeping Flesh* to a point 6 feet above its first peg where there is a *Friend 1½* slot and an incipient crack branches off rightwards. Follow the crack delicately to reach a more friendly area at 25 feet, which is supplied with some chunky wire placements. Gain a crystalline finger-edge above and continue diagonally rightwards to a comfortable foothold (hand-placed short knife-blade in existing peg placement). Make a long reach to a line of finger-jugs and swing right along these to the *Hellbound* belay.
2 50 feet 6a/b. *Hellbound* pitch 2.

★Hellbound 150 feet E6 (30.4.90)
[Photos p.96a,b.] A brilliant route. Extreme slab-climbing up a faint diagonal 'weakness' right of *Creeping Flesh*. Two sets of micro-wires should be carried as well as a set of standard wires. Start as for *Creeping Flesh*.
1 100 feet 6b. Follow *Creeping Flesh* for 10 feet and climb the thin diagonal crack up right until below a peg. Climb directly up to it on good pockets. Continue up a faint crack above using tiny flakes to a *Rock 3* placement and make very difficult moves up right. Follow the crack with increasing difficulty and make a wild move to gain the belay ledge. Peg belays.
2 50 feet 6a/b. Make bold moves above the belay to reach a peg (with relief), and continue direct to the top. Stake belay.

★★Smoothtalkin' 160 feet E5 (2.8.92)
Technically amenable, but still a tremendous line with bold climbing towards the end of the first pitch. It climbs the lower curving crackline just above the arching overlaps. Start below a corner formed by the main arching roof.
1 110 feet 6a. Climb the corner for 30 feet to where it becomes a roof and make a tricky pull left (peg) to gain the crack. Follow the crack rightwards to where it becomes horizontal. Move up and slightly left to reach another diagonal crack, which is climbed up right and then horizontally rightwards for 6 feet (cams). Above is a line of pockets and edges which are followed past a peg to reach a hand-ledge and the peg belays of *Hellbound*.
2 50 feet 6a/b. *Hellbound* pitch 2.

Some 30 yards right of The Great Slab, a curving crack runs the full height of the cliff. Cliff-top stakes for the next three routes are not in place.

World's Weird Wall 210 feet E3 ‡ (15.7.84)
A serious but potentially outstanding route which follows the continuous central crack, now sadly overgrown. Pegs should be carried. Start beneath the crack, beside some perched boulders.
1 60 feet. Scramble up the grassy groove to where it steepens. Peg belay (removed).

2 70 feet 5b. Follow obvious holds leading diagonally right (peg at 20 feet) until a difficult move gains large holds (peg). Continue straight up on creaky holds (two further pegs in small pockets) to large loose ledges (peg). Move up to a foothold by the obvious hole. Peg belay up and to the right, and nuts in a crack.
3 80 feet 5a/b. Climb the sinuous crack until moves left gain large flakes. Easier climbing leads to the top. Stake belay removed.

Right again is a smooth concave face with a wide overlap low down. The following route climbs the left-hand side of the face and the corner above.

Flight Path 200 feet E2 †† (15.5.81)
The first pitch is very serious owing to the unreliable nature of the rock. Start at a large boulder which abuts the face.
1 80 feet 5a/b. Climb diagonally right on small flaky holds to the shallow blind corner, which is followed, past a peg at 60 feet, until a short traverse left gains the terrace.
2 60 feet. Wander left to climb the chimney to grass leading right to a stance beneath a corner. Peg belay removed.
3 60 feet 4c. Climb the corner. Stake belay removed.

★**Open Day** 90 feet E3 6a ‡ (19.7.86)
An excellent sustained crack pitch on the pale wall right of the last pitch of *Flight Path*, which requires a cleaning before an ascent. Approach by abseil (from stake to be placed). Climb the obvious sinuous crack in the wall, which provides sustained difficulties, to finish up the arête and grass above. Belay to whatever it was you abseiled from!

Right of the main cliff is an unpleasant expanse of horizontal strata, up the centre of which **Vaudeville Jazz Pooftah** (150 feet E1 4c) wends its way with nothing to commend it.

Damehole Point

OS Ref 223 263

An attractive headland, which has received a fair amount of attention of late. It has a long, low, south-facing wall which can be approached either from Hartland Point as for Smoothlands or, slightly further, from Hartland Quay.

During the winter storms of 1998/99 a huge rockfall took out the roof of the shallow cave half-way along the promontory together with a route appropriately entitled **Strip-Teaze** (7.4.96). Surprisingly, the rockfall does not appear to have affected the traverse of *Wine Dark Sea* or the low-level *Basketball with the President* and, although the track along the top of the promontory is still traversible, cracks in the earth next to the path indicate general instability in the area.

The long, easy-angled slab of **Celsius** (120 feet Very Difficult 14.4.79) can be seen to the north. Little or no protection.

At the front of the point, well above the sea, is a prow with an overhang near the top. The following route climbs the cleaned groove right of the prow.

Blood Brothers 70 feet Very Severe 4c † (22.5.94)
This pleasant route starts on the sloping ledge at the front of the point, which can be reached by abseil if the tide forbids access along the base of the cliff. Climb easily to a ledge below the groove and follow the groove with interest to the top. Good spike belays on the ridge above.

The long south face of Damehole Point is split by a large shallow recess half-way along its length, left of which is a smaller, seaward recess in the centre of the seaward wall. The next route climbs the left-hand section of the wall left of this recess.

☆**Flying Blind** 60 feet Hard Very Severe 5a † (22.5.94)
Dynamic climbing on solid rock. Start 15 feet in from the left-hand edge of the wall, beneath a vertical line of flakes. Move right up a ramp until it is possible to follow a crack up left to the flakes, which are climbed to a resting-place at the brown scar. Move up and traverse left to the arête, which is followed delicately to a belay ledge. Nut and cam belays. Either continue up *Blood Brothers* or down-climb easy rock at the front of the Point.
Variation Finish
Cracking Up E2 5b † (7.4.96). Climb the roof above the brown scar direct.

Sprain Stop Play 70 feet E2 5b † (7.4.96)
Not well protected. Start directly under the brown scar. Climb the right-hand of two rightward-trending ramps; then move up and left into a niche. Exit right from the niche and climb up past a ramp to the large ledge above.

★**Under Pressure** 70 feet E2 5b (5.86)
A good route that climbs the obvious thin slanting crack in the wall 15 feet left of the left-hand edge of the seaward recess. Tougher than it looks. Climb the crack, and at the ramp pull up and gain the large ledge above via a little left-facing groove (bold).

☆**Sugar Puff Power** 70 feet E3 6a † (7.4.96)
Sustained and high in the grade but thoroughly enjoyable: the plum line. Start below the left-hand edge of the seaward recess. Climb the arête to good flake holds and a spike runner. Make improbable moves diagonally rightward along the lip of the recess before ascending the wall above its apex to a half-height ledge. Climb the centre of the black wall and exit via a solid, left-slanting groove.

Up the Damehole 70 feet E1 5a (15.8.93)
This route climbs the through-hole at the back of the seaward recess, thus reversing the route taken by outdoor activities centre groups who abseil 'Down the Damehole' as part of their preparation for the great outdoors; it is only slightly less daft. The dubious pleasures of this so-called 'entertaining struggle' can be extended by splitting the pitch at the ledge at half height. Graded for loose rock and dodgy holds. Start beneath the hole and climb it on the left.

If you climb it on the right you will find a distinct **Absence of Inselbergs** (E1 5b 1995)

Carboverdrive 80 feet E4 6b † (7.4.96)
A fine line, easier for yoga-freaks. Ascend a rightward-leading glacis on the right-hand edge of the seaward recess, and climb black rock on jugs to an awkward position beneath the right-hand apex of the roof. Contort though this to reach a flake and then the half-height ledge. Continue more easily up the left-facing flake above and step left to finish up the exit groove of *Sugar Puff Power*.

Reunion 70 feet E1 5a † (7.94)
Start in the middle of the landward wall and climb direct to the horizontal break; then climb up, bearing left, to a slanting break and finish just left of the prominent nose (peg). Belay on a stake well back.

Left for Dead 70 feet E3 5c † (7.4.96)
Deceptive. Start 6 feet left of an obvious elliptical pocket in the right-hand side of the face. Climb up to meet a rightward-rising crackline and follow it almost to its top. Swing left onto the compact headwall and climb direct just right of the prominent nose.

Training for The Eiger 70 feet E4 5c † (7.4.96)
Start 25 feet left of the right-hand arête of the face. Climb straight up 6 feet right of the elliptical pocket until increasingly tenuous moves and poor rock lead to the shattered right-hand of two rightward-rising cracks. Climb the crack and finish carefully over two shaky pockets.

★**The Wine Dark Sea** 300 feet E1 (8.4.79)
[Photo p.112a.] A fun route, and a fine traverse which makes the best of the horizontal nature of the south face. Best done either with a swell running at half tide, or at high tide on a calm day. Start at the base of an easy-angled slab right of the wall.
1 140 feet 5a. Climb the slab to its top and step left onto the wall. Traverse left to a scoop and gain a line of flakes; then step down to a diagonal crack leading to a large ledge.
2 70 feet 5b. Climb down into the first shallow recess; then move left and climb a slab. Swing down left and gain a small ledge (peg useful for a back rope). Climb down with increasing difficulty to ledges just above the sea.

3 90 feet 4b. Climb down into the seaward recess and traverse across this to gain a ramp leading across the final wall to ledges at the front of the promontory. Belay on nuts and cams.
Either stay roped-up and scramble carefully up a loose wide ramp or, better, finish up the obvious groove of *Blood Brothers*.

Basketball with the President (350 feet E3 5c 1995) follows a lower leftward traverse-line than *The Wine Dark Sea* (just above the high-water mark). Steady climbing until the best and hardest (sustained) is reserved for the traverse of the smoother, seaward face just above the sea. Escape as for *Wine Dark Sea*. Best soloed on a calm and sunny summer's day.

Big Sea Swimmer 40 feet Very Severe 4b † (15.8.93)
Climb the small clean slab on the left side of a narrow inlet at the landward end of the Point. Pleasant but protectionless.

South of the promontory are a number of slabs with easier, unnamed climbs used for 'training' novices, which are well supplied with stakes at the cliff-top. An inset slab and corner, **Bumpers** (80 feet Severe 14.4.79), has been recorded, but climbers may prefer to avoid this area.

The final route climbs a clean slab 100 yards further south.

Out of Season 70 feet Hard Very Severe 4c † (10.10.93)
Climb the slab, taking a central line and passing two pegs which constitute the only protection. Reasonable climbing though the rock is a bit flaky.

Dyer's Lookout

OS Ref 224 256

The rather sombre main cliff above an isolated beach is the setting for a number of the most powerful and daunting routes on the Culm Coast. In complete contrast, the delicate climbing on the Blisterin' Barnacle Slab offers some light relief. The area is best reached from the car-park just beyond the toll booth at the top of the hill descending to Hartland Quay. Follow the coast path north along the cliff-top for a quarter of a mile until it descends to an isolated cottage. From the beach just beyond the cottage can be seen the seaward slab containing *Blisterin' Barnacle*. The unmistakable sweep of the *Earth Rim Roamer* wall is a hundred yards further north across the boulders. Just north again is the very steep concave slab of *The Culmination*.

Opposite this is an easy-angled, south-facing slab with **Easy Culm, Easy Go** (60 feet Very Difficult 19.7.92) up the seaward arête and crack, and **Dyer Need** (60 feet Very Severe 4c 19.7.92) up the smoother slab just to the right.

★★**The Culmination** 80 feet E6 6b (24.7.89)
A testing pitch. Scramble up to belay at the wide crack at its base. Follow the crack to where it closes and move diagonally right to gain another crack. Follow this with increasing difficulty to two pegs. Step right and up to a good fingerhold. Fingery moves lead up right to another peg. Step left; then climb direct past a final peg to finish on large flat holds. Belay to notices warning of a dangerous cliff!

A little further south is the impressive *Earth Rim Roamer* wall, the scene of a number of dramatic rockfalls which have served only to extend the featureless expanse of holdless rock.

Dyer Straits 120 feet E8 6b † (3.8.98)
[Photo p.32a.] A tremendous route and an obvious challenge which had been attempted by a number of leading climbers. The line takes the tenuous seam that leads left from the first stance of *Earth Rim Roamer II*, and is protected with thirteen *in-situ* pegs (some of which were placed years before the first ascent and must therefore be regarded with some suspicion).

☆☆☆**The Earthsea Trilogy Part I** 160 feet E6 6b † (24.7.89)
One of the great routes of the Culm Coast and a stupendous pitch. Start below a very thin crack below a notch in the seaward arête. Climb to a peg at 30 feet (bold) and follow the crack to join the arête where it steepens. Climb the crack left of the arête to where it is possible to swing round right. Continue up the arête in a wild position to a ring-peg and another out left (difficult to clip). Pull up left onto the wall where forceful climbing first left, then back up right (peg) regains the arête leading to the top. Belay to an *in-situ* stake just below the top.

★★**Earth Rim Roamer II** 180 feet E4 (9.5.82)
The original, harrowing lead on this wall, climbed after the original *Earth Rim Roamer* (and its wall) succumbed to natural forces.
1 60 feet 4b. Climb the seaward arête to a stance where it steepens. Peg belay.
2 120 feet 6a. Follow the crack on the left of the arête until hard moves gain better holds leading back to the arête. Move right around the arête and climb to a projecting ledge. Follow the shattered crack-and-groove-system above to the top. Stake belay.

Further south, a tall slab sprouting a motley collection of pegs may have been climbed. This steep slab looks impressive but the upper half has a surface composed of interwoven shards of rock that disintegrate when touched – not very pleasant. The slab is bounded on the right by a narrow 30-foot groove.

Seal Clubbing 80 feet E2 5c †† (6.7.86)
Climb the groove to a ledge at 30 feet. Follow the arête to where it begins to impend and move out onto the slab (peg removed). Go back right to the arête above the steep section and follow it to the top. Escape off the back

with care. This route may have suffered a rockfall affecting the grade.

Crab Slab

Further south again is a squat slab containing a long diagonal crack.

O'Sullivan's Conundrum 50 feet E5 6a † (22.8.98)
An extremely committing lead up the right edge of the white streak near the left end of Crab Slab. Its seriousness is proportional to the size of the fallout zone's pebble/boulder material. Follow an intricate series of tiny holds directly up the right margin of the white streak to a slight horizontal break, better holds, and a peg (25 feet of solid 6a to the peg, the first protection). Swing right and make a final hard move to a better break. Finish straight up without further difficulty.

The Pastafarian 60 feet E3 6a (22.7.89)
Technical and bold, this route climbs straight up the centre of Crab Slab via the shallow niche half-way along the crackline. Start beneath the obvious peg at 20 feet. Deceptively thin moves lead past a finger-ledge to the peg, which is clipped with some relief. More difficult moves lead to the diagonal crack and the niche. Continue in a direct line up easier rock to the top.

Bulging Speedeye Wall 60 feet E1 5c (1982)
To the right of the shallow niche of the preceding route are two obvious pockets above the crackline. Start beneath these and climb delicately past two pegs in the lower wall to the crackline. Climb easily, without further protection, to the top via the two pockets.

Spring Surprise 50 feet Hard Very Severe 5a (15.4.79)
Further right, near the seaward end of the slab, are two other, larger pockets. Start beneath these pockets and climb to the first. Gain the second with difficulty and follow the crack out left until it is possible to climb direct to the top.

Crab Slab 100 feet Very Severe 4b (6.76)
An enjoyable lateral excursion along the lower crack is taken until, at the left-hand end, it becomes preferable to climb direct to the top rather than to continue along the same line. Well protected with cams and large nuts.

Blisterin' Barnacle Slab

Further south, and out to sea, is an isolated, north-facing slab of solid smooth rock which becomes inaccessible at high tide.

★**Briny Walk** 80 feet Hard Severe 4a (5.79)
A pleasant, well-protected route taking the shallow groove in the left arête of the slab. From a corner on the landward half of the slab, traverse right to the groove, which is climbed direct. Step right at the top.

Access to the remaining routes on this isolated slab is by scrambling up easy rock at the back of the slab and down the seaward end to reach the half-tide platform beneath the smoother right-hand section of the slab. For the next three routes, continue leftwards along a narrow foot-ledge.

★**The Plumed Serpent** 80 feet Severe (1979)
Climb the obvious snaking crackline 10 feet right of *Briny Walk* at the left-hand end of the slab. A well-protected delight.

Crumbs... 80 feet Hard Severe (1979)
Start 10 feet right of the obvious crack of *The Plumed Serpent*. Climb the initially smooth rock direct to reach disjointed cracks, which are followed to the top.

Further right the centre of the slab is composed of flakes, incuts, and small ledges.

Stuffed Badger 80 feet Hard Severe (5.79)
Climb the centre of the slab (little protection).

★**Jazz Discharge Party Hat** 70 feet Hard Very Severe 5a (1982)
Ten feet right of a short corner formed by a vertical overlap is a thin crack. Climb the crack on incuts until a hard move gains a narrow ledge. Continue direct to the top.

★★**Blisterin' Barnacle** 70 feet E2 5b (5.79)
A superb, sustained route (but at the bottom end of the grade) on perfect rock. Small wires required. Start in the centre of the smooth right-hand section of the slab, beneath a bottomless quartz crack. Move delicately up the slab to a thin crack; step left and climb up to the quartz crack, which is followed to the top.

★**Not Blisterin' Barnacle** 70 feet E1 5b (30.7.82)
This climb may have a personality complex but it is only slightly less fine (and difficult) than its neighbour. Start as for *Blisterin' Barnacle* and follow the thin crack further right to finish on the seaward arête.

Ripsnorter 150 feet Hard Very Severe 5a (11.86)
A girdle of the slab, starting on the seaward arête. Climb the arête until it is possible to gain a weakness at mid height. Keep stepping left to the other arête and finish up this.

The smaller slab further out to sea can be soloed pleasantly anywhere at or below Severe standard with the exception of a poor old **Languishing Limpet** (19.7.92) fighting its way up the thin straight crack in smoother rock 15 feet right of the landward arête at Hard Very Severe 5a.

South of the Blisterin' Barnacle Slab are two impressive but easy-angled south facing slabs containing three 110-foot Severes on smooth rock that unfortu-

DYER'S LOOKOUT ~ BLISTERIN' BARNACLE SLAB

1 The Plumed Serpent S
2 Crumbs HS
3 Stuffed Badger HS
4 Jazz Discharge Party Hat HVS
5 Blisterin' Barnacle E2
6 Not Blisterin' Barnacle E1

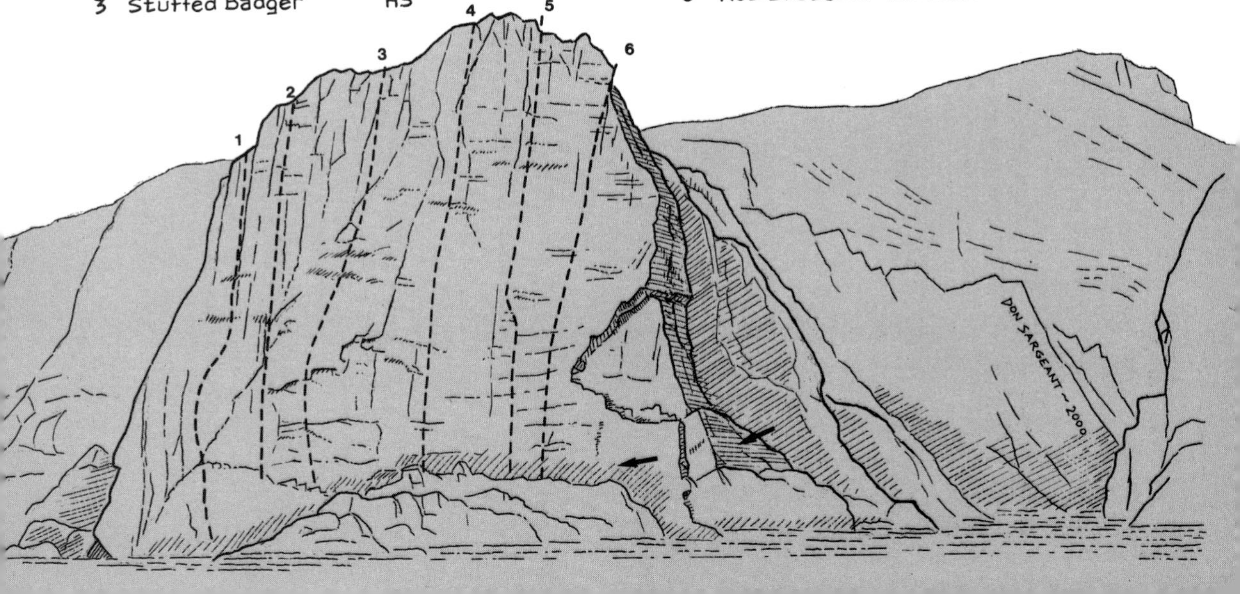

nately lacks any real identity, difficulty, or protection. From left to right they are **Sukharita** (23.4.82), **Clover** (7.5.81), and **Shamrock** (7.5.81). However, the grade appears to reflect the low technical difficulty and not the feeling of being 100 feet up without protection or the possibility of a rest!

Bear Rock

OS Ref 224 253

Bear Rock is the conspicuous double pinnacle (split by a smooth narrow chimney) some 500 yards north from Hartland Quay and is easily seen as one drives down the toll road to the car-park outside the pub. The Rock can be reached across the boulder-beach between half and low tide.

Barely Possible 80 feet Hard Very Severe 4b †† (1961)
Climb the loose landward arête of the lower pinnacle (possible rockfall) or the seaward end of the chimney, move across the flat summit, and attain the top of the upper pinnacle by a tricky move. Poor belay; simultaneous abseil descent.

The smaller, blunt pinnacle on the landward side of Bear Rock provides a pleasant scramble to reach and climb a narrow chimney, **Consolation** (Difficult 1959).

Hartland Quay

OS Ref 222 247

Hartland Quay is reached via a toll road (50p during the summer) and in good weather is a popular spot with the tourists – the coast scenery both north and south being particularly spectacular. To the north lie Bear Rock and the impressive strata formations of Warren Beach Cliff, and to the south are the smooth slabs of Screda Point. There are a number of small zawns and slabs west of the pub – all the slabs have been climbed and claimed in the past.

Warren Beach Cliff

Two shale horrors have been climbed on this geologically renowned precipice.

Stag Night Fright 350 feet Extremely Severe † (8.3.97)
Frightening, loose, prickly, and generally dangerous! Start at the far end of the beach, at a collapsing fin beneath a shallow, hanging shale gully.
1 100 feet 5a. Climb the right-hand side of the fin. From its top, step precariously left across a slab (two pegs removed) to take a stance on a mound of rubble at the bottom left of the gully (no belay).
2 100 feet 4c. Climb up and left through mixed vegetation and rubble,

taking extreme care with the man-sized loose blocks, to gain a more solid rib. Follow the rib to a good stance at its top.
3 150 feet 4c. Climb steeply straight up to gain the hanging field of thorn bushes. Bash up and right to exit via a shallow grass and mud slope.

Jerusalem 350 feet Extremely Severe † (20.7.96)
A very serious undertaking in the *Breakaway* mould, climbing the highest part of the cliff. The route gains a good ledge at half height before finishing by the prominent black chimney near the cliff-top. Pegs, *Warthogs*, slings, hexes, and helmets are essential. Start at a rib just right of the first small cave.
1 100 feet 5a. Climb the rib right of the cave and move up right at 40 feet. Continue up shallow grooves and trend right on poor rock to belay at the base of a thin vertical crack.
2 80 feet 5b. Move diagonally left to a short corner and pull round a small rib onto projecting holds. Go up to slanting ledges leading up left, then right. Climb right again to steep rock, then back left to a short detached chimney. Climb this; then move up to an excellent ledge belay beneath a bulging wall.
3 50 feet 5b. From a spike at the left end of the ledge, use a series of grass holds to gain a small cave in an exposed position. Pull left around the rib, climb the slim corner, and bear right to steep grass ledges below the dark chimney. *Warthog*/peg belays.
4 80 feet 5b. Ascend steep grass to the base of the dark chimney. Climb up and right via a large detached flake; then continue via two further cracks/flakes to the base of a shallow chimney. Climb the chimney direct (*in-situ Warthog*) and exit right to earth ledges. Belay beneath the final earth/shale cliff.
5 40 feet 5a. Finish grimly up jutting ribs and steep earth (serious) just left of the belay to reach the 'green and pleasant land'.

Screda Point

OS Ref 223 245

Screda Point lies to the south of Hartland Quay. It is easily reached and, having a spread of enjoyable routes on solid rock, is a good area for a first visit to the Culm. However, it is greatly affected by the state of the tide and it is wise to consult the tide-tables and arrive an hour or two before low water, especially if you wish to climb the easier routes on the seaward pinnacles. The slabs are at their best on a summer afternoon when the sun reaches them.

The climbs lie on the slabs and pinnacles, which can be well viewed from the car-park of the Hartland Quay Inn – indeed the antics of climbers provide a colourful side-show for the visitors. In summer, the pub offers a welcome lunchtime or evening break from entertaining the other patrons. The climbs can be reached along the beach between half and low tide, or via the coast path to the level grass above The Landward Slab.

Just north of The Landward Slab is a smaller slab with a diagonal right-to-left crack in it, which can be climbed at Severe. The rib on the right is **The Cleaver** (Moderate 27.9.59). Up the wide crack in the overhang behind *The Cleaver* is a **Micro Non Entity** (30 feet E4 5c † 24.8.86), a short route that packs a punch.

At the extreme left-hand end of The Landward Slab is a triangular cave, above which are impressive overhangs. The whole area appears to remain damp even in the driest of periods. The following three routes are centred on this cave and are graded for the normal damp conditions.

Water off a Duck's Back 80 feet E1 5b † (23.7.99)
Start in the triangular cave. Climb the foul-looking crack and the bulging, slanting chimney above, and continue up easier terrain to finish.

☆**The Visit to the Quack Doctor** 80 feet E5 6a † (22.7.99)
Start in the cave. Climb the crack as for *Water off a Duck's Back* until it is possible to 'duck' right under the overhangs to a good resting-foothold on the edge of the slab. Make blind moves through the roof to a poor peg and another peg just above. Overcome the final roof on good but spaced holds past a final (good) peg, and climb rightward to finish.

☆☆**Canard** 80 feet E6 6b † (20.7.99)
[Photo p.112b.] Start in the corner right of the triangular cave, and climb it until able to step left into the middle of the slab. Climb the slab to a massive chockstone (thread). Make bold moves through the roof above to two pegs. Pull over another roof (poor peg) and finish up the slab above.

The Landward Slab

The broad, smooth-looking slab with a prominent dark water-stain just right of centre contains the best climbing on the point. Stakes have been placed above the slab to facilitate an abseil approach and to act as a belay for those who have completed the return journey. Fortunately, the climbs are not as holdless as they appear from a distance but, that said, protection (mostly small wires and pegs) is usually well spaced and the rock, although solid, can have a smooth, frictionless feel to it.

Macho Duck 90 feet E3 5b (20.4.82)
Good climbing with spaced protection. Climb cracks up the left-hand edge of the slab and trend left above the cave to a peg (now defunct). Finish direct.

★**Naughty Sneaky** 140 feet E2 5b (20.4.82)
Sustained delicate climbing. Climb a faint sloping line of weakness across the slab from bottom left to the obvious pocket near the right arête. Finish up right.

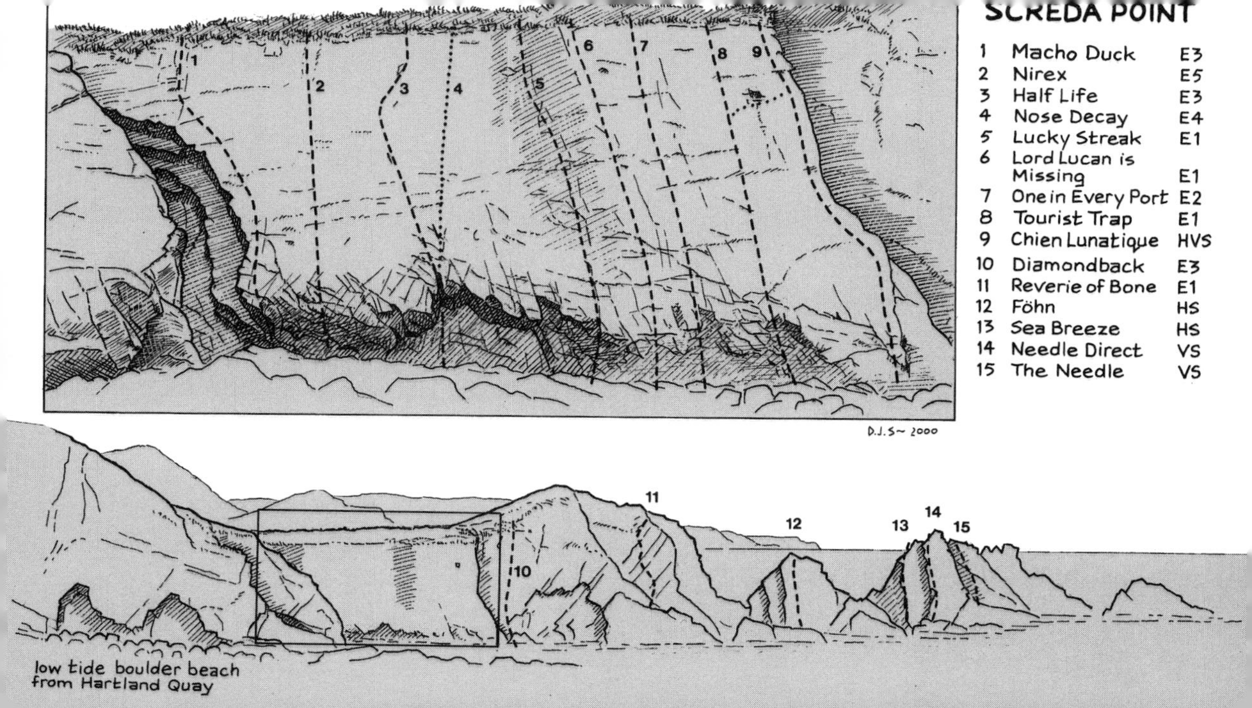
SCREDA POINT
1 Macho Duck E3
2 Nirex E5
3 Half Life E3
4 Nose Decay E4
5 Lucky Streak E1
6 Lord Lucan is Missing E1
7 One in Every Port E2
8 Tourist Trap E1
9 Chien Lunatique HVS
10 Diamondback E3
11 Reverie of Bone E1
12 Föhn HS
13 Sea Breeze HS
14 Needle Direct VS
15 The Needle VS
D.J.S~ 2000
low tide boulder beach
from Hartland Quay

★**Nirex** 90 feet E5 6a (5.5.87)
Climb the slab direct between *Macho Duck* and *Half Life*. Bold and technical.

★★**Half-Life** 80 feet E3 5c (15.3.80)
A superb pitch, sustained and technical, very sparsely protected with micro-wires, and at the top of its grade. Start at an overhang 20 feet right of the left-hand edge of the slab. Surmount the overhang and climb a vague line of discontinuous cracks leading up and slightly left to a blank section. A difficult step right gains more positive holds and the top.

★**Nose Decay** 80 feet E4 6a (1982)
Very bold. Check that the peg is still *in situ* before you start out! Surmount the overhang as for *Half Life*, and climb straight up on small holds, past a prominent peg at 50 feet (crux), in a direct line to the top.

★**Lucky Streak** 80 feet E1 5b (30.5.89)
Another good climb, following a fine crack in the dark water-stain. Spaced protection on the first half.

Lord Lucan is Missing 80 feet E1 5b (1988)
Follow a crackline immediately right of the stain.

★**One in Every Port** 80 feet E2 5c (20.4.82)
Climb the crack 10 feet right of the stain.

An eliminate has been climbed between the cracks of *One in Every Port* and *Tourist Trap*: **Hobson's Choice** (80 feet E2 5c 1989).

★★**Tourist Trap** 80 feet E1 5b (28.4.79)
The first route to be climbed on the slab, and a good introduction to its delights. Climb the crack which runs directly up the slab to the immediate left of the obvious pocket at two-thirds height. The last 10 feet constitute the sparsely-protected crux (though this can be avoided by stepping right into the pocket and finishing on the right at HVS 5a).

Sundare 80 feet E1 5b (16.4.83)
Climb the thin crack leading directly to the pocket, and finish on thinner holds above. Very close to *Tourist Trap*.

★**Chien Lunatique** 80 feet Hard Very Severe 4c (29.4.80)
Climb the right-hand arête of the slab. Spaced protection in the middle section.

Magnox 150 feet E2 5b † (6.87)
This is a counter-diagonal to *Naughty Sneaky* and no doubt covers the last few square inches of rock on this slab that had not otherwise felt the touch of the chalked hand of man. Start on the seaward arête as for *Chien Lunatique*. Head up and leftwards, aiming for the prominent peg on *Nose*

The Wine Dark Sea (E1) Damehole Point
Climber: Mark Garland Photo: David Hope

Canard (E6) Screda Point
Climber: Simon Young Photo: Young coll.

Sea Breeze (HS) Screda Point
Climber: John Hooper Photo: Rick Abbott

Magical Staircase (S) Marsland
Climber: Andy Elliot Photo: Andy Grieve

Decay. Cross *Half-Life* and continue leftwards above the cave to finish at the landward end of the slab.

A right-to-left girdle of The Landward Slab has also been climbed at E2 5c (1987).

Right of The Landward Slab is a higher, diamond-shaped slab containing the next route.

Diamondback 90 feet E3 5b † (26.7.99)
Start at the lowest point of the slab. Climb steeply right to a peg at 40 feet and continue direct to a good wire and a *Friend 1* in a slot. Climb straight above the slot for 30 feet until it is possible to reach better holds and some placements in a diagonal crack. Follow the crack for a couple of moves (peg on the right) and finish up the grassy tufts.

Right again is another slab, rising from a small zawn, with a rippled surface and four diagonal cracks.

Reverie of Bone 110 feet E1 4c (1 pt aid) ‡ (29.4.79)
An uninviting climb that is now very grassy in its upper reaches. Start below the second crack from the right. Climb the crack easily for 30 feet; then traverse left into the next crack, which is followed until it is possible to reach a crack on the left. Continue left to the thin fault, which is climbed (peg removed) to another peg. Tension right into the groove and finish on insecure grass holds.

At the seaward end of the point are two shark's-teeth pinnacles. The inner and smaller of them gives one route, although more lines of a similar grade are possible.

Föhn 60 feet Hard Severe 4a (29.4.79)
Pleasant. Climb the centre of the slab to the top.

The Snuffler 60 feet Very Severe 4b † (9.10.90)
Just to the right of *Föhn* is a small cave. Climb up its right edge onto the slab, then straight up to the arête at a notch. The next move is the crux, above which the top is soon reached.

The most seaward pinnacle is known as The Needle and, not surprisingly, can be approached only at or near low tide. The central slab is bounded on either side by a chimney with a connecting cave – The Needle's Eye.

Sea Breeze 80 feet Hard Severe 4a (28.4.79)
[Photo p.112c.] Climb the landward arête of the pinnacle left of the left-hand chimney.

The landward chimney is **Tide's In** and Very Difficult.

★**Needle Direct** 80 feet Very Severe 4b (4.74)
The most substantial of the routes at the seaward end of the point. Climb up the centre of the pinnacle and move left just below the summit.

The Needle 80 feet Very Severe 4b (27.9.59)
Climb the right-hand side and arête of the central slab.

The right-hand side of The Needle's Eye can be climbed at Very Difficult – some loose rock near the top.

☆**Give Us a Break** 60 feet Very Severe 4c † (1994)
Climb the quartz break that snakes up the middle of the seaward slab right of the slot. Sustained, delicate, and enjoyable.

St Catherine's Tor

OS Ref 224 241

The tor is the conspicuous conical 'breast' of a hill sliced in half by the forces of erosion. A pleasant stroll south from Hartland Quay.

Three Slab Pebble 250 feet Severe † (11.9.82)
The Culm Coast's answer to the Froggatt test-piece! Climb the three easy-angled south-facing slabs stacked one upon another on the seaward side of the tor. Carry pegs for belays.

Speke's Mill Mouth

OS Ref 226 236

A small compact area consisting of an impressive concave slab/wall right of a picturesque waterfall. Structurally speaking, it is part of the same strata of rock as Brownspear Point further out to sea, but it has the ambience of a separate area, being enclosed and idyllic.

Speke's Mill Mouth is best approached from Hartland Quay by a pleasant half-mile stroll past St Catherine's Tor, although the lazy may prefer to park their cars on a grassy area above the cliff, reached by a very rough track from Lymebridge (OS Ref 237 228).

Access to the waterfall and the concave wall to its right is made down a steep path. The condition of both waterfall and wall is affected by the amount of rainfall and severity of the wind on the day. The waterfall has been ice-climbed by Mick Fowler! Stakes at the top (in place at the time of writing) provide belays for all the routes on the wall.

☆**Streamline** 60 feet E4 6a † (15.6.97)
[Photo p.336b.] A good, atmospheric, and very photogenic route up the very left edge of the waterfall. Start left of the waterfall. Straightforward climbing leads to a mid-height ledge. Arrange protection for the smooth crux slab above, which is climbed to a peg. Further hard moves past another peg lead to a clean exit just left of the fall. Fencepost belays.

Sacred River 60 feet E3 6a/b † (23.7.89)
Good climbing up the very thin cracks just right of the waterfall, passing a peg (now deceased). Feasible only during drought conditions.

Red Tape 60 feet Hard Very Severe 5b (19.8.84)
Climb the thin crack right of the waterfall and left of the rather grassy, wider crack of *Cuchulain*.

Cuchulain 60 feet Very Severe 4c ‡ (16.6.84)
The rather overgrown crack leading to unpleasant material at the top, for which a prefixed rope is advisable.

Finn McCool 60 feet Very Severe 4b (23.6.84)
An enjoyable climb up the obvious central crackline – not as overgrown as it appears.

Right of *Finn McCool* is a rubble-filled unclimbed crack. Twenty feet right again, in the centre of the wall, is the curving crack of *Pressure Drop*.

★★**Pressure Drop** 120 feet E3 5c (23.6.84)
The classic of the area, and quite reasonable for the grade. Climb the crack, indistinct at first, past a peg to a small pocket and another peg. Difficult moves lead to its continuation and a resting-pocket. Move right and follow the crack above on good holds to the top.

☆☆**Ed** 110 feet E5 6a † (18.6.97)
Excellent climbing up the slab right of *Pressure Drop*. Start beneath a ring peg 20 feet right of the start of *Pressure Drop*. Climb up to the peg and make difficult and committing moves up to a slot and another peg. Step up and gain a standing-position on the higher of two grassy breaks. Make bold moves up to good pegs and traverse left with difficulty for a couple of moves to the second peg of *Pressure Drop*. Follow that route for 10 feet to a good pocket; then break out left and climb the wall above with no further protection to the top.

Right again are two peg-protected routes delineated by their original *in-situ* placements (these pegs may now be showing their age).

★**Surface Tension** 100 feet E5 6a (20.7.89)
Start from the top of a boulder below and right of the line of pegs. Climb the slab for 15 feet and traverse 10 feet left to finger-ledges. Climb to the break and two pegs, bold but straightforward. Move up with difficulty past

another peg (poor) and continue in the same line past two more pegs to join *Pressure Drop*, which is followed to the top.

★★Down to a Sunless Sea 120 feet E5 6a (8.7.89)
An excellent route, with widely-spaced protection provided by the pegs, and on rather brittle rock. Start from boulders at the extreme right-hand end of the wall and climb boldly up the slab, trending slightly left past a peg to a break (peg). Sustained climbing leads slightly rightward past two pairs of pegs to a shallow niche (peg). Climb straight up on good holds at the narrow overhang (wires in the wall above) and make a hard move to get established on the headwall; then climb to the top.

Brownspear Point

OS Ref 224 236

This dramatic promontory has some impressive features and contrasting climbing on both sides of the point. The north side is steeper, and dominated by the central black wall, unclimbed except by the 'washing machine' routes which encroach onto its upper left-hand edge; it is bounded on the right by the structurally unstable remains of a fine-looking corner (*Headbanger*). Further out to sea the climbs are shorter and the rock is more reliable. At the tip of the point is a fragile arch, and round on the lighter, south side of the promontory the slabs lie at a pleasantly low angle to give climbs of a nature radically different from their northern counterparts.

The point is approached as for Speke's Mill Mouth.

The North Side

The main feature of The North Side is the smooth black wall in its centre. Right of the short unstable corner bounding the wall on the left are three routes: all begin at a belay in the scree gully level with an obvious rising foot-ledge leading across the wall, which is reached by scrambling up the steep scree below or by abseiling from blocks on the ridge above. The first four routes are non-tidal.

★Front Loader 90 feet E3 5c (13.9.85)
A technical and serious route near the left-hand edge of the upper slabby wall. Step right onto the foot-ledge and traverse easily rightwards to a peg. Move up via pockets to another peg. Step left and climb fragile black flakes with increasing difficulty to a large hold. Move up and then right to gain a diagonal blind crack and another peg. Climb with difficulty in a direct line past a peg to the top.

★Zanussi 120 feet E2 5c (10.6.85)
A well positioned route, protected by five *in-situ* pegs and nothing else.

Brownspear Point
The South Side

	Route	Grade
1	The Red O	VD
2	Gangway	VD
3	Berlin	XS
4	Eric Pode's Route	XS
5	Steam Power	E1
6	Mainsail	HVS
7	Hatchway and Rigging	S
8	The Wager	HVS
9	Up the Ante	E1

Start as for the preceding route, level with the obvious foot-ledge. Follow the foot-ledge for 50 feet past a peg to another peg. Step up and left past another peg; then climb a series of incut holds and small slots to a good handhold (peg). Ten feet above is a smaller hold, from which a difficult traverse right gains a thin crack (peg). Finish direct to the crest of the point.

★**Hotpoint** 120 feet E1 5b (6.5.87)
Bold for the grade and in a tremendous position. Start as for *Front Loader*, follow the foot-ledge for 50 feet to the second peg, and climb up to the peg above (so far as for *Zanussi*). Then traverse right for 15 feet and move up via pockets to another peg. Technical climbing gains a crack, which is followed to the top.

Beyond the smooth black wall and the corner bounding it on the right are shorter walls leading down to the seaward extremity of the point.

Avoiding the Touch 60 feet Hard Very Severe 5b † (26.9.93)
An intimidating route climbing cracks beneath a large overhanging block. Climb overlaps to the start of the obvious widening crack left of the shallow cave half-way along this section of the promontory. Climb the crack, move left where it fades, and climb the continuation crack. Exit with care past the block to avoid disturbing its delicate equilibrium (for the sake of the belayer!).

Further right are a number of routes with exits, which require care, onto unstable ground at the top. Similar care is necessary for the descent of the crest and rib on the southern side of the point.

★**Parallel Flow** 60 feet E1 5b (3.4.86)
A fine route with some unpredictable rock. Start below the shallow cave and climb up to gain the vertical crack. Follow this; then move left to another crack, which is followed strenuously to the top.

★★**Tetrapod** 50 feet E3 6a (27.3.86)
A miniature classic, well protected but sustained. Climb the next crack right of the shallow cave, passing a peg.

☆**Both Ends Burning** 50 feet E4 6a † (17.9.93)
Climb the very thin crack right of *Tetrapod*, past a peg, to the top. Painful on both toes and fingers!

Gabion 60 feet Severe (27.3.86)
Climb the arête of the wall.

The Flying Limpet 45 feet E3 6b † (9.97)
The final crack on the right of the wall. Mantel onto a small ledge at the foot of the crack and make very tenuous moves to leave it. The crack eases as height is gained.

Further round, the tip of the point has been pierced, leaving a delicate arch. The next route replaces **Somewhere over the Rainbow** (50 feet E1 5b 20.6.87), which started up the wide crack and then stepped across the apex of the arch to the crack on the right.

★**Madam Sixtoes** 50 feet E2 5c (8.5.95)
The disjointed cracks in the wall on the left-hand side of the arch. Short and intense, but well protected and with some surprising holds. Enter the deep crack and climb to its close. Step left (peg) and climb delicately into the stepped crack, which is followed with interest to the top. Peg belay.

☆**Penny for the Guy** 50 feet E4 6a † (26.5.97)
A fingery route up the arête and wall above on the left-hand side of the arch. Three pegs provide protection together with a *Friend* ½ in the crack on the left. Peg belay.

☆☆**Mighty Wurlitzer** 50 feet E4 6b † (9.97)
Superb unusual climbing up the curving right arête of the arch. A bold start up the lower arête leads to a balancy step left and the undercut upper arête (crux). The final crack is climbed in a fine position to the top.

Archie Andrews 40 feet Very Severe 4c (28.3.86)
Climb the crack right of the arch. Descend the seaward arête.

On the south side of the arch is:

Living with the Loonies 30 feet E4 6b † (9.97)
Start from a high ledge-system. Fingery climbing just left of the arch leads to a quartz traverse right to a hanging crack, which is followed to the top.

The South Side

Access to the south-facing slabs can be gained by descending grass and scree slopes at the landward end of this side of the point. In the centre of the cliff is a prominent shallow cave known as The Hatchway. Left of this and beyond a rib is a smaller slab with another arched cave at its base. It is wise to carry pegs whilst climbing here.

The Red O 90 feet Very Difficult (18.8.84)
Climb the clean slab left of arched overhangs past two faint red circles. Pleasant and solid but undistinguished. Belay to a large block around the rib to the left. Descend the easy inset slab below the block with care.

At the extreme left-hand end of the main slabs and adjacent to The Hatchway is a subsidiary slab forming an easy-angled pillar.

Gangway 190 feet Very Difficult (1961)
A serious route for the grade owing to lack of protection and loose rock. Start at the foot of the subsidiary slab.

1 60 feet. Climb the slab to a ledge at its top; then head left towards the arête. Go up to a peg belay on the rib. A loose pitch.
2 130 feet. Follow the rib direct until it curves leftwards near the top. Move right onto the slab and finish direct.

Berlin 210 feet Extremely Severe (1974)
An exhilaratingly loose climb taking an arbitrary line up the expanse of slab above and left of The Hatchway. The holds resemble loosely-packed playing cards and should be left unshuffled. Start beneath The Hatchway.
1 130 feet 4c. Ascend a small slab in the left side of The Hatchway until beneath the overlap (peg). Step left and surmount the overlap, and continue more or less straight up for 50 feet (placing two pegs constitutes the crux). Trend right to the vertical overlap and follow this to a stance on the rib.
2 80 feet. Climb the rib, and move right near the top.

Eric Pode's Route 200 feet Extremely Severe (10.10.78)
Another exciting excursion on exfoliating rock.
1 120 feet 4c. Start as for *Berlin* and climb leftwards out of the cave until is possible to traverse right to a shallow corner formed by the overlap. Climb the corner direct and continue leftwards to a stance on the rib (as for the two preceding routes).
2 80 feet. *Berlin* pitch 2.

Steam Power 200 feet E1 (10.6.85)
Very much an eliminate, but with some interesting moves on the second pitch. Start to the right of The Hatchway at the foot of a rib.
1 80 feet 4b. Climb the rib easily to the grassy gully. Step left onto the slab and climb direct to vague ledges on *Mainsail*. Follow these left to belay in the corner.
2 120 feet 5b. Move back right and climb easily at first on knobbly rock (as for *Mainsail*) for 20 feet; then step left to gain some very thin cracks in the smooth slab. Climb up with more difficulty past a peg to easier ground beneath the upper slab (peg removed). Go up and left past a flake to reach the rib of *Gangway* and the top.

Hatchway and Rigging 190 feet Severe (1961)
A loose and undistinguished climb. Start as for *Steam Power*.
1 70 feet. Climb the rib; then go easily up the gangway leading right. Peg belay.
2 50 feet. Follow the edge of the overlap and keep to the left edge of the slab until a traverse can be made to a grassy chute on the right. Peg belay.
3 70 feet. Traverse left to regain the edge of the slab. Continue direct and then climb the most solid line to the top.

★★Mainsail 200 feet Hard Very Severe (1961)
One of the earliest and still the best climb on The South Side. Sound rock with technically interesting climbing and a sparsely-protected crux. Start

beneath a subsidiary triangular slab, 20 feet right of The Hatchway.
1 60 feet 4c. Climb the centre of the slab on small holds to a stance in the gully left of the rib of *Hatchway and Rigging*.
2 140 feet 4c. Traverse left and slightly up for 20 feet; then climb the centre of the slab, bearing right, on curious knobbly rock. At 60 feet a delicate step up and to the right gains the easier upper slab. Climb direct on large but sometimes loose holds to the top.

The Wager 220 feet Hard Very Severe (9.12.78/1984)
The first pitch is very good. The second has no real protection and is loose in places. Start at the foot of the narrowing slab, identified by a slanting overlap at mid height, about 40 feet right of The Hatchway.
1 110 feet 5a. Climb up and slightly left to gain the edge of the slab at the point where it curves leftwards. Move right and climb direct on small holds to the slanting overlap. Follow this leftwards and step left to a stance and peg belay in the gully left of the rib.
2 110 feet 4c. Traverse right into the centre of the slab and climb direct on friable holds to the top.
Variation
2a 100 feet 4c. The left edge of the slab can be followed in its entirety. Slightly easier than the original.

Up the Ante 200 feet E1 (25.11.84)
1 130 feet 5b. Climb up the middle of the slab to a peg. Move right and follow a line of weakness to gain a band of easier rock which leads left to the arête.
2 70 feet 4c. Move onto the slab on the left and finish direct as for *The Wager*.

The small bay south of Brownspear Point is bounded at its southern end by an isolated buttress which is split by a fine-looking crack. **Javelin** (90 feet Severe 1.86) climbs this crack to a ledge below large poised blocks. Descend on the right with care.

Some three-quarters of a mile further south from Brownspear Point are two offset, south-facing slabs. **Duff Hunch** (120 feet Very Difficult 13.4.89) climbs the seaward end of the larger, landward slab.

Hole Rock

OS Ref 222 226

This pleasant and compact little crag lies on the north side of a promontory about half a mile south of Brownspear Point. The top of the ridge leading down to the promontory can be reached by a footpath from Elmscott, or by the coast path from the road at Dixons Well (OS Ref 224 212).

Follow the ridge down until it steepens; then contour north and descend to a faint track that leads back south to the ridge, which is followed down to the top of the crag. The base of the cliff is reached by an easy descent route in the middle of the promontory or by abseil from the *in situ* stake (which serves also as a belay for the routes).

The crag gets its name, presumably, from the small hole that pierces the base of the crag half-way along its length. To the left of the hole is a steep sheet of rock incised by thin leaning cracks which provide the lines for the routes. The widest crack is *The Butterfly Boy*.

☆☆**Titanic Nights** 75 feet E2 5c † (12.5.90)
The thin discontinuous crack left of *The Butterfly Boy*. Delicate and sustained but well protected. Start just right of the foot of the crack. Step up and move left into the crack and climb this past a peg to where it curves sharply left. Step right to the continuation crack, which is followed past another peg to the top.

★**The Butterfly Boy** 70 feet Hard Very Severe 5b (15.8.87)
The obvious wider, zigzag crack near the right-hand side has a sting in its tail. Start just right of the crack. Tricky moves lead left into the crack, which is followed to where it peters out. Move up steeply left to a peg protecting a hard move to reach holds at the top of the wall.

Propeller 70 feet Hard Very Severe 5a † (31.8.87)
The crack right of *The Butterfly Boy*. Follow the crack to its end (peg). Climb straight up on incuts to a diagonal line of flakes and follow these up right to a long reach for the top.

Nabor Point

OS Ref 214 201

This is one of the most remote areas on the Culm coast. The climbs, though short, are solid and set in wild and beautiful surroundings, making this a cliff for the connoisseur of Culm. Tide and topography are complicating factors and a certain amount of 'nous' is required to avoid the embarrassment of being trapped in the central bays by the incoming tide.

From the top of Nabor Point three promontories can be seen below; the central promontory provides most of the climbing. The best way to approach the area is to descend steep grass just south of Nabor Point itself starting down the southern edge of the shallow gully leading down toward the beach. A stake can be found just before the grass gives way to rock, some 80 feet above the beach, from which it is advisable to leave a fixed rope to facilitate access to and eventual exit from the central bay. This method avoids the possibility of being caught in the central bays between half and high tide.

Approach can also be made along the beach from Embury Beacon, but half-to-low tide is required to negotiate the notch in the guarding southern promontory.

Far North Area

This is an area of steep slabs 100 yards north of the main area and is easily recognized by the distinctive right-to-left diagonal crack of *Two Williams' Wall*.

☆**Luminarc** 60 feet E2 5c † (4.11.90)
A delicate and well-protected route that blasts up the middle of the steep slab left of *Two Williams' Wall*. Succulent finger-slots appear quite miraculously. Start just right of the little pool at the bottom of the face. Pull up left and climb straight up between two converging cracks with holds and small wires in the right-hand crack. A very thin move allows better holds to be gained. Continue direct to the top of the rock and then up easy ground to a stake some 30 feet up the ridge. Abseil off.

Two Williams' Wall 60 feet Hard Severe (13.4.89)
Climb the right-hand arête to reach the start of the diagonal crack, which is climbed, initially by foot-traverse, to the top with good protection. Continue up the ridge to a stake belay. Abseil off.

North Area

The northern promontory provides **Nemo** (50 feet Severe † 23.7.84), which climbs the thinner crack just left of the obvious groove on the right of the slab.

Mythical Wall

The climbing on the central promontory is located on three distinct north-facing areas – Mythical Wall is the steep triangular face at the landward end of the promontory. The wall is seamed with cracks and sports a bulge in its upper half. The three routes on this wall offer exhilarating climbing on superb finger-jugs. Descent is by the landward side – care required near the top.

☆**Cyclops** 60 feet E1 5b † (11.1.90)
In the centre of the wall is an upright oval patch of white quartz with parallel cracks running up either side. Climb the twin cracks, surmount the bulge centrally, and climb the thin crack in the middle of the headwall. Peg belay in the back wall.

Minotaur 60 feet E1 5b † (11.1.90)
Climb the deep crack 15 feet right of the twin cracks of *Cyclops*. Where the crack closes, step right and climb straight up the wall to the bulge. Step right and climb the bulge (peg) to the thin crack above, which leads to the top. Peg belay.

Medusa 60 feet E1 5b † (2.5.93)
Steep and surprising. Climb the dog-leg crack left of the right arête to good quartz holds. Continue straight up the wall left of the crack to where this begins to fade (committing). Climb strenuously over the bulge and continue up the vertical crack to the top. Peg belay.

The Trials of Isosceles 70 feet Very Severe 4c † (2.5.93)
Climb the right-hand arête of the wall via an awkward bulge. Harder than it looks.

The Sanctuary

The main feature of The Sanctuary is the steep and smooth back wall with the diagonal crack of *Lifeline* running from right to left. Approach to The Sanctuary at low-to-half tide is best achieved by scrambling up the back (south) of the central promontory and descending an easy stepped ramp on the right-hand side (facing out) of the back wall.

☆**Lifeline** 70 feet E2 5b † (26.11.89)
The long diagonal crack in the back wall gives a route with a 'big' feel to it. Climb easily to a peg at the start of the line. Move left to the crack itself and follow it, well-protected but strenuous, to the top of the wall. Block belays well back.

The Short Walls

Low tide and calm seas are required to gain access to this area near the end of the central promontory. The walls are reached by scrambling down easy rock on their landward side from the south. There are two long strip walls separated by a three-foot-wide ledge. The routes finish at the ledge and the 20-foot upper wall provides excellent soloing on magnificent finger-jugs.

Gizmo 40 feet Hard Very Severe 5b (26.11.89)
A little gem. Steep and well protected. Climb the obvious thin crack near the left-hand end of the lower wall – a thin start and an awkward finish.

Avalon 35 feet Hard Severe 4b † (2.12.90)
The obvious wider crack in the lower wall. Short and sweet.

The South Area

The southern promontory is long, low, and undercut. A notch at the seaward end provides the key to access from the south if the Nabor area is approached from the Embury Beacon beach. If the notch is cut off, then variations on **Nautilus** (220 feet Severe 23.7.84) can be used to escape. This route follows a traverse-line above the undercut base of the promontory starting at the slabby, landward end.

Knaps Longpeak

OS Ref 211 187

An area of low-angled slabs in the bay to the north of Foxhold Slabs. It shares the approach to that crag – along the foreshore between half and low tide after parking at Welcombe Mouth. On the north side of the bay is a south-facing slab with an obvious crack in its left-hand section and an overhung base.

'My Word Is My Bond' 90 feet Very Severe 4c † (31.10.92)
Pegs should be carried to back up the single *in-situ* belay/abseil peg. Start on a small pinnacle 15 feet right of the base of the slab. Swing up from the pinnacle using side-pulls until established on the stratified wall. Move up and left to the base of the slab and climb it to the top, using the crack. Peg belay; abseil off.

Opposite, on the southern side of the bay, is a broad area of slabs which can be divided into three sections: the steep Landward Slab, which is bounded on its right by a vegetated, rightward-slanting crack; the large Central Slab, seamed with cracks and vegetation; and the smooth Seaward Slab, bounded on its left by a deep corner.

The Landward Slab

Shaken Not Stirred 180 feet Hard Very Severe 4c † (16.6.94)
Start 15 feet left of the obvious crack of *Destination Unknown*. Climb the easy-angled slab until it steepens and then a thin crack until a delicate move can be made to reach handholds on the left edge of a pocket in the steepest section of the slab. Mantelshelf into the pocket. Exit from this using a crack up and left to easier but looser ground. Go up grass to the full extent of a 50-metre rope and belay on blocks (sling *in situ*). Scramble up and right to the crest of the ridge and abseil from pegs at the top of *Silk* down the south-facing Foxhold Slabs.

Destination Unknown 180 feet Hard Very Severe 4c † (26.8.91)
Start in the middle of the slab at the base of the obvious crack. Climb the crack, which becomes a slight overlap higher up, to its vegetated top. Exit onto steep grass and continue up left for 60 feet to a block belay. Descend as for the preceding route.

The Central Slab

The distinctive features of The Central Slab are the wide crack of *Playing with the Boys* and a cutaway section in the middle of the base of the slab.

Thin Lion 90 feet Very Severe † (6.76)
Start at the left-hand end of the cutaway and climb cracks above to steep grass at the top. Peg belay (removed).

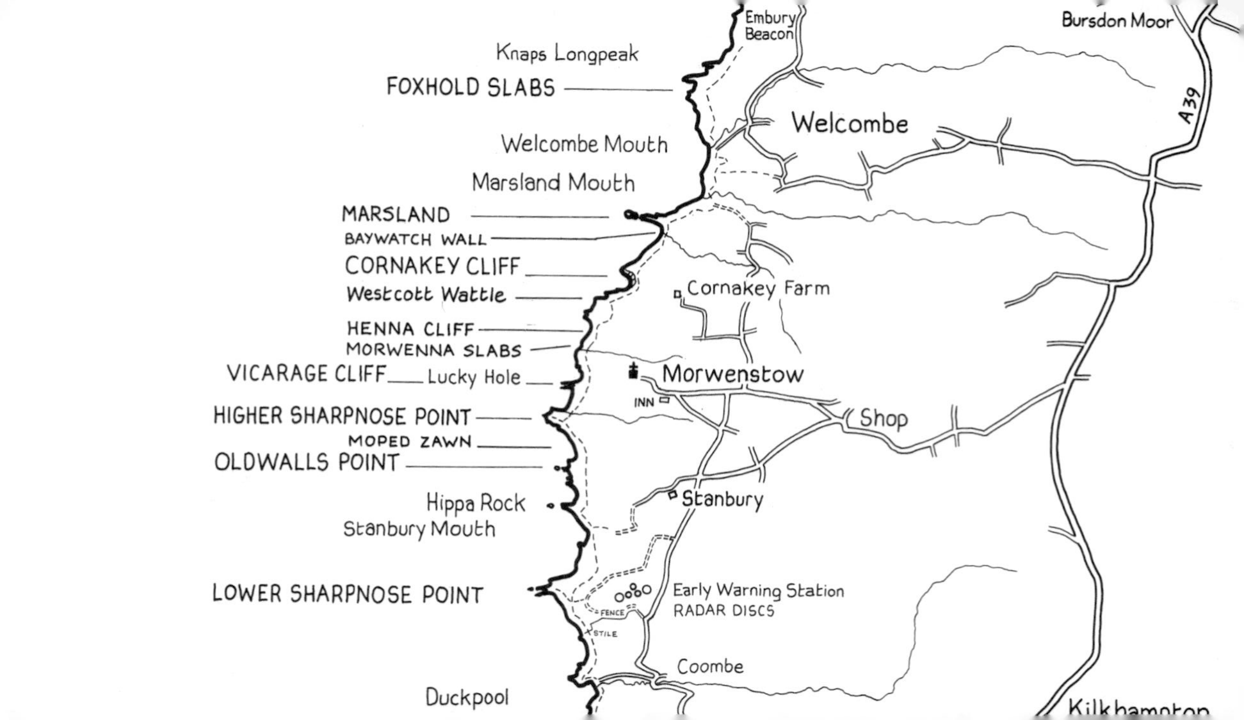

Embury Beacon
Bursdon Moor
Knaps Longpeak
FOXHOLD SLABS
Welcombe
A39
Welcombe Mouth
Marsland Mouth
MARSLAND
BAYWATCH WALL
CORNAKEY CLIFF
Cornakey Farm
Westcott Wattle
HENNA CLIFF
MORWENNA SLABS
VICARAGE CLIFF
Lucky Hole
Morwenstow
INN
HIGHER SHARPNOSE POINT
Shop
MOPED ZAWN
OLDWALLS POINT
Hippa Rock
Stanbury
Stanbury Mouth
LOWER SHARPNOSE POINT
Early Warning Station
RADAR DISCS
FENCE
STILE
Coombe
Duckpool

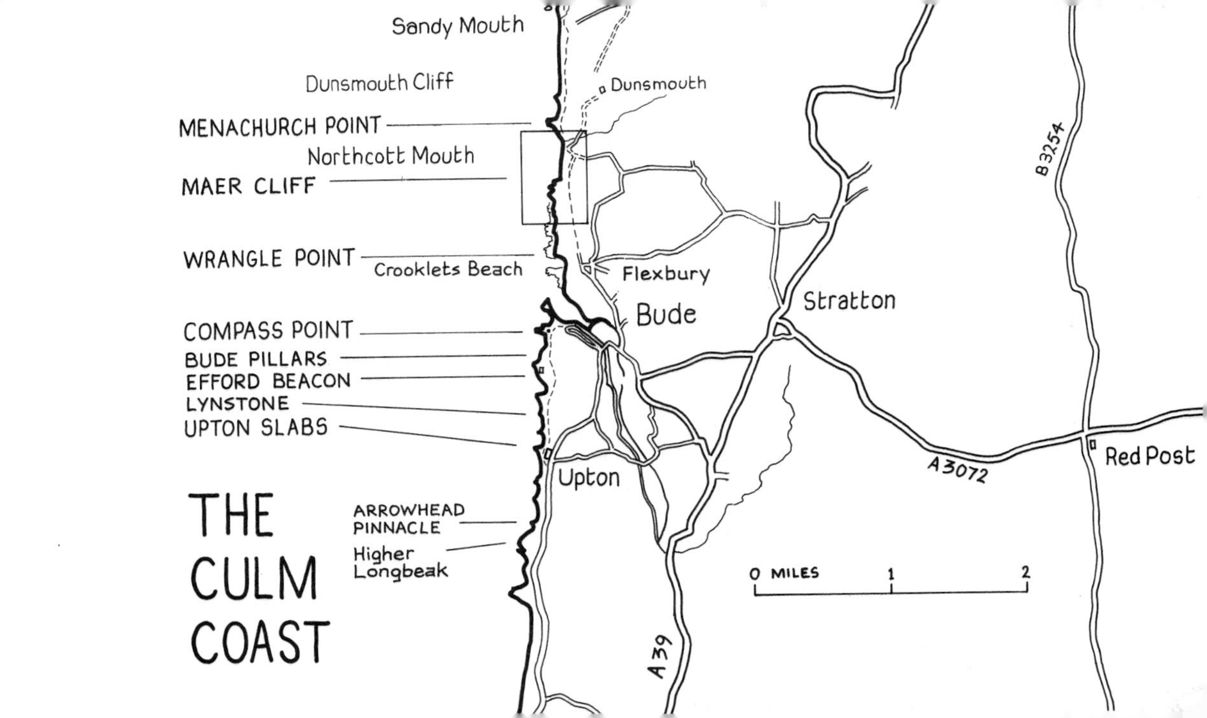
THE
CULM
COAST
Sandy Mouth
Dunsmouth Cliff
Dunsmouth
MENACHURCH POINT
Northcott Mouth
MAER CLIFF
WRANGLE POINT
Crooklets Beach
Flexbury
Bude
Stratton
COMPASS POINT
BUDE PILLARS
EFFORD BEACON
LYNSTONE
UPTON SLABS
Upton
ARROWHEAD
PINNACLE
Higher
Longbeak
B3254
A3072
Red Post
A39
0 MILES
1
2

Playing with the Boys 120 feet Severe † (6.76)
Climb the wide and winding crack to a peg belay in the crevasse.

Take My Breath Away 130 feet Severe 4a † (18.8.91)
Right of the cutaway is another crack. Climb this to the crevasse and peg belay of the preceding route.

Heaven in Your Eyes 130 feet Hard Severe 4b † (14.8.91)
Climb thin cracks left of the right-hand arête to a small vegetated scoop. Leave the scoop by the clean finger-width crack. Eventually, move left into the finishing-crack of *Take My Breath Away* and belay as for that route.

The Seaward Slab

The left-hand bounding corner, **Great Mills** (6.76), has been climbed at a modest grade. The smooth slab to the right has two cracks, and the slab merges into loose mixed ground, which should be treated with caution. **Gog** and **Magog** (both 100 feet Hard Severe 4a 2.4.77) climb the left and right-hand cracks respectively; **Gonad** (100 feet Very Severe 4c 14.4.85) climbs boldly between the two cracks without protection.

Foxhold Slabs

OS Ref 211 185

A sunny, south-facing area of middle-grade slab climbs on solid white rock: a pleasant introduction to the lighter side of Culm. The slabs lie some 500 yards north of the bathing-beach of Welcombe Mouth, where there is usually adequate parking. Approach to the slabs along the boulder-beach is generally restricted to between low and half tide, although with determination and a willingness to accept a soaking in the event of a miscalculation it may be possible to negotiate at higher tides.

There are three distinct slabs: a clean seaward slab, a narrow central slab with an undercut base, and a large landward slab. The slabs form the southern side of a spur, above which a long and exceedingly tedious escape can be made to the cliff-top – this is not recommended. It is far better to abseil back down from the belay pegs of *Mozambique* or *Silk*.

What Goes Up 80 feet Very Severe 4c † (12.4.92)
Climb the conspicuous crack set in dark grey rock left of the seaward slab and traverse right onto the slab to gain the peg belay of *Mozambique*.

Malawi 80 feet Very Severe 4b † (6.8.94)
Climb the left arête of the slab to join *Mozambique* for its final crack.

★Mozambique 80 feet Very Severe 4c (5.3.77)
A pleasant climb, with a thin start, up the crack in the left-hand side of the seaward slab to a peg belay.

Breakaway (XS ~ first ascent) Henna Cliff
Climber: Mike Morrison Photo: Mick Fowler

Harpoon (E2 ~ first ascent) Vicarage Cliff
Climber: Brian Wilkinson Photo: Wilkinson coll.

Zambia 80 feet E2 5c (6.8.94)
An artificial but exacting line between the cracks of *Mozambique* and *Angola*. Climb direct up the slab, using micro-wires of dubious value (one in *Angola*) to gain the mid-height ledge. Continue direct; then move left to the peg belay of *Mozambique*.

Angola 80 feet Hard Very Severe 5b (6.5.81)
A testing pitch up the thin crack and blank slab right of *Mozambique*.

Joker Man 80 feet Very Severe 4c † (14.4.85)
Climb the corner bounding the seaward slab on the right. At the top, traverse left to the belay of *Mozambique*.

The French Connection 210 feet Hard Very Severe † (26.3.86)
A serious route that climbs the narrow, central, bottomless slab after a difficult start over the overlap (using holds on the right wall).
1 140 feet 4c. Climb the slab past the narrow restriction and continue until it is possible to step right to the belay at the first stance of *Silk*.
2 70 feet 4a. *Silk* pitch 2.

★Silk 160 feet Severe (20.3.77)
A pleasant introduction to Culm slabs up the left-hand section of the landward slab. Start 30 feet up loose shale beneath the obvious crack.
1 90 feet 4a. Climb the crack to a ledge. Follow the shallow groove above and then thin parallel cracks on the left to a ledge and peg belay.
2 70 feet 4a. Climb up for 10 feet; then take the diagonal crack on the right. Move back left and go straight up to a ledge beneath the short headwall. Peg belay and abseil point.

☆Satin 150 feet Hard Very Severe † (25.9.94)
A delicate and sustained first pitch provides enjoyable and surprisingly well-protected (with micro-wires) climbing. Start 20 feet right of the start of *Silk*, on a higher ledge beneath twin cracks.
1 80 feet 5a. Climb the cracks and continue direct up the hairline crack above with sustained interest to the extreme left-hand end of a quartz break. Climb direct to a grassy ledge and on up to the peg belay of *Silk*.
2 70 feet 4b. Step right and climb the centre of the slab on pockets (bold); then move left to the top belay of *Silk*.

White Sabbath 140 feet Very Severe 4c (20.3.77)
A long and winding pitch. Start on a sloping ledge, higher and further right than that of *Satin*, unfortunately covered with debris. Step left onto the slab and climb direct on small holds to a quartz break. Step right to cracks and gain a ledge; then climb to a ledge 10 feet higher. Follow the thin crack above past shallow pockets; then climb diagonally left to the peg belay of *Silk* beneath the short headwall.

Marsland

OS Ref 206 174

[Photo p.16.] One of the Culm Coast's most delightful crags, its lack of height being more than compensated for by the idyllic sunny setting and the enjoyable nature of the climbing. Gull Rock is the small stack separated at high tide from a long rocky promontory which runs seawards from the high headland forming the southern side of Marsland Mouth. At low tide the area can be reached by traversing the foreshore south for half a mile from Welcombe Mouth or from Marsland Mouth. It is possible to scramble down the headland via a faint steep path to gain the crest of the promontory – this is quite difficult to locate on a first visit and recent rockfalls have made the descent more precarious and therefore not recommended.

The promontory consists of a number of south-facing slabs of which the central, light grey slab left of the shallow cave is the most attractive and the most popular. Abseil/belay pegs are in place above this slab and use of these is the recommended method of descent for all routes on the promontory itself. However, care is required as the pegs have probably passed their sell-by date and now need replacing.

Gull Rock

The stack can be approached only for one and a half hours either side of low spring-tide, and descent from the routes is made by the seaward arête, or by the back (north) of the stack if the tide is coming in. The stack is used by seabirds as a nesting-site and is best avoided during the nesting-season (March to July inclusive). The first routes are on the south-facing, most seaward slab of the stack, left of the through-cave known as The Devil's Hole.

Gullible Too 40 feet Severe † (2.8.92)
Climb the cracks and pockets near the left arête.

Tha' Wer' Easy 40 feet Hard Severe † (1994)
The second crack from the left arête.

Fitzharber 40 feet Hard Severe † (11.10.92)
A bouldery start leads to a pocketed crack, which is followed past a recess to the top.

Little Lambs 40 feet Very Severe 4c † (4.4.92)
Start at the mid point along the base of the slab and climb direct to the top at it highest point.

Deimos 40 feet Very Severe 4c † (2.8.92)
Climbs the series of diagonal cracks left of the landward arête.

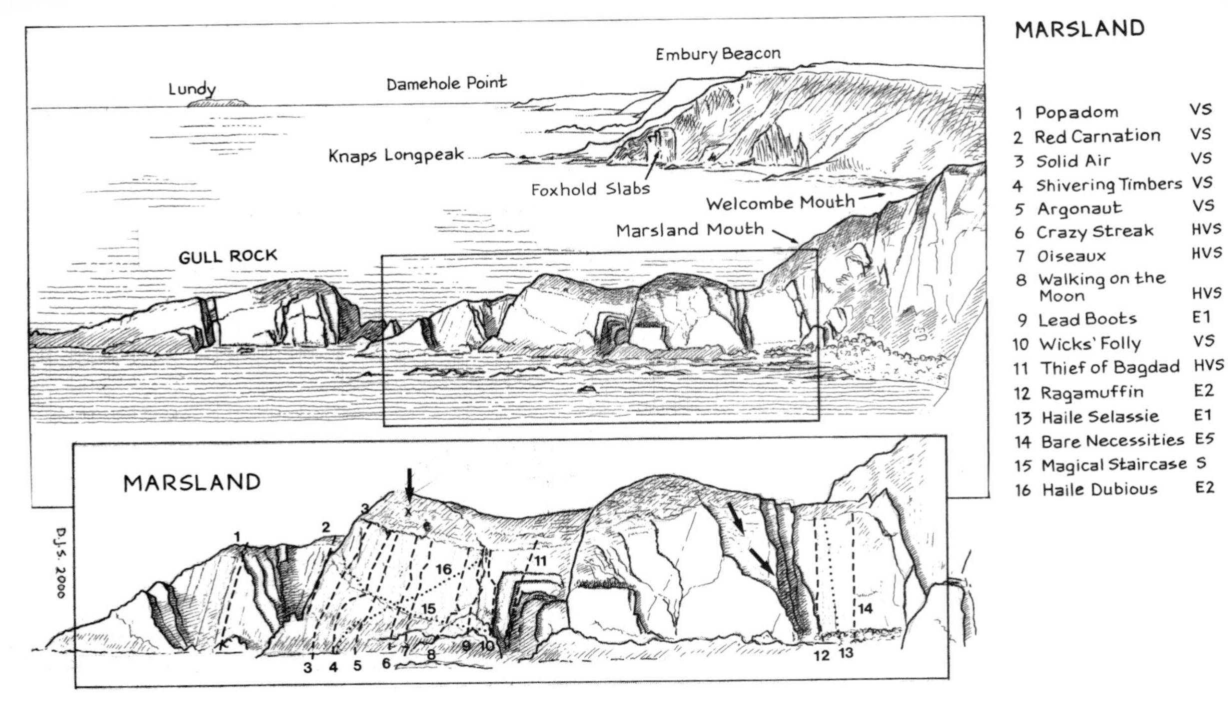
MARSLAND
Embury Beacon
Lundy
Damehole Point
Knaps Longpeak
Foxhold Slabs
Welcombe Mouth
Marsland Mouth
GULL ROCK
MARSLAND
1 Popadom VS
2 Red Carnation VS
3 Solid Air VS
4 Shivering Timbers VS
5 Argonaut VS
6 Crazy Streak HVS
7 Oiseaux HVS
8 Walking on the Moon HVS
9 Lead Boots E1
10 Wicks' Folly VS
11 Thief of Bagdad HVS
12 Ragamuffin E2
13 Haile Selassie E1
14 Bare Necessities E5
15 Magical Staircase S
16 Haile Dubious E2
D.J.S. 2000

Silence of the Lambs 80 feet Very Severe 4b † (4.4.92)
The arête at the right edge of the slab. Poor protection. Start on a ledge just above the pool at the entrance of The Devil's Hole, and climb the arête and over the overhang. Continue up the arête to the top, with occasional moves on the slab.

Right of The Devil's Hole are two more slabs. The following four routes take lines up the landward slab.

The Teardrop Explodes 50 feet E4 5c (13.8.95)
Poorly protected and serious. Climb the right arête of The Devil's Hole via a low traverse from the right. Loose rock near the top.

Electric Lemonade 50 feet E1 5b † (1994)
Climb the thin, rightward-trending crack, which starts 5 feet left of the obvious deep crack, to the small overlap. Climb carefully up the loose slab above until a traverse right can be made to easy ground and a stake belay higher up.

Tha' Wer' 'Ard 50 feet E1 5b † (1994)
Climb the pair of converging cracks left of the landward arête to the overlap. Surmount this with care and follow the crack above to easier ground and the top. Stake belay.

Elend 50 feet Very Difficult † (4.4.92)
Climb the folded wall in the landward end of the stack to finish up a groove on the right.

Main Cliff

The first climbs right of the through-gap between Gull Rock and The Main Cliff are located on a short triangular slab left of the rock-pool. **Maxland Armadillo** (40 feet Severe 1994) climbs the left-hand section, avoiding the arête; **Popadom** (40 feet Very Severe 4b 5.1.80) climbs the slab centrally to finish on its landward arête; and **Savage Poodle** (40 feet Very Difficult 1994) climbs the obvious layback crack on the landward edge.

The next three routes are located on the larger slab further right containing straight parallel cracks.

Red Carnation 70 feet Very Severe 4c (8.84)
Climb the left-hand of two parallel slanting cracks in the inset face above a rock-pool.

Rock-Pool Crack 70 feet Hard Severe 4b (5.1.80)
The right-hand crack.

Rock-Pool Slab just right of *Rock-Pool Crack* has been climbed at Very Severe 4c (4.4.92).

The Central Slab

The Central Slab is a fine open expanse of rock seamed with thin cracks and friendly little holds. A central peg belay/abseil point serves all the routes on the slab.

The crack and arête starting just right of the seaward edge can be climbed at Hard Severe 4a and is a good introduction to The Central Slab.

Solid Air 70 feet Very Severe 4b (18.2.73)
Start 25 feet in from the left-hand edge of the slab below a quartz patch and climb direct to the top on good but hidden holds.

Shivering Timbers 80 feet Very Severe 4c (5.1.80)
Start 20 feet in from the left-hand edge at an obvious crack and below an overlap at 20 feet. Climb up to the overlap; then step right to another crack and move up to the stepped shelf. Move a few feet right to a ledge and finish up the crack above.

Argonaut 80 feet Very Severe 4c (20.7.68)
Climb a vague thin crack, about 40 feet in from the left arête, to the stepped shelf. Go left along this for 10 feet to another ledge. Move left and climb the slab above.

Crazy Streak 70 feet Hard Very Severe 5a (28.6.81)
Climb the slab in a direct line to the top, starting left of the peg in the centre of the slab. Minimal protection.

★**Oiseaux** 70 feet Hard Very Severe 5a (28.6.81)
Pleasant, but with spaced protection. Climb direct up to the peg. Step right and climb straight to the top on spaced pockets.

★★**Walking on the Moon** 80 feet Hard Very Severe 5a (5.1.80)
The best pitch on the slab. Start 20 feet left of the right-hand corner, left of a quartz patch at 20 feet. Climb thin cracks leading up rightwards to the left of the quartz patch. Step up, then left to a narrow foot-ledge, and continue with more difficulty to the top. The foot-ledge can be reached direct; this is harder than the normal way.

★**Lead Boots** 70 feet E1 5b (7.83)
Eliminate but fun. Start just left of the corner and climb with difficulty to a prominent peg. Make a hard move above this and continue direct.

Wicks' Folly 60 feet Very Severe 4c (1970s)
The shallow stepped corner, which is unexpectedly tricky.

The Traverses

This relatively small slab is now blessed with the luxury of three traverses.

Haile Dubious 120 feet E2 5c † (9.7.89)
The best name on the slab. A rising left-to-right traverse, increasing in difficulty. Climb the first few feet of *Shivering Timbers* and then head diagonally right to the peg on *Oiseaux*. Continue to the narrow foot-ledge of *Walking on the Moon*. Move diagonally right (crux) and continue in the same line to finish at the top of *Wicks' Folly*.

★**Magical Staircase** 120 feet Severe (4.2.73)
[Photo p.112d.] Follow the obvious stepped gangway running from right to left across the slab past the obvious peg in the middle of the slab. A fine route at this grade.

★**Summer Wine** 120 feet Hard Very Severe (25.10.83)
An excellent girdle of the slab at half height. Start in the right-hand corner. Climb the corner until level with the narrow foot-ledge on *Walking on the Moon*. Traverse left with difficulty in the same line to the ledge. Continue left with interest until the gangway of *Magical Staircase* is reached. Finish up the left arête.

The Landward Slabs

The smaller slab right of *Wicks' Folly* contains two minor routes: **Sheikh of Araby** (50 feet Very Severe 4c 27.5.84) and **Sinbad** (50 feet Very Severe 4c 27.5.84).

★**Thief of Baghdad** 80 feet Hard Very Severe 5a (27.5.84)
The left side of the large cave contains a narrow subsidiary slab. Start below the slab and climb it until delicate moves lead right to the edge (ancient peg). Step up to the overlap, pull over on good holds, and finish direct.

★**Arabesque** 90 feet E1 5b (20.4.85)
Climb the back wall of the cave diagonally left over two overlaps until below a slab just right of the left-bounding groove. Move up and left with difficulty to gain the groove (peg); then layback the crack to a hold on the slab on the left (on *Thief of Baghdad*). Continue as for that route over the overlap and finish direct.

Wolf Solent 80 feet E2 5b † (28.4.84)
This route climbs the right edge of the arched cave. Start in an overhung recess right of the cave. Climb the corner above the recess for 15 feet (peg high up on the right) until a long step left gains the rib. Follow the shallow groove above and step left at its top. Climb through the overlap and follow the diagonal crack above. Block belays well back.

Right of this is a vegetated slab and right again is an inset slab, the 'neck' the promontory, containing the following four routes.

Ragamuffin 70 feet E2 5b † (4.4.92)
Climb direct up the slab, just left of *Haile Selassie*. No protection; poor rock near the top.

★**Haile Selassie** 70 feet E1 5b (13.4.84)
A brilliant little route which climbs the continuous crack in the left-hand side of the slab. It eases off at the top. Hidden belay on the other side of the neck.

☆**Bare Necessities** 70 feet E5 6a † (18.7.94)
Climb the middle of the slab, right of *Haile Selassie* (very thin); then swing right to a large rounded pocket. Step left and continue to the top. Three pegs.

Gardener's Delight 70 feet E2 5a (5.84)
A dangerous route. Start just right of the centre of the slab, beneath a faint curving overlap. Climb up to a ledge (peg removed), move right and up with difficulty to a narrow ledge (peg removed). Thin fragile flake holds lead to the top.

Baywatch Wall OS Ref 207 170

South of Gull Rock and easily seen from it is Litter Mouth Waterfall. Left of the waterfall is a pillar of rock, the north face of which is a steep bubbly wall capped by rubble. To the left of the pillar is a pale buttress of good rock that unfortunately deteriorates at half height into vertical mud and grass.

Pale Fire 80 feet E2 5c † (4.4.92)
Climb the buttress direct to the end of the usable rock. Use a prefixed rope to pull out or lower off.

★**Booby Prize** 80 feet E6 6b (8.8.94)
This superb, unusual, and sustained route climbs up the middle of the Baywatch Wall. After a bold start, climb the centre of the wall, protected by pegs and micro-wires. There is a *Friend 1* placement at half height and the crux is at three-quarters height. Belay to a stake, and a peg in the stream bed behind the stake.

Cornakey Cliff OS Ref 204 165

The archetype of Culm crags, full of tradition, vegetation, and, as a special bonus, a fair amount of loose rock. *Wreckers' Slab* is the classic ascent and a magnificent expedition up the right-hand and most continuous of the three enormous slabs. The lower, northernmost slab is, in contrast, steeper and cleaner, and has a number of very good routes along its length.

Owing to the popularity of *Wreckers' Slab*, the former parking arrangement at Cornakey Farm has become untenable. Climbers are therefore asked to park at The National Trust car-park at Morwenstowe, gain the coast path, and walk north across the top of Henna Cliff until the long slabs of the cliff can be clearly seen below. The cliff forms the northern side of Yeol Mouth and consists of a series of long overlapping slabs which increase in height from left to right. Those wishing to climb *Wreckers' Slab* are advised to gear up and leave their sacs in a grassy bay at the top of the climb before descending. A faint, prickly path zigzags down the spur on the north side of Yeol Mouth, skirting round the steep mixed ground near the summit. Eventually, a graffiti-ridden hovel is reached, from where steeper terrain is descended on the north side to boulders on the beach below. The last 40 feet of descent has become seriously destabilized, and extreme caution or an abseil is recommended. (Fifty minutes from Morwenstowe.)

Half tide or lower is required to reach the boulder-beach at the back of Yeol Mouth. At higher tides and in calm seas, an entertaining traverse, **The Nose** (Very Difficult 1959), can be made across the various slabs and corners.

The Seaward Slab

The northernmost, concave, seaward slab provides a number of short routes on good rock. If the sea forbids access, then routes on the right-hand side of the slab can be gained by abseil from nut and cam anchors in a bluff of rock above the slab.

★Stormy Weather 80 feet Hard Very Severe 5a (3.6.84)
An enjoyable route. Start 10 feet right of the seaward arête at a boulder. Climb easily to a slanting break; then go diagonally right to a large flat foothold. Ascend the deep cracks above. Peg (removed) and/or small cam belays in a bluff of rock up the grassy slopes above.

★★Sunday, Bloody Sunday 80 feet E1 5b (3.6.84)
An excellent climb taking the thin crack in the face right of *Stormy Weather*. Climb directly up to a scoop at 20 feet; then traverse up and left past a shallow ramp to gain the thin crack, which is followed to a good foothold on the right below a thinner crack. Make a difficult move to reach better holds and then the top. Belay as for *Stormy Weather*.

★Sailing the Seas of Cheese 80 feet E4 5c (5.2.92)
Fine climbing. Start directly below a triangular recess at two-thirds height right of *Sunday, Bloody Sunday*. Climb boldly to the recess (cam placements) before stepping right to a quartz vein, which leads to the top.

Bradworthy 5 70 feet Hard Very Severe 5a † (19.7.84)
A diagonal right-to-left crystalline ramp peters out below the steepest section of the slab. Climb the slab 20 feet left of the base of the ramp in a direct line to its vanishing-point. Move up and right via a flake to gain a small ledge, and continue to the top.

Cornakey Cliff

1	Stormy Weather	HVS
2	Sunday, Bloody Sunday	E1
3	Sailing the Seas of Cheese	E4
4	Bradworthy 5	HVS
5	Cancer Crack	VS
6	The Plank	HVS
7	Smugglers' Slab	VS
8	Jo	HVS
9	Heaven and Hell	HVS
10	Jolly Roger	VS
11	Wreckers' Slab	VS

Cancer Crack 70 feet Very Severe 4b † ‡ (16.1.94)
Start at a shallow cave 40 feet in from the left arête. Climb the crack rising from the top of the cave to a triangular niche. Continue up the now vegetated crack to a grassy finish.

Thirty feet further right is a double cave in the centre of the slab. Further right again there are three diagonal cracks. The following routes take the first two of these.

Spanking Colonel 80 feet E1 5a † (17.9.90)
Start 30 feet left of the landward end of the slab, just above a step in the zawn bed. Climb easily up a wide broken crack to reach a rising foot-traverse and follow it to a peg. Climb the crack above to the top, with a temporary diversion to the left some way up. Belays in a bluff of rock 20 feet above.

Dinner with the Creggs 80 feet Hard Very Severe 4c † (23.12.90)
Start just right of *Spanking Colonel* and just left of the dirty groove at the back of the zawn. Climb the crack and make hard moves over an overlap at 20 feet. Follow the deep crack above (good protection) to the top. Belays in a bluff of rock 20 feet higher.

★Gun Money 100 feet E1 5c (24.9.84)
A right-to-left girdle of The Seaward Slab giving good delicate climbing with sparse protection. Start at the base of the crystalline ramp, which is climbed to a *Friend* 2 placement below a small, right-angled overlap. Step down and move left with difficulty to gain reasonable footholds; then climb up and traverse horizontally to a belay ledge on the arête. Finish up or down.

The Left-Hand Main Slab

The Plank 160 feet Hard Very Severe ‡ (2.12.72)
A variety of pegs should be carried for runners and belays. Start at parallel cracks near the right-hand edge of the slab.
1 60 feet 4c. Climb the cracks until beneath an overlap; then step up right onto a rougher tongue of rock in the corner.
2 100 feet. Go up to a grass ledge and climb on widely-spaced incuts until level with a traverse-line at a change in the rock's texture. Move across to a smooth pocket and a grass-filled crack. The next 50 feet require the use of levitational techniques. Climb mixed terrain (in the fullest sense of the phrase) to a ledge beneath a tottering wall. Climb this to the top; it may well be that cracks on the left have slightly more inherent stability.

The Central Slab

★Smugglers' Slab 230 feet Very Severe (1959)
A worthwhile adventure route wandering up the next slab right of *The Plank*. Medium-to-large cams required.

1 140 feet 4a. Climb the obvious central crack and move left onto the large detached block. Go up to the overlap and step right. Then climb easily up the slab to belay on a diagonal ledge.
2 90 feet 4a. Climb the crack above to a ledge; climb the 15-foot wall, and belay on the arête at the top.
Descent: scramble over the arête and down the back, eventually to join the descent path well above the hovel.

Jo (230 feet Hard Very Severe 9.72) climbs the long corner forming the right-hand groove of the slab. Two pitches of 140 feet and 90 feet, with a belay on a diagonal ledge requiring large nuts.

Between The Central Slab and Wreckers' Slab are two narrower, bottomless slabs. *Heaven and Hell* climbs the right-hand and thinner of these two, while the esoteric *Jolly Roger*, after starting on Wreckers' Slab, crosses over to climb the broader one, mainly by its left arête.

☆**Heaven and Hell** 450 feet Hard Very Severe † (16.1.94)
'Full of real North Coast adventure'. Start at a diagonal crack, 20 feet left of the start of *Wreckers' Slab*.
1 140 feet 5a. Climb the crack and 'a sort of' a chimney and ascend the slab and steep grass above until the base of a further slab is reached. Peg and cam belay.
2 160 feet 5a. Climb the centre of the slab via superb cracks to its top. Belay in cracks using cams and nuts.
3 150 feet 4c. Climb the break through the overlap above (loose) to a subsidiary slab, which is followed until it is possible to traverse rightwards to finish up *Wreckers' Slab*.

Jolly Roger 250 feet Very Severe † (9.71)
Carry pegs for belays.
1 120 feet 4b. Climb just right of the left-hand arête of Wreckers' Slab for 40 feet until it is possible to traverse diagonally left across unpleasant material to reach the bottomless slab. Belay on a ledge a few feet higher (multiple-peg belay).
2 60 feet 4c. Climb the left-hand arête of the slab (loose) until it is possible to step right to belay in a vague corner on nuts and a peg.
3 70 feet 4a. Continue up the slab above and escape left under the upper broken wall.

Wreckers' Slab

★★**Wreckers' Slab** 410 feet Very Severe (1959)
A Culm classic, which should not be missed by those who still possess the spirit of adventure. It climbs the largest and most impressive slab, the furthest of the main three from the sea, in three long pitches. Start beneath the centre of the slab.
1 120 feet. From the beach, step up onto the slab and climb it via a

groove. Go up and across the easy-angled slab to its left edge and then ascend a groove until moves can be made back onto the main slab. Peg and nut belay on ledges below the overlap.
2 150 feet 4b. Climb up the crack to the overlap (nut runners), step up and left onto the upper slab, and follow this directly to good nut belays in the pillar on the terrace.
3 140 feet 4a. Climb the crack behind the pillar to gain the final, easy-angled slab. Climb this (numerous ways are possible) to belay on the ridge at its top.
Exit by scrambling along the ridge to the grassy bay.

The Landward Slab

Immediately right of Wreckers' Slab is another area of slab, tapering downwards to a point well above the beach. The slab is roughly 100 feet high and ends at a broad, sloping, scree terrace beneath smaller, more broken slabs. Left of centre are two cleaned cracklines which, surprisingly, are much more solid than their neighbours and provide enjoyable climbing in impressive surroundings. They are approached by abseil from the top of Wreckers' Slab, and start at the base of the tapering slab on small foot-ledges in the bounding groove.

☆**Duty Free** 110 feet Very Severe 4c † (22.2.87)
Climb the thin broken crack-system 10 feet right of the left edge of the slab. Belay on pegs (not in place) up and to the right across the scree terrace.

Bootleggers 100 feet Very Severe 4c † (22.2.87)
Climb up to gain the obvious deep central crack and follow this to an awkward finish past a small overlap. Belay on pegs (not in place) up and to the right.

From the terrace a further 100 feet of easier slab-climbing and scrambling leads to the upper terrace beneath the top pitch of *Wreckers' Slab*. Finish as for that route.

Yeolmouth Waterfall Cliff OS Ref 202 162

Salute to the Admiral 300 feet Grade III † (15.1.87)
Hidden across the bay to the south of Wreckers' Slab is a waterfall. If this freezes (perhaps once every 50 years or so) it provides an excellent ice climb in two or three pitches. On the first and only ascent the upper fall was avoided by a marginally easier subsidiary gully on the left. Belay to the foot-bridge.

Westcott Wattle

OS Ref 199 160

An isolated area of smooth, low-angled slabs, the sparsely-protected climbs of which require a cool head. South of the Yeolmouth Waterfall is a grassy combe, which is approached from Morwenstowe Church. Meander down the grassy combe to a short steep scree slope (*in-situ* rope for assistance) that leads down to the beach (40 minutes from Morwenstowe). Low-to-half tide is required to reach the climbs.

Immediately south (or left looking out) is a low-angled slab as yet unclimbed. Further south is a larger area of slabs, smooth and streaked with grey on their left. Escape for the following three routes is by crossing the grass slope on the left of the top of the climbs to a slabby break in the slanting retaining wall which, after a few moves, leads to the upper slopes.

Visco-City 230 feet Hard Very Severe † (26.1.86)
Etive-style padding minus the frictional properties of granite, and with even less protection. Carry pegs for protection and belays. Somewhat dusty looking. Start at the centre of the grey-streaked area of slab.
1 150 feet 4c. Climb directly up the slab to a peg (not *in situ*) at 130 feet, and traverse rightwards onto grass (peg belays in the slab on the right).
2 80 feet 4a. Scramble up to the rounded rib, which is followed to block belays on the grassy meadows.

Widowmaker 300 feet E1 † (28.9.86)
Similar in style to the preceding route, but harder. Carry pegs for protection and belays. Two long grass tongues terminate some 30 feet above the ground, and the narrow purplish slab between is characterized by a thin line of weakness that vanishes at 30 feet.
1 150 feet 5a. Climb easily at first to the faint crack, and where this fades head directly up, passing isolated little incuts to a reasonable peg placement at 110 feet. A final delicate step up on more lichenous rock leads to better holds and a stance on a narrow ledge just left of the rounded rib. Peg belays.
2 150 feet 4a. Follow the crest of the rib to finish as for *Visco-City*.

CJW Arête 350 feet Severe † (26.4.87)
The obvious arête to the right of *Widowmaker* – a mountaineering experience rather than a rock climb.
1 150 feet. Climb the arête to poor peg belays.
2 150 feet. Continue up the arête.
3 50 feet. Continue a little further; then climb the rounded rib as for the preceding routes.

Further south is another easy-angled slab, better supplied with holds.

Alaska 120 feet Very Severe 4b (9.3.87)
Start beneath the centre of the slab, on the sixth boulder in from the mouth of the trench below the slab. Climb up to gain and follow a thin crack-system and continue in a direct line to the top. Block belays. Sparse protection.

The Dimpsy 120 feet Hard Severe 4b † (9.3.87)
Climb the slab directly above the third and largest boulder bridging the trench. Little protection.

Tom's Route 120 feet Difficult (26.4.87)
A pleasant beginners' route. Start in a niche to the right of the jammed boulder and climb up and right on big holds to a narrow, angled shelf. Delicate moves lead to the crest of the slab and up to good belays. Descend steep mixed ground at the back or abseil down the route.

Henna Cliff

OS Ref 200 158

Surprisingly, in view of its description in the last guide, *Breakaway* appears to have achieved a level of unexpected popularity and is reputed to have had at least eight ascents to date. Perhaps, if this state of affairs continues, polish will have to be added to the long list of objective dangers to be encountered on this impressive route! The new area of Morwenna Slabs is added as it shares the same approach and may prove useful as a means of mental recuperation for those overpowered by the sight of the 'Henna Horror' beyond.

Henna is the highest precipice on the Culm coast, and the most frightening. The beach at the bottom of the crag can be reached by following the coast path north from Morwenstowe Church to a point half-way down the steep southern slope of the stream valley from where a faint path leads back south and down, eventually over easy-angled slabs, to sea-level. Boulder-hopping and easy scrambling north then follows. This is possible only at lowish tides. Alternatively, an abseil can be made from the bridge across the stream, avoiding the waterfall if possible. A huge boulder lies beneath the central faultline. A hammer, long pegs, ice-screws, *Warthogs*, a helmet, and a strong belief in one's immortality are the main requirements for an ascent.

Breakaway 500 feet Extremely Severe (7.7.79)
[Photo p.128a.] A serious and committing route. After pitch 2, retreat would be at best extremely difficult or at worst terminally easy. The climb takes the central fault. All the equipment mentioned in the introduction is essential. Start on the rock rib running up the cliff left of the initial overhanging section of the fault. Scramble up this to a stance and peg belay at its top.
1 110 feet 5b. Climb the rock rib to gain a grey ramp leading up rightwards. Follow this (poor rock) until it is possible to enter a groove in

the wall above. Climb the groove to a stance and peg belay on a collapsing earth ledge on the left.
2 90 feet 5b. Climb up slightly left of the stance to gain an ascending line of weakness beneath overhangs. Follow this line rightwards (which becomes a chimney after 70 feet) and gain the top of a sort of pinnacle in the main faultline. Surmount the overhangs above, and belay on ice-screws in a niche.
3 80 feet 5a. Continue up the faultline over two awkward bulges; then trend right up easier ground to a peg belay where the cliff steepens again.
4 80 feet 5b. Take the rightward-trending line above until, after 40 feet, it is possible to traverse a ledge-line leftwards and gain the top of a huge triangular block in the main faultline.
5 70 feet 5c. Climb the sandy shallow chimney above to overhangs. Swing out right to a bulge and return left above the overhang into the continuation crack of the chimney. Move up to a flake, and belay on top of it.
6 70 feet 5b. Continue directly above the stance (peg *in situ*) to gain a grassy ramp, which leads up leftwards to the top. Fencepost belay.

Morwenna Slabs

Just north of the waterfall mentioned opposite are two pleasant south-facing slabs.

Time Critical Injury 70 feet Very Severe 4c (27.11.93)
Enjoyable and well protected. Start in the middle of the seaward slab and climb direct up cracks until the rock becomes smoother. Move to the left side of the slab and climb a wider crack to the ridge. Scramble carefully up the ridge. Stake and nut belays up along the ridge.

Frats in a Rage 70 feet Very Severe 4c † (19.11.93)
Start at the left edge of the landward slab and climb the slab just left of the arête to an overlap. Surmount this and climb direct to the top. Stake and nut belays.

Green's Goolies 70 feet Very Difficult † (27 11 93)
Start in the centre of the landward slab, right of where the horizontal overlap ends. Climb the slab direct to a hole and continue, slightly left, to the top. Belay as for the other routes.

Vicarage Cliff

OS Ref 197 151

Sunny, south-facing, and sheltered, this remarkable little crag has a lot to offer in the lower and mid grades, and a couple of good harder routes to get the pulse racing: the place to remind yourself that climbing should also be about enjoyment.

From the car-park outside the famed Vicarage Tea Rooms at Morwenstowe (cream teas during the summer months!) walk out toward the coast path and head south. Once you are over the stile the headland soon comes into view, as does a sign pointing the way to Hawker's Hut (the 'Wrecking Reverend's' eyrie). The quickest descent is past the hut, which proves initially very thorny and then very steep, direct to the beach by the promontory. This can be quite unnerving for the inexperienced and a better way, at least for the first visit, is to continue along the coast path to the Tidna stream and descend a fisherman's path above the southern end of the beach.

Climbing at Vicarage Cliff is located in three distinct areas: Lucky Hole is the first area described and is situated behind The Promontory; The Promontory itself; and lastly The Landward Slabs above the beach.

Lucky Hole

This can be reached at lowish tides by skirting round the seaward end of The Promontory. The climbing is found on the low-angled slabs at the back of the zawn, the most seaward of which is in fact an arch pierced by a hole at sea-level. Keep an eye on the incoming tide: it would not be difficult to get trapped in this secluded little zawn.

★**Claire** 70 feet Difficult †† (26.4.86)
A pleasant romp, and one of the few 'delectable Diffs' on the coast, though the route may have been affected by a recent rockfall. Start just left of the arch. Go directly up the slab and over the overlap to a good finishing-crack. A block at the top will accept a long sling for a belay provided you keep low. Descend by scrambling carefully down the back.

Bison Bison 70 feet Very Difficult † (13.3.94)
Start to the right of the arch and climb the slab, using the corner, to where the rock becomes friable. Move up and left and follow a thin crack to finish just right of *Claire*. Belay as for *Claire* and scramble off.

Right again is another narrow slab of light-coloured rock.

★**Romping Robert** 100 feet Very Severe 4c (23.10.88)
A good sustained route, quite high in the grade. Start at the shallow groove on the left of the slab. Climb the groove and surmount the overlap with difficulty. Follow the crack above, and step left after 30 feet to a wider crack, which leads to a point just left of some overhanging blocks. Continue up the loose but easy ground above to belay on blocks on the ridge. Descend by scrambling with care down the back.

Rectory Tearooms 100 feet Hard Very Severe 5a (14.9.88)
Another good route, which starts at the shallow crack/groove in the centre of the slab. Climb the groove, using the crack on the right for runners and holds, to where it bends over to form a sloping ledge. Climb thin cracks above with difficulty to the top. Belay and descend as for *Romping Robert*.

VICARAGE CLIFF

No.	Route	Grade
1	Pandora	HS
2	Sunstruck	VS
3	Little Dribbler	HVS
4	Box of Delights	HS
5	Joi de Vivre	HVS
6	Tombstone	HS
7	Sol	HS
8	Wellington's Stand	VS
9	Vicarage Tower	VD
10	Spotted Dick	S
11	Harpoon	E2
12	Crazy Paving	E1
13	In Memorium	HS
14	Mad Mag's Parasol	VS
15	Choss and Chips	S

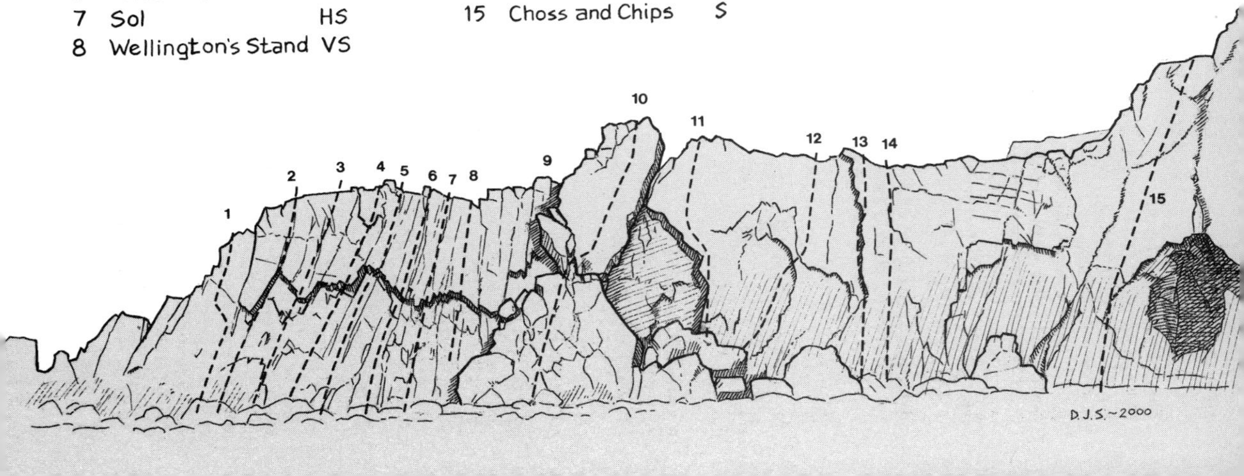

The Promontory

The Promontory presents a long line of south-facing slabs, with the conspicuous Vicarage Tower half-way along and a large shallow cave at the landward end. Climbs left of the tower are accessible between half and low tide, and descent from all the routes here is either down the seaward groove between the tower and the slab (*Vicarage Tower* in reverse) at V Diff or, easier, by scrambling down the back of The Promontory behind the tower.

The short thin crack left of *Pandora* is **A Dying Art** (50 feet E1 6a 28.4.96) and is well protected with micro-wires.

Pandora 60 feet Hard Severe 4b (13.1.85)
A pleasant introduction to the easier routes here. Near the seaward end of The Promontory is a short, bottomless, seaward-facing groove. Gain this from the right (or direct at 5a) and climb it until it is possible to move right round the arête to a crack, which leads to the top.

Sunstruck 70 feet Very Severe 4c (29.11.89)
An interesting route on solid rock. Start right of *Pandora*, below a protruding pointed block. Climb to a standing-position on the block and move up and right to midway along and beneath the slanting overlap. Pull over and follow the crack above to the top.

Little Dribbler 70 feet Hard Very Severe 5a (3.2.85)
High above the overlap is a large raised pancake of rock. This route follows with interest the conspicuous crack that runs through the overlap and arrives immediately left of the pancake.

★**Box of Delights** 70 feet Hard Severe 4b (4.1.85)
A well-named route that follows the crack through the highest break in the overlap to finish right of the pancake.

★**Joi de Vivre** 70 feet Hard Very Severe 5a (28.4.90)
An enjoyable eliminate breaking through the diagonal overlap right of *Box of Delights*. Climb up to the middle of the slanting overlap from the left. Sustained climbing over and above the overlap leads, via gradually easing parallel cracks, to the top.

Tombstone 70 feet Hard Severe 4b (30.3.86)
Climb up to and over the lowest point in the overlap, and finish up the slightly wider crack above.

Sol 70 feet Hard Severe 4a (28.12.89)
A pleasant climb. Start beneath the overlap right of its lowest point. Climb to the overlap, and follow the left-hand crack to the top.

Wellington's Stand 70 feet Very Severe 4c (3.2.85)
Climb the deeper crack just left of the tower past a downward-pointing spike in the overlap.

Cuboid 90 feet Very Severe 4c † (3.2.85)
A slightly barmy route for the eccentric who has done everything else on the seaward slab and wants more. Starting at the tower, this climb girdles the slab just below the line of the overlap and finishes along the diagonal break left of *Pandora*.

Vicarage Tower 70 feet Very Difficult (1957)
The first properly-recorded route on the Culm Coast! Climb the seaward groove between the tower and the slab. Useful as a means of descent for nearby routes. The original continued along the ridge to the top of The Promontory – this is not recommended.

An 'indirect start' to *Vicarage Tower* has been recorded which climbs up inside the chimney formed by the blocks of the Tower and emerges through a hole onto the half-way ledge. **Exceptionally Smooth Bit Underside** (70 feet Severe 4a 7.99) is fun, well protected, and named after a curious area of rock within.

Spotted Dick 80 feet Severe (4.10.92)
Climb up the middle of the Vicarage Tower. The line is easily identified by large reddish spots – unique. The main difficulty lies in surmounting the overhang half-way up and in convincing yourself that the whole, huge, delicately-poised edifice is going to remain *in situ* long enough for you to climb it. Keep to the right on the upper part of the tower, where rock and protection are better. Belay with a large sling around the top of the tower and escape by climbing down the back.

★★**Harpoon** 80 feet E2 5b (27.12.89)
[Photo p.128b.] An elegant and sustained route on good rock – the best on the crag – which climbs the concave slab right of the tower. Low in the grade but slightly 'run out' at the top. Start just right of the arête immediately right of the tower. Follow thin cracks over a small overlap to a hidden spike runner (tape) on the arête at 35 feet. Continue directly up to another overlap. Step left and climb straight up the centre of the concave slab with difficulty past a peg to the top.

Crazy Paving 70 feet E1 5a † (28.4.96)
The route optimizes use of the crazed slab right of *Harpoon* – proceed with caution. Start at the foot of the groove right of *Harpoon*. Follow the groove for 20 feet to the point where it veers left (good cams). Move 5 feet right and climb the slab (*RPs*) to a narrow ledge. Finish up thin cracks above.

Further right a slim, seaward-facing groove runs the full height of the cliff and ends in an overhang. The following route uses the groove's right arête.

In Memoriam 80 feet Hard Severe (29.3.86)
Start right of the arête and climb the slab before stepping onto the arête at 25 feet and then back right onto the slab 20 feet higher. Belay round the

block at the top of the groove. Descend by scrambling landward along the ridge for some 50 feet (stay roped up) and abseil from an *in-situ* sling round a block.

Mad Mags' Parasol 80 feet Very Severe 4c (25.9.93)
High up on the slab right of the groove of *In Memoriam* are two conspicuous patches of grey rock. This climb steers a course between them using small wires for protection. Start beneath the patches and climb to a shallow recess at 20 feet. Follow thin cracks out of the top of the recess and climb between the patches to stand on top of the left-hand one. Continue in a direct line to the top. Belay and descent as for *In Memoriam*.

Further right is a large cave.

Choss and Chips 140 feet Severe † (13.10.88)
Just what The Doctor ordered – for sufferers of constipation! Start left of the cave. Climb easily up the slab and over an overlap onto a loose slab that gets looser as you go up and right to reach the ridge just before it steepens. Dubious belays. Descend by abseil from a long sling.

The Landward Slabs

At the extreme landward end of The Promontory is a long slab starting 100 feet above the beach, easily seen from Hawker's Hut. This used to contain the historic **Hawker's Slab** (250 feet V Diff 1959), but sadly an essential component of the initial crack (the left hand side of it) took off for a beach holiday and, not surprisingly, failed to return. However, all is not lost as **More Tea, Vicar?** (230 feet Severe 23.11.97) and **The Bitch from the Bush** (210 feet Severe 23.11.97) climb obvious cracks in the remnant slab.

Flaky Pastry (130 feet Very Severe †† 23.7.94) climbed the slab below *Hawker's Slab* by its left-hand side, left of a loose 'vertical overlap' (is this what they used to call a groove?). Said to be loose at the top and now, in view of recent earth movements, the components are almost certainly lying in a heap on the beach.

One hundred yards south of The Promontory is another narrow slab with black streaks down its right-hand side, ragged cracks on the left, and a smaller, pale, skull-shaped slab above.

★Atom Head 130 feet E1 5c (20.9.92)
A fine sustained lead at the top end of the grade, tracing a sweeping line up the slab. Not affected by the tide. Start up the narrow slab right of the ragged cracks, and move right where it opens out. Climb cleaned cracks up right to a peg. A hard move gains the thin crack above (wires), which is followed until it is possible to step left and climb boldly up the black streaks to a peg out left. Move up right to a pocket and the final peg. Very thin moves (crux) lead to a scooped ledge near the top. Move up right using the

edge of the slab and climb over blackthorn to peg belays 15 feet above. Abseil off.

Higher Sharpnose Point   OS Ref 195 148

The south-facing slabs at this location are something of a disappointment, being rather low-angled and vegetated. The climbs lack any real merit or character. From Morwenstowe Church, follow the coast path south for half a mile to an old Coastguard lookout behind the point. Scramble down scree and blocks to the base of the slabs. **Bubbly** (80 feet Difficult 1962) climbs the curious acned slab near the seaward end of the point. **Half-Mast** (220 feet Severe 13.5.79) climbs the highest, central section of the slabs left of a vertical overlap, and **Quarter Deck** (300 feet Very Difficult 1959) climbs the slab left of an obvious vegetated fault. Two other routes, **Port** and, not entirely unexpectedly, **Starboard** (both Severe 6.3.83), are the left-hand and large central cracks respectively.

Moped Zawn   OS Ref 198 240

This sheltered little zawn lies fifty or so yards north of Oldwalls' Point and has a handful of enjoyable routes on its southern wall which will provide an afternoon's entertainment. Approach as for Oldwalls' Point. Descent from the top of the wall is by abseil from *in-situ* tapes on a spike at the left-hand end of the ledge.

Schwarzchild 70 feet E1 5b † (14.6.98)
An eliminate starting at the thin crack just right of the corner, and left of the more prominent crack of *The Snake*. Climb the crack past some suspect rock until it peters out. Step right and finish up *The Snake*.

★**The Snake** 80 feet Hard Very Severe 5a (4.7.81)
An enjoyable climb with a tricky start. Follow the thin but widening crack in the centre of the slab toward the back of the zawn. Finish up the right-hand fork and short wall above.

Vickers 80 feet E1 5a† (6.94)
Eliminate. Immediately right of *The Snake* is a narrow expanse of wall. Climb the middle of this until it is possible to move right to the arête. Climb the arête with little protection.

Starfire 60 feet Very Severe 4b (6.7.79)
Climb the groove formed by the hanging vertical overlap in the centre of the wall after starting up the thin crack beneath.

Bantam 60 feet Very Severe 4c (6.7.79)
Climb the deep crack right of *Starfire*.

Grapejuice Cocktail 60 feet Very Severe 4b (9.10.94)
Enjoyable climbing up the enticing clean crack a few feet left of the right-hand arête of the wall.

Nippy Norman 60 feet Hard Severe 4b (6.7.79)
Climb the corner near the seaward arête, and move right to finish up a groove.

The following route provides an unrecommended alternative to the abseil descent.

Exit Route 100 feet Hard Severe 4b (17.5.86)
Start 20 feet above the fixed descent-point at a large spike. Move left into the open corner above the zawn and climb the cracks in its right wall to a large overhang. Pull around to the left to reach further cracks, which are followed to ledges. Go up the looser arête to block belays on the right.

Oldwalls' Point

OS Ref 198 140

A fine piece of rock in the shape of a steep, 150-foot slab of good-quality sandstone. Unfortunately, it suffers from acute regrassing and the erosive effects of an amorous sea which has nibbled away at its extremities. Formerly worth a visit, if only to climb the regional classic, *Matchless*, which itself is looking a bit shaggy in its upper reaches (only half an hour's gardening for an altruistic Culm enthusiast), it now also sports an excellent E3.

Approach from the car-park at the end of the road beyond Stanbury Farm (OS Ref 205 137). Take the path due west from here that leads out to the coast path. This is followed north for 300 yards to a large combe just beyond the first stile. Go down the south rim of the combe, straight down fine scree of shale shards; then tack back south to find the easiest way down steeper scree. The point is a little further north and looks unimpressive from this side. The action, however, is on the other side and this can be reached below half tide by skirting round the front of the promontory. When the tide is too high it is possible to traverse the crest of the point, abseil down the seaward face, and belay on the sloping platform below, which is out of the reach of all but the highest seas. *Matchless* can be started from here by a delicate descending traverse to the route's obvious crackline.

Dominator 160 feet E1 5b ‡ (15.7.79)
This good climb needs a friend: someone prepared to excavate its treasures from beneath the copious vegetation now adorning its cracks.

Near the left-hand side of the face is a tall grass-filled groove. Start right of this, below an overhanging crack. Climb over the overhang and up discontinuous cracks above leading to a small niche at 100 feet. Step right and climb widely-spaced holds to the top. Large hex and/or peg belays (removed).

☆**Mountain Biker** 150 feet E3 5c † (8.91)
A fine climb right of *Dominator*. Climb over the roof with difficulty at its widest point and follow thin cracks, easing, to the top.

☆☆**More than a Match** 150 feet E3 5c † (27.4.96)
'More than a match for *Matchless*' said the first ascensionist in a kind of inverse tautology which would be worth at least a paragraph of metaphysical contemplation in a guidebook written by Nick White. In this less weighty tome, however, it is necessary to say only that it was considered to be one of the finest routes of its grade on the Culm Coast. Start immediately right of the foot of the right-hand of two niches in the overhanging base of the cliff.
Climb the very steep crack/groove past a useful slot in the bulge to a good rest above (hard). Step up to a straight thin crack and follow it for 50 feet to a small irregular nick where the crack branches. Go up the right-hand branch (bold at first); then bear slightly left to gain a juggy niche 30 feet below the top. Finish straight up a pocketed crack and the easy wall above. Nut belays.

☆**Aimless** 150 feet E4 6a † (27.4.96)
A clean eliminate line left of *Matchless*. Start 15 right of the right-hand niche. Pull up a slight groove to a long overlap, undercut left for 6 feet, and rock up delicately onto the slab. Move right to a good slot in the break and tiptoe on tinies to another break (crux). Climb direct via a tiny shallow scoop to a narrow double break. Follow the spidery crack above, eventually to step right into the wide crack of *Matchless* just left of the base of the pancake. Follow *Matchless* to the top.

★★**Matchless** 150 feet Hard Very Severe 5a (3.7.79)
One of the great climbs on the Culm coast. Solid, safe, and enjoyable crack-climbing of the highest calibre. Start in a niche directly beneath the left-hand side of a large pancake high up on the face near the seaward arête. Gain a ledge at 10 feet and climb the obvious thin crack rising from its left-hand end (crux and peg at 15 feet). Continue up the crack until it is possible to step right into the crack and groove formed by the left-hand side of the pancake. Continue to the ledge on top of the pancake and climb a line of holds above to the top. Nut and sling belays.

Hippa Rock

OS Ref 198 137

Situated on the northern side of the low headland north of Stanbury Mouth, Hippa Rock is a compact but excellent little area with short but sustained routes on solid rock. Straightforward scrambling down the ridge due west of the Stanbury car-park (OS Ref 205 137) leads to the top of the crag where a stake, hidden in a grassy hollow, allows the base of the cliff to be reached by abseil. It is advisable to leave the abseil rope in place to belay to, as the stake is some distance back from the tops of the climbs.

The cliff consists of two overlapping slabs at the end of the promontory. The smooth landward slab is split by the conspicuous diagonal crack of *Coitionary Tales*. The routes on this slab use curious but solid load-cast formations. The rock being very compact means that the routes are protected mostly with spaced micro-wires and the occasional peg. The pegs are beginning to show their age and should be used with caution.

Virgo 50 feet Very Severe 4c † (4.4.90)
Just right of the corner at the left-hand end is an obvious crack in the top half of the slab. Climb easily up to the crack and follow it to a difficult exit and a grassy ledge.

Blackwater Down 60 feet E1 5b (4.4.90)
Climb the line of the distinctive black stain on the left-hand section of the slab (peg) to an awkward exit. Sustained.

★Sensual Seas 60 feet E1 5b (17.3.90)
Right of the black stain is a very shallow scoop running from mid height. Start beneath this. Climb up and right to the break, and move up left along it to beneath a peg just left of the scoop. Climb straight up past the peg to the top (delicate).

★Volupte 60 feet E3 5c (9.3.90)
A fine, sustained, and fairly bold route. Start 20 feet left of *Coitionary Tales*. Climb easily up to the diagonal fault beneath two pegs. Step up right to essential micro-wire placements, then up and left to the first peg (crux). Move up to the poor second peg, step right, and climb to the top.

Psycho-soma 60 feet E1 5b (11.8.90)
An enjoyable eliminate which crosses *Coitionary Tales* from left to right. Start directly beneath the top of the diagonal crack of *Coitionary Tales*. Climb to the diagonal fault and move onto the upper slab via an obvious small foot-ledge. Climb straight up, then left to a peg. Climb up to the next peg and move up and right into *Coitionary Tales*. Place a high runner and move right; then climb a shallow column to overhanging blocks and the top.

★Coitionary Tales 60 feet Hard Very Severe 5a (1983)
The obvious diagonal crack, and the original route here, it must have been dirty and dangerous when it was first climbed on-sight at E2. Cleaning has rendered it an enjoyable and well-protected crack-climb.

☆Consenting Adults 60 feet E4 5c † (23.8.89)
Bold climbing up the smooth slab starting right of *Coitionary Tales*. Trend left to the foot of a micro crack, which is followed past a peg, and climb the wall to finish.

★Tales of Don Juan 60 feet E1 5b (1989)
Pleasant climbing up thin cracks just left of the right arête of the landward slab, well protected with wires.

Katabatic 80 feet E2 5c † (23.8.89)
Climb the corner on the left-hand side of the seaward slab until it is possible to move right to a thin crack, which is climbed (crux) to a sloping ledge. Continue up easier rock direct to the top.

Hippodrome 85 feet E2 5b † (28.4.96)
An interesting climb up the centre of the slab where 'plant clusters do not prove an impediment'. Climb an arête easily leftwards and move left above the roof for 5 feet to the foot of a grey streak, which is followed until a long reach gains a good break. Follow an intermittent crack to a wide finishing-crack.

Polar Airstream 130 feet Severe (27.12.81)
Climb the seaward arête of the slab, and move left at 100 feet to finish up a wide loose crack.

Lower Sharpnose Point OS Ref 195 127

Lower Sharpnose Point is without doubt the unchallenged premier crag on the Culm Coast and contains a concentration of quality face-and-crack-climbing on its narrow fins to match any in the South West. The rock is, for the most part, as good as it comes. It has to be! For the three fins stand precariously balanced in the turbulent Atlantic seas that only the soundest of materials could withstand. The drawback, as with most Culm Coast crags, is that nearly all the climbs are affected by the tide to a greater or lesser extent. However, with a little ingenuity, common sense, and an abseil rope, access to the more landward routes between the fins can be made when the tide encroaches. But the message remains; to get the most out of your visit, check the likely state of the tide before you arrive (see below).

The climbing is steep and exhilarating but on generally good holds, and a confident approach combined with some upper-body strength and a wide selection of camming devices works wonders. Of course, further up the scale, stamina and technical finesse coupled with a cool head begin to play their part.

The cliff lies beneath the CSOS tracking station, the cluster of whirring white discs which can be seen for miles around. Cars can be parked on grass verges near a metal gate located half a mile north of the main gates of the establishment's compound – do not block the gate entrance. Surmount the gate and follow the tarmac track for about half a mile until it meets the compound perimeter fence. Continue right along the fence until a metal field-gate is reached. The top of what was once the upper crag can be seen out right towards the sea. From here, walk along the fence and continue in the same straight line until another tarmac track is reached. Continue along this for 50 yards to a coast path waymarker. Follow the path out to sea past a stile to another waymarker. One hundred yards beyond this, fork right off the path (small cairn) along a narrow track through gorse to the top of the cliff. (Twenty minutes walk from the parking-area.)

The base of the crag can be reached by descending obvious paths at either end of the crag, although continuing erosion of the earth and shale slopes means that caution must be exercised. Unhindered access to, and between, the fins is possible between half tide and low tide. However, above half tide it is possible to abseil into the bay between the North and Middle Fins from blocks near the landward end of the top of the North Fin. In the event of a misjudgement, escape can be made via an easy ramp at the back of the bay, opposite the start of *Lunakhod*. Heavy rain reduces the friction of the dark rock to zero, especially on north-facing climbs; be warned.

To escape from the top of the Baby, North, and South Fins, just walk (with care) along the crest to terra firma. Escape from the top of the Middle Fin can be made by a precarious retreat along the crest, but this is not recommended; it is better to abseil from slings (*in situ* at the time of writing) at the top of *Lunakhod* or *Fay*.

Finally, it cannot be over-emphasized that many of the pegs *in situ* on the climbs will almost certainly have been affected to a greater or lesser extent by the corrosive effects of the sea air. Always back up the pegs with natural gear where possible.

Baby Fin

North of the North Fin is a smaller, 40-foot-high edifice which has been dubbed the Baby Fin. With five intense little routes on its solid south face, it offers a sample of the delights to be found on the adult fins further south.

Cold Snap 40 feet E4 6b † (4.5.87)
Climb the obvious pods on the left-hand side of the wall to the third pod (peg). Hard moves up right lead to good holds near a slanting crystal break. Step left to a vertical crack, which is followed to a finish on the right.

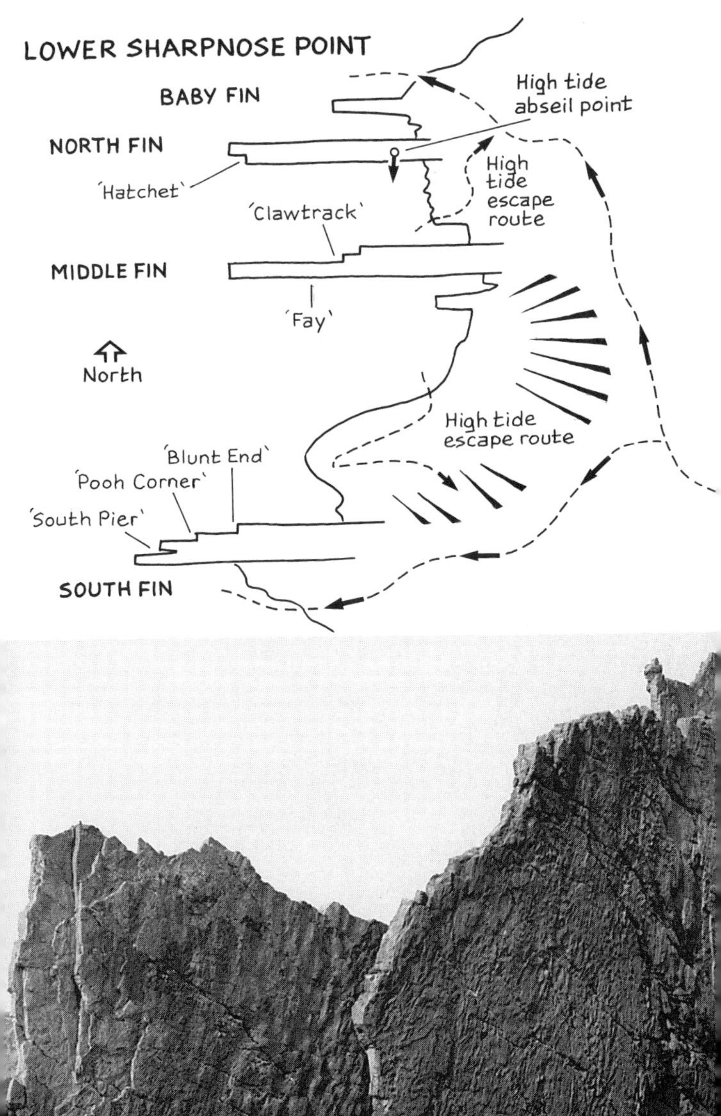
LOWER SHARPNOSE POINT
BABY FIN
High tide
abseil point
NORTH FIN
High
tide
escape
route
'Hatchet'
'Clawtrack'
MIDDLE FIN
'Fay'
North
High tide
escape route
'Blunt End'
'Pooh Corner'
'South Pier'
SOUTH FIN

Grypt-Up Phynne 40 feet E4 6a † (4.5.87)
Start 5 feet left of a large boulder close to the wall and climb boldly up horizontal holds to a peg. Hard moves past this lead to a good hold at the upper crystalline break and a hand-placed peg. Exit left of the block overhanging the wall.

☆**Early Ming** 40 feet E4 6a † (22.4.87)
A good route. Start on the large boulder at the foot of the wall and climb to the horizontal break. Step left and move up (peg); finish rightwards via a slot.

American Excess 40 feet E3 5c † (4.5.87)
Climb the discontinuous crack left of *Ning Nong*, starting 10 feet right of the large boulder. Step right at the top to finish.

Ning Nong 40 feet E3 5c (22.4.87)
Start at the foot of the ramp on the right-hand side of the wall. Climb to an oval pocket and move left to a diagonal crack. Follow the crack past a spike runner (bold) to better holds. Climb the wall above past a peg to the top.

North Fin – North Face

A dark forbidding wall of quality rock that remains in eternal shade. It is characterized by two diagonal quartz breaks. *Blackthorn Winter* takes the higher and more prominent one, and *Village Idiot*, the lower one. The obvious deep vertical crack of *Mascon* is near the right-hand end.

Wafer Phynne 70 feet E3 5b (23.8.87)
At the landward end of the face is an obvious flake-line. This is climbed past three ageing pegs (the first two are poor). From the top of the flake, climb direct to finish.

☆**Dogsbody** 75 feet E5 6b/c † (1989)
Start 10 feet right of *Wafer Phynne*, at a thin crack. Climb the crack (peg) and continue direct to an obvious undercut. Move up right; then crimp desperately past a good peg to gain slots leading to good holds; finish direct.

★★**Culm Dancing** 80 feet E5 6a (28.5.87)
Sustained and fingery climbing. Start at a thin crack 30 feet from the left (landward) end of the wall, as for *Blackthorn Winter*. Climb the thin crack on sideholds to reach a pocket. A difficult move gains more pockets at the start of the upper diagonal quartz break. Swing up left to good holds and then climb direct up the wall past two pegs. Move left just below the top to avoid loose rock.

★**Blackthorn Winter** 130 feet E5 6a (14.5.87)
A sweeping crossing of the Face, serious in its second half. Start at a thin

crack 30 feet right of the landward end of the wall. Climb the thin crack on sideholds to reach a pocket. A difficult move gains more pockets at the start of the upper diagonal quartz break. Follow this rightwards in its entirety, passing a peg, eventually to join the crack of *Mascon*, which is followed to the top.

★**The Devonian** 100 feet E5 6a (18.5.87)
A fine wall climb. Start as for *Poker Face*, at the base of the lower diagonal quartz break. Move up slightly leftwards to reach a thin crack and climb it to the upper quartz break. Follow the break rightwards for 20 feet to a peg (on *Poker Face*). Swing left from the peg; then climb fairly directly past the second peg, and exit left just below the top.

★**Poker Face** 120 feet E3 6a (28.9.85)
A sustained route wandering up an impressive wall. Start at the foot of the lower diagonal quartz break. Climb the break for 10 feet; then go up a shallow ramp to handholds on top of a narrow shelf on the left (peg). Swing left across the shelf and move up with difficulty to reach the upper diagonal quartz break. Follow this strenuously rightwards (as for *Blackthorn Winter*) to finish up the final crack of *Mascon*.

★★**Helsinki** 100 feet E5 6b (1988)
The blank-looking wall right of *Poker Face*. Start just right of *Poker Face* and climb a short undercut diagonal flake to the lower diagonal break. Move up to a hidden finger-flake, and use this to move into the middle of a blank area (crucial *Friend 1*). Move up and slightly left past the *Friend*; then continue trending up and right until a move straight up gains the upper diagonal break. Finish up a cracked area above the break, trending left.

A Handful of Rust 100 feet E6 6b † (5.89)
A bold and direct climb up the centre of the wall taking a similar line to *Helsinki*. Start as for *Helsinki* and climb a short undercut diagonal flake to the lower diagonal break. Move right 8 feet and climb up to hollow flakes. Climb past a thin crack (peg, crux) to better holds and continue direct to the top; or, harder, step right and climb the face just left of the deep crack of *Mascon*.

★★**Mascon** 100 feet E1 5a (27.8.72)
A classic excursion, seeking out and climbing the exposed crack in the upper part of the right-hand half of the face. Carry large nuts or cams for the crack. Start at a large block adjoining a short cracked wall below the large platform on the front face of the fin. Climb a crack, which is surprisingly awkward, to an optional stance on the platform. Make a committing traverse left across the wall to gain the deep crack, which offers strenuous, well-protected climbing on good holds to the top.

Variation Starts

Village Idiot 50 feet E2 5c (6.83)
The long left-hand start. Climb the lower diagonal break leading to the base of the upper crack of *Mascon* (peg just below).

★**Bolder Boulder** 40 feet E4 6a (6.3.83)
Sustained, technical, and bold. Climb the thin crack leading directly into the upper crack of *Mascon* (peg out left just below).

☆**Athabasca Falls** 90 feet E4 6a † (12.8.90)
An exciting and well-positioned pitch, right of the crack of *Mascon*, taking the left-hand side of the fin's arête. High in the technical grade but not too bold. Follow *Mascon* to the platform below the arête. Launch up the arête with a committing move to reach a peg. Continue, mainly left of the arête, to a niche just below the top. Sprint on jugs to the summit.

★**Weekend Millionaires** 110 feet E3 6a (6.3.83)
An exposed climb up the front face of the North Fin. Start below the narrow face. Climb direct to the platform (stance if required); then continue up the corner above to a square-cut roof. Pull over the roof with difficulty, step right, and finish up the wide crack above.

North Fin – South Face

A steep, sunny face of excellent rock that can get oppressively hot in summer. There is a good spread of grades. Near the left-hand edge is the large corner of *Hatchet*. The obvious deep diagonal crack is taken by *The Smile*, while the shorter, lower crack provides the start of *Last Laugh*.

Hatchet 90 feet Hard Very Severe 5a (7.2.71)
Awkward. Climb easily to the foot of the corner, which is followed to an uncomfortable niche. Pull steeply over the bulge to the ledge above. A wide crack leads to the top.

Slice of Life 90 feet E4 6a † (23.7.94)
A fine, bold, but escapable route up the arête right of *Hatchet*. Start beneath a short, bottomless crack right of *Hatchet*. Climb steeply to the crack and follow it until it is possible to reach left to big holds. Climb up to more broken rock and follow this past a very loose block to a layback flake on the left. Climb the projecting arête to a good hold (*Friend 1*); then swing right and climb the wall nervously on 'snappy' flakes.

Misery Goat 90 feet E2 5c (23.8.87)
Start 10 feet left of *Last Laugh*, on the left-hand side of a scooped recess. Pull steeply through the bulge above to the diagonal crack of *Last Laugh*. Climb up the wall above, trending right, on reasonable holds to a peg at 40 feet. Continue up, trending slightly left, to the niche of *The Smile*. Pull strenuously onto the steep wall above and continue on improving holds to the top, as for that route.

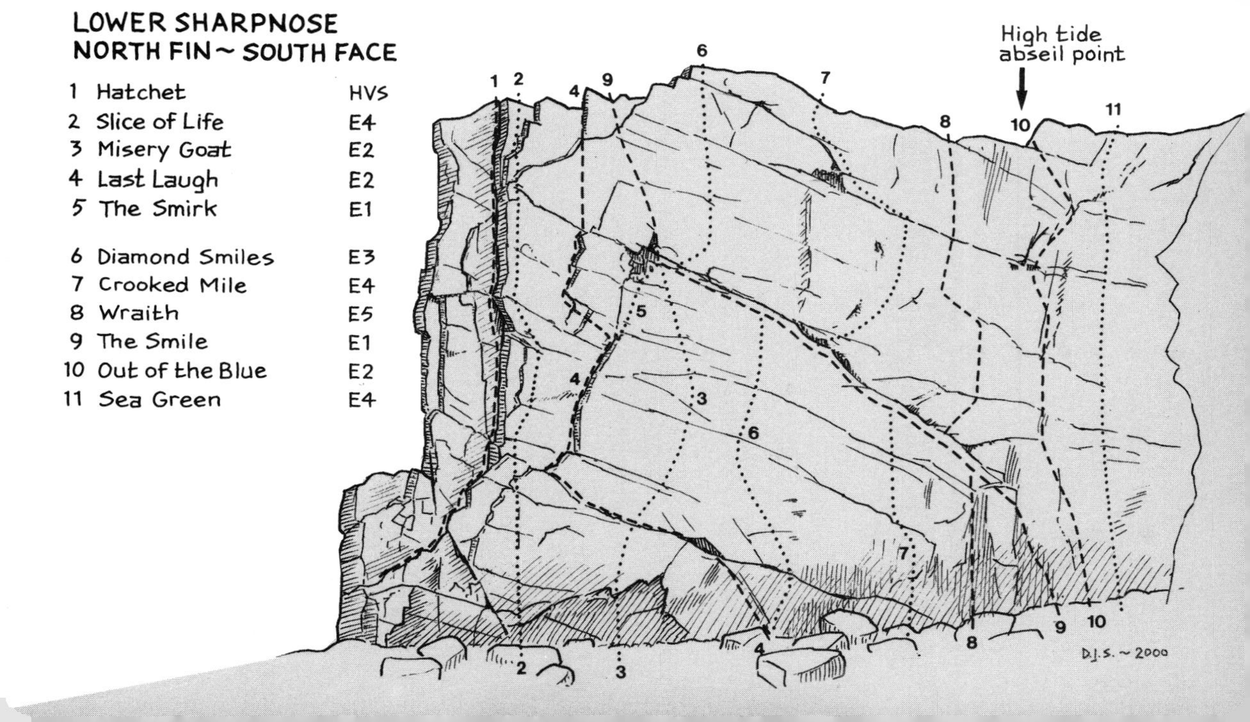
LOWER SHARPNOSE
NORTH FIN ~ SOUTH FACE
1 Hatchet HVS
2 Slice of Life E4
3 Misery Goat E2
4 Last Laugh E2
5 The Smirk E1
6 Diamond Smiles E3
7 Crooked Mile E4
8 Wraith E5
9 The Smile E1
10 Out of the Blue E2
11 Sea Green E4
High tide abseil point
D.J.S. ~ 2000

When the Goat Comes In (E3 5c 4.88) climbs the lower half of *Misery Goat* to the slanting break of *The Smile* and finishes up the narrow area of wall between the niche of *The Smile* and the finish of *Diamond Smiles* (peg on the latter).

★Last Laugh 90 feet E2 5c (25.4.81)
This interesting route climbs the serrated groove high up and right of the corner of *Hatchet*. Start at the foot of the lower diagonal crack, 40 feet in from the left-hand arête of the wall. Follow the crack to a shallow slanting corner right of the bigger corner of *Hatchet*. Climb the corner to where it peters out at a vertical crack. Traverse left into the serrated groove and climb it (crux) to a rightward-curving flake. Follow the flake and finish up the short wall above.

The Smirk (100 feet E1 5a 1982) follows the preceding route to the vertical crack, breaks out right to the niche of *The Smile,* and continues to the top as for that route.

★★★Diamond Smiles 110 feet E3 5c (16.8.84)
A brilliant climb, swaggering up the middle of the wall. Strenuous, sustained, and high in its grade. Bold to begin with, but better protected on the upper wall. Start just right of the start of *Last Laugh*, on top of a boulder. Climb steeply right past a star-shaped hole and then back left following a line of weakness, past crystal-lined cracks and quartz veins, to the slanting break of *The Smile*. Follow this leftwards almost to the niche, swing right to a peg, and continue, trending right, to the top.

★★Crooked Mile 120 feet E4 6a (15.5.86)
Another major excursion up the wall. A bold start. Twenty-five feet left of the start of *The Smile* is a series of small holds leading up the smooth lower wall. Follow these for 10 feet, move left to better holds, and climb up to the first quartz break. Move up on the right to more good holds; then climb diagonally right to a junction with the slanting break of *The Smile*. Move leftwards along this to a depression, and then climb steeply up and diagonally rightwards to reach a good horizontal crack after 25 feet of very sustained climbing. Hand-traverse left to a brown scoop and finish up a diagonal crack.

Another route, **Mustard** (100 feet E4 6a 7.87), appears to follow a similar line to *Crooked Mile*. Start as for that route and climb direct to a 'hole' in the slanting break of *The Smile*. Trend up and right and climb the yellow wall (peg); move left to finish.

★★Wraith 100 feet E5 6a (23.8.87)
An excellent wall climb, direct and sustained. Start 15 feet left of *The Smile* at a thin crack. Climb the crack; then follow an obvious line of holds leading to a junction with the slanting break of *The Smile* at 25 feet. Step right and climb up to a good hold beneath a blank-looking grey scoop.

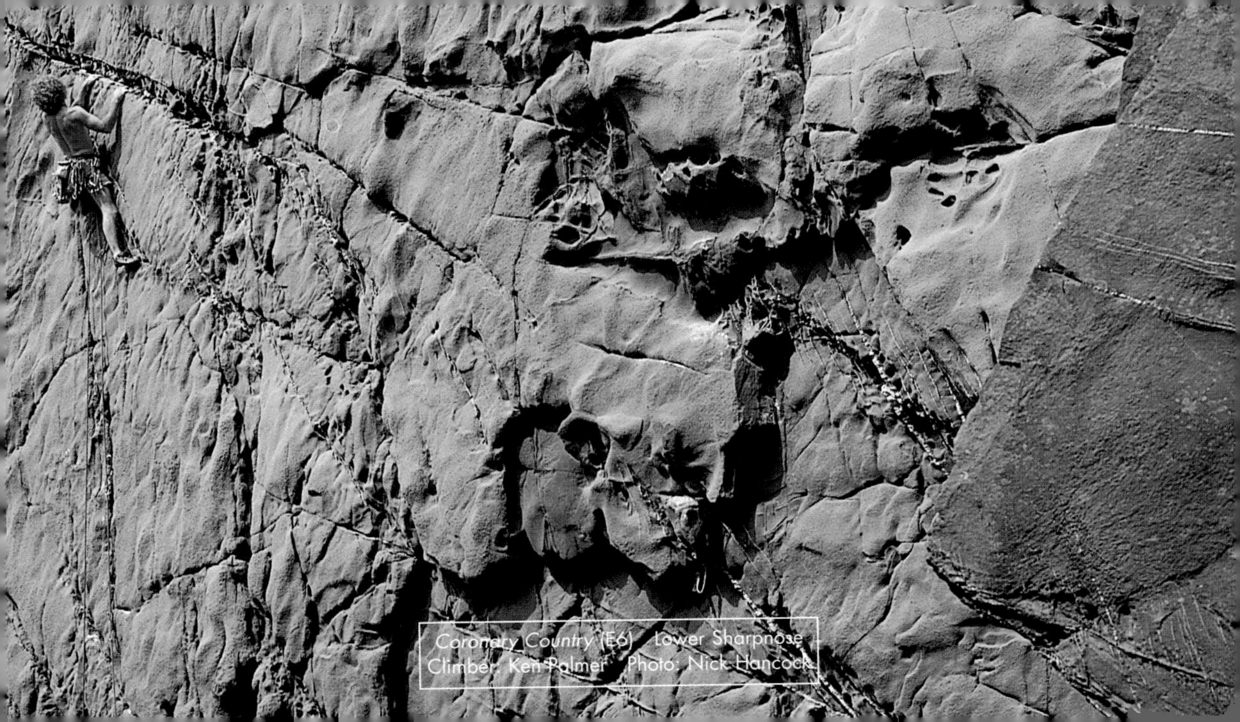

Coronary Country (E6) Lower Sharpnose
Climber: Ken Palmer Photo: Nick Hancock

South Pier (D) Lower Sharpnose
Climber: 'Tig' Photo: Mike Lee

Break on Through (E4) Lower Sharpno
Climber: Unknown Photo: Rich Mayfie

Continue up to a peg (a bold clip) and aim for another good hold on the left. Make a long, bold reach to the break and move back to the right towards another peg. Move left on very small holds to a hard finish, the crux. It is possible to avoid this finish by moving further left. *Friend 2½* and peg belays.

The Smile 120 feet E1 5a (3.4.71)
A steep route on which care should be taken with the protection to avoid rope-drag. Start from the toe of a large oval slab of rock beneath the lower right-hand end of the conspicuous slanting break. Gain the break, which is followed to a shallow brown niche. Pull strenuously onto the steep wall above and continue to the top on improving holds.

Out of the Blue 90 feet E2 5c (27.7.80)
A beautiful and sustained wall-climb on superb holds. Protection on the initial section is somewhat spaced and it is therefore high in the grade. Start 10 feet right of *The Smile*. Climb up bearing slightly left, linking a series of scoops and breaks and a unique circular finger-pocket, until 25 feet from the top. Continue directly up the wall with steep moves to finish.

Sea Green 90 feet E4 5c (6.87)
Another excellent route. Start just right of *Out of the Blue* and climb up the wall, boldly at first, in a more or less direct line to the top.

Honeypot 80 feet Very Severe 4b (4.75)
This is the ragged corner formed by the junction of the South Face with the back wall. Reasonable rock.

To the right, **Help Save the Rhino** (40 feet E3 6a †† 21.2.88) has been affected by rockfall.

Kung Fu Kecks 50 feet E4 6a † (17.10.99)
In the back of the bay, 25 feet right of *Honeypot*, is a protruding buttress of rock made of thicker strata. The buttress is flanked on its right by a zigzag flake. Contort strenuously up the deceptive flake-line, which is tougher than it looks but low in the grade.

Middle Fin – North Face

Another shady face, with big challenging routes. The main features are the two classic groove-lines of *Lunakhod* and *Clawtrack* toward the landward end of the fin.

The Flying Finn 150 feet E4 6a † (27.5.91)
A big pitch which climbs the obvious clean crack left of *Spoils of War*. Follow *Spoils of War* for 50 feet until a traverse left is possible at the level of the second of two pegs. Difficult moves follow to gain the crackline, which is climbed past two further pegs.

★★Spoils of War 150 feet E4 5c (12.4.86)
The long, long crack in the wall left of the groove of *Lunakhod*. An excellent route, strenuous and bold at first, but easier on the immaculate final section. Start 20 feet left of *Lunakhod*, beneath the thin crack. Climb the crack up to and over the bulge to a welcome resting-place. Step left and climb the next bulge on good but dubious holds to a diagonal break leading up to the right to stand on a semi-detached block. Continue up the crack above past a steep section; then bear left in a magnificent position to the top. There are good block belays 10 feet down on the south side.

A splendid expedition can be made at E1 5b by climbing the first 70 feet of *Lunakhod*, moving left around the arête, and finishing up the crack of *Spoils of War*.

★★★Lunakhod 130 feet Hard Very Severe 5a (30.4.71)
A classic sustained route. Well-protected in its upper reaches (large cams useful). Start below the long left-hand groove. Follow broken corners, boldly at first, to a small ledge at 60 feet. Continue up the immaculate groove above to a wild move over the top overlap to gain the short final crack. Belay on the 'Rabbit's Ears' tower.

★Clawtrack 130 feet Hard Very Severe 4c (4.71)
Another strong line, based on the right-hand crack. Bold and, unless very large nuts or cams are carried, sparsely protected. Go up the obvious ramp leading via flake cracks into the main crack, which is followed to a small ledge beneath the corner (stance possible). Climb the wide corner-crack to the top.

The next three routes start up *Clawtrack* and fan out across the impressive wall to the right.

☆☆☆Culm to Mother 140 feet E5 6b † (21.2.88)
Climb *Clawtrack* for 10 feet, then direct to a ring peg. Trend right and up to good holds. Climb up left to a peg; step right, and then up and left to another peg. Continue left, then up and diagonally right to finish. Spike belay on the left.

Challenger 90 feet E4 5c (6.83)
Sustained, loose, and poorly protected – a real challenge! Start up the ramp of *Clawtrack*; then follow the obvious diagonal break to a downward-pointing flake. Traverse 10 feet right to a small loose pinnacle, and climb direct for 15 feet before traversing right to a large ledge. Climb the wall above, not without interest, to the top. A direct start has been climbed to this route at 6a (4.88).

★★Twilight Zone 120 feet E3 5c (16.5.86)
Absorbing and interesting. Start up the ramp of *Clawtrack*; then follow the obvious diagonal break for 20 feet until below a bulge. Climb straight

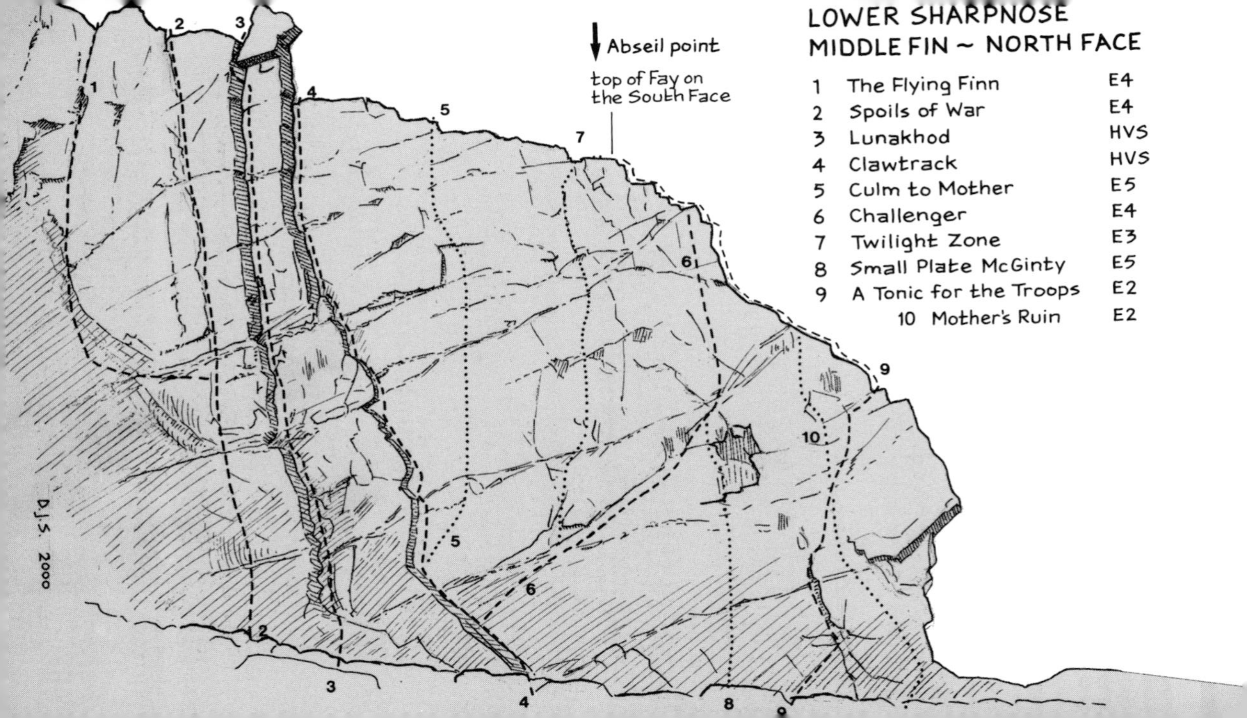
LOWER SHARPNOSE
MIDDLE FIN ~ NORTH FACE
1 The Flying Finn E4
2 Spoils of War E4
3 Lunakhod HVS
4 Clawtrack HVS
5 Culm to Mother E5
6 Challenger E4
7 Twilight Zone E3
8 Small Plate McGinty E5
9 A Tonic for the Troops E2
10 Mother's Ruin E2
Abseil point
top of Fay on the South Face
D.J.S. 2000

through the bulge and continue to a weakness leading up rightwards. Follow this for 15 feet and climb fairly directly up the wall to a crackline, which veers slightly left and leads to the top.

Small Plate McGinty 90 feet E5 6a (21.2.88)
Start 20 feet left of the starting ramp of *A Tonic for the Troops*, beneath a rounded boss 20 feet up. Climb pockets and quartz to the boss (jug on top). Step left; then go up on sidepulls to a break. Continue to a brown area with some blocks. Climb up to the large ledge and the finish of *Challenger*.

★**A Tonic for the Troops** 80 feet E2 5b (16.8.84)
A compact route on good rock. Twenty feet left of the right-hand arête of the wall is a shallow, bottomless groove that starts 20 feet up. Start at a short, rightward-slanting ramp below and left of the groove. Climb the ramp and steep rock to gain the base of the groove. Climb this and step right to a ledge. Step back left and climb more steep rock until 8 feet below the top. Swing right to the arête to belay. To escape, stay roped and continue easily up the ridge to the abseil point at the top of *Fay*.

☆**Mother's Ruin** 110 feet E2 5b † (26.9.99)
An obvious line of weakness sweeping up from the right-hand arête of the wall. Start at the far right-hand side of the wall directly beneath the prow of the seaward face at a short diagonal crack leading up right. Climb the crack to gain the weakness leading up left. Follow this to the ledge at the top of the groove of *Tonic for the Troops* and continue up left in the same line, with awkward moves to pass a left-facing flake, to a brown scoop and the ridge. Climb the ridge airily to belay at the abseil station at the top of *Fay*.

The narrow frontal face of the Middle Fin has been climbed using lassoes, prusiks, aid, etc., and called **Alpine Groyne** (7.4.73), a debilitating malaise.

Middle Fin – South Face

This beautiful stretch of rock contains the cream of the crag's hard classics. The face is a maze of diagonal cracks, quartz veins, and breaks with no really prominent features other than the almost continuous diagonal crack/break of *Heart By-Pass* running across the centre of the wall and the wide diagonal quartz break on the right-hand section taken by *Malefactor*.

★**Finesse** 40 feet E5 6a (21.2.88)
Fine but short. Start below the arête left of *Break On Through*. Climb easily until the arête steepens; then step right onto the wall and go up to a quartz break. Finish blindly, diagonally to the left.

★★★**Break On Through** 90 feet E4 5c (24.4.86)
[Photo p.160b.] This excellent route gives superb and sustained climbing near the left-hand edge of the face. Start on the sloping platform beneath

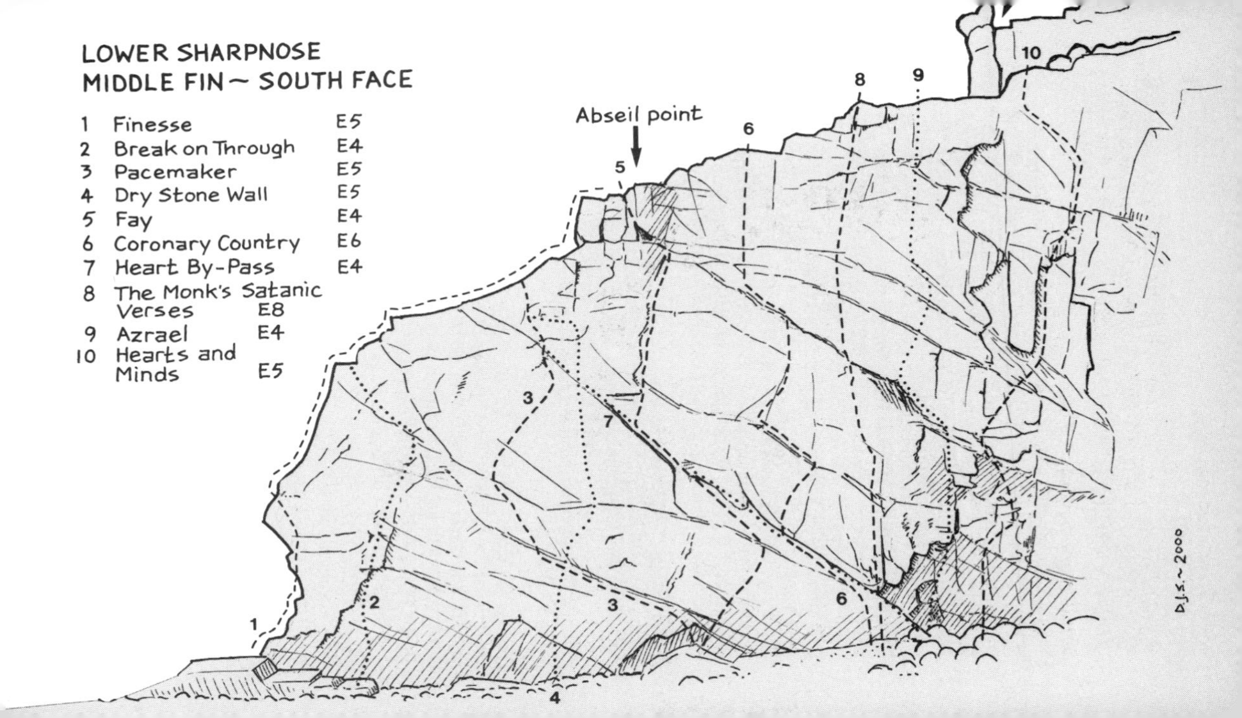
LOWER SHARPNOSE
MIDDLE FIN ~ SOUTH FACE
1 Finesse E5
2 Break on Through E4
3 Pacemaker E5
4 Dry Stone Wall E5
5 Fay E4
6 Coronary Country E6
7 Heart By-Pass E4
8 The Monk's Satanic Verses E8
9 Azrael E4
10 Hearts and Minds E5
Abseil point
D.J.S. ~ 2000

the seaward arête. Move up and right to some good holds, and continue, bearing slightly right, until 15 feet below the top. Bold, strenuous moves diagonally left gain the crest of the fin.

★**Sunscape** 100 feet E5 6a (1.5.94)
Fine climbing. Start 15 feet left of *Pacemaker*, at a diagonal break. Climb this for 15 feet; then climb a vertical crack to a higher break. Step left; then move up to another break, which is traversed leftwards to sidepull flakes. Climb these and continue in the same line to meet the break of *Pacemaker*. Move left along the break for 10 feet; then follow a line of weakness up to a small overlap. Finish slightly left of this.

★**Dry Stone Wall** 100 feet E5 6a/b (1988)
Start 15 feet left of *Pacemaker*, at an obvious ground-level block. Climb directly up cracks to the diagonal break of *Pacemaker*; then climb up right to a friendly area. Continue up slightly, bearing right until level with the wide slanting crack on *Fay*. Move up left to the break above and continue left along *Heart By-Pass* to *Pacemaker*'s last few moves.
An alternative to continuing along *Heart By-Pass* is the **Magic Carpet Finish** (6a † 9.5.94), which climbs with difficulty directly up the wall left of the two pegs on *Fay* to a good crack. Continue to the top on better holds.

★★★**Pacemaker** 100 feet E5 6a (16.5.86)
A superb, sustained pitch. Start at a pointed block some 50 feet right of the seaward arête. Climb the diagonal break up and left for 30 feet; then move up to a quartz vein and follow this leftwards to a peg. Go diagonally right for 30 feet to reach another peg in a slanting quartz break. Continue steeply to the top.

☆**Fanny Calder** 100 feet E5 6a † (8.4.95)
Start as for *Pacemaker*. Climb the diagonal break for 6 feet and use sideholds to climb up (crux) to the next major break (of *Hellhound on My Trail*). Follow this left for 3 feet; then climb up on sideholds to the big diagonal break of *Fay*. Continue left along the thinner break, past a peg, to the finish of *Pacemaker*.

★★★**Fay** 120 feet E4 5c (15.5.86)
Now the classic of the wall, sustained and excellent, taking a central and direct line. Difficulty increases as height is gained. Start as for *Pacemaker*, on the pointed block, and climb on good holds, bearing slightly right to the first quartz break and a thread runner. Move up to an excellent spike; then climb leftwards to the start of a wide slanting crack (peg above). Using the crack for your feet, follow it to its end; then climb steeply past two pegs and bear right up a thin crack to reach a horizontal break. Move left to a niche and continue to the top.

The next two routes sweep from right to left across the wall from the start of *Coronary Country*.

★Hellhound on My Trail 130 feet E4 5c (4.5.92)
An excellent route, well protected. Start as for *Coronary Country* and follow the diagonal crack/break leftwards, dropping down to the lower break at the obvious spike on *Fay*. Where this becomes thinner and divides, step down to its lower branch and follow this leftwards to finish on the crux of *Break On Through*.

★Heart By-Pass 110 feet E4 5c (10.4.94)
Another very fine route. Start as for *Coronary Country* and climb the diagonal crack/break, past the spike on *Fay*, to where it narrows to a thin crack at 60 feet. Continue leftwards along the crack (crux, peg) to the finish of *Pacemaker* (peg).

★Coronary Country 140 feet E6 6a/b (17.5.87)
[Photo p.160a.] A powerful route up the highest part of the wall. Easier but serious in the lower part, it then becomes increasingly technical. Start 25 feet right of the pointed block at the base of *Pacemaker*, at a leftward-slanting diagonal crack. Climb the crack for 20 feet to the good spike on *Fay* and pull up to reach a thin vertical crack, which is followed to a higher diagonal quartz break. Move left and up along this for 8 feet to a line of thin discontinuous cracks running up and to the right. Climb these past two poor pegs to gain another quartz break. Move up to another peg; then traverse left along the break for 6 feet before launching straight up the wall to the top on bigger but more fragile holds.

☆The Monk's Satanic Verses 140 feet E8 6c † (5.89)
A sensational direct line straight up the wall right of *Coronary Country* with a poorly-protected and very demanding crux. Start as for *Coronary Country*, beneath a vertical weakness. Climb with relative ease up the weakness for 30 feet to a diagonal break. Climb a thinner crack/seam above the break to its end. A difficult sequence is made to gain another crack/seam. Follow this with increasing difficulty (crux) to the diagonal break of *Malefactor*. The more featured rock above is climbed in a direct line (care with rock) to the top.

☆☆Malefactor 140 feet E5 5c † (23.7.94)
Climb *Azrael* to the quartz break and follow this leftwards to the finishing niche of *Fay*. Serious and fragile.

★★Azrael 140 feet E4 5c (31.5.89)
A very good route, mainly on large but somewhat sandy holds, serious in places. Start 10 feet right of *Coronary Country*, below a white tape under an overhang at 20 feet. Climb up to the right of the thread (past a peg) on good pockets to a ledge. Step right; then climb back up left along the big quartz break (peg) until beneath the obvious vertical, widening crack. Climb the crack to gain a standing-position on a jug; then step left to the base of a discontinuous crack (peg). Climb the crack; then move up left to a peg, and continue past it to a good jug and twin pegs (one poor).

Traverse left along a line of big pockets to a good horizontal nut-slot. Continue up to the top via the occasional dubious hold. Huge block belay.

Hearts and Minds 140 feet E5 6a (1 pt rest) † (12.88)
Start just right of *Azrael* at a shallow left-facing corner. Climb direct to a large flat hold at 15 feet. Carry on in a very direct line on poor holds past two quartz breaks, an undercut flake, and a hidden, poor peg to a large shallow niche with stepped overhangs forming its left-hand side. Climb up to a large thread at the apex of the niche. Trend right to a resting-area; then traverse strenuously back left along the top quartz break to the final wall below a small overhang. Climb this wall strenuously (peg) to a slot below the small overhang (nut to rest). Go over the overhang and up the tiny but still strenuous wall to belay pegs.

Rising Moisture 160 feet Hard Very Severe † (7.4.84)
The landward corner-system of the South Face. Very sandy rock.
1 80 feet 5a. Climb the corners and continuation chimney to a stance on the right below a 20-foot chimney.
2 80 feet. Step right and ascend steeper rock until it is possible to move across left to the top.

The Stunted Razor Snout (25 feet E4 6b † 15.6.97) is a contrived route which hand-traverses the lip of the scrappy-looking wall opposite the South Face of the Middle Fin. It is necessary first to climb the slab/ramp and place long slings over the edge on the pegs.

South Fin – North Face

An impressive face containing some long adventurous pitches, although the rock in the upper reaches of the more landward climbs leave something to be desired. Left of centre is the corner of *Blunt End*, further right is the deep chimney of *Heffalump Trap*, and right again is the smaller *Pooh Corner*.

The big wall left of *Blunt End* contains three, fairly serious climbs.

Cool, Culm, and Collected 100 feet E3 6a/5c † (19.5.84)
Start 10 feet right of the back wall, at a steep thin crack below a ragged overlap. Climb up to and over the overlap to a small ledge at 15 feet. Move up a few feet and follow a zigzag crack out right for 10 feet to a ring-peg and the start of a vertical crack. Climb the crack with difficulty past two more pegs to a ledge right of a broken corner. Step left into the corner and climb it to the top.

Leprosy 100 feet E3 5c (16.7.83)
Sustained, awkward, and quite serious. Start 15 right of the thin crack of *Cool, Culm, and Collected*. Climb direct for 15 feet; then move right along sloping footholds to below the vertical line of 'stuck-on' flakes. Climb these with difficulty to a narrow ledge on top of the last flake, 20 feet from the top. Climb the crack on the left to a difficult, loose finish.

The Lemming 100 feet E3 5b (7.81)
Start 50 feet left of the corner of *Blunt End*, at a rightward-slanting crack. Climb the crack until a foot-traverse leads right to beneath a circular niche at 40 feet. Gain the niche and climb out of it using the jammed flake above. Continue in the same line until it is possible to swing right to the large sloping ledge on *Blunt End*. Finish, as for that route, leftwards and up the easy-angled corner above.

Blunt End 110 feet Hard Very Severe 5a (7.4.73)
The obvious corner/groove splitting the left-hand side of the wall. Climb the steep corner for 50 feet to a large ledge leading up left. Scramble up this and finish up the easy-angled corner above.

Right of *Blunt End* is another impressive wall containing two parallel cracks, both of which are fairly serious in their upper reaches.

★**Angle Grinder** 100 feet E3 5c (1982)
Climb the left-hand crack, which is difficult at first until more broken but still steep rock is reached. Climb this in the same line on better but suspect holds with spaced protection.

★**Uphill** 100 feet E3 5c (27.8.72)
The deeper, right-hand crack in the centre of the wall gives a fine but serious route. The first 30 feet are quite sustained, after which friendlier holds appear, although protection becomes spaced.

★**Eeyore** 110 feet E3 5c (20.5.92)
The obvious slim groove right of *Uphill*. Climb the easy ramp from the right to below the slim groove. Poorly protected climbing (*Friend* ½) leads to a peg at 40 feet, which is passed with difficulty. Climb direct on better holds up the wall to the top.

Tigger 110 feet Hard Very Severe 4c (2.8.81)
Climb the rib immediately left of *Heffalump Trap* and step right into a steep inset corner. At the top, move left into a slabby open groove. Finish up this.

Heffalump Trap 90 feet Very Severe 4b (2.71)
This is the obvious deep chimney/groove, which is climbed to a loose finish.

★**Dulcima** 90 feet Hard Very Severe 5a (7.4.73)
A very fine pitch which climbs the crack and shallow groove in the wall right of *Heffalump Trap*.

★**Xanthoria** 80 feet Hard Very Severe 5a (6.71)
A good route. Climb the left arête of *Pooh Corner* to a large platform at 40 feet; then step left onto the wall and climb up to pass a loose block and gain the rib. Finish on smaller holds.

Pooh Corner 40 feet Severe 4a (2.71)
Climb the obvious clean-cut corner.

Cool Moon 40 feet Hard Very Severe 5b (1983)
Climb the thin slanting crack to the right of *Pooh Corner*, and move onto the open wall at 30 feet.

The front face of the South Fin gives one of the Culm Coast's better easy climbs:

★**South Pier** 150 feet Difficult (1963)
[Photo p.160b.] Climb the front face of the fin, finishing up the interesting squeeze chimney on the right.

South Fin – South Face

The last and unfortunately least of the six faces, it is more broken and has poorer rock. Except for the first, the climbs start from a large ledge beneath the face, gained by 30 feet of scrambling. There are two major cracks.

Poodle Power 90 feet Severe (4.97)
Start at the foot of the step left of *Illiteracy*, climb an obvious crack to a ledge, and finish up the right arête.

Illiteracy 60 feet Very Severe 4c (6.82)
Climb the left-hand and better crack. Take care with rock at the top.

Stone Man 60 feet Very Severe 4c (2.71)
Climb the right-hand crack, named after the petrified effigy (imagination required) encountered half-way up.

Bonk 60 feet Very Severe 4c (12.70)
Start as for *Stone Man* and climb the steep ramp on the right wall to a ledge at 40 feet. Continue up the corner on the right.

Pit Bull 60 feet E4 6a † (26.6.91)
The thin vertical crack 15 feet right of *Stone Man*. The tough crack is climbed, with the use of hidden holds inside it, to the ledge on *Bonk*. Finish up the easy corner above.

The upper crag collapsed in late 1996, and with it went **Edge of the West** (100 feet Very Severe 4c), **Sita** (90 feet Very Severe 4b 4.75), **Sparrow** (90 feet Very Severe 4c 7.4.73), and **Never Too Slate** (90 feet E4 6a 9.3.96).

Duckpool

OS Ref 200 115

Between Lower Sharpnose and Sandy Mouth a mile and a half away are a number of routes on isolated slabs and walls which can be reached along the foreshore from the car-park at Duckpool. The first is on the south-west face of Block Cliff, which is located at the seaward end of a line of easy-angled slabs running out to Steeple Point on the north side of Duckpool beach. The route starts at the lowest point on the right-hand section of the cliff and can be approached at up to half tide.

Out to Lunch 50 feet Difficult (18.5.95)
Climb easily up the buttress on good holds to a thread; move left onto the steep south-west face and climb cracks just left of the arête. Belay to two stakes 25 feet back. Abseil descent.

The next, painful-sounding route lies on a narrow south-facing slab on the first headland south of Duckpool beach and can be reached in five minutes from the car-park at all but the highest states of the tide.

Bill the Bollock-Biter 70 feet Severe (22.5.95)
Climb directly up the middle of the slab, step left to use the arête at two-thirds height, and move back right to finish. Belay to a good thread in the jumble of blocks above. Abseil descent.

Two hundred yards further south is another south-facing slab of better rock, with a cave on its landward side.

de Genieter 50 feet Very Difficult (22.5.95)
A good route for this grade. Climb the central crack to a horizontal crack. Move up and right into a groove, which is followed to the top. Belay by lowering a rope down the back of the slab for the second to tie to thread belays in the boulder-beach. Abseil descent.

Sandy Mouth OS Ref 200 100

This relatively quiet tourist beach has its own car-park and toilet block. Climbing is situated on a shapely pinnacle called The Flame, the largest and landward of two pinnacles 200 yards north of the bathing-beach, and in the vicinity of Stowe Cliffs a quarter of a mile further north.

Stowe Cliffs

The first route takes the right-hand of two cracks in a prominent south-facing slab 100 feet above the beach.

Turmoil 80 feet Very Difficult (3.11.95)
A good route with excellent protection. Climb the forked-lightning crack. Belay to two *in-situ* stakes and descend by abseil.

Across the tidal beach is a dark, north-facing wall with an undercut base. On the right of the wall is a prominent crack leading up and left to a grassy hole.

Wall of Holes 80 feet Hard Very Severe 4b (22.5.95)
Start beneath the crack. Move up to the crack and climb it using holds either side to pass to the right of the grassy hole. Delicate moves up juggy holes just right of the arête lead to looser rock, which is climbed direct to the grassy ridge (bold at the top). Belay by lowering a rope down the south side for the second to tie to thread belays on the beach. Abseil descent.

The Flame

There are four routes on The Flame, descent from which is made by abseil down the south face from *in-situ* tapes around the summit block. The shorter, seaward pinnacle has a few minor pitches on brittle rock which are left for rediscovery.

The Flame 140 feet Very Severe 4b (5.8.76)
Slightly more serious since a minor rockfall affected what was the initial corner. However, this climb is still the easiest way to the summit, but care is required with some of the holds. Start at the seaward edge of the south face. Climb the edge direct on pocket holds until forced to step left onto the arête, which is followed more easily to the top.

The south face is smooth and attractive, and has three obvious cracklines which may need recleaning before an ascent. A rockfall has affected the first two climbs.

Avon Calling 100 feet E3 5c †† (16.1.83)
Climb the left-hand crack, which is strenuous and sustained.

The Wick 90 feet E1 5a †† (14.1.83)
The central crack looks straightforward, but the holds are not positive and the protection is not easy to arrange.

Local Hero 100 feet E2 5c (16.1.83)
The right-hand crack is climbed to the arête and easier ground, which is followed to the top.

Dunsmouth Cliff OS Ref 202 092

This minor area, containing two loose routes, can be reached by heading north along the coast path for half a mile from Northcott Mouth as far as a conspicuous concrete shelter, beyond which a path leads down to the beach. The first, most northerly slab one encounters is vegetated and has a loose pillar in its centre. Right of the slab a brown wall slants up to the right and is bounded on the right by a large black seam.

Intensive Care (150 feet E2 5b † 24.7.79) climbs the brown wall, crack, and groove to a loose finish; and **Mortal Coil** (60 feet E2 5b 4.11.84) ascends the thin, widening crack in the upper half of the steep slab further right.

Menachurch Point

OS Ref 201 088

A varied collection of interesting and unusual routes is to be found on the north-facing slabs and seaward tip of the promontory forming the northern arm of Northcott Mouth. The slabs are accessible by descending grass slopes on the northern side at the landward end of the promontory at most states of the tide. Low-to-half tide is required for climbs at the tip of the headland.

The steep slabs on the northern side are easily identified by three cracks on the left and a flat, 'arrowhead' pinnacle leaning against the slabs on the right. Belay for all the routes on this part of the cliff on a well-hidden stake in the grass just below the top, or on blocks on the crest of the promontory.

Trident 80 feet Very Severe 4c (11.75)
The left-hand of the three converging cracks using the common start in the centre. A little grassy through lack of use.
The Direct Start (E1 5b † 6.6.93) is a solid, independent way to start *Trident*. From 15 feet up the trench on the left-hand side of the cliff, climb the thin crack-system leading diagonally right to the deep crack of the parent route.

Menachurch Wall 80 feet Very Severe 4b (1974)
The central and best of the three cracks. Climb the crack to the crux transition from rock to earth.

Lightfingers 80 feet Very Severe 4c (11.75)
Climb the right-hand crack.

☆**Kalashnikov** 100 feet E2 5c † (6.6.93)
A fine technical eliminate between *Lightfingers* and *Britannia*. At the upper end of the grade if the line is adhered to. Start just left of the corner of *Britannia*. Climb the wall direct to a large scooped hold at 25 feet. Move up right to a small ledge and on up with difficulty past a peg to another scooped ledge. Follow the fine crack-system directly above until a bulging ramp leads horizontally out right to the spike at the top of *Britannia*. Finish up the arête.

Britannia 100 feet Hard Very Severe 4c (5.8.76)
Climb the obvious corner past an ancient peg at 40 feet. Not as good as it looks. Finish up the arête.

Stiff Upper Lip 100 feet E1 5b (28.10.85)
A sustained route, bold in places, which climbs the thin crack up the centre of the flat 'arrowhead' pinnacle. Finish up the arête.

Aphrodite 100 feet Severe (8.77)
Climb the loose right arête of the 'arrowhead' easily, but very carefully.

Dynamo Hum 80 feet Very Severe 4c (8.77)
Climb the narrow buttress right of the arête on unstable rock.

Further right is a long strip slab, and the following route climbs the obvious thin crack at the seaward end, just left of an easy groove.

☆**Klingon Kulture-Shok** 50 feet Hard Very Severe 5a † (13.6.93)
A smart little route which is very well protected and on good rock. Beam up the crack with increasing difficulty to good finishing-holds leading to a sloping ledge strewn with asteroids. Peg belay. The bold will wander off left through the astral debris, the insane will climb the impending rotten wall above the ledge, and others will lower off from the belay peg (ensuring first that it is able to take the strain).

In the tip of the headland is a deep low cave, a dark lair for a family of routes which snake their way out of its improbable confines.

The Kiss 40 feet E4 5c † (3.9.91)
At the seaward end of the overhanging south-facing wall of the cave is a series of disjointed cracks some 20 feet in from the left-hand edge. Climb these strenuously to finish up the left-hand edge on jugs.

☆**Tunnel Vision** 40 feet E5 6b † (4.9.91)
The obvious crack up the impending left wall of the cave; very strenuous but well protected. At the junction with *Abandon Hope…*, continue up the headwall as for that route.

☆☆**Abandon Hope...** 80 feet E4 6b † (15.6.91)
A weird and wild route which is undoubtedly the longest-lowest roof on the Culm. An interesting experience featuring a variety of body-bar and jamming techniques. Low tide and dry conditions required. Start in the dark at the back of the cave, ascend a short wall to the apex, and aim for daylight. The crux is entering and struggling through the 15-foot inverted-V section, which proves somewhat uncomfortable. Continue up the headwall to belay on the ridge above.

The Flight of the Laden Swallow 100 feet E2 5b † (13.10.91)
A traverse above the mouth of the cave. The rock is mostly suspect.
1 70 feet 5b. Climb the break right of the cave and follow the ledge to the cave entrance. Move out (peg) and over the cave to the opposite side, and belay at the base of a crack leading to the top.
2 30 feet 4b. Climb the crack on suspect rock but with good protection. Spike belays.

Maer Cliff

OS Ref 201 080

One of the most diverse, interesting, and complex areas on the Culm Coast, it has benefited greatly from fairly recent developments in a wide spectrum of grades. Routes of all types of difficulty, style, seriousness, and character are to be found here. Furthermore, the commodious car-park at Northcott Mouth is only five or ten minutes' easy walking away from the climbs. There are three main approaches to the cliff. On first acquaintance it is best to turn right out of the car-park and walk down the road that leads to the beach at Northcott Mouth. From there, walk back south along the beach to the stumpy pinnacle of Unshore Rock and the brooding façade of The Black Wall. Alternatively, turn left out of the car-park, pass the white buildings of an outdoor pursuits centre, and go through a gate and out rightwards to the cliff edge. An obvious path leads down left (facing out) of easy-angled slabs to the base of The Black Wall. A third alternative is to continue along the cliff edge until another easy path leads down to a boulder-beach north of The Wafer.

Unshore Rock

The south face of the diminutive *Unshore Rock* has become the home of the following four hard, peg-protected routes. There is no belay at the top so ingenuity is required to facilitate a belay and an escape. Anyone operating at these grades should be able to work it out.

☆**Dark Night** 30 feet E5 6a/b † (17.6.99)
Excellent fingery and committing climbing up sloping bosses and scoops at the left-hand end of the wall. Start beneath the obvious line of holds and climb easily to a break (protection in a small slot above). Make hard moves (peg) and finish direct.

☆**Angry Cockroaches** 35 feet E6 6c † (6.99)
Good and sustained. Start 10 feet right of *Dark Night* and climb easily to the break (peg). Move up and left to a vague crack (peg) and climb to a short diagonal ramp (two pegs). Finish up the ramp via a long reach.

☆**After Dark** 35 feet E4 6a † (6.99)
Good moves up the obvious vertical crack in the right-hand side of the wall. Start beneath the crack. Climb up the wall to the crack (wires), make a hard move to a slot (peg just below), and finish, moving slightly left past another peg.

Mexican Blackbird 35 feet E6 6b † (6.99)
Reachy climbing between *After Dark* and the right-hand arête. Climb the awkward and friable wall past a peg to the break and a second peg. Reach up with difficulty to clip a third peg and place a *Rock 1*. A long reach gains a good hold and a pumpy finish past a very poor final peg.

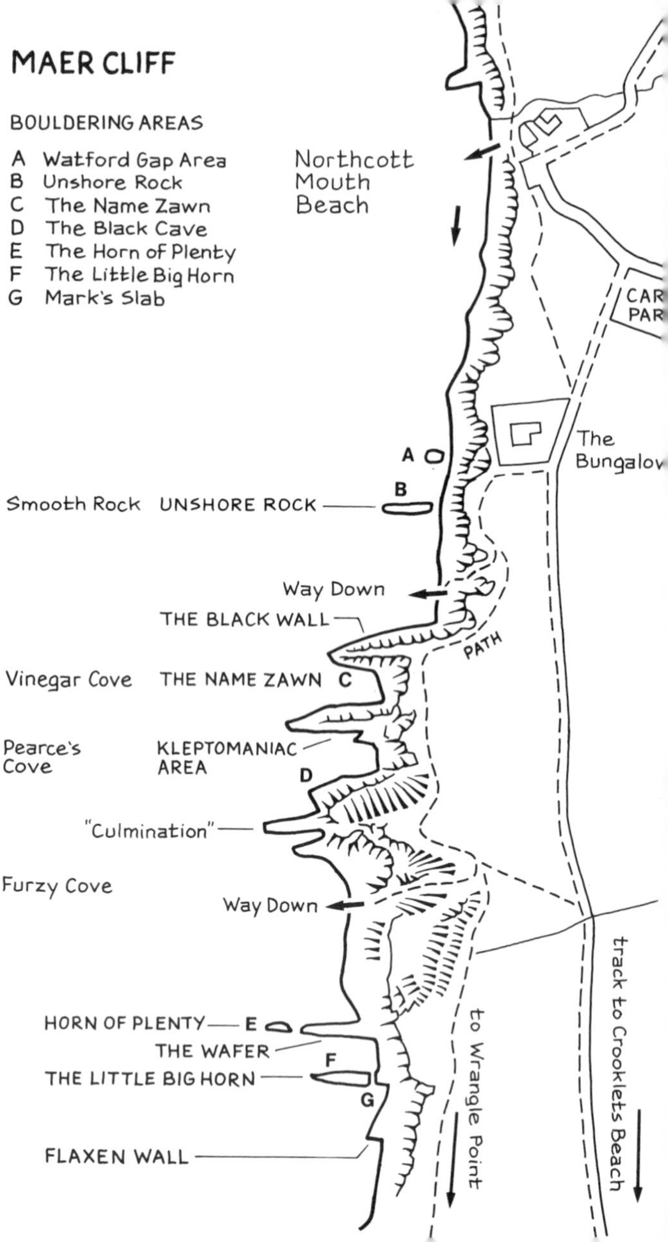

MAER CLIFF

BOULDERING AREAS

A Watford Gap Area
B Unshore Rock
C The Name Zawn
D The Black Cave
E The Horn of Plenty
F The Little Big Horn
G Mark's Slab

Northcott
Mouth
Beach

CAR
PAR

The
Bungalov

A

B

Smooth Rock UNSHORE ROCK

Way Down

THE BLACK WALL

PATH

Vinegar Cove THE NAME ZAWN C

Pearce's
Cove

KLEPTOMANIAC
AREA

D

"Culmination"

Furzy Cove

Way Down

HORN OF PLENTY E

THE WAFER

F

THE LITTLE BIG HORN

G

FLAXEN WALL

to Wrangle Point

track to Crooklets Beach

The loose landward arête of Unshore Rock is **Bronco Belayer** (40 feet Hard Very Severe † 11.9.93), which finishes on the right.

The Black Wall

At the southern end of the Northcott Mouth beach is a big black wall, 120 feet high and 400 feet in length. The obvious central buttress of the wall is rhomboid-shaped with a smooth left-hand face and arête taken by the first major hard route to be climbed here, *Bugsy*. At the left-hand end of the wall is the shattered buttress of lighter rock taken by *The Needle Tree*, while right of the central buttress is a big light-coloured recess, and further right is the wedge-shaped seaward wall containing *Night Maer* and *Ground Fall*.

The Black Wall routes were nearly all climbed with *in-situ* pegs and have been written-up accordingly. However, most of the pegs have subsequently been removed by agencies known or unknown. Even though *Bugsy, Big Black*, and *Fortune Faces the Brave* have all been soloed (after practice), it is highly recommended that pegs are carried. Some routes also require a preplaced hanging rope for escape over the loose terrain at the top: check descriptions before starting out.

The Needle Tree 120 feet E3 5a † (4.8.94)
'Shaped like a Christmas tree and when you touch it the needles fall off!' The tottering cracked arête at the landward end of The Black Wall. Follow the main crack and the thin crack above to the mud cornice. Pull out onto a hanging-rope belay set up prior to the ascent.

The Ungrateful Seconds 120 feet E6 6a † (4.8.94)
Climb the wavy compact wall 30 feet left of the arête of *Bugsy*; then move slightly left across poorer rock to a loose finish. Four pegs (three removed). Preplaced hanging rope advised for the final 20 feet.

★★**Bugsy** 120 feet E6 6a (14.6.91)
[Photo front cover.] A very bold route. Start in the centre of the wall in the central buttress. Climb to a flat pocket at 35 feet (no meaningful protection before a poor nut in the pocket). Hard moves up to and past a peg allow a leftward-diagonal traverse to another peg near the arête. Climb the right-hand side of the arête (bold) to easier ground (wires) and then past another peg in the continuation arête to an easy grass exit.

Further right is a curving overlap; the following two routes take lines up the impressive wall above. The pegs on both routes were removed by a local outdoor activities centre.

★**Big Black** 130 feet E6 6a (24.7.94)
Another big, bold route. Climb ledges to the left-hand end of the overlap. Pull round this to a slot below a poor peg. Follow slots until a hard move (crux) gains better holds next to two pegs. Climb straight up for 10 feet;

then trend up slightly right past a thin slot (*Friend 0*) to larger holds at a break. Climb carefully up slightly left to another slot (wires and *Friend 1½*) and then directly to the top. Pull out on a preplaced belay rope.

★★**Fortune Faces the Brave** 130 feet E6 6a/b (24.7.94)
A powerful line. Start just right of *Big Black*. Climb to a peg at 15 feet (*RP* just above) and make 'interesting' moves to the overlap (two pegs just above). Follow the red streak (reach left to a peg on *Big Black*) to a marginal peg below good holds. Climb directly up keeping right of the nut-slot until a step left gains a sandy groove and a preplaced belay rope.

Twilight Waters 110 feet E4 5c †† (1995)
Climb the first groove right of the overlap for 30 feet until a swing can be made to the left onto the slab. Climb this direct until a crack in the top slab is gained and followed to a preplaced belay rope. Possibly affected by the rockfall.

The next groove right of the overlap was **Oceans** (130 feet E5 6a †† 5.8.94), but the top section has suffered a rockfall. [Photo p.192a.]

Forty feet further right is an obvious deep, slanting, chimney/crack that peters out in the middle of the seaward wall; this is the location of the next route.

Night Maer 120 feet E6 6a (1994)
Serious. Climb the chimney/crack (one peg removed) and snappy wall above.

Ground Fall 90 feet E1 5a † (24.11.85)
Another serious route. Start 50 feet right of *Night Maer*, below a ragged overlap at 15 feet. Follow a pocketed crack over the overlap to a foot-ledge. Step right and climb another crack to the top (three peg runners removed).

The Name Zawn

Around the other side of the promontory is a very narrow zawn, the overhanging left wall of which is taken by the following two routes, which are protected by stainless steel pegs. Left of the first route is a short boulder-problem utilizing an undercut (E3 6b).

☆☆**The Name Doesn't Matter** 50 feet E6 6b † (7.96)
Very steep, technical, and pumpy climbing. Start beneath two pegs on the left-hand side of the impending wall. Climb up to a shallow break; then make a couple of bold moves up to opposing sidepulls, from where it is possible to clip the tat attached to the first peg. Make hard moves up left of the peg (in a very shallow corner) to a line of fragile pockets leading rightwards to a good undercut directly above the peg. Move up to good holds and a second peg, and finish direct on even better holds. Top out, or abseil from a preplaced rope.

☆**Bodysnatchers** 50 feet E6 6b † (7.96)
Not quite as good or hard as its neighbour. Start right of *The Name Doesn't Matter*, beneath a peg at 10 feet. Climb up with difficulty to the peg, move boldly over the bulge above, and follow a very fragile flake up rightwards until it is possible to stand up on the flake and place a cam in a hole. Move up to a second hole and cam placement, and make a long reach up to holds and a peg. A pumpy traverse left, past two more pegs, leads off the wall onto steep grass. Top out or abseil from a preplaced rope.

Just south again, **Warts** (30 feet E3 6a 3.97) climbs an overhanging 'warty' wall past two pegs near the left arête to a hard finishing-move.

Kleptomaniac Area

A hundred yards further south is an easy-angled rib, on the south side of which is a shallow arched overlap of good rock breached by the following three worthwhile routes. Numerous easier lines either side are left for rediscovery.

Sun 50 feet Very Severe 4c (1993)
Climb the obvious crack slicing through the overlap at the left-hand end of the arch, starting from a boulder. The bulge at 20 feet is climbed on good holds, and a peg protects the overlap at the top.

Sea 50 feet Very Severe 4b (1993)
Weave through the overlaps in the centre of the arch (spaced protection).

Sand 50 feet Hard Very Severe 5b (1993)
The most substantial route on this wall. Climb strenuously leftward through the bulges at the right-hand end of the overlap, starting from a large flat boulder. Well protected.

★★**Kleptomaniac** 70 feet E1 5b (28.11.93)
An elegant climb on solid rock up the sweeping arête just south of the arched overlaps. The technical difficulty is low but the exposed arête requires a cool head. Start a few feet in from the base of the arête. Climb straight up to reach the arête at the first peg. Follow the edge with interest and exposure past a second peg to brittle holds at the top, resisting any temptation to deviate. With cunning, adequate supplementary natural protection can be arranged.

Note: this arête was mistakenly identified as the route *Culmination* in the 1988 guide. *Culmination* in fact climbs the much bigger arête 100 yards further south.

Hadrian 70 feet E2 5b (22.11.85)
Bold climbing on spaced protection. Start 15 feet right of the arête of *Kleptomaniac* and climb straight up past a peg at 30 feet to another 15 feet higher. Traverse right across the overlap to a third peg and follow the obvious line above to finish.

★★Bronte 70 feet E2 5c (7.93)
A varied and well-protected climb that crosses the stepped overhang on the right-hand section of the wall. Climb to an obvious small circular niche 15 feet up (*Friend 0* up right beneath the overlap). Climb up left until it is possible to step right across the overhang into a niche, and move delicately up to clip the first peg. Follow the crack to the next peg and make hard moves on thin holds to reach a stepped ledge and then the top.

On the leaning wall directly opposite *Bronte* is the following route.

Foxman and Robin's Zawn Duel 70 feet E3 5b † (11.5.99)
Loose and quite serious. Start beneath the shallow corner. Layback the finger-crack in the back of the corner (peg) and climb on sloping holds to the top of the impending wall. Continue up the arête to belay on blocks on the ridge above.

A little further south is another wall, with a stepped arête on the left and a corner on the right, which provided the line of the route **Tears for Fears** (1982) before the emotional departure of the upper section.

★Kicking Over the Traces 70 feet E1 5b (2.10.93)
A fine varied route, starting 20 feet in from the stepped arête, and beneath a short deep crack right of the arête in the upper part of the wall. Climb thin cracks to a peg where they fade out. Continue with difficulty to good holds in the base of a large scoop. Pull into the scoop, step right, and climb the deep cracks with interest to the top. Stake belay well back.

★The Wall 70 feet E1 5b (1982)
The wall and deep crack between the stepped arête and the corner on the right. Start 10 feet left of the corner. Bold but straightforward climbing to reach the first peg at 30 feet; thereafter, sustained climbing continues past another peg up the widening crack to the top.

It'll End in Smears 70 feet E2 5b (16.11.96)
Start up the corner. Climb the corner (peg) to where it steepens, step left, and climb the steep slab to the top.

The following route has been recorded, but its precise location has not been established.

Midst of a Trauma 80 feet E5 6a † (20.9.98)
Start 6 feet right of the small arête and below a peg at 12 feet. Climb direct to the poorish peg, and follow square-cut flakes to a peg with tat. Step right on flakes and fit a wire over a strange 'pin and washer' affair. Make hard committing moves up towards the next peg and then a hard step right. Pull up to better holds past another peg.

★Tormented Tendon 70 feet E4 6a (14.10.90)
The crack and blank wall just right of the corner. Follow the crack until it is

possible to step right to a small foot-ledge. Climb to a peg (removed) 15 feet from the top (crux) and move right to a good hold and up to finish.

AWOL (60 feet E1 5b 24.11.85) climbed a pocketed crack right of the corner to a difficult finish but has since taken its name to heart.

Just south is another, shorter wall.

Dangerous Driver 50 feet E1 5b (31.5.87)
Climb directly up the middle of the wall, with runners half-way.

Twenty yards further south is an impressive but rather dubious-looking arête that runs the full height of the cliff.

Culmination 120 feet E3 5b † (1982)
This could be the culmination of a climbing career if not treated with the respect it obviously deserves. Climb the line of the arête, placing four pegs for protection. The top crack may be somewhat vegetated.

The next climbing area is located a couple of hundred yards further south and is easily identified as that surrounding the pointed pinnacle, the Horn of Plenty. The original and eponymous route up this attractive little fang trudged up the seaward arête at V Diff (1957), but better is:

South Face of the Horn 40 feet Hard Severe 4b † (31.10.93)
A worthwhile and enjoyable climb to the summit, following the obvious crack and huge holds up the middle of the south face. Steep and smooth to start but well protected. Some ingenuity will be required to belay and get down without leaving gear behind.

The Wafer

Landward of the Horn of Plenty is a thin, precariously-leaning wafer of Culm, miraculously impervious to the onslaught of storm and gravity. *The Suicidal Optimist* showed what was possible but the collapse of **Shivering Chimney** (7.9.69) showed what was likely on this impressive curtain of rock. Belay and escape for the routes on The Wafer are arranged by dropping a rope down the back for the second to secure.

Dutch Departure 110 feet E2 5c † (18.2.98)
A left-to-right rising traverse of The Wafer. Start 10 feet right of the seaward arête. Climb steeply up on good holds to reach a traverse-line that goes right of the lower edge of the obvious large shallow pocket crossing two vertical lines of weakness. From the pocket, step down and right to cross the wide crack of *Skull and Crossbones* and continue the traverse (increasing in difficulty) to the second, shallower pocket. Hard moves up right join *Turbid Legacy*, which is followed to the top. Belay as for that route.

Skull and Crossbones 90 feet Hard Very Severe 5a (6.9.69)
Climb the obvious slanting crack in the centre of the wall on friable holds. Vegetated at the top.

★**The Suicidal Optimist** 90 feet E3 5c (31.5.87)
The name says it all. Good climbing but loose and wafer thin at the top. High up to the right of *Skull and Crossbones* is a large pocket above a vague line of weakness. Climb slightly leftwards past two hand-placed pegs (removed) to reach the pocket. Move left and finish past another peg (also removed).

★★**Turbid Legacy** 90 feet E2 5c (1992)
Fine sustained climbing taking a direct line up the right-hand part of the wall. Protection is by medium and small wires and cams at three-quarters height. Start at a short vertical crack some 20 feet right of the central, triangular cave. Climb the crack and take a line direct up the wall above to the top, the last 20 feet being easier in angle but unprotected.

Probing Phobia 100 feet E3 5b † (7.97)
A bold and sparsely-protected route. Start as for *Turbid Legacy*. Climb the crack for 15 feet (peg removed) and move right on small holds; then climb steeply up right, past a peg at 30 feet, to enter a shallow, reddish-orange groove at 50 feet. A sling over a small spike and a marginal wire 'protect' progress up to the top of the groove. Step left onto the headwall and finish direct.

In the main cliff behind and south of The Wafer is a band of disintegrating shale, the left-bounding wall of which contains the impressive crack of *Freedom* (widening ominously near the top) and, further right, the finger-crack of *Cry of Love*. Both are fine climbs but may require cleaning before an ascent. **The Right to Silence** (120 feet E4 6a †† 15.7.94) took the arête left of the crack of *Freedom*, but a serious rockfall in the upper half has rendered this unclimbable.

★**Freedom** 120 feet E4 6b ‡ (1982/15.7.94)
A great route. Start at the base of the shale band and grovel upwards to the peg at the base of the wall. Start the superb crack with finger-jams and finish on arm-locks (steep and very tiring). Belay to a rather small *in-situ* stake.

☆**Cry of Love** 120 feet E3 5c † ‡ (23.8.98)
Climb the thin finger-crack right of *Freedom*. Sustained. Stake belay.

Flaxen Wall

Thirty yards south of the 'stubby' fin opposite the wafer is a tall, south-facing wall of pale yellow rock with the snaking crackline of *Millennium* on the right.

★**Till Dreaming's Done** 90 feet E1 5c (16.1.94)
A fine climb following a compelling line of disjointed cracks and pockets left of centre of Flaxen Wall. Very well protected with wires and small cams, but tough for the grade. Start in the middle of the wall and climb on pockets up and left, following the crack through a smooth oval patch until it peters out at a large nut placement. Move left and climb the zigzag crack above with interest to a narrow ledge. Step right and climb up until it is possible to hand-traverse right to the top of *Millennium*. Belay by pulling one rope through, throwing it over the back, and asking your second to clip the peg at eye-level.

★**Millennium** 90 feet Hard Very Severe 5b (24.10.93)
An excellent crack climb, elegant and sustained at a reasonable grade but well protected. Start beneath the crack on the right-hand side of the wall. Climb on pockets to reach the base of the finger-crack at 30 feet. Climb it and the wider continuation to its end beneath a niche. Gain the niche with difficulty using cleaned holds on the right, and climb to the top keeping to pockets and thinner cracks on the right. Belay as for the preceding route.

Bouldering – Northcott Mouth and Maer Cliff

As a general rule the Culm Coast does not provide a great deal in the way of concentrated high-quality bouldering such as that found in the Peak District. Isolated problems crop up here and there but the structure and angle of a lot of the rock does not lend itself to sequences of steep technical moves close to the ground/sand. The exception is the fine collection of tough problems on the stumpy fin opposite the Horn of Plenty, which has been dubbed The Little Big Horn. A resumé of these and other bouldering opportunities in the vicinity is set out below, and they are easily located on the accompanying map. All problems are given English technical grades although the variable beach height can in some cases affect these quite drastically.

Watford Gap Area

This is the first narrow gap between the landward cliff and a free-standing rock as one walks south along Northcott Beach. The arête on the landward side is 6a. In the cave to the left of the gap is a traverse at 6a and other problems at the same grade. Through the gap on the landward side is an amenable wall with problems in the 4b to 4c category.

Unshore Rock

This is the flat-topped pinnacle north of The Black Wall. The north-facing wall has a number of good problem starts at 6a. It is not advisable to continue up beyond the half-way mark as the quality of the rock deteriorates considerably.

Across the way from Unshore Rock, The Black Wall has been traversed at sea-level at high tide: **Sundance** (6a/b 1995).

The Name Zawn

The zawn with the impending left-hand wall containing *The Name Doesn't Matter*. The classic pump-out is the excellent **Ben's Traverse**, which starts 20 feet left of *The Name*... and continues until it is possible to finish straight up (6b). The starts of *The Name*... (6b) and *Bodysnatchers* (6b) are excellent problems in their own right and the slabby wall opposite provides more excellent problems of all grades. The free-standing boulder just south of the zawn has many fine problems and a good traverse.

The Black Cave

The superb cave opposite the wall containing *Dangerous Driver*: many problems on 'slopers', 6b or harder. The lip traverse is good (6b), as is the problem that emerges from the back (6b).

Horn of Plenty

The low traverse on the south side (6a).

The Little Big Horn

An excellent concentration of steep fingery problems. Although it is possible to top-out above the looser material on some of the vertical problems, it is undoubtedly safer and less frightening to reverse back down. The dark, sea-washed rock low down is excellent but the wall is prone to retaining any early dampness, and in such conditions the problems become harder. The following is a list of the easier problems, numbered in relation to the accompanying drawing; there are other possibilities.

1 5b. Climb just right of the arête to a massive jug in a hole.
2 5c. The wall and crack to jugs.
3 6a. Climb up and left to a pedestal and mantelshelf easily onto the top.
4 6a. As for 3, but move right to gain the obvious porthole.
5 6b. Climb direct to the porthole on crimps.
6 5b. The crack.
7 5c. Climb the wall just right, and traverse the break to a crack.
8 5c. Climb the crack and groove, and exit right.
9 5c. Climb the wall to the sloping ledge.

There are two traverses: the high one is 5c/6a and the low one is 6b. On the south face of The Little Big Horn lies easier fare – 4a to 4c, but care is required with brittle rock, especially near the top.

Mark's Slab

The landward slab south of the gap between The Little Big Horn and the main cliff provides a desperate 6b traverse, the difficulty of which is acutely dependent upon beach height. The twin cracks at the right-hand end of the slab are not quite so demoralizing (5a/b).

'Little Big Horn' bouldering area

1	5b	5	6b
2	5c	6	5b
3	6a	7	5c
4	6a	8	5c
		9	5c

Simon Young '99

Wrangle Point

OS Ref 201 075

Rumours of the death of this crag have been greatly exaggerated! The main slab is still in the land of the living at the time of writing although the slab further south has definitely deceased. The unmistakable broad white slab is reached between low and half tide along the beach from Crooklets on the northern side of Bude. At higher tides the base of the slab is cut off by the incoming waters. The climbing has a distinctly esoteric flavour but is not without its rewards.

Surfers' Slab 200 feet Very Severe 4a (5.9.69)
Technically easy, but there is a need to remain calm. Start beneath the seaward arête and climb the slab direct to the edge, which is followed to the top. No belay.

★**Hassle** 160 feet Hard Very Severe 4b (6.5.73)
An essential rite of passage for the student of the esoteric Culm slab. The difficulty is not high but it is unrelenting, and the lack of meaningful protection or rest and the fragile nature of some of the holds keep the adrenalin flowing. Start below the point where a curving overlap forms a narrow corner. Climb up and left, heading towards the corner. Climb the corner and continue up and left to reach the arête, which is followed to a grass and mud shoulder below the cliff-top. No belay.

Hussle 160 feet Hard Very Severe 4b (12.83)
A similar experience to *Hassle*. Climb the centre of the slab direct, starting 15 feet right of the shallow corner of that route. Illusory protection. No belay.

Prevarication 150 feet Hard Very Severe † (10.4.83)
A rising traverse from the bottom right-hand corner to the arête. Unsubstantiated rumour of pegs used. No belay.

Inland of the slab is/was another slab which habitually shed its surface. **Serpico** (150 feet E1 5b 6.9.80) took its left arête, and **Ironside** (150 feet Hard Very Severe 4c 1974) wandered up the slab itself by a line of least resistance.

Compass Point

OS Ref 200 063

An attractive promontory of south-facing slabs containing a number of fine routes which are easily accessible and well worth seeking out. However, the rock on the less popular routes can be rather brittle and unpredictable, and the usual warning regarding pegs, some of which have been in place for many years, cannot (like the pegs themselves) be over-stressed. Unfortunately, the northern side of the landward end of the cliff is becoming more unstable and this has affected the previous ridge-top access.

Approach by driving along the narrow lane on the south bank of the Bude Canal to limited parking just before the lock. Continue by foot along the lane, through a white wooden gate, and up to the conspicuous Compass Tower directly above the landward end of the promontory (seven minutes walk).

Most of the climbs lie on south-facing slabs which form the south side of the promontory. Access to the climbs can be made along the landward crest and down a steep central ramp leading to the beach (three stakes are in place at the top of the ramp for those who wish either to rope up for this tricky descent, or to abseil to the beach). Recent rockfalls have left the crest of the ridge in a dangerous condition and, although it is still possible to negotiate it with caution, it is probably better on a first visit to continue south along the coast path to a straightforward descent above the southern end of the beach and walk back to the cliff (another five minutes from the Compass Tower). During low-tide conditions, it is possible to scramble round the end of the promontory from the north or to follow an interconnected series of caves and tunnels from the northern side to the *Westerlation* zawn.

On the north side of the point is a narrow zawn leading to a through-cave. The first three routes are on the left wall of the entrance to the zawn and start beneath double-tiered overhangs.

Boj Wolb 50 feet Severe † (1991)
Start just right of the seaward arête of the wall. Climb up to a vague crack leading to the left-hand end of the overhangs, and follow the corner above.

Crutch upon Crutch 50 feet Very Severe 4c † (1991)
Climb the crack beneath the centre of the tiered overhangs and surmount the overhangs above, using the left-hand of two cracks.

Yorkshire Pud 50 feet Very Severe 4c (9.75)
Start 10 feet to the right of the crack of *Crutch upon Crutch*. Climb the wall to a downward–pointing boss in the overhangs. Pull left over the overhangs and finish direct.

Further back into the zawn is a cave, in the roof of which is a man-sized slot. The following route climbs into and up the slot and replaces the route **Dark Attraction** (4.81), the initial flake crack of which had collapsed.

☆**Inch In, Inch Out** 80 feet E3 5b † (14.7.99)
An unusual, shadowy excursion. Start beneath the slot and climb the northern wall of the cave to an overlap at 35 feet (peg). Bridge the cave roof to climb into and through the slot to emerge into the sunlight. Belay to stakes 15 feet above.

Compass Point

1	North Ridge	VD
2	Westerlation	S
3	Troy	VD
4	Samantha	E1
5	Sugar Magnolia	HVS
6	Corinth	E4
7	Tydomin	HVS
8	Fruichon	HS
9	Wharf Rat	E1
10	Pipsqueak	VS
11	West South West	E1
12	The Beast	E1
13	Snapping Bubblies	E3
14	Crimtyphon	E2
15	Every Rose Has Its Thorn	E3
16	Salt Lake City	E1
17	Detroit	E2
18	Chicago	E3
19	Second Coming/Easter Risings	E3
20	Caravanserai	HVS
21	Dreadlock Holiday	E5
22	Compass-tures Green	E3
23	Frog Abuse	XS
24	The Entertainer	E3
25	Father Christmas's Nightmare	E3
26	Fisting Groove	HVS

12
13
14
15
16
17
18
19
20
21
22
23
24
25
26

At the entrance to the zawn, a wide ramp on the right-hand side leads to an overhanging wall with a hanging flake near the top. The following very steep route takes a dynamic line up the wall.

☆**Full Tilt** 50 feet E4 6a † (25.6.93)
Climb the wall direct past three pegs to the large hanging flake, which is used to gain the top. Short but very strenuous.

The crest of the northern arm of the promontory gives, not surprisingly, **North Ridge** (100 feet Very Difficult c. 1930) with an exposed move rightwards near the top.

★**Westerlation** 80 feet Severe 4a (6.5.73)
An enjoyable wall climb on good holds. Start at the third large boulder leading into the dividing zawn, and climb the wall on the left to a broken crack leading up and left to a diagonal break. Move right and finish direct.

Cool Canute 80 feet Very Severe 4c (22.9.79)
This route climbs the obvious shallow crack/groove, further into the zawn, beyond the boulder-bridge, and just before a 'through-hole' at ground-level. Very tricky unless absolutely dry.

The southern ridge provides a straightforward but exposed scramble, which can be made more interesting by balancing across the boulder-bridge and climbing the short wall above, **Troy** (Very Difficult c. 1930).

Right of the ridge the cliff is comparatively low and a right-to-left diagonal crack (unclimbed) divides the slab left of the conspicuous groove of *Corinth*. Left of the diagonal crack is a long overlap at 40 feet.

Samantha 50 feet E1 5b † (1991)
Start 30 feet right of the ridge, below a peg. Climb up to and past the peg to the overlap. Surmount this and continue direct to the ridge above. Arrange an awkward belay at the boulder-bridge.

★**Sugar Magnolia** 60 feet Hard Very Severe 5a (1974)
Climb the thin crack 15 feet left of the right-to-left diagonal crack to a small niche. Move left along a shallow ramp to a technical finish. Belay as for *Samantha*.

Corinth 80 feet E4 5c (1974)
This is the conspicuous groove with a smooth left wall and curious pitted flutings on the overhanging right wall. A difficult and taxing climb with marginal protection from long pegs driven directly into the soft shale at the back of the corner.

★★**Tydomin** 90 feet Hard Very Severe 4c (1974)
The fine arête and slab right of *Corinth*. Technically straightforward but with sparse protection. Climb just right of the arête until it curves left (peg).

Move onto the slab above and finish either direct or diagonally right. One other peg occasionally reappears.

Fruichon 80 feet Hard Severe 4b (1974)
The corner right of *Tydomin* is climbed to a small cave. Move left and gain the layback flake above.

Wharf Rat 80 feet E1 5a (1974)
Climb the narrow broken wall right of the corner of *Fruichon* up various cracks. Pegs were used on the first ascent but may not now be necessary.

Pipsqueak 80 feet Very Severe 4c †† (1974)
This climb has suffered a rockfall in the initial groove, which has rendered its left wall smooth and holdless and has undoubtedly increased the grade given above. Climb the slim groove on the left-hand side of the narrow buttress, step right, and follow the ramp rightwards to the top. Two pegs (removed).

Right of *Pipsqueak* and left of the descent ramp, the buttress is split by a crack which, at ground-level, starts as a 15-foot chimney and tapers to a mud-filled crack. The crack has been climbed but no details are known. To the left of this crack are the flakes of *West South West* and to the right is the large flake of *The Beast*.

West South West 80 feet E1 5b † (17.8.84)
Start 15 left of the chimney and climb direct up the flakes and the slab above (peg) to finish up the obvious crack.

The Beast 50 feet E1 5b † (1984)
Climb the large flake and finish up the arête with care.

Twenty feet above the foot of the descent ramp is an inset wall beneath a square-cut roof.

Snapping Bubblies 80 feet E3 5b (20.3.81)
Climb up to and over the roof (dubious tied-off peg), and continue direct for 15 feet to an oval pocket (twin pegs). Climb diagonally left for 15 feet to another, shallow pocket. Continue directly up the slab past two more pegs to belay on the ridge above using large nuts and cams.

★Crimtyphon 100 feet E2 5b (1974)
Still the best, most enjoyable pitch at Compass Point! Start 10 feet right of the descent ramp and climb to the left-hand side of a large pocket at 10 feet. Climb up steeply left to a peg at 20 feet and continue in the same line to another pocket at 40 feet (peg in the top rim of the pocket). Traverse left 10 feet to a smaller, oval pocket (twin pegs) and climb direct for another 10 feet to a fourth pocket. Step left to a smaller pocket and climb direct, past a final peg, to the top. Belay on the ridge above using large nuts and cams.

Direct finish
Every Rose Has Its Thorn (80 feet E3 5c † 1991) continues in a direct line up the slab above the second pocket of *Crimtyphon* (peg at 80 feet).

Salt Lake City 110 feet E1 5b (24.8.79)
Right of *Crimtyphon,* at half height, is a curving flake. Climb the dièdre directly below the flake, and move left at 30 feet into the groove formed by the flake (place a peg above and right). Follow the flake up and left with difficulty to a ragged crack left of the roof. Finish direct on loose rock.

★**Detroit** 100 feet E2 5b (30.3.85)
A good climb which uses the start of *Salt Lake City* to reach the fine slab above and right of the groove. Climb the dièdre for 25 feet and step left into the groove. Move right immediately onto the slab and go up past a deep short slot to a thin ledge (peg). Continue up and left on small holds past another peg to finish direct.

Right of *Detroit* the rock degenerates into a series of loose, vegetated corners and unattractive slabs. An unpleasant route has been climbed in this area but not recorded. Right again is the large curving groove of *Chicago*, and beyond this is the conspicuous straight and narrow groove of *Caravanserai* with its accompanying crack just to its left.

Chicago 110 feet E3 5b (2.75)
A serious route on fragile rock. Start below the left end of the obvious sloping ledge at 15 feet, as for *Caravanserai*. Gain the ledge and continue up a shallow crack to a niche and grassy ledge beneath the curving groove. Climb the groove and traverse beneath the roof to the arête. Finish up this.

★★**Caravanserai** 120 feet Hard Very Severe 4c (1.75)
A good climb taking the narrow groove, with the accompanying crack supplying holds and protection placements. A bit of a 'soft touch' but sustained; care is required at the top. Start below the left end of the obvious sloping ledge at 15 feet. Gain the ledge and traverse up and right along it until beneath the groove. Climb the groove direct and belay to stakes and/or fenceposts. A worthwhile direct start up a thin crack directly below the groove is a delicate 5b.

★**Second Coming/Easter Risings** 100 feet E3 5c (3.9.91/10.4.85)
Start midway between the ordinary and direct starts to *Caravanserai*. Climb the blank wall and continue direct up a thin crack to the niche of *Chicago* (poor peg runner). Follow the arête and gain the thin crack on the right. Climb the crack (three pegs) to a large hold on the arête. Continue up brittle rock to a pocket (peg).Go left to another pocket to regain the arête. Climb this with care.

Oceans (E5 ~ first ascent)   Maer Cliff
Climber: Paul Twomey   Photo: Ian Parnell

Mine's a Point
(E3 ~ first ascent)
Upton Slabs
Climber: Sean Hawken
Photo: Andy Grieve

Borderline (E4 ~ first ascent) Bude Pillars
Climber: Sean Hawken Photo: Andy Grieve

Dreadlock Holiday 110 feet E5 5c (9.8.79)
A very serious climb up the thin crack in the centre of the wall right of *Caravanserai*. Protection is poor and the quality of the rock decreases as height is gained. Start uncomfortably close to the moving shale at the back of the zawn. Climb the slab just left of this to a thin horizontal shelf at 40 feet. A vague crack leads up the slab past a peg at 70 feet. Continue in the same line until it is possible to tiptoe gently to the top of the final groove of *Caravanserai*.

Facing the landward end of the promontory is an arch. Above and south of this is an area of cliff especially reserved for loose-rock fanatics. Mysteriously, the number of routes in this locality has increased since the last guide and some of the earlier routes have been repeated. The first route takes the arête directly above the arch. The belay for all routes in this area is the wooden fence between the Compass Tower and the cliff, or the Compass Tower itself.

Compass-tures Green 100 feet E3 5b † (12.10.90)
Climb the cracked arête left of the groove of *Frog Abuse* to a slabby finish right of the arête (peg removed). Follow the tottering wafer *à cheval* to the pasture above with heart in mouth.

Frog Abuse 120 feet Extremely Severe 5b (6.4.85)
Climb the grey groove to the left of the blunt rib of *The Entertainer*, and exit right at the top. Pegs removed.

The Entertainer 120 feet E3 5b (2.75)
[Photo p.336a.] An impressive route with a loose finish, which climbs the blunt arête left of the obvious chimney. Climb the arête until about 30 feet from the top. Move right and tackle the loose finish.

Father Christmas's Nightmare 120 feet E3 5a (1974)
Climb the chimney to the loose finish of *The Entertainer*.

The next groove to the right is easy-angled and technically straightforward, but serious.

Fisting Groove 100 feet Hard Very Severe 4b (6.4.85)
Climb the groove for 60 feet to reach loose scree leading rightwards to the top.

Compass Mentis 60 feet E3 5b † (17.8.91)
Dangerously loose. Climb the arête right of *Fisting Groove* with one peg.

Bude Pillars

OS Ref 200 062

Some 300 yards south of Compass Point is an isolated collection of near vertical pillars. Approach from the cliff-top is down an easy path 250 yards south of the Compass Point folly. The pillars are a little further south along the shore from the base of the path. The main pillar of fine sandstone stands proud from the other walls and chimneys and provides three excellent climbs.

☆☆**Brainchild** 80 feet E5 6a † (8.4.96)
Unusual climbing on the curved impending wall up formations which resemble a brain. Climb the obvious line up the centre of the wall, past three pegs, and step left to finish up the crack. Belay and escape as for *Zinfandel*.

★★**Borderline** 80 feet E4 6a (10.10.95)
[Photo p.192b.] Climb the steep, narrow, southern face of the main pillar just right of the arête. Only one good nut (at two-thirds height) protects the thin top section. Belay and escape as for *Zinfandel*.

★★**Zinfandel** 80 feet Hard Very Severe 5a (16.8.92)
A fine crack climb right of *Borderline* on the main pillar. Well protected once the crack is reached. From the centre of the face, climb up and left to a thin sling runner on the arête. Step right and follow the thin crack, which gradually widens, to the top. Peg belay (not *in situ*) at the top of the pillar. An additional belay (a wise precaution) can be arranged by dropping one rope down the back of the pillar for the second to secure. Scramble with care up loose ground above or (better) abseil off.

Some 5 yards further right is the deep chimney of *Sigmoidoscopy* and the next route starts beneath a subsidiary rib immediately left of the chimney entrance.

The Curate's Egg 70 feet E1 5a † (10.4.85)
Climb the rib for a few moves; then step right onto the wall (peg removed). Climb cracks in the wall to reach the short ramp (peg removed). Make a difficult step up to an obvious flake, and climb this before moving right into the chimney to finish. Block belays well back.

Sigmoidoscopy 70 feet Hard Very Severe 4c (15.5.86)
The chimney. Those suffering from a depraved desire to repeat this route should consult a certain local GP.

Further to the right is a south-facing slab with a crack above a pocket in the left-hand side.

Up Yours 50 feet E1 5b † (1.8.91)
Climb easily to the pocket and follow the well-protected crack above on diminishing holds to the top. Block belays well back.

Further south is another fin.

Waisted Youth 40 feet Hard Very Severe 5a † (26.7.91)
A short fun route on the south face between the seaward arête and the corner. The last few moves constitute the well-protected crux.

Efford Beacon

OS Ref 200 058

Below the Efford Beacon trig-point is a large, steep, and serious cliff with a couple of quality routes requiring an experienced hand.

☆**Fantasy Land** 240 feet Extremely Severe † (21.9.91)
The obvious rightward-slanting ramp immediately below the trig-point. Pegs used and removed. Start below the bottom of the ramp.
1 110 feet 5b. Climb straight up to a block below the right-hand arête of the ramp. Pull up and make an awkward move to gain a good foothold on the arête. Traverse horizontally right for a few feet to gain a thin ramp, which is followed to a belay in a corner below an overhang.
2 90 feet 5a. Step left to regain the ramp and follow the left-hand side until it is possible to step right to gain a good crack. Belay at the top of the ramp. An excellent pitch.
3 40 feet 5a. Traverse right and step down with difficulty onto a shale ramp. Climb this for a few feet until it is possible to regain the rock on the left, which is followed to a large spike vertically above the belay. A few steps up the shale and mud bank gain the top and the trig-point belay.

Further south is another buttress.

★**Slippery Mhic** 260 feet Extremely Severe (20.4.84)
The obvious right-to-left-slanting fault. Retreat would be dangerous in view of the poor belays and the overhanging nature of the crag. Start at the top of the projecting rib which abuts against the face. Pegs used throughout.
1 120 feet 5b. Ascend to the faultline (peg for the second's backrope), and traverse left for 25 feet to gain a prow. Step down under a large overhang and continue traversing until it is possible to regain the main faultline, which leads to a stance in an obvious scoop.
2 140 feet 5a. The conspicuous left-slanting, slabby chimney gives an excellent pitch.

Lynstone

OS Ref 200 054

The area comprises of three 50-foot fins of rock on a secluded beach some 500 yards south of Efford Beacon. Though short, the climbs are steep and intense. Use the rather grandly-named Efford Farm Business Park car-park (OS Ref 205 058) situated at the end of the narrow lane just outside Bude, off the Bude–Widemouth road. Follow the public footpath west across Efford Down to the coast and take the obvious path down to the beach south of the Beacon (five minutes from the car-park). The fins lie 250 yards south of the beach and are accessible between half and low tide.

The first fin reached, the north fin, has a fine-looking south face, which is as yet unclimbed. The central, pierced fin, The Arch, has a deep diagonal crack running out of the through-cave. The south fin, very close to The Arch, has a hold-plastered south face and a smooth dark northern aspect – The Black Wall, on which the following three routes are situated.

☆**Black Dog Bite** 50 feet E2 5b † (22.8.93)
A rare commodity on the Culm Coast, an impending crackline (with a bite worse that its bark). Strenuous. Climb the obvious steep crack towards the landward end of the wall (well protected with large nuts) until near the top where the crack opens out. Move onto the left side of the crack and climb straight up to the top. Belay by dropping one rope down the back of the fin to be clipped into a thread belay at ground-level.

La Bella Negra 50 feet E2 5c † (11.7.93)
Steep and strenuous. Start at the rounded ear of rock half-way along the wall. Use the ear to gain the slanting crack with difficulty. Hand-traverse 10 feet right to a slot. Climb straight up (hard) using the rounded diagonal crack above and continue direct on improving holds to the top. Stake belay.

☆**Obsidian Rose** 50 feet E2 5c (1 pt aid) † (22.8.93)
Steep dynamic climbing on superb rock. Start beneath shallow cracks 10 feet left of the seaward arête. Follow the cracks with difficulty past a peg to a horizontal break (nut used to rest at the break on the first ascent). Climb directly above on small holds until diagonal cracks can be followed left to finish just right of *La Bella Negra*. Stake belay.

The south face of the south fin has weathered into a surface of bizarre protruding knobbles.

Holdrush 50 feet Hard Very Severe 5a † (17.7.93)
Good climbing centred on a shallow square recess half-way up. Harder than it looks but well protected. Start directly beneath the recess some 25 feet from the seaward edge of the fin. Pull onto the wall and climb on huge holds to the recess. Fix a sling, pull into the recess, and climb the steep wall above on hidden holds to a difficult exit at the top. Stake belay.

The obvious right-to-left diagonal break in the centre of the face starting at the small ground-level through-cave is **Barefoot Lee's** (55 feet Severe 1993).

Hold-up 50 feet E1 5a (28.6.97)
Start just right of the small through-cave. Climb the highest part of the wall on the south face on amazing holds, and then through the overlap direct (with care).

Upton Slabs

OS Ref 200 049

This is an impressive expanse of slabs but, on closer acquaintance, it becomes apparent that the quality of the rock leaves something to be desired. The slabs are best approached at below half tide along the beach from Upton. Descend to the beach by an easy path from near Upton Junction (OS Ref 201 048) along the Bude–Widemouth road where the road, the coast path, and the cliff edge almost converge. The climbs are all on the southern side of a promontory and below a prominent wooden post. There are four sets of slabs separated by three distinctive corners, the landward slab being the highest and having a convex appearance. Rockfalls at the back of the promontory have removed an earlier descent path and destabilized the crest previously used for belaying, and there is now a substantial stake at the top of *Crocus Cat*. It is advisable to use the stake for belaying and abseil descent from the crest.

The seaward arête of the seaward slab is **Triton** (70 feet Severe 5.87) and should be treated with care.

Zinc Silhouette 80 feet E2 5b (17.4.83)
Climb the centre of the seaward slab on curious rusty flakes and edges to a prominent narrow edge at 30 feet. Move left (peg removed), then diagonally right (peg). Step left and follow a line of small finger-pockets to the top.

Lounge Lizard 80 feet Hard Very Severe 4c (12.82)
The left-hand of the three corners. Serious. Two pegs; cams useful.

★**White Rasta** 100 feet E2 5c (1.83)
The right arête of the first corner gives some interesting climbing. Start 10 feet right of the arête. Climb a very thin crack and move diagonally left up to a ledge and overlap at 30 feet. Surmount the overlap with difficulty and move left to the arête (peg), which is followed to a small ledge (peg removed). Step right and finish direct.

Starkadder 100 feet E1 5a (12.82)
A serious route, sparsely protected. Start as for *White Rasta*, beneath the ledge and overlap. Climb up to the ledge, and move up and right (peg removed) to a pocket. Step back left and go straight up past another peg to the top – bold.

Parsley Pig 110 feet Very Severe 4b (10.82)
The middle corner, loose and unpleasant.

Cold Comfort 110 feet Severe (12.82)
The right arête; care with the rock required.

★**Two Pints to Capel** 120 feet Very Severe 4b (10.82)
A pleasant route. The central, triangular slab is split left of centre by an obvious wandering crackline. Climb the crack to ledges at 40 feet. Step right into a continuation diagonal crack; then move left onto the clean upper slab, which provides pleasant, open climbing in a direct line to the top.

Ocean Rendezvous 120 feet Very Severe 4c (17.4.83)
Similar in style to the preceding route but slightly more difficult. Climb the thinner cracks 10 feet right of *Two Pints to Capel* to ledges near the right-hand arête, which is followed to the top.

Crocus Cat 120 feet Very Severe 4b (10.82)
Climb the third curving groove by starting in the miniature groove immediately to its left. Loose and unpleasant: not a very nice pussy at all.

The huge, landward slab has been breached by three long serious pitches. The friability of the rock and the sparseness of protection must be taken into account before embarking on these exploits. Pegs should be carried.

Private Enterprise 130 feet E2 5a (4.84)
The least of the three routes nevertheless has a serious start on dubious rock. Left of the niche at the start of *Big Business* is a discontinuous crack, which is climbed to the rightward-sloping ramp. Move left and finish up the left-hand side of the slab. Four pegs all removed.

★**Big Business** 130 feet E3 5b (1.83/5.83)
A fine but serious line up the centre of the convex slab. Start in the overhung niche just right of the centre of the slab. Climb leftwards out of the niche to a small ledge left of a whitish corner. Follow the crack above, steeply at first, past a good peg (removed). Continue up the line by a series of delicate moves (poor peg removed) to reach the rightward-sloping ramp. Climb the easier-angled slab above, and move left beneath the loose headwall, which leads to the top.

Broken English 130 feet E3 5b (6.83)
Start as for *Big Business* and climb leftwards to the base of the whitish corner. Move up right into the corner and follow it until it peters out. Difficult moves lead up to a pocket (peg removed); then climb up via more pockets in a direct line to easier ground (peg removed), and move left near the top to finish.

Fifty yards south of Upton Slabs is a south-facing slab that finishes at a grassy ridge abutting the main cliff.

Absence 70 feet Very Severe 5a † (30.4.94)
Start just right of the landward edge of the slab. Climb the slab delicately (4c if the right-hand retaining material is bridged) to a *Friend* 2 placement at 20 feet. Climb directly and delicately up the slab above to cracks near

Upton Slabs

1	Zinc Silhouette	E2	7	Two Pints to Capel	VS
2	Lounge Lizard	HVS	8	Ocean Rendezvous	VS
3	White Rasta	E2	9	Crocus Cat	VS
4	Starkadder	E1	10	Private Enterprise	E2
5	Parsley Pig	VS	11	Big Business	E3
6	Cold Comfort	S	12	Broken English	E3

the top. Continue to the grassy arête above. Stake belay, which should be backed up by dropping a rope down the back for attachment to nuts and a peg.

On the south side of the small bay south of the slabs is a pinnacle with a series of loose overlapping slabs on the south side. The landward slab has an obvious thin crack near its left-hand edge.

Foul Brood 70 feet Hard Very Severe 4c (1.83)
Climb the crack to a loose finish on the right. The top of the pinnacle is loose, there is no belay, and the escape is also loose – get out of that! Not recommended.

Bolivian Consummation 120 feet Very Severe 4b † (2.5.93)
The slab on the landward cliff opposite and 50 feet south of the pinnacle. Start on the left of the slab and climb the better rock near the left-hand arête to finish on the shoulder of the slab. Block and nut belays. Abseil descent by dropping a rope down the back of the slab to be attached at sea-level.

Arrowhead Pinnacle

Further south in the bay, before Higher Longbeak, is a spectacular arrowhead-shaped pinnacle.

Half a Point 60 feet Extremely Severe 5b † (1996)
Climb the narrow seaward face of the pinnacle (pegs) to the top. Abseil descent.

★Mine's a Point 60 feet E3 5c (23.2.95)
[Photo p.192b.] Climb the crack on the left-hand section of the south face to gain a small ledge on the seaward arête 10 feet from the top. Climb up and back onto the south face to reach the top (room for one only!). Three pegs. Abseil descent from *in-situ* sling around the top of the pinnacle.

The Atlantic Coast

The rock architecture, particularly near Boscastle, is stupendous and here adventure, commitment, and seriousness are regarded as essential ingredients of a rock climb. There has been some development since the last edition of the guide but this still represents only the merest tip of the iceberg.

Thorn's Beach Slabs OS Ref 151 978

Park at St Gennys, which is a little over half a mile north-east of Crackington Haven. Take the footpath that runs due north, past the old vicarage, direct into the valley round the edge of the field. Continue across the steps in the overgrown stream and climb steeply up through vegetation to join the coast path at a signpost on the ridge of Cleave Cliff. Directly behind this sign is a vague path that leads steeply down through scrub to Thorn's Beach. Walk along the beach for 200 yards to the north-east until below the obvious, overlapping, north-east-facing slabs, which have a large scree-covered ledge in their centre at one-third height. The base of the cliff is awash one hour either side of high tide. The poor friction of the slaty rock would make any routes here extremely difficult in the wet.

Smugglers and Rockpools 210 feet Hard Very Severe † (4.6.89)
Start on the beach, towards the left-hand end of the cliff and below the cleanest-looking slab, which leads to the obvious ledge.
1 60 feet 4b. Climb easily up a narrow slab, which gives access to the more prominent slab with a crack near its right edge. Go up the left corner and step right to the crack, which is followed as it steepens to the scree-covered ledge. Belay to two *in-situ* 3-foot stakes.
2 150 feet 4c. From the belay, move up and right to step round the slab into a corner. Make hard moves up the corner to gain a small ledge at the base of a good crack which runs up the right-hand slab. Follow this crack to a ledge. Climb up the continuation groove to another ledge. From here, move up and left to vegetation. A belay (nuts and stakes *in situ*) will be found further up and to the left in a small rocky bluff. Descend a faint thorny path, with care, rightwards (facing out) to reach the beach.

Great Barton Strand OS Ref 142 974

Park at St Gennys and take the footpath west from here to join the coast path. Follow this north down into the St Gennys valley. The north-facing, wave-like slab, New Wave Slab, is visible in the cove below on this descent. Cross to the north side of the stream and walk out to the headland beyond the waterfall. From the headland a scrambling descent can be made back towards the base of the waterfall and into the cove. For about two hours either side of low tide it is possible to cross the boulder-beach to the obvious 80-foot-high, long, wave-like slab that gradually increases in steepness to an overhanging top.

Malibu 80 feet Very Difficult † (7.9.89)
A spare rope is needed for belays up and right from the route top. Start at the left edge of the long slab. Climb straight up with negligible protection until the capping overhang is reached. A move up and left enables the top and steep grass to be gained.

Belly Board 80 feet Very Severe † (7.9.89)
A spare rope is needed to reach an *in-situ* stake belay. Start a third of the way along the slab from its seaward end, and just right of a wet groove where a subsidiary slab joins the base of New Wave Slab. Climb directly up the steepening slab to a prominent pocket hold. From here, step up among the overhanging blocks and make an interesting traverse right to gain steep grass.

Descend from both routes by abseiling off a prominent horizontal block at the seaward tip of the slab.

Crackington Haven

OS Ref 140 970

This, the first of the great shale precipices which dominate the next ten miles of coastline, is unmistakable as you look out to sea from the village. A prominent feature on the skyline is an overhang at 100 feet with a sloping ledge above. The only route starts to the right of this and trends left past a prominent 25-foot-long band of lighter rock near the top.

Muffin Man 400 feet Hard Very Severe † (10.5.80)
Start below and to the right of the overhang, which appears as a prow.
1 100 feet 4b. Climb diagonally left to beneath the prow and then traverse right for 20 feet to a ledge. Peg belays.
2 150 feet 4b. Leave the ledge at its left-hand end by an awkward move; then continue without further difficulty to the highest point of the easy ground above.
3 150 feet 4c. Climb the wall above, trending left to below the band of lighter-coloured rock. Traverse left just beneath this, climb up to its left-hand edge, and pull through an overhang to easier terrain.

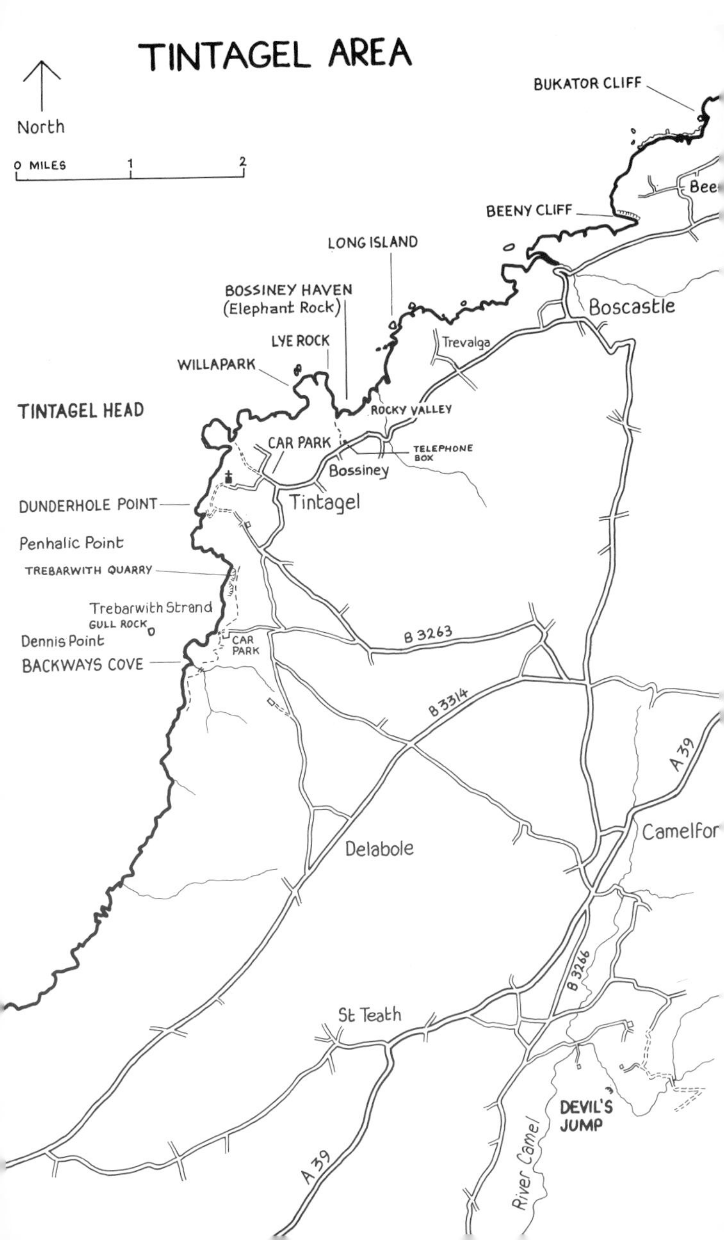
TINTAGEL AREA
North
0 MILES
1
2
BUKATOR CLIFF
Bee
BEENY CLIFF
LONG ISLAND
BOSSINEY HAVEN
(Elephant Rock)
Boscastle
LYE ROCK
Trevalga
WILLAPARK
TINTAGEL HEAD
ROCKY VALLEY
CAR PARK
TELEPHONE BOX
Bossiney
DUNDERHOLE POINT
Tintagel
Penhalic Point
TREBARWITH QUARRY
Trebarwith Strand
GULL ROCK
Dennis Point
CAR PARK
B 3263
BACKWAYS COVE
B 3314
A 39
Camelfor
Delabole
B 3266
St Teath
DEVIL'S JUMP
River Camel
A 39

Coastal Traverses

The eastward traverse from Crackington Haven to Millook requires low tide and quiet seas, but takes in wonderful rock scenery. Approximately five miles long with a 'sting in the tail' just before Millook is reached (183 001). The first section under Pencannow Point (138 974) is probably the hardest section (V Diff). There are a number of escape possibilities, some easy, some through dense undergrowth, and some exciting (if chosen unwisely).

The traverse of Cambeach (129 966), **Longevity** (Severe † 7.7.99) is feasible only in dry weather and with a quiet sea. Start with a scramble down the combe and damp gully that divides Big Cam from Tremortha Haven; then boulder-hop west for 300 yards. Climb a series of steps (V Diff) to reach a slab, and cross the slab to the headland's ledge. Swim across to the back of a zawn, and then traverse out (Severe) to reach a scrambling section, followed by 40 feet of Severe climbing to a horizontal ledge with a bulging wall above it. V Diff climbing just above the sea leads past four coves to a scree ledge. The coast path can be reached up steep slopes above Little Strand.

Bukator Cliff

OS Ref 118 935

The cliff is marked as such on the OS Map, and as one of Cornwall's most distinctive features, is not likely to be confused with other lesser crags. Approach by scrambling down steep landslide debris to the forlorn little beach below the landward end of the crag.

Pegs, *Warthogs*, and helmets are essential for all three routes.

Private World 540 feet Extremely Severe (5.5.79)
Aptly named. It takes the prominent (when viewed from below) chimney/groove at the left-hand end of the crag. All pegs have been removed. Start beneath the huge black overhanging corner.
1 150 feet. Traverse left out of the corner to gain easy slabby rock. Climb this to ledges at its top left-hand corner. Peg belays.
2 80 feet 4c. Climb up diagonally left to gain a groove leading up to the chimney-line. Climb the groove past an old peg to a ledge on the left. Peg belay.
3 110 feet 5a. Surmount the bulge above the stance to gain the main chimney-line. Move right at 50 feet (peg) to gain the right-hand branch, which leads to an easy chimney. Go up this to a good stance on the left. Peg belay.
4 70 feet 4b. Climb straight up for 20 feet (peg); then follow a ledge-line leftwards to a peg belay in a corner where the ledges run out.
5 70 feet 5b. The shallow groove directly above leads past two pegs to a loose exit beneath huge overhangs. Move up right to gain a pinnacle stance. Poor peg belay.

6 30 feet 5c. Traverse right on the obvious line (two pegs) to gain the arête and a sloping ledge around the corner. Peg belay.
7 30 feet 5a. The shallow groove above (peg) leads to the top.

In Memoriam 600 feet Extremely Severe (30.5.81)
Easier and less sustained than *Private World*.
1 & 2 230 feet 4c. *Private World* pitches 1 & 2.
3 70 feet 5a. Move back right for 10 feet from the stance and climb directly into the bottom of the obvious wide chimney capped with overhangs. Place a peg and move right across the wall at the first opportunity (about 20 feet below the capping overhangs) to gain the right arête of the chimney. Climb this for 25 feet (peg) to a small stance and good peg belays.
4 120 feet 4a. Trend diagonally right up easier ground to a stance below a vague depression (two pegs) on the right-hand side of the easy-angled central section of the cliff.
5 140 feet 5b. Ascend the depression to the overhangs and move diagonally right between them (pegs) to gain grass tufts with difficulty. Move right again to gain the obvious grassy area below the top.
6 40 feet. Climb easily to the top.

Where There's a Will... 500 feet Extremely Severe † (29.4.90)
A serious route up the wall right of *In Memoriam*. Start towards the right-hand end of the wall, at the base of a slabby groove leading to a leftward traverse-line.
1 120 feet 4c. Climb the groove to the traverse-line at 70 feet. Go left along ledges and up to a ledge near a steep shallow corner.
2 70 feet 5b. Move left and up through a bulge; then climb the left wall of the corner (poorly protected) to a belay up left.
3 70 feet 5c/6a. Climb diagonally up and right beneath overhangs on jutting quartz holds, and break through the roof/bulge at the only weakness (serious). Move up to protection in a groove, then right to a poor belay on a small ledge.
4 60 feet 5a. Climb up and left to easier ground, and belay at the base of an open groove.
5 140 feet 5b. *In Memoriam* pitch 5.
6 40 feet. *In Memoriam* pitch 6.

Beeny Cliff

OS Ref 108 920

Another North Cornish esoteric masterpiece. The cliff extends northwards from Pentargon Bay as far as the offshore rocks of Beeny Sister. The route described lies on the section within the bay itself. A prominent feature left of centre is a scree slope at one-third height. Start beneath the left end of this and scramble to ledges where the cliff steepens. The route is easy in its lower reaches but becomes serious and hard in its upper section.

The Tourist 530 feet Extremely Severe + A2 † (2.10.79)
The main cliff forms the north side of Pentargon Bay. Start beneath the left end of the prominent scree slope at one-third height. Scramble for 50 feet to belay on ledges where the cliff steepens.
1 150 feet. Climb diagonally right to gain the left edge of the central scree slope after 90 feet. Move onto the slope and belay on its upper edge.
2 120 feet. Traverse the slope to its right-hand end.
3 80 feet. Climb up right via a loose wall to gain the second scree slope (much smaller than the first). Belay at the left end of this, below a shallow overhanging groove (with an orange right wall) leading up to a prominent niche.
4 60 feet 5b+A2. Aid the overhanging groove using *Kingpin* or *Lost Arrow* blades; then free-climb up right to a stance in the niche (two pegs in place).
5 120 feet 5b. Traverse leftwards along the obvious horizontal line (peg for aid after 25 feet) to gain ledges after 80 feet. Follow the groove above more easily to the top. A serious pitch.

Long Island

OS Ref 074 907

There are two fine routes on the exposed and surprisingly impressive seaward face. However, there is one slight drawback – an approach in the form of a 100-foot swim!

☆☆**Little and Large** 400 feet Hard Very Severe † (14.4.84)
Swim and traverse round to the seaward side of the island. The route takes the central depression and finishes up the prominent overhanging chimney.
1 150 feet. Solo up to a prominent band of red rock and belay at the left end of a good ledge (thread) where a right-trending line leads to the foot of the chimney.
2 95 feet 4c. Follow the obvious line rightwards to a good ledge just right of the foot of the chimney.
3 60 feet 5b. Surmount the first overhang, and traverse 15 feet left under the large second overhang to reach a short crack leading up into the chimney. Follow this to an excellent stance and thread belay.
4 75 feet 4c. Move up left from the belay to gain a right-trending line beneath an overhanging groove. Belay 20 feet from the top.
5 20 feet. Finish up the obvious line. The summit is 20 feet above.

☆**Bloodbath** 375 feet Hard Very Severe † (21.4.84)
This climbs the west arête of the seaward face, which is seen in profile from the coast path. Start from a large platform, exposed at low tide, below the arête.
1 150 feet. Solo up to a belay below the prominent red overhang at 150 feet. The final bulge beneath the roof is passed on its left.

2 50 feet 4b. Pass the red overhang on its left and trend up right, crossing another overhang, to a good ledge on the crest. Thread belay 6 feet higher.
3 60 feet 5a. Climb the weakness through the overhangs directly above to reach a prominent jamming-crack that leads to another good ledge at the start of more broken terrain leading up to the right.
4 115 feet. Move left of the arête and climb for 20 feet to a ledge. Surmount the next band of overhangs on the crest and avoid the final roofs on their left. The belay is 15 feet below! Easy climbing remains.

Trewethet Cliff

OS Ref 073 899

Trewethet Cliff lies just north of Trewethet Gut (marked on the 1.25,000 map) about half-way between Bossiney Cove and Long Island, and is easily identified by a prominent band of overhangs at three-quarters height. Approach from the cliff-top via a grass/rock ramp. There are two obvious lines of weakness in the overhangs.

Chossy Chimney 70 feet Very Severe 4a † (16.9.95)
At the left end of the steep wall is a chossy right-angled corner.

Slugs on Jugs 130 feet E1 † (16.9.95)
This route climbs the wall left of *The Urge* and traverses left under the overhangs to finish.
1 70 feet 4c. Follow the obvious leftward-slanting ramp/flake for 20 feet before making a rising traverse right to join the last 10 feet of *The Urge* pitch 1.
2 60 feet 5a. Traverse horizontally left with increasing exposure until a large hole is reached. Make sensational moves up and leftward from the hole to the top.

☆☆**The Urge** 160 feet Extremely Severe † (16.9.95)
This takes the left-hand fault through the band of overhangs gained by climbing direct up the lower wall. An excellent climb. Start from the rocky lower section of the ramp where it is possible to step reasonably easily onto the wall.
1 90 feet 5b. Climb direct to a small flat ledge and then go up left to a shallow brown groove. Follow the groove until it is possible to trend leftwards to a small but fine stance beneath roofs. Peg belays.
2 70 feet 5c. Move up right to the roofs and a large dubious block. Traverse right across the lip of the first overhang and climb the second direct via a crack. Finish out to the left.

☆**Baffler** 100 feet Extremely Severe 5c † (16.9.95)
The right-hand line of weakness, approached via a usually slimy chimney half-way up the ramp. Atmospheric and exciting, though relatively short.

Enter the chimney and follow it to overhangs. Move up and left beneath these until it is possible to climb steeply up and out rightwards to a small ledge on the lip of the main overhang. Follow a steep right-trending crackline to easier ground and the top.

At the top right-hand side of the impressive overhanging wall is a large platform.

Molly's 29-Hour Party 60 feet Severe 4a † (1.5.99)
Start on a recessed ledge at the base of the corner on the seaward face, and climb the corner with ease until just below the platform on the right. From here, climb diagonally left under the overhang to finish with increasing exposure on good holds.

Rocky Valley East Headland OS Ref 072 898

Park in the large lay-by on the B3263 half-way between Bossiney and Trethevy. Follow the path along Rocky Valley to the coast and take the right-ascending path over a small bridge. Continue directly up the cliff path until beside the campsite; then bear left through a wall and follow the cliff edge to a large flat area beneath a steep rock outcrop.

Must Be Mental 80 feet E2 5b † (14.8.89)
Start at the bottom right-hand end of a ramp, by an overhanging corner. Move up and over the corner to a sloping ledge and continue directly up the wall to a small niche. From the niche, climb the steep wall above (crux) with very poor protection.

Why Me Mum? 90 feet E1 5b † (14.8.89)
Start as for *Must Be Mental*, and then traverse rightwards to a corner. Move up the corner onto a sloping ledge and continue leftwards up the short bulging wall (slimy) to a small groove at the base of an overlapping corner. Follow the groove up to the corner and finish on loose holds.

Rocky Valley Zawn OS Ref 070 895

There is an initially impressive-looking 180-foot slab in the first zawn west of the headland on the west side of Rocky Valley between Boscastle and Tintagel. It is best viewed from the fishermen's scramble down the headland on the west side of the zawn. Approach either from the coast path after parking at Rocky Valley, or as for Bossiney Haven. A series of soft rock belays can be found in a bluff directly above the slab. Abseil to a ledge at the base of the slab, which is clear for two hours either side of low water; a knot changeover can be made on the easy-angled slab. The slab is nasty in the wet.

Mary's Journey 210 feet Hard Severe † (20.7.89)
This climbs the left wall of the zawn to cross the chimney onto the slab, and then goes up and across right to exit on the slab below the final overhangs. Start at the base of an obvious ramp that runs up the north wall of the zawn.
1 130 feet 4b. Go up the easy-looking ramp until a difficult step is made up to overhangs, and then make a series of moves to the right to pass them on the steep wall. Once in balance, turn to face out from the wall and jump across the top of the chimney that bounds the left edge of the slab. Continue easily up and across right to belay as for *Piran P*.
2 80 feet. Continue up to the headwall and go right below this to reach grass and belays in the soft rock of the headwall.

Piran P 200 feet Severe † (14.5.89)
Start at the right edge of the ledge below a slight pillar that abuts the steep base of the slab.
1 120 feet. Climb up the right side of the pillar. Move boldly up using flat holds, stepping left and back right, until the angle eases and runners appear. Continue up the easy slab, trending slightly left, and use a crack to the left of a bay to reach a belay ledge.
2 80 feet. Go up easily to the left and climb a steep nose to the left of overhangs to reach a grassy bay, which is exited via rock to its right. Belay to the abseil rope.

Bossiney Haven

OS Ref 065 896

Approach from the Bossiney Haven beach car-park (public toilet and phone). Take the beach path until it crosses the coast path. Turn left steeply downhill on the latter and then wind up between crags to a cliff-top field. Follow the edge of the field to its lowest point, where a faint fisherman's path winds down to the top of the buttress that forms the southern edge of Lye Rock bay.

Elephant Rock

A prominent flying buttress at sea-level and a popular postcard subject. Pegs (removed) were used on pitch 2 on the first ascent.

Elephantitis 120 feet Extremely Severe (6.8.82)
The obvious chimney/crack in the landward face.
1 60 feet. Climb the chimney to a stance where it widens just before closing completely

2 60 feet 5b. Surmount the overhang and trend right for 25 feet before moving back horizontally left for 15 feet to enter the jungle of the cliff-top.

Bossiney Haven Buttress

The routes take the north-east-facing buttress, which contains a large sea-cave. The start of the first is reached directly by abseil.

Open Claw 60 feet E4 6a † (6.7.97)
Left of the cave, there is a peculiar gash shaped rather like an open claw in a projecting roof at the top of the crag. At low-to-mid tide, climb a steep undercut crack in a horizontally-striated face to beneath a sharp rock lip. Overcome this athletically on its right and so gain a ledge underneath the gash. Pull steeply up to the roof and exit by a spectacular move through the gash.

The next three routes are best climbed solo at high tide: fun outings in a magnificent position. Descent is simplest is by a 60-foot abseil down the Lye Rock side of the buttress. Abseil and belay stake *in situ*; it can be backed up if a spare rope is used. A belay can be taken on the right edge of the buttress on a big ledge.

Kill 90 feet Hard Severe 4b † (6.7.97)
A dramatic little line. From the foot of *Rick*, traverse horizontally left to a sharply projecting ledge. Move up to a quartz rail, bear left, and then traverse the very lip of the cave roof horizontally leftwards to finish immediately right of a crack.

Pat 80 feet Severe † (7.9.89)
From the belay, swing left onto a foot-ledge on the face of the buttress. Trend up and left at about one-third height to take the easiest line and keep just above the lip of the sea-cave.

Rick 60 feet Severe 4a † (6.7.97)
The handsome right-angled arête facing Lye Rock.

Lye Rock

OS Ref 064 897

The routes are found on the seriously tidal cliff above the boulder-choke connecting Lye Rock to the mainland. Descent is a little to the north-east of the south-east (right-hand) arête. Walk across grass to the rocky promontory in the middle of the upper section of the south-east slope. Now descend steep grass southwards for 50 feet to a 60-foot abseil. Traverse left to the boulder-choke – with difficulty dependent upon tidal conditions.

☆**Bird Brain** 380 feet Extremely Severe † (17.4.82)
A bold and impressive route up the most obvious line on the face and finishing up the prominent orange flake. Start from the extreme left edge of the boulder-choke.
1 100 feet 5a. Traverse horizontally left for 80 feet to an overhanging crack, which is climbed to a stance.
2 120 feet 5b. Climb the overhanging flake above until it ends (peg); then move rightwards up a discontinuous crack to a good ledge in the centre of the wall.
3 120 feet 5b. Go diagonally left on the obvious line, and break through the overhangs (peg) to reach the base of the prominent flake crack. Climb this, which becomes a chimney, and move precariously left over the top of the pinnacle to climb to a stance just below the top. A peg is advisable in the wall behind the pinnacle in case the latter's top falls off.
4 40 feet 4b. Climb directly through the overhang in the corner to reach the top.
Variation
No Brain E4 (6.7.97)
1a 100 feet 5a/b. A worthwhile higher-tide start. From the left-hand side of the boulder-choke, follow the obvious right-to-left ramp-line to its end. Place a couple (or more) poor pegs; then go up the wall above on quite good holds to belay (nuts) two-thirds way up pitch 2 of the main route.

☆**Under Pressure** 150 feet Extremely Severe † (10.4.82)
An obvious rising traverse-line leads up right beneath the huge roofs. Start from the right-hand side of the boulder-choke.
1 120 feet 5c. Traverse right, easy at first, to a difficult step round an edge to a very smooth slab (two pegs). Continue with difficulty along the same line to a stance at the obvious thin crack.
2 30 feet 5a. Step down from the belay and traverse across to the arête, after which a few steep moves up lead to grass.

Willapark Cliff

OS Ref 061 897

An extremely steep cliff with very loose rock. Walk out from Bossiney Haven and turn west on the coast path across the headland. Descend steepening grass slopes and a rock step to boulders, and cross these back to the north-east. At low tide, 200 feet of straightforward climbing, left and up, then leads to the foot of *King Arthur's Crack*. At half tide the traverse is at a higher level with moves of 4b.

★**King Arthur's Crack** 250 feet Hard Very Severe (11.5.80)
Left of centre of the crag the most obvious feature is a straight chimney/crack, easily visible from the descent, giving the line of the route.
1 100 feet 5a. Climb the crack to a good stance in a shallow cave, 15 feet below where it finishes in an overhang. Thread belay.

2 60 feet 5a. Move diagonally right up the steep wall and trend left to a grass ledge.
3 90 feet 4a. Continue diagonally left to finish at a block on the skyline.
Direct Finish
3a 90 feet 5a (4.90). Instead of trending left, climb straight up the wall to finish up a short overhanging crack. Not as loose as appearance would suggest.

★★Cockney Disorder 280 feet Extremely Severe (2.6.84)
Right of *King Arthur's Crack* is an overhanging groove and a smooth wall. Start on the slabby area of rock beneath *King Arthur's Crack*.
1 30 feet. Climb up to a stance on the right wall of the shallow depression above.
2 70 feet 5b. Step left from the stance and climb, trending slightly right, to the foot of the groove (good nut runner). Pull over the overhang to enter the groove, which gives sustained climbing until a rightwards traverse is possible for 10 feet to a stance and peg belays.
3 60 feet 5b. Climb directly above the stance to reach the obvious groove in the smooth wall. Follow this to an easing of the angle, and transfer to a line 10 feet to the right, which leads to a good stance.
4 120 feet 4c. Move diagonally right beneath the overlap to easier ground leading back leftwards to the top.

Seal Appeal 380 feet Extremely Severe † (10.4.82)
1 30 feet. *Cockney Disorder* pitch 1.
2 100 feet 5b. Traverse horizontally right round the arête to gain a traverse-line between overhangs. Follow this (peg) to an awkward swing round a corner. Cross dubious blocks to reach a good stance.
3 50 feet 4c. Move up right to a ledge, surmount an overhang, and trend slightly left on the wall above to reach a stance.
4 80 feet 5b. Climb the overhanging corner above the right end of the ledge to reach a slabby area. Move left to the arête and up and around it before traversing left to a stance at the base of a crack/overlap.
5 120 feet 4b. Climb the overlap and slab above, trending right to easier ground, which leads back left to the top.

Tintagel Head

OS Ref 048 892

This is a magnificent windswept headland, complete with the stark remains of a medieval settlement, notorious for the part it plays in the endless exploitation of Arthurian Legend. English Heritage and the BMC have negotiated an access agreement to the cliffs (please refer to the details of this on page 15). It is most important that no damage is done to the fabric of the medieval ruins. In addition, there is evidence of ancient field terrace-systems

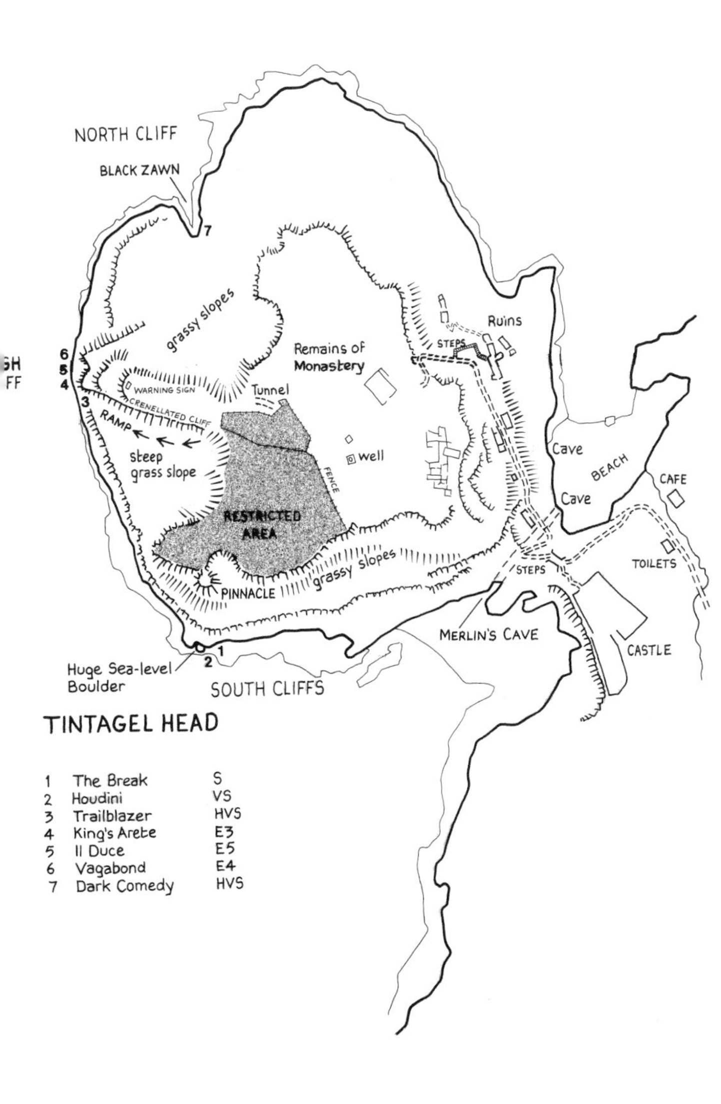
NORTH CLIFF
BLACK ZAWN
7
grassy slopes
Ruins
STEPS
Remains of
Monastery
6
5
4
3
WARNING SIGN
Tunnel
CRENELLATED CLIFF
RAMP
steep
grass slope
well
FENCE
Cave
BEACH
CAFE
Cave
RESTRICTED
AREA
grassy slopes
STEPS
TOILETS
PINNACLE
MERLIN'S CAVE
CASTLE
1
2
Huge Sea-level
Boulder
SOUTH CLIFFS
TINTAGEL HEAD
1 The Break S
2 Houdini VS
3 Trailblazer HVS
4 King's Arete E3
5 Il Duce E5
6 Vagabond E4
7 Dark Comedy HVS

on the slopes between High and South Cliffs. These field-systems should be avoided as far as is possible (see map).

The seaward point of the headland is known as The Island, by virtue of a narrow gulf spanned by a wooden bridge. The routes lie on the cliffs forming the west side of the headland. These are in three sections known as North, High, and South Cliffs, of which High Cliff is far and away the most impressive, containing one of the South West's most powerful and inspiring lines, that of *Il Duce*. Once on the cliffs you are in a climber's Camelot, a wonderland of vertical, towering slate-gardens, of dreamtime routes and stunning lines. The area is surprisingly dry. North Cliff receives sun in the late afternoon, and the *Il Duce* area is intensely arid on hot summer days; water is a recommendation for your rack. The rock is sound and the tide does not affect the cliffs, but high seas can render the starts a little more exciting and, of course, wet.

The nature of the cliff-top makes identification of the different crags difficult, though an obvious feature is the pinnacle above South Cliff adjoining the hillside.

North Cliff

Towards the north of the headland, grass slopes lead down to terraces above sea-level. Follow these to reach a black zawn. The original entry involved lassoing pegs (placed in 1972 and now gone) at the foot of a slabby ramp from the lowest of the ledges on the south-west side and making a Tyrolean traverse to reach nut belays. Nowadays, traverse above the far wall and abseil in.

Dark Comedy 90 feet Hard Very Severe 5a † (9.9.72)
A serious route on small holds and with minimal protection. The abseil approach leads directly to its start. Step up right and climb to a ledge. Traverse right for 40 feet to the blunt nose of a buttress. Climb this to a short corner, which leads to the top.

Extending south-west from the black zawn is a series of 80-to-90-foot-high walls, interrupted by corners and striking arêtes. Bear leftwards across the grass mentioned above to intercept the north end of a ledge-system. This leads, after an initial bold step at the top of the corner of *Astroslide*, to a commodious terrace – Dinnerplate Terrace, from where the climbs are approached by abseil. All routes commence from large sloping ledges 15 to 20 feet above high-water mark. The rock is flawless, although it rapidly becomes greasy in damp conditions. If you come here to do only *Il Duce* you will be passing by some very worthwhile climbing.

★**A Weekend on Mars** 150 feet E3 5c (5.7.97)
Fine climbing. Start as for *Astroslide*. Climb a line of weakness and reach the foot of a slight groove at 12 feet. Swing right to a ragged crystalline crack and follow it past a ledge into an unmistakable triangular niche.

Climb the crack leftwards out of a niche to a good thread on the arête. Finish up the crack in the right-hand side of the arête.

☆**Astroslide** 130 feet E3 5c † (31.7.94)
Destined to become a Cornish classic? Abseil from a good thread and big hex 15 feet left of the bold step. From the right-hand end of the ledge, climb diagonally rightwards on the edge of the abyss to foot-ledges on the left arête of an obvious tapering groove above the roofs. Climb the black wall just left of the groove to a good break. Step right, surmount the roof, and continue direct up the steep slab (thread runner) to another wide break. Step right and finish up the corner.

☆**Overkeel** 80 feet E5 6b † (30.7.94)
The staggering overhanging arête which forms the right-hand edge of the wall of the black corner. Abseil from the terrace 30 feet south of the arête (as for the next three routes). Walk to the left end of the ledges. Grovel up the corner to an outward-sloping shelf. Traverse leftwards to good holds around the arête; then go straight up to a flake (thread runner) and a rest above. Innovate rightwards up the arête and finish over the right-hand side of a small capping roof.

The loss of a large block beneath the roof has removed two routes: **Pengenna Pie** took a central line up the undercut wall to the right of *Overkeel*; and **Seadogger**, the open, rightward-slanting groove (both 70 feet E4 6b †† 30.7.94).

☆☆**Wicked Gravity** 70 feet E4 6a † (18.7.94)
Climb the central, left-facing groove to the right of *Seadogger*. Fine varied climbing and one thread runner.

☆☆**Chancelot** 70 feet E5 6a † (31.7.94)
Bold and exacting climbing on the right-hand arête of *Wicked Gravity*. Abseil to a big ledge in an alcove, 70 feet right of *Overkeel*. Belay on a huge thread and take a stance at the left-hand end of the ledge, beneath a short left-facing corner. Ascend this for 10 feet and cross leftwards to reach the arête (thread runner). Step up to a ledge, reach right around the arête, and boldly gain better holds and a thread runner. Continue up (peg); then take the right-hand side of the arête to finish on frayed nerves and withered arms.

☆☆**One Stood against Many** 80 feet E5 6a † (18.7.94)
A brilliant face route finding an intricate path up the black west-facing wall left of the large corner. Belay on the huge thread. Follow a series of right-facing holds and step up left onto a projecting foot-ledge. Move up for 10 feet and traverse left to a good side-jug. Continue direct with limited protection to a flake, swing right, and finish up a shallow groove.

☆**Knights of the Intriguing Niche** 70 feet E4 5c † (30.7.94)
A line to the right of *One Stood against Many* with intriguing features and a worrying upper wall. Follow the ragged crack into the niche and pull out to reach a good ledge (thread runner). Take the groove above to a roof. Step left (crucial *Friend 1½*); then bear slightly rightwards on improving, threadable holds.

☆**Legend Has It** 100 feet E2 5c † (31.7.94)
The prominent large corner just before the cliff swings around the arête to High Cliff. Climb the lower corner rightwards to ledges below the main corner. Straightforward at first; then tricky moves lead rightwards below the capping roof near the top. Pull over on good holds to a belay. Traverse left to gain the terrace.

☆**Frank's Crack** 90 feet E2 5b † (31.7.94)
Climb as for *Frank's Corner* to the ledges. In between the capping roof of *Legend Has It* and the corner of *Frank's Corner* is a crack leading to a curving groove. Gain this to reach the top.

☆☆**Frank's Corner** 90 feet E3 5c † (31.7.94)
Climb the slim groove to the right of *Legend Has It* to reach the ledges below the main corner. Step left and follow the left-leaning corner to the top.

☆☆☆**Gypsy Queen** 140 feet E6 † (18.7.94)
The compelling left-hand arête of High Cliff. Approach as for *Chancelot* etc.
1 40 feet 4a. From the ledge, traverse right to a sloping black ledge below the undercut arête.
2 60 feet 6b. Somehow gain entry to the groove piercing the arête, and reach a good crack in the face above. Climb direct (peg on right); then improvise to get wrapped around the arête and reach a rest and thread runner above. Move right across a small roof to reach a short crack leading to a swing left, and belay on a sloping ledge.
3 40 feet 5c. Go diagonally right to a pocketed crack and climb the overhanging wall to exit left to ledges. Belay, and then traverse left to Dinnerplate Terrace.

High Cliff

In contrast with most of the other cliffs on this coast, first impressions of its spectacular nature can be gained only by committing oneself to a route. Between the pinnacle above South Cliff and the highest point of the headland, descend grassy slopes until it is possible to walk north to gain a sloping ramp leading beneath a huge vertical wall rimmed by strange horizontal serrations. The corner of *Il Duce* lies beyond this wall, out of sight to the north.

Note: the first five routes are reached via the traverse comprising pitch 1 of *Il Duce*: start at the toe of the ramp, step down, and traverse left to a spacious stance beneath the roofs at the base of the main groove (60 feet 5a).

☆**Isle of Avalon** 130 feet E5 6b † (17.5.92)
In the same class as *Vagabond* but direct and harder. Start as for *Vagabond*.
1 60 feet 6b. Move up and leftwards to the foot of the short groove of *Vagabond*. Move left again and make a hard move up the rib to reach a good crack and a rest on the left. Climb the crack to some pockets for large cam placements; then launch strenuously up the wall on their left to better holds and the *Vagabond* belay ledge.
2 70 feet 5c. Climb the crack behind the stance, swing right into its continuation, and follow it to a good ledge. Finish carefully up the short but intimidating, leaning wall above. Scramble off to the left across Dinnerplate Terrace.

★**Vagabond** 280 feet E4 (26.5.78)
One of the original trio of routes centred on the *Il Duce* groove, finding the easiest (!) path up the wall and overhangs to the left of the groove. It is an excellent route on good rock. Start 30 feet left of *Il Duce* pitch 2, at the left-hand end of the ledge.
1 60 feet 5c. Climb up left to a small groove leading through the first overhangs. Follow the groove until it closes (peg); then move up and diagonally rightwards to reach a narrow ledge. Trend back left to another ledge. Nut belays.
2 60 feet 5c. Follow a diagonal line to the right to a slanting overlap. Climb beneath this, and where it ends make difficult moves left to a ledge. Follow the ledge rightwards over a short step to a good stance.
3 80 feet 5a. Climb the corner behind the stance to the overhangs, step right onto the rib, and move up again to a ledge, which leads rightwards to the third stance of *Il Duce*.
4 80 feet 4c. Climb the crack above and finish as for *Il Duce*.
Variation
2a (10.6.90). Instead of moving right to the overlap, climb straight up broken cracklines to gain the left-hand end of the ledge; then continue as for *Vagabond*.

☆☆**Ocean Colour Dream** 190 feet E6 6a † (17.5.92)
A major route with a demanding start and splendid but serious face-climbing on the wall immediately left of *Il Duce*. Start 20 feet left of *Il Duce* pitch 2, beneath a corner leading up to the big roof.
1 40 feet 6b. Place some good gear in the corner, and then make a very difficult traverse leftwards across the lip of the roof (two pegs) until bold and pumpy moves up the short leaning arête lead to a good ledge on the right. Wires, *Friend* ½ and 1, and a thread above the left-hand end of the ledge are needed for the belay.
2 70 feet 6a. Climb the awkward and unprotected wall behind the belay to reach jugs and a fine runner-slot after 20 feet. Follow the intermittent crack-system above, twice side-stepping right, until a runout and a final reachy move gain the right-hand end of the *Vagabond* belay ledge. Innovation is required to protect this pitch: two *Friend* 3s will be of use and

there is a good thread (for a pull-through wire placement) at about 40 feet.
3 80 feet 4c. *Vagabond* pitch 4.

★★★**Il Duce** 260 feet E5 (23.4.72/1980)
[Photo p.224a.] An outstanding route, which takes the impressive, though hidden groove up the highest point of the cliff. In stark contrast with the milling crowds above, the climb has a distinct air of seriousness and remoteness, particularly in its middle reaches; and it is still well worth E5, given that the original pegs are now long gone. Start at the toe of the ramp.
1 60 feet 5a. Step down and traverse left before swinging left onto the large ledges below the overhangs guarding the entry to the main groove.
2 60 feet 6a. Climb the right-hand of two converging cracks, with increasing difficulty and limited protection, to holds beneath the overhang. A series of bold moves to the left gains a short chimney on the lip of the roof. From its top, difficult climbing leads up and left across the wall to a stance and a peg belay at the base of the groove.
3 60 feet 5c. Small positive holds in the groove provide encouragement for the first 40 feet, above which the rock becomes bulging. Hard moves around the left side of the bulges allow good ledges above to be reached. Peg and nut belays.
4 80 feet 4c. Climb the crack on the right and move left into the groove, which is followed to a thread below the roof. Move right and stroll across the huge flake to an obvious break, which leads to the top.

☆☆**Faschisti** 180 feet E5 6b † (17.5.92)
A thrilling pitch up the right-hand arête of the *Il Duce* corner. (*King's Arête* keeps mostly right of the arête). Difficulties are unrelenting and the protection is sparse, awkward to find, and then of only marginal security. Start as for *Il Duce* pitch 2.
1 130 feet 6a. From the thread 10 feet up the *Il Duce* crack, swing right and climb boldly to get established on the sloping projecting nose from its left. Pull up right to a small ledge (thread runner on *King's Arête*) and then traverse leftwards across the lip of the roof (above *Il Duce*) to a crack-system near the arête. Follow the crack to a good jug and resting-place after 20 feet. Move up again (poor thread); then bear leftwards up a technical shallow groove (hidden poor peg) to pull over a small roof onto a good ledge. Climb up to a good crack and follow this, as for *King's Arête*, to the belay niche.
2 50 feet 5a. Above the stance is a bulge, which is passed on the right. Move up and right to the obvious crack, which leads to the exit of *Il Duce*.

★★**King's Arête** 250 feet E3 (3.7.82)
A spectacular route based on the right arête of *Il Duce*. Start at the toe of the ramp.
1 30 feet 5a. Follow the obvious leftward traverse-line of *Il Duce* as far as the projecting ledge.
2 60 feet 5c. Climb direct above the ledge for 20 feet and move left to gain the arête, which is followed over a bulge to a narrow ledge leading

right. Stance and peg belay at the right-hand end of the ledge.
3 80 feet 5b. Trend diagonally left from the belay to rejoin the arête and follow this, eventually gaining a short steep crack on the right-hand side, which leads to a stance in the niche. Peg belay. (Pitches 3 and 4 can be run together to avoid using the peg belay.)
4 80 feet 5b. Avoid the overhang above on its right; then move back left to the arête and go up to reach the huge flake on *Il Duce*. Finish up the break on the right.
Variation
1a The Republican Start E2 5b (1997). From the toe of the ramp, follow a line of flakes up and left for 30 feet; then make a rising leftwards traverse to reach the belay at the end of pitch 2. Good but poorly protected.

Trailblazer 240 feet Hard Very Severe (16.4.71)
Compared with the preceding routes this line up the huge wall is disappointing, and protection is not always readily available. However, the situations are good. Start at the toe of the ramp.
1 120 feet 4c. Move left onto the wall and bear left to a flat, narrow ledge. From its left end, climb to an obvious sidehold and continue to a larger ledge. Go up to a good crack (peg); then traverse right to another ledge, from which a short corner on the right can be reached. Climb the corner and the rock above to a terrace and nut belays.
2 120 feet. Move right and wander up past various ledges to the top.

Travelling Man 300 feet E4 (9.6.90)
A good traverse of High Cliff. Start as for *Trailblazer*, at the toe of the ramp.
1 60 feet 5b. Climb diagonally leftwards to a narrow flat ledge, and then move up and left to gain a crack leading to the right-hand end of the *King's Arête* belay ledge. Peg and nut belays.
2 40 feet 5c. Climb for 10 feet; then traverse left and move around the arête to gain the corner of *Il Duce*. Step down to belay as for *Il Duce*.
3 80 feet 5c. Step down and traverse left for about 15 feet to a good sidepull. Climb up and left via a rightward-slanting diagonal crack to gain the overlap on *Vagabond* pitch 4. Climb the wall above to gain a ledge (as for *Vagabond*); then traverse left across a wall to gain the obvious spiky ledge on the arête.
4 120 feet 4c. Climb the rightward-slanting grooves to finish above the corner of *Il Duce*.

☆☆**Pathfinder** 340 feet E5 † (5.7.97)
An improved version of the *Travelling Man* line with two trying additional pitches that extend the traverse across North Cliff. If these are omitted in favour of a finish up *Frank's Corner*, the most amenable Extreme (with *King's Arête*) on High Cliff results.
1 60 feet 5b. *Travelling Man* pitch 1.
2 40 feet 5b. Traverse left across the lip of the roof on *Faschisti*, and move up its crack to regain the original.
3 80 feet 5c. Climb diagonally down left from the *Il Duce* belay for 10

feet (tricky). Traverse horizontally left on generally superb holds, across *Vagabond*, to a sloping overhung niche on the far arête (belay of *Gypsy Queen*).
4 40 feet 5a. From the left side of the niche, swing down on a good thread hold; then proceed easily leftwards, descending a little, to a good belay immediately right of the roofed corner of *Frank's Corner*. Either finish up this or change gear for pitch 5.
5 50 feet 6a. Traverse strenuously left just above *Knights of the Intriguing Niche* to its flat hand-ledge on the left. Continue left into the middle of the black face and make a few moves down *One Stood against Many*. Reach left to the arête of *Chancelot* and with protection from its *in-situ* thread (back-rope for second vital) reverse one of its cruxes to reach the thread belay.
6 70 feet 6a. Move up the corner of *Wicked Gravity* for 10 feet to a point just short of its *in-situ* thread (*Friend 0* nice to have). From a reasonable hold on the left wall, traverse left to pockets and an *in-situ* thread on *Pengenna Pie*. Move down leftwards and across beneath the foot of the black face to a position 6 feet short of the terminal arête (*Overkeel*). Finish daringly up a line of positive holds in the wall just to the right of the arête. A superbly located and committing lead.

South Cliff

The following two routes lie on the cliff below the obvious pinnacle attached to the grassy hillside. Abseil down the cliff beneath the pinnacle to a huge boulder.

Houdini 90 feet Very Severe 4c (1 pt aid) † (8.9.72)
Climb the corner behind the right-hand side of the boulder, approached via a chimney.

The Break 80 feet Severe (8.9.72)
This is the next groove to the right of the corner. Climb it to a ledge and from there to the top.

Dunderhole Point

OS Ref 046 881

This is the small blunt promontory south of Tintagel Head, and the following routes are on the cliff between the Youth Hostel and the actual point. Descent for *Bandstand* is by abseil down an obvious corner on the north side of the crag to large ledges 30 feet above the sea. For *Silver Lining*, abseil (at low tide) straight down the buttress to sea-level ledges below and to the right of The Bandstand; then scramble up to another ledge beneath a prominent left-facing corner.

★Bandstand 170 feet E2 (27.4.74)
A good route with superb stances, especially the second, which could easily accommodate an entire brass section.
1 40 feet 4c. From the end of the ledges, traverse right to the seaward face and continue to a good stance below the corner. Belay on cams in the boreholes.
2 40 feet 4c. Climb the corner to The Bandstand. Good nut belays at its right-hand end.
3 40 feet 4c. Move right for a few feet to a groove with a good crack, which is climbed to another large ledge.
4 50 feet 5b. Climb the steep wall into a shallow groove leading to a ledge. Climb more easily to the top.

☆Silver Lining 170 feet E2 † (8.4.85)
Similar in style to *Bandstand* but without its fine stances.
1 60 feet 4c. Climb the corner and exit right to a scoop. Peg belays.
2 60 feet 5b. Pull out rightwards onto a ledge and climb easily to a steep wall below a right-slanting break. Climb the wall, using the break where necessary, until the ledge on the right is reached. Small nut belays at the right-hand end.
3 50 feet 5a. Climb diagonally right for 20 feet; then break left and continue up the final wall on excellent holds. Belay to the rock outcrop on top of the point.

Trebarwith Quarries OS Ref 051 870

From the village of Trebarwith Strand, follow the coast path north for 500 yards to reach the quarries.

Cornish quarried slate is, in general, much more suited to roofing than to climbing, and the rock here is no exception. However, there is a shapely pinnacle boasting two routes which share the feature of a highly unusual descent: the see-saw abseil is yet another example of the extraordinary, which ensures that Cornish climbing is never dull. The ground rules are simple:
- ropes should be placed on opposite sides of the pinnacle;
- absolute trust in one's partner is essential;
- if body weights are disparate, arrange suitable extra ballast;
- the first person to reach the ground should resist any impulse to untie and walk away.

Non-observance of these rules is likely to be painful and may place friendship under strain.

★Udolpho 80 feet E1 5a (15.9.73)
A good but serious climb. Extra pegs should be carried. Start at the left-hand side of the landward face of the pinnacle. Climb a short wall;

then bear left around a pillar to the groove formed by its left edge. Continue to the foot of the overhanging corner (large hex or poor peg). Climb the corner to ledges leading to the summit (where the fun begins).

★Carbonek 120 feet E2 (27.10.73)
A fine line on the seaward face of the pinnacle. Protection is sparse. Start at the pillar which abuts the face.
1 50 feet 4c. Climb the face of the pillar by its right-hand side (peg at 20 feet) to a good stance on top.
2 70 feet 5a. Go up to a ledge on the arête (poor peg) and continue up the face to a sloping ledge. Step right past a peg into the groove and pull around the overhang to easier ground and the summit. Belay by looping the rope around the summit prow and, before descending, read the paragraph above!

★★Trebarwith Strand to Backways Cove Coastal Traverse
2000 feet approx. E1/2 (15.9.73)
One of the best sea traverses in the South West. A serious expedition requiring favourable tide and sea conditions and competence in the variety of manoeuvres which are typical of such enterprises. The first eight pitches are described in detail; thereafter the climbing becomes more serious and less enjoyable. OS Ref 047 862 to 044 860. Start about 2½ hours before low tide and allow the maximum amount of daylight.
1,2 300 feet 4b. Follow a line near sea-level across the sandy floor of a cove to the obvious rocky promontory.
3,4,5 200 feet 5a. Continue right around a nose, go up a leaning wall, and belay on the left of a slab. Climb round an arête and take the easy ledge-system to the edge of a deep zawn. Climb up to a block with a thread then descend and swing boldly across the zawn to a good ledge on the far side. Pull the second across and retrieve as much gear as possible.
6,7 190 feet 4c. Climb up and right onto the face of the zawn, which is traversed strenuously to the arête and round to the seaward face. Continue rightwards, heading for an obvious corner and nose of rock; then follow the large ledges to a huge sea cave. An escape of Difficult to Very Difficult can be made from here if necessary.
8 Traverse into the back of the cave and then out again. Continue along the lines of least resistance to another large zawn, which, according to the second party to complete the route, necessitates a swim.
After this, interest is maintained past many different obstacles until Backways Cove is reached.

Backways Cove

OS Ref 044 859

[Photo reverse frontispiece.] This is the next cove south of Trebarwith Strand, reached by a pleasant walk from Trebarwith (OS Ref 056 860). The south side of the cove is slabby, whilst the north contains an impressive box zawn with two striking corners. Low tide is necessary to reach the routes.

Fever 80 feet Hard Very Severe 5a (15.9.73)
A line up the left-hand side of the orange-coloured seaward face. Start beneath it, at a groove. Climb the groove and the line of flakes above; then move right onto the wall proper via a smooth narrow ramp. Move up and right, then back left to a spike near the arête. Peg and nut belays; then scrambling to finish.

Snakebite 150 feet E2 (1974)
Not to be underestimated. The rock deteriorates alarmingly near the top of the first pitch, and the pinnacle is none too firm. Start at the foot of the right-hand groove in the face.
1 75 feet 5a. Climb up to an overhang and move round beneath it to the right. Step right and go up a steep wall to a ledge.
2 75 feet 4c. Climb up, preferably without heavy breathing, to the pinnacle on the arête; then continue up the chimney behind, definitely without heavy breathing, to a peg on the arête. Move right in an exposed position and resume normal respiration.

The Obelisk 70 feet Very Severe 4c (15.9.73)
This is the obvious square-cut pinnacle on the north-east side of the cove. All the faces are sheer. Start at the foot of the north-east face. Climb the centre of the face for 40 feet (peg). Move out to the seaward arête and climb this to the top; the final section is loose.

The next four routes are in the box zawn, which is, in fact, an old quarry.

☆**Back to the Old Ways** 130 feet E3 5b † (13.5.95)
The seaward corner requires many small wires and a steady approach. Climb the slabby wall just left of the corner; then continue up the corner with occasional excursions onto the left wall.

☆☆**The Strangest Secret** 150 feet E6 6a † (6.90)
Continuous bold and difficult climbing, with the crux right at the top. Start in the centre of the backwall, on a pedestal just left of the huge blowhole. Climb a quartz vein to an overlap (peg) and move right to a sickle-shaped groove (peg). Climb the edge of the groove to a slot, then boldly to cracks 20 feet above. Traverse diagonally left on sloping holds for 20 feet to a niche (peg and spike). Go direct (peg out left) to the red headwall (shallow *Friend 3*) and up to a further peg just beyond the crux. Move left and up to finish up an easy wall.

☆**North Coast Fever** 130 feet E4 5c † (1.7.95)
Start 30 feet right of *The Strangest Secret* and climb a series of short walls and ledges for 50 feet (with no protection) to a short groove (wires) and a crystal bulge. Move left around the bulge (crux), then up to better holds and a peg out right. Finish direct.

☆**Bend Over Backways** 120 feet E3 6a † (2.7.95)
Start on the right-hand side of the landward arête of the zawn. Climb up and move left around the arête at 25 feet (crux); then continue directly up the arête on better holds to finish.

On closer acquaintance, the seemingly impressive slabs on the south side of the cove prove to be disappointing.

Ahab 190 feet Severe (17.4.71)
Start at the right-hand end of the large blowhole.
1 40 feet. Climb the slab, bearing right to a terrace and peg belay.
2 150 feet. Climb for 50 feet to a peg. Traverse right and continue to another peg near a grassy area. Care is needed at the top, possibly owing to the fact that the final belay is around an anthill.

Baha 170 feet Hard Severe † (7.83)
Start 30 feet right of the blowhole.
1 70 feet 4a. Climb up, bearing left to a ledge (peg belay).
2 100 feet. Move up and right; then traverse right to a scoop. Climb this by its right edge and move right again to reach a short groove, which is followed to finish. Belay well back on grassy ledges.

Lobber Point

OS Ref 994 812

A small headland of pillow lava. From the harbour in Port Isaac, follow the footpath north into a field. Climb over a wall onto the headland and descend to a platform, from where it is possible to look back into the harbour. Just to the west is a dark slab of solid rock. Low-tide access only: scramble across the slab or abseil in.

Alice 75 feet Very Difficult (27.9.86)
Climb the right edge of the slab and make an awkward move left across the wall. Continue up the left corner to the top. Stake and nut belays well back.

Scarnor Point

OS Ref 978 512

Approach via the coast path from Port Quin or Port Isaac until the headland is reached. Go directly down grass to the tip of Scarnor Point.

The Point is made of pillow lava (spilite), in common with its bigger neighbours, Kellan Head and Pentire. The crag faces north-west, and it is approximately

Il Duce (E5) Tintagel Head
Climbers: Dave Turnbull and Dave Scott-Maxwell Photo: Nick Hancock

Rock-a-Bye-Baby (E3) Kellan Head
Climber: Dave Henderson Photo: Ian Parnell

80 feet high from the ledges at its base, which are above high-tide level (but not the swell). At the west end is a massive overhang that takes a bite out of the headland and is clearly visible from the coast path at Kellan Head. In Downgate Cove, just to the south, are two massive boulders that must be the remains of the cliff's face.

The topography is as follows. On the left (facing the cliff) are the descent walls and ramps with a diamond-shaped wall on their right and overhangs to the right of this wall. To the right again is a wall with a steep corner on its right. Further right, a loose-looking buttress bristles with overhangs, and then steps back to give a short wall terminated by a steep corner-crack above the zawn, where massive overhangs fall away into the sea.

An abseil can be made down the ramps and walls on the left to reach the base of the diamond-shaped wall.

Polymorphus Pervert 90 feet Hard Very Severe 4c † (5.7.92)
Harder and more perverse than it looks, it takes the black, diamond-shaped wall by its right edge. Scramble easily up to the base of a crack formed by the overhang and the right edge of the wall. Move up to a very cramped niche, where a step left enables moves to be made up to the left edge of the overhang. From here, bridge up into a bottomless groove, and pull round to the left to reach easier ground; then climb direct to the top.

Pilot Hotel 100 feet Very Severe 4c † (26.9.92)
This takes the obvious line of weakness between *Polymorphus Pervert* and *Spacewalker*. Start at the left side of the loose-looking buttress bristling with overhangs. Step up to the obvious, rising, right-hand traverse-crack below the overhangs, and jam along this to the top of the steep wall. Here, climb up a crack and a steep faulted wall to reach a beak-like pedestal from its right-hand side. The short wall above is very loose, but a step up and left brings you out on top of the buttress.

Spacewalker 100 feet Severe 4a † (5.7.92)
This takes the extreme right-hand edge of the cliff. Climb the immaculate corner-crack at the right-hand end of the cliff until a traverse right can be made across the wall to a big ledge on the lip of the overhang. Go up the groove above, and trend right to the arête until below the final wall. Step back left and climb to the top. Belay well back on a bluff of rock above.

Kellan Head

OS Ref 969 811

This is the northernmost of the two headlands enclosing the narrow inlet of Port Quin, and, like its counterpart Doyden Point, is an excellent steep crag of

PADSTOW AREA

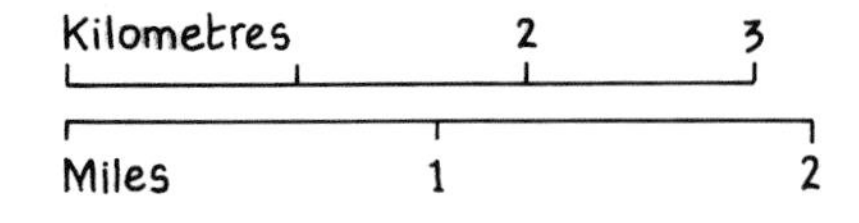

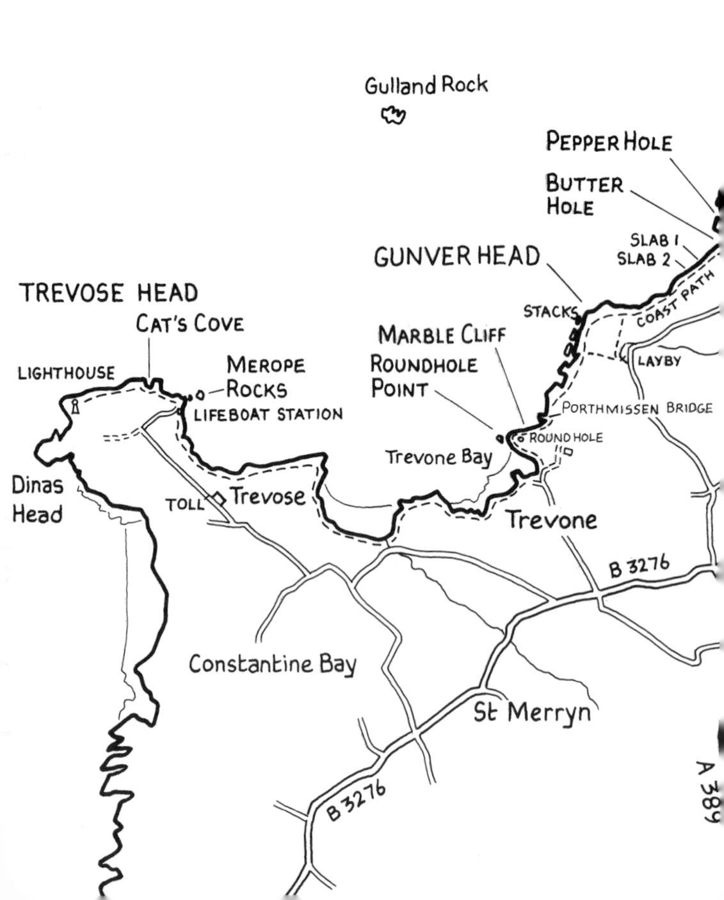

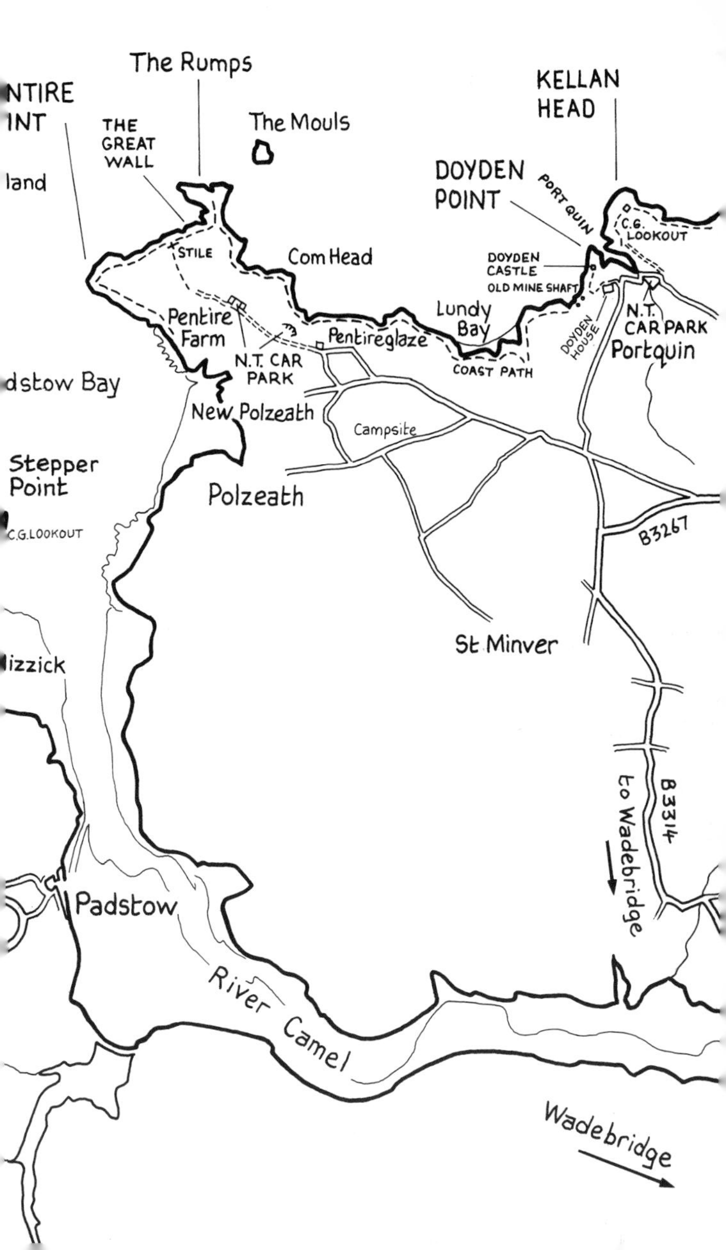

The Rumps
NTIRE
INT
THE
GREAT
WALL
The Mouls
KELLAN
HEAD
DOYDEN
POINT
PORT QUIN
land
C.G.
LOOKOUT
STILE
Com Head
DOYDEN
CASTLE
OLD MINE SHAFT
Pentire
Farm
Lundy
Bay
DOYDEN
HOUSE
N.T.
CAR PARK
Pentireglaze
Portquin
N.T. CAR
PARK
COAST PATH
dstow Bay
New Polzeath
Campsite
Stepper
Point
Polzeath
C.G.LOOKOUT
B3267
St Minver
izzick
to Wadebridge
B3314
Padstow
River
Camel
Wadebridge

pillow lava. The upper section of Waterslide Wall is a diminutive version of its illustrious neighbour, The Great Wall at Pentire, and provides an interesting introduction to the type of climbing found on *Eroica* or *Darkinbad the Brightdayler*.

There is a National Trust car-park at Portquin, from where the coast path is followed to the north alongside an intrusive post-and-rail fence. Shortly after the path makes a turn to the north it runs along the top of the large, easy-angled Kellan Slab with its conspicuous undercut base. Seventy-five yards beyond, the path starts to climb steeply. Contour across grass slopes to an easy-angled ramp leading down beneath a very steep grey wall, again with an undercut base. This is Waterslide Wall, and the ramp ends at a wet corner carpeted with bright green algae. A large, flat-topped pillar defines the left end of the wall, and a ledge-system leads across the pillar about 40 feet up above the sea, starting at the same level as the base of a short vertical step in the waterslide. These ledges allow access, after a tricky start, to the seaward face of the pillar and the aptly-named Hidden Amphitheatre beyond, the central feature of which is a large triangular slab topped by an extremely impressive sloping roof on the left and an impending headwall on the right. Beyond the slab are a steep face with a groove-line just left of the roof and a wall split by a number of deep cracks. All the routes start well above the high-water mark though, as is the case with most crags on this coast, not necessarily above the reach of the waves.

Immediately after Port Quin harbour is left, a buttress of orange rock is encountered.

The Mighty Quin 80 feet E2 5b † (9.89)
An impressive, serious line on rock which is generally sound but which deteriorates on the upper easy slab. The route follows the right-hand of a pair of grooves in the buttress of orange rock. Climb easily over ledges right of the groove. Step over an area of algae to gain a short layback crack. Continue up the groove past a peg to a steep sequence of moves leading to an easy but loose slab. From the top of the slab (peg), traverse left beneath the big roof to an awkward step leading up to easy ground.

The next two routes are situated beyond and to the left of the Hidden Amphitheatre, and two approaches are possible: either, from the Hidden Amphitheatre, traverse over greasy rock around a corner to the brown slab; or abseil down a short vertical wall 30 yards beyond the Hidden Amphitheatre and then scramble easily right.

☆**Divergent Thinking** 60 feet E2 5c † (8.89)
A good route with a long crux right at the top. Start as for *Darkness Visible*. Climb the short boulder-problem groove and follow the easy line rightwards to ledges below a slab. Pull onto the slab and follow a leftward-slanting diagonal quartz weakness to the top with increasing difficulty.

☆**Darkness Visible** 110 feet E3 † (23.7.89)
A magnificent second pitch with sustained and bold climbing in a dramatic situation. Start beneath a short V-groove at the top of a brown slab with a chimney on its right.
1 40 feet 5b. Climb the short groove with difficulty; then go easily up the rightward-slanting groove to good ledges and large nut belays.
2 70 feet 5b/c. Follow a line of flat holds above the belay (crucial *Friend 1* in a pocket), and gain a standing-position on the last of these. Step right to below a thin crack and climb it with difficulty over bulges until it terminates. Step up and right; then exit left to peg and nut belays on a well-positioned ledge.

Hidden Amphitheatre

The best means of access to the left-hand section of Hidden Amphitheatre is by abseil from the terrace below the pathside promontory.

Solace 70 feet Very Severe (22.5.88)
A pleasant route at the extreme left end of the cliff. Descend slabs on the north-east side of the cliff and belay about 20 feet left of the first groove in from the edge of the crag. Traverse right and climb the groove; finish rightwards.
☆Variation Start 70 feet Hard Very Severe 5a † (7.7.89)
From ledges below and to the right of the *Solace* groove, climb up and left to join the parent route.

★**Consolation** 50 feet E3 6a (30.7.89/14.4.95)
Good wall climbing with continuous interest. The route basically takes the central ledgy line of weakness in the middle of a narrow 50-foot wall right of *Solace*. Start on a sloping ledge at the bottom of the wall. Climb up to the overhang and reach a small projecting hold. Just above this hold is a peg, which can be backed up with a good *Rock 3*. Use the hold to get established on the wall (hard). Climb up to a ledge with a peg out right and another (marginal) higher in the groove. Bridge up towards the third peg; then move off left to wire placements on the wall. Continue directly to the top.

★**Deliverance** 80 feet E2 5b (30.7.89)
Excellent steep climbing with good holds and good protection. The route follows a line parallel to the curving groove right of the *Consolation* wall. Start at the same point as *Consolation*. Climb up easily over ledges to a short undercut wall. Move leftwards across this to gain a slanting crack, which is climbed up and right to a hard move onto a large ledge. Follow a crack and good jugs to a hollow flake. Step up and reach left to a good hold, from which committing moves lead to another ledge. Make more steep moves up and finish leftwards.

☆**Living Time Warp** 80 feet E5 6a † (14.4.95)
An exciting pitch up the line of thin cracks in the blunt right-hand arête of the curving corner immediately right of *Deliverance*. Committing and strenuous. Start on a brown glacis below a short overhanging black wall with a brooding black chimney to the right. Climb the short black V-groove overhead and continue up ledges beneath the right-hand side of the arête. Swing left over the bulge to reach the crack and so gain a positive foot-ledge on the arête. Swing left again (peg) and finish up the crack and pockets above.

Kellan Corner 80 feet E1 5b (14.4.95)
A route of some character. Climb the obvious corner to the right of *Living Time Warp* (and left of *Kellan Arête*); exit past a peg in the short headwall.

★★**Kellan Arête** 70 feet E6 6a (9.4.95)
The dominant line of Kellan Head: the big bulging arête in the centre of the Hidden Amphitheatre; wild and withering, with protection, mainly small wires, hard to place. It just misses three stars because of the escapability to the left. Scramble up leftwards from the foot of the triangular slab to a short corner. Reach the good ledge beneath the arête and stack in maximum gear. Climb the radical-angled arête, using some pockets just to its left, and so gain a beautiful black-lip jug on the left – good shakeout. Launch out right and follow the sloping handrail on the edge of the arête to crux moves onto the final headwall. Exit direct.

☆☆☆**Kellanesis** 90 feet E6 † (14.4.95)
The fantastic 40-foot sloping ceiling which runs between the chimney of *Endgame* and *Kellan Arête* holds many potential lines on a similar theme. This one, probably not its easiest, takes an irresistible line of beautifully sculpted flakes and holes some 20 feet right of *Kellan Arête*.
1 40 feet. Follow a line of your choice and assemble sense and kinetic energy on a good small platform beneath the line.
2 50 feet 6c. From a big spike (sling) follow a rising flake-line leftwards (peg) to a difficult move for a none-too-obvious hole (twin pegs). Gain the undercut flake above and out (peg and *Rock 1*), and with some power pass the lip to reach pockets above (*in-situ* thread) and a straightforward exit.

★**Endgame** 130 feet E1 (6.4.86)
An excellent first pitch, taking the angle formed by the right-hand edge of the triangular slab and the impending headwall, leads to a weird finish. Start beneath a thin vertical crack leading to the main corner.
1 90 feet 5a. Climb the crack to a narrow ledge beneath the wall; then follow the wider crack leading up and left to a small stance just below the apex of the slab. Rusty peg belay.
2 40 feet 5b. Climb the deep slot above.

The Rook 150 feet Very Severe (10.86)
Start at the right-hand end of the easy-angled platform below *Endgame*, beneath the left side of the arête taken by *Gambit*.

1 80 feet 4b. Climb the wall just left of the arête to the large platform.
2 70 feet 4c. Move slightly right and climb a steep crack to a ledge. The steep slab above is taken to a pedestal and doubtful rock to finish.

Gambit 110 feet Severe (6.4.86)
A pleasant but slight route, taking the left arête of the pillar and the hanging slab above. Start on ledges beneath the arête.
1 60 feet. Follow the rib more or less direct via ledges and walls to the broad ledge on top of the pillar.
2 50 feet. Step down and left into a short corner, which is climbed to a steeper move onto the hanging slab. Exposed but straightforward moves lead directly up the slab. Belay 20 feet higher.

☆**Knight's Move** 80 feet E1 † (23.7.89)
A rather short crux, but with elegant and well-protected moves on sound rock. Start at the right-hand side of the Hidden Amphitheatre, at a shallow cave below a slab leading to a terrace.
1 40 feet 5a. Climb the wall 10 feet left of the cave until level with the cave roof. Traverse right to good footholds above the cave; then climb directly up the centre of the slab to a terrace.
2 40 feet 5c. Above the centre of the terrace is a thin slanting crack above a large flake. Climb up to stand on the flake, and make committing moves up the impending wall to a peg. Easier climbing leads to the top.

Frostbite 120 feet E1 (6.12.85)
Deceptively steep. Start 10 feet left of the vertical step in the waterslide, below a steep corner capped by a roof.
1 50 feet 5b. Climb the corner to the roof. Step right and continue straight up to ledges.
2 70 feet 4c. Above and to the right is a steep corner-crack. Climb the crack with care and step left to finish. Belays are 20 feet higher in a low bluff of rock.

The Waterslide Wall

This is the impressive steep grey wall, guarded by a horizontal band of overhangs, rising above the lower section of the descent ramp. The first routes climb the wall to the left of the left-hand of two slanting bottomless corners.

★**Tiger's Eye** 90 feet E3 (1.7.89)
Sustained, thin climbing up the steep wall left of *Zugzwang*.
1 50 feet 5a. *Zugzwang* pitch 1.
2 40 feet 5c. Pull up onto the exposed wall to the left of the belay. Climb up and left (passing a shallow *Rock 4* placement) to a point near the arête of the wall. Continue direct to a peg near the top and exit leftwards.

★**Zugzwang** 120 feet E2 (6.4.86)
A very good climb, sustained, steep, and varied. Start in the centre of the wall at a (usually) wet slate corner beneath the roofs.

1 50 feet 5a. Climb the awkward corner and use excellent holds above the first roof to move up and right into a niche. Exit leftwards and then step left across the lip of the main overhang to a stance on the horizontal faultline.
2 70 feet 5b. Climb the deep cracks in the wall behind the stance, aiming for a prominent circular niche to the left of the corner. Move right above the niche into the corner and make a difficult step left (peg) onto the obvious prow. Continue rightwards onto the upper section of the wall (peg) and finish direct. Belay 50 feet back in an outcrop.

Master of Deceit 100 feet Hard Very Severe 5a (31.12.85)
Like a politician, it starts with good intentions but avoids the issue as soon as possible. Start as for *Zugzwang*. Climb the corner; then move right, using holds above the roof, to the niche. From here, go up to the obvious faultline, follow it rightwards to a steep crack, and finish lamely on a ramp.

☆**The Bishop** 110 feet E1 † (30.7.89)
An eliminate but worthwhile right-to-left diagonal of The Waterslide Wall, borrowing lots of goodies from other routes. Start as for *Play It Straight*.
1 50 feet 5b. Make the steep initial move to gain the horizontal slot and swing left to good holds. Move up; then traverse off left along the obvious ledge to the belay of *Zugzwang*.
2 60 feet 5b. Climb up and left onto the exposed wall of *Tiger's Eye*. Continue leftwards to projecting holds on the arête. Move left again for 8 feet and finish direct up a narrow crack with a pointed projecting hold on its right. Belay on an outcrop on the left and another higher up on the right.

★**Play It Straight** 80 feet E3 5c (21.5.88)
Good, bold climbing up a compelling line taking the obvious curving corner avoided by *Master of Deceit*. Start 12 feet right of *Zugzwang*. Gain a horizontal slot 10 feet up and swing left to big holds. Move up to the right-slanting break of *Master of Deceit*; then make some bold moves up into the corner. Climb the corner to the lip of the overhang, go straight up to a crack, and finish leftwards up the face past a peg on *Zugzwang*.

★**Rock-a-Bye-Baby** 70 feet E3 6a (1.7.89)
[Photo p.224b.] A sustained and power-packed route on good rock. Start as for *Play It Straight*, and climb to its horizontal slot. Either climb direct to the overhang, or swing left to big holds and make thin moves up and right to it. Gain a layback position beneath a peg out to the right and pull onto the short wall above with difficulty. Climb to a sloping ledge in a niche and finish up the groove on the left.

Fifty yards west of the approach ramp beneath The Waterslide Wall is a narrow zawn with a striking groove-line at its back, the line of *Passchendaele*. Approach by descending easy-angled slabs on the eastern side of the zawn.

☆**The Somme** 80 feet E3 5c † (1.7.89)
A good route, which is more technical than it looks. Start in the slanting corner at the top of the slab left of *Passchendaele*. Follow the crack to the overhang and make wild committing moves out across the roof-crack to gain a hanging slab on the right. Step up and right into a groove, which is climbed to an exit on the left.

The following route should be attempted at low tide in calm seas and requires a period of dry weather to come into condition. The bottom pitch is likely to remain wet at all times. An extra rope will be required to reach the fenceposts beside the path.

★**Passchendaele** 160 feet E2 (26.4.87)
1 30 feet 5b. Move right into the groove and climb it to a sloping ledge.
2 55 feet 5c. Move out onto the right wall and climb up to reach good holds; then a difficult move gains the cleft. Continue up for a few feet, step left, and then move back up right on good holds. Make a series of spectacular moves right to reach a ledge.
3 75 feet 5a. Climb the easy-angled slab on the right until it is possible to move out left to the slab above the roof. Climb the slab with some difficulty (peg). Fencepost belays.
Variation
3a 75 feet 5b (5.91). Climb the obvious crack above the belay direct to the foot of the slab; then finish as above.

Nanda's Delight 140 feet Hard Very Severe 5a (5.91)
Climb the crackline to the right of *Passchendaele*.

Kellan Slab

Though this looks impressive from Doyden Point across the inlet, appearances are deceptive, for the angle is low and the climbing, apart from short, much steeper entry-pitches through the overhanging base of the slab, lacks identity. Descend (at half-to-low tide) the rib just east of the slab to wet terraces below the roof. Only the first pitches are described; above these, a line taken anywhere will do to reach belays on the fenceposts.

Sea Thrift 70 feet Very Severe 4c (4.81/12.85)
From the corner at the left side of the main overhang, traverse left on barnacles around the rib to another open corner. Climb diagonally right back to the rib and belay on the slab above.

Sunstorm 60 feet Hard Very Severe 5a (4.81)
Toward the left-hand side of the roof is a prominent V-groove. Pull over the initial overhang with difficulty to gain the groove; then continue up the slab above.

Back to Grand Falls 60 feet Very Severe 4b (1974)
Start at the right end of the overhang. Step up and left onto the wall, and follow a vague groove rightwards to a steeper section of the slab.

Shady Pete 110 feet Very Severe 4c † (3.11.88)
At the right-hand end of the slab, from ledges above the sea, move easily left and up a crack to rejoin the arête where it is flat. Step up; then move left with interest onto the slanting, undercut slab of the headwall. Make a move up on the left and continue to the top.

Doyden Point

OS Ref 966 806

A pleasant compact cliff which faces west and gets the afternoon sun. The rock is pillow lava, and is generally solid except near the top. Rough seas would make the starting-platform uncomfortable at any state of the tide.

Cars should be left at The National Trust car-park at Portquin, from where the point is easily visible, appearing as a rounded headland with a curious crenallated folly near its summit. Walk up the steep hill to a signposted right-of-way leading past a large house, and then cross grassy slopes to the folly. Follow the edge of the cliff down easy rock to a wide sloping gully and, beneath it, a flat ledge some 40 feet above the sea. It is easier and safer to abseil in from here. Alternatively, traverse back across a steeper groove to another ledge overlooking a slabby corner and descend this corner – not recommended.

The left-hand side of the crag consists of a large grey slab beneath a steeper, blocky headwall. To the right the cliff becomes vertical, and at its centre is the conspicuous orange groove of *Decumanus*. Very steep rock continues beyond this to the partially hidden green corner of *Sick Rose* and an impressive sea-cave beneath large stepped roofs. Finally, the right-hand end of the cliff is marked by a platform.

The first route lies on the steep right wall of the slabby corner descended on the approach.

Watergate 70 feet E1 5b (4.81)
Start on a ledge at the base of a slabby corner and climb the steep crack in its right wall past a niche; then move right to a slanting narrow slab. Climb the slab (two pegs) to the rib and finish up this.

Dynamo Hum 100 feet E2 (13.7.85)
Above the flat-topped pillar, the left arête of the slab of *Caprice* contains a smooth groove on its left flank. Start, at low tide, at the base of the pillar beneath a corner running up its left side.
1 30 feet. Climb the corner to the top of the pillar.
2 70 feet 5c. Climb the groove to a small overhang (peg); then step onto the right arête and move up to where the groove fades. Continue directly up the slab to a junction with *Caprice* near the top.

Doyden Point

1	Watergate	E1
2	Flying Circus	E2
3	Caprice	VS
4	Caprice Direct Start	VS
5	The Shrink	E1
6	Decumanus	E1
7	Yogic Flyer	E5
8	Lotus	E1
9	Illegal Alien	E3
10	Sick Rose	E4
11	Wilting	E6
12	Visage	E2

x abseil point

★Flying Circus 120 feet E2 5c (26.4.86)
An enjoyable route based on the left arête of the *Caprice* slab. The crux is in a fine position. Start on the sloping platform directly beneath the arête. Climb leftwards to an overhung niche, step up and left, and then traverse right beneath the undercut arête to a foot-ledge at the base of a shallow groove. Go up the groove a short way and move left on thin incuts to the arête. Climb the thin cracks above before stepping left to an obvious large foothold. Difficult moves lead up to the rib above and onto the arête at the top of the slab. Belay as for *Caprice*.

★Caprice 120 feet Very Severe 4c (26.10.71)
A pleasant pitch which takes a natural diagonal line up the large slab. Start 15 feet left of the orange corner of *Decumanus*. Climb leftwards across an easy subsidiary slab to the overlap. Go up on quartz holds to reach a small fang on the edge of the main slab. Traverse left to a thin crack leading out of the shallow depression in its centre. Steep moves gain a series of broken ledges, which are followed leftwards to the arête and belays. (A finish direct over precariously-poised blocks is not recommended.)
Direct Start 70 feet Very Severe 4c (2.1.83)
Climb pitch 1 of *Dynamo Hum*. Traverse right to reach a slim groove in the slab and follow this to join *Caprice* at the shallow depression.

The Shrink 150 feet E1 5b (1974)
This takes the right-hand section of the *Caprice* slab to a strenuous finish. Follow *Caprice* to the obvious small fang on the edge of the main slab; then continue direct on steeper rock to ledges beneath an overhanging corner-crack (peg) on the left. Climb the crack onto a steep wall, and go up the shallow groove to the roof (peg), which is turned on the left to reach ledges. Finish more easily.

★Decumanus 140 feet E1 5b (17.4.71)
The striking, central orange groove. The crux is slightly worrying. Start at the top of the sloping shelf beneath a crack leading into the main groove. Climb the crack and turn the first overhang on the right. Continue up the corner past a more difficult bulging section at 60 feet. Difficulties ease as the line above is followed, but the quality of the rock deteriorates until a final loose corner is reached. Avoid this on the left.

★★Lotus 160 feet E1 (26.6.77)
An exposed and exhilarating climb on good holds, taking the diagonal crack leading rightwards from the top bulge of *Decumanus*.
1 125 feet 5b. Climb the corner of *Decumanus* over the first roof and past the bulging section at 60 feet. Move right immediately and follow the diagonal crack until it is possible to move up to a narrow hanging slab. Go up to its top (tape runner) and move down and right to easier-angled rock. Nut and spike belays.

2 35 feet 4c. An awkward move round a rib on the right gains another slab. Step up onto a broad sloping ledge; then pull steeply across the short headwall to the grass slopes. Iron ring belay above the slope.

Yogic Flyer 100 feet E5 6a † (8.4.95)
Climb to the first overhang on *Decumanus*. Traverse right to below a short crack and climb up to the right-hand end of the *Lotus* traverse. Move left for 5 feet and take the exposed wall above on pancake holds to a slightly loose finish.

★★Illegal Alien 165 feet E3 (13.7.85)
A demanding and impressive route up the very steep walls left of the green corner of *Sick Rose*. Start 30 feet left of the corner, beneath an obvious line of weakness.
1 50 feet 5c. Climb steeply to a large overhang. Traverse right beneath this and swing round its right-hand end onto an overhanging wall (peg). Climb the wall, trending slightly left to a ledge on the left. Peg belays.
2 80 feet 6a. Move left into the obvious smooth groove, which is climbed with difficulty (peg) to an equally smooth slab. Go left onto the arête and ascend a short crack/groove to a niche. Exit right via a dubious flake to gain the stance of *Lotus*.
3 35 feet 4c. *Lotus* pitch 2.
Variation
1a 50 feet 5c (8.4.95). A spectacular entry to the route, free of tidal problems. From the right-hand side of the sloping terrace, traverse right along the base of the orange wall, above the roofs, until it is possible to climb down right on good holds and bear rightwards around the arête to the belay ledge just above.

★Sick Rose 145 feet E4 (27.5.78)
An unfriendly and strenuous route centred on the green corner. Start at half-to-low tide from a lower platform reached by descending the steep wall beneath the main shelf.
1 120 feet 6a. Climb the wall bearing right and then up steep biscuit-like rock to narrow ledges leading left. Move rightwards into the main corner, which is followed to a difficult exit onto a sloping ledge on the left. Continue up bulging rock; then move right onto a slab. Nut belays.
2 25 feet 4b. The short wall above leads to more broken rock and belays well back.

☆Wilting 150 feet E6 6a † (8.4.95)
This takes the compact, sandwiched 'slab' of light-coloured rock leading rightwards between roofs from the foot of the *Sick Rose* corner. Mentally draining, with no secure protection on the traverse.
1 100 feet 6a. Follow *Sick Rose* to the niche (peg at 40 feet). Traverse right to a good break and pull over a small overhang onto the compact 'slab'. Climb the 'slab' rightwards, very sustained, around a rib at its end to a good small ledge.

2 50 feet. Amble up an easy groove to the top.

☆**Visage** 150 feet E2 † (1982)
A traverse in a dramatic situation between the two sets of striking roofs above the lip of the sea-cave. Start on the lower platform 10 feet right of *Sick Rose*, at the base of a diagonal line of weakness.
1 100 feet 5c. Climb up and right to gain the upper horizontal band of very compact rock between the roofs. Traverse across to the right to a large ledge on the edge.
2 50 feet 5a. Climb the wall above directly to the top.

Pentire

OS Ref 924 805

The coast from the headland of Pentire Point on the north side of the Camel estuary to The Rumps half a mile to the north-east is littered with outcrops and a rich variety of sea-cliffs offering a unique climbing experience. The centrepiece of this collection is undoubtedly The Great Wall, a 'cathedral' which compares favourably with any other rock architecture in the country.

However, it is not only The Great Wall that provides climbing of high quality. For those prepared to step off the beaten track, a discovery of many unique climbs is waiting. Although overshadowed by the dramatic aura of The Great Wall, the smaller cliffs at Pentire offer a wide variety of short but good-quality climbs on rock varying from a hard, compact, *Darkinbad*-like nature to huge-jugged with gabbro-like friction. They should not be passed by if you have the time to browse for there are a few gems that match anything else on the North Coast in quality, even though they are relatively short.

The headland itself is close to the popular resort and surfing centre of Polzeath, and campsites and caravan sites are plentiful, the Trennant Steading site having a large population of partying surfers and a friendly landlord. Cars can be driven to The National Trust car-park in the yard of Pentire Farm, where a small fee is payable in an honesty box. A well-marked and signposted track leads across fields to a junction with the coast path at a wooden gate. Directly seawards of this gate is a wooden bench, a few yards below which is the top of Redwall Cliff. A hundred yards to the north-east an insignificant rounded hump of rock and grass can be seen. This turns out to be the summit of The Great Wall, which faces north-west and thus tends to remain cool, providing relief on a hot summer's day. Most of the cliffs have a similar orientation which can lead to problems of drying out after rain. Two hundred yards further towards The Rumps (a headland with a series of pinnacles descending the ridge to the sea), the path cuts through the remnants of a small drystone wall. Immediately left of this is a steep ravine, choked with huge boulders at its top. This is the central gully of North Cliff.

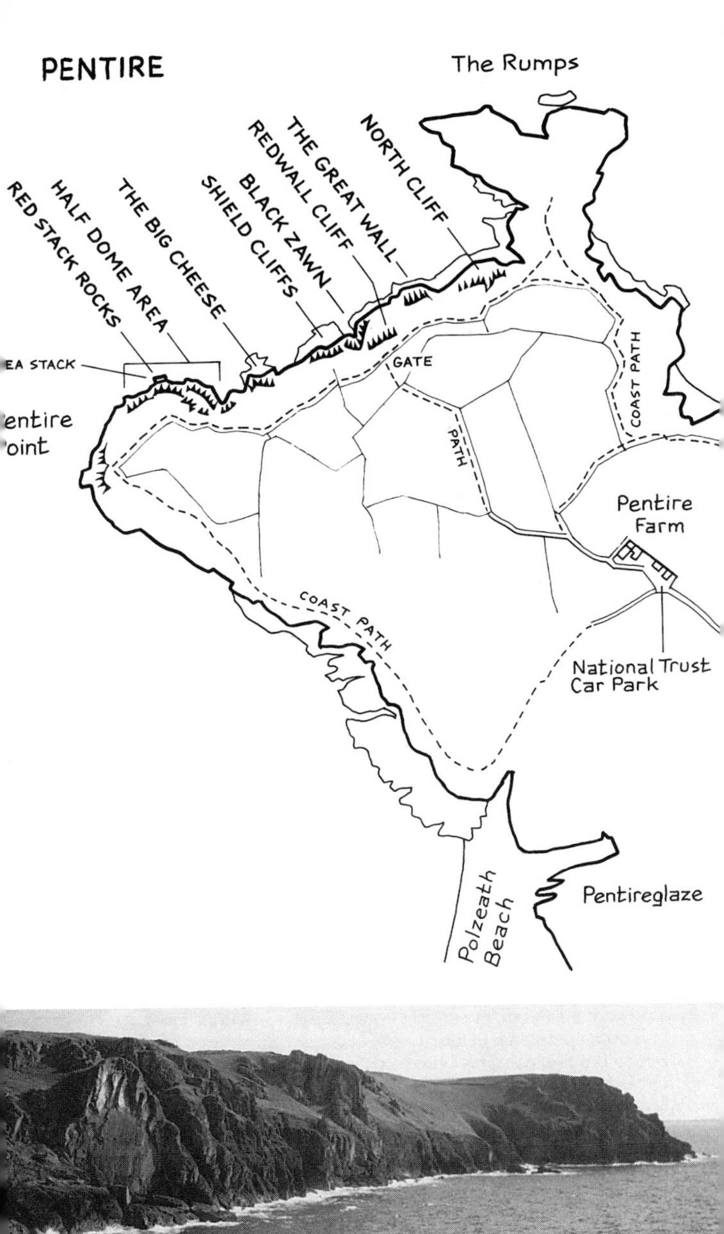
PENTIRE
The Rumps
NORTH CLIFF
THE GREAT WALL
REDWALL CLIFF
BLACK ZAWN
SHIELD CLIFFS
THE BIG CHEESE
HALF DOME AREA
RED STACK ROCKS
EA STACK
entire
oint
GATE
PATH
COAST PATH
Pentire
Farm
COAST PATH
National Trust
Car Park
Polzeath
Beach
Pentireglaze

North Cliff

This impressive little cliff is set into the hillside above a boulder-strewn beach, and is split into two halves by the central gully. The left-hand buttress is marked by a prominent hanging prow and the right-hand cliff by its obvious central groove-line with a slabby left wall. Approach the climbs by abseiling down the central gully.

The Concrete Trampoline 100 feet E3 5b † (8.8.94)
Climb the obvious rib on the buttress, just left of the gully, until it is possible to step left into a niche (peg removed). Continue to a second niche, which is exited on the left to belays well back (the abseil point).

Robert of Pentire 100 feet E3 6a † (31.8.87)
This good climb follows the obvious central groove-line on the right-hand cliff. Start beneath the groove, by a large block of rock separated from the main face. Climb the groove to a grassy ledge. Move across right and climb the wall to the right of the groove until it is possible to gain the groove again beneath the overhang. Climb to the overhang and then traverse left below it (crux) to good holds. Continue up the groove to grassy ledges and go up these to belay well back.

The Great Wall

From the grassy mound at the top of The Great Wall, a faint path meanders down the grassy slopes to the east of the col until an easy-angled ramp is reached leading back to the cliff. From here the unmistakable and inspiring profile of the wall is observed, the flake crack of *Eroica* demanding immediate attention. A large glacis below the wall protects it from the tide, and boulders prevent any real disturbance by the waves or all but the heaviest of seas, as well as providing excellent viewpoints for studying the routes.

The Great Wall is shaped like a wedge, its narrow upper third sculpted into a series of open corners, arêtes, and slanting grooves, while its lower two-thirds is a planed sheet of shining ebony. Only the overlaps forming the great flake left of the centre of the crag, and the angled, stepped corners right of *Darkinbad the Brightdayler* break the unity. The long diagonal groove of *Lost Leviathan* is the boundary of the right-hand side, while the open wall and flakes of *Cobra* lead up to the hanging groove of *Through the Looking-Glass* to form the left-hand side.

★Through the Looking-Glass 100 feet E3 5c (12.10.86)
Start on the flank of the left-hand edge of The Great Wall, on a grass ledge level with the bottom of the groove, taking a belay from a pinnacle further up the grassy bank. Step right onto the nose, and then move round right again to gain the overhanging face and a lot of exposure. Cross the wall with difficulty (peg at start) to reach the foot of the groove and a welcome ledge. Follow the groove to the top (peg below the final moves).

Pentire
The Great Wall

1	Through the Looking-Glass	E3
2	Reflections	E4
3	Cobra	E2
4	A Groove Full of Mirrors	E7
5	Eroica	E2(E3)
6	Black Magic	E5
7	Darkinbad the Brightdayler	E5
8	Urco's Revenge	E5
9	Siren's Cry	E5
10	Last Leviathan	E4
11	Over My Head	E1
12	Twilight	HS

★★Reflections 120 feet E4 6a (31.8.87)
A great climb, with sensational exposure, taking the slim groove-line to the right of *Through the Looking-Glass*. Technically low in the overall grade, but the distances between runners give a different impression. Start as for *Through the Looking-Glass* to gain the ledge at the foot of the first groove. Step right to a short V-groove, climb the groove to good holds, and continue to a ledge beneath the final wall. Climb steeply to a peg and finish up the hanging groove.

Pete's Route 80 feet E2 5b † (4.89)
The obvious open groove to the left of *Cobra* is followed to a finish on the grassy slopes at the start of *Through the Looking-Glass*.

Cobra 130 feet E2 5c (4.75)
Interesting climbing up the prominent leftward-slanting crack in the lower left section of The Great Wall. The rock is of the spitting variety and not to be trusted. Start at the foot of the crack 20 feet left of *Eroica*. Climb the groove to an overhang. Cross this with difficulty and continue to an obvious flake crack slanting right. Follow the crack until it steepens; then use underclings to the left to gain a short broken corner, which is followed to the grass slopes at the start of *Through the Looking-Glass*.

☆A Groove Full of Mirrors 240 feet E7 (1 pt aid) † (8.9.91)
A historic line, the fulfilment of which will be the elimination of the aid point. It is the link with the hanging groove in the left-hand side of the headwall, providing probably the most intimidating, daring lead on the crag.
1 70 feet 4c. Follow *Eroica* to a small ledge between double cracks 15 feet below the double overlap. *Friend* and thread belays above.
2 90 feet 6b. Undercut the lower, left-hand of the two flakes and follow the flake-line above quite reasonably leftwards to a horizontal break and overlap; in view of the forthcoming excitement, the peg for the right-hand rope should be supplemented with wires under the roof for the left-hand rope. Step right and make totally committing moves up the thin black wall to a jug in the middle of nowhere. Still with no protection, traverse delicately left to clip two poor pegs in the leaning wall below the roof and then a downward-pointing aid peg, which enables a finger-crack and then the stance of *Reflections* to be gained.
3 80 feet 6a. *Reflections* pitch 2.

★★★Eroica 210 feet E2 (1 pt aid) (E3 free) (11.4.71/1975)
[Photo p.256a.] A magnificent route, which fully deserves its status as one of the all-time sea-cliff classics of Britain. Despite a bold and intimidating appearance, the route is low in the grade, for the holds, apart from a short section of the second pitch, are positive, and protection is adequate. Judicious use of the crucial peg will enable the spectacular situation to be enjoyed in comparative comfort. Start at a shallow undercut corner marking the junction of the steep central section of the wall with the more slabby rock of its left-hand side.

1 100 feet 5a. Climb the corner, which soon eases, to the first roof. Step out to the right to gain friendlier holds in the cracks above and aim for a cramped niche beneath the double roof. The traverse left on undercuts between the overlaps is more difficult to contemplate than to execute. Enjoy the bite of the exposed and exhilarating layback move into the deep crack leading to a narrow stance on top of the flake. Peg and nut belays.
2 110 feet 5b (6a free). Above is a short leaning corner and an obvious peg in an interesting state of decay. Climb the corner with difficulty (*RP4* useful), or with the greatest of ease by lassoing the peg or clipping the usual collection of bleached slings hanging from it. Then make a series of delicate moves up the smooth ramp on the right to a welcome handhold in the corner above. Traverse right to a sloping shelf (stance possible). The open corner above is steep and strenuous to start, but gradually eases until moves right lead to a gully, which is followed to the top.

Dislocation Dance/Pulses Unreal 130 feet E4 6a (6.81/6.81)
Start as for *Eroica* and climb up and right across a pocketed wall to a junction with *Darkinbad the Brightdayler*. Continue up to the main break on *Darkinbad...* (hanging stance possible). Move left and climb the obvious thin crack to reach the flake-top stance on *Eroica*. Abseil off or finish as for *Darkinbad the Brightdayler* pitch 2 or *Eroica* pitch 2.

★**Black Magic** 220 feet E5 (27.5.87)
[Photos p.256b.] An exhilarating and sustained counter-diagonal to *Darkinbad the Brightdayler*. Plenty of small-to-medium wires and lots of extenders should be carried. To the right of the start of *Eroica* is an overhung base, above which is a thin discontinuous crack-system.
1 150 feet 6a. Climb the crack-system until it is possible to move right to *Darkinbad the Brightdayler* at the two pegs. Move up right to reach a prominent crystalline hole and then make a series of committing moves up and right to a good flake. Continue on this line past a peg to a final difficult move to reach easier ground and a belay at the foot of the top corner of *Last Leviathan*.
2 70 feet 5c. Either climb the corner or (5a) move right to an easy groove.

★**Darkinbad the Brightdayler** 205 feet E5 (25.4.72/1976)
One of the few five-star routes in the country. A worthy companion to *Eroica*, though much harder and more sustained, giving wall-climbing of the highest calibre. Start 40 feet right of *Eroica*, on a large boulder resting against the cliff.
1 140 feet 6a. Step from the boulder onto a line of small flat holds leading to a ledge. Lack of protection hereabouts and the deep trench below add to the air of commitment. Climb the steep wall above and continue up to the left of a small overhang, following a thin crack which curves left (two pegs). Move left for 20 feet and then climb with difficulty to a line of overhangs. Ascend diagonally right using a discontinuous crack. Transfer to a thin crack on the right and move up with difficulty. Continue in

the same line to the sloping shelf below the final corner of *Eroica*.
2 65 feet 5c. Traverse left into the groove above the crux of *Eroica* (peg), and climb fairly easily to where it overhangs. Move up to good jams and continue by difficult laybacking to a ledge. On the left is a thin line of weakness in the wall, above which all is horizontal.

★Urco's Revenge 180 feet E5 (7.87)
A powerful climb, accepting the obvious challenge of the groove and overhangs which *Darkinbad the Brightdayler* avoids.
1 130 feet 6b. Climb the initial wall of *Darkinbad the Brightdayler* until it is possible to move right into the groove. Continue up the groove with increasing difficulty to a roof and two pegs. Using holds on the wall above, move diagonally right (crux) to gain a good handhold on the lip of the second roof. A hard move over this leads to easier but still demanding climbing to reach the belay on *Last Leviathan*.
2 50 feet 5a. Climb the small groove above, and move right to finish.

Another Nervous Breakdown 230 feet E7 † (4.8.91)
The hardest and perhaps the most serious route on The Great Wall. It takes a totally independent line to the right of *Urco's Revenge* via the prominent thin flake crack. Marginal *RP* protection protects the extended 6b sequence to gain entry to the crack, and the final groove is scarcely less committing. Start 15 feet right of *Darkinbad the Brightdayler*, on top of a boulder.
1 130 feet 6b. Climb boldly, diagonally leftwards from the boulder, to reach a good flat hold in the base of a tiny groove. Continue straight up (wire on left) to the ledge at 30 feet. From near the right-hand end of the ledge (good *Rock 1* slot), make very extending moves up the bare wall to reach the flake crack. Climb the flake more easily to a resting-ledge on the right. Take the open groove above to reach a good handhold (poor peg on the left-hand side and poor *RP4* on the right). Make committing moves up a thin ramp and a wall to reach easier ground above a little undercut roof; then step right to the belay ledge of *Last Leviathan*.
2 100 feet 5c. *Last Leviathan* pitch 2.

Your Funeral, My Trial 230 feet E6 † (6.88)
This bold route takes the shallow rib to the right of *Urco's Revenge* and *Another Nervous Breakdown*. Start as for the latter.
1 130 feet 6b. Traverse right into a short, overhung groove, and climb this boldly to the right-hand side of the large ledge of *Darkinbad the Brightdayler*. Step right to sloping ledges and climb the vague rib (crux) to a rest. Continue up shallow grooves above until *Last Leviathan* is reached. Go up this to the belay ledge.
2 100 feet 5c. *Last Leviathan* pitch 2.

★★Siren's Cry 240 feet E5 (8.83)
Superb, sustained climbing up the crack-system right of *Urco's Revenge*. Start 30 feet right of *Darkinbad the Brightdayler*, beneath a thin crack up a faint slabby depression.

1 140 feet 6a. Climb the crack (peg) until moves left gain ledges and a groove (hands-off rest). Continue up the groove until it is possible to traverse right to join *Last Leviathan*. Continue up this to reach the belay ledge.
2 100 feet 5c. *Last Leviathan* pitch 2.

☆**Beneath Black Waters** 190 feet E6 † (4.8.91)
Brilliant, high-standard face-climbing on a direct line up the triangular wall right of *Siren's Cry*. Apart from a slightly bold start, all principal difficulties are protected with good small wires. Start from the large flat-topped boulder below the face, some 20 feet right of the short overhung groove of *Your Funeral, My Trial*.
1 90 feet 6b. Ascend the lower slabs easily via a faint groove to reach a narrow ledge at 35 feet (poor projecting stainless steel peg). Go up and rightwards to a good pocket (*Hex* 8 or similar) and then step left to a good wire-slot where the wall steepens yet further. Move left and climb direct to a thin rightward-trending crack. Follow this with difficulty over a small steep roof (crux, peg), step left to a rib between two very slight grooves (peg), and then climb steeply rightwards on surprising holds to join *Last Leviathan* at its large flake and continue to the belay.
2 100 feet 5c. *Last Leviathan* pitch 2.

Last Leviathan 230 feet E4 (4.75)
The compelling leaning groove-line which forms the right-hand edge of The Great Wall. Rather gloomier than its neighbours. Start a few feet left of the ominous black corner that rises from the sea at the right-hand end of the crag, where another boulder reaches the crag.
1 130 feet 5c. Follow the diagonal weakness into the corner and climb the corner to a poor ledge. Continue over a flake and up another corner to a good ledge on the right or another up and to the left. The upper section of this pitch is quite serious with loose rotten rock and poor protection.
2 100 feet 5c. Climb cracks leading diagonally left to the foot of a steep corner with an overhanging flake on the right wall. Climb up the corner and the flake until it is possible to reach the right rib. Finish up this.

Over My Head 150 feet E1 (5.78)
1 75 feet 5c. Start as for *Last Leviathan* at the black corner, and climb as far as the poor ledge.
2 75 feet 5a. The subsidiary corner above is climbed on good holds to flake belays at the top.

Twilight Cliff
Immediately landward of the top of The Great Wall is a small cliff dominated by an easy-angled leftward-rising ramp that leads to a short groove.

Daylight 90 feet Very Difficult
Twenty feet left of the start of *Twilight* is a broken crack. Follow the crack to reach the gully above and climb it.

Twilight 80 feet Hard Severe 4b (12.10.86)
Well worthwhile. Climb the ramp diagonally up to the left until the base of the groove is reached. Pull through the initial crack and overhang and continue up the groove to the top.

Redwall Cliff

From the foot of *Twilight*, follow a sheep track to the west. After 30 yards the track skirts a steep gully to seawards before passing below a small buttress with a prominent overhang. From here, a small black buttress can be seen down at sea-level about 100 yards further west. Immediately landwards is a larger grey and red buttress bounded on its right-hand side by a set of prominent grey corners. This is Redwall Cliff. This cliff lies immediately below a wooden bench seat by the gate of the Pentire Farm path.

At the left-hand side of the cliff is a prominent slabby red wall that is steeper than it first appears.

Warrior Mouse 50 feet Hard Very Severe 5a (21.8.94)
Well worth doing for good situations on positive holds. Start beneath an obvious, overhanging, chimney-like groove. Climb steeply and strenuously up the groove to a ledge to the right of the red wall. Step left onto the red wall and climb steeply up good holds to its top. Traverse precariously left over ledges to reach boulder belays at the top of the buttress's left-hand gully.

The next three routes are best belayed by using a preplaced rope to an outcrop back by the coast path.

Bloodbeak 90 feet E1 5b (7.96)
Climb up the arête as for *Ironbeak* to a good ledge. Step right into a groove and go up to another ledge. Traverse left across the undercut red wall and then climb a very slim groove and the wall to its left to reach a precarious finish.

Ironbeak 80 feet Hard Very Severe 5a (8.89)
Something of a ramble up the central section of the cliff. Start at the foot of a steep arête to the right of the overhung cave below *Warrior Mouse*. Climb up a thin crack just to the right of the arête to reach a good ledge. Step right into a groove and follow it for 10 feet to another ledge at the base of the red-coloured headwall. Go diagonally right up cracks to reach the corner of *The Joseph Bell* and finish as for that route.

★**The Joseph Bell** 90 feet Hard Severe 4b (21.8.94)
This takes the series of corners in the right-hand side of the buttress.

Imposing exposure in the upper corner. The climb maintains its interest throughout. Start by a crack below a slabby, grassed area. Step up the crack and go easily over the slabs to the foot of the first open-book corner. Climb this to a good ledge; then step left into the upper corner, and climb ever steepening rock on excellent holds. Step right at the top of the corner and pull over a precarious bulge to finish.

Triple Groove Buttress

Below Redwall Cliff is an easily identifiable cliff consisting of three prominent grooves.

Groove of Illusions 70 feet Very Severe 4c † (13.8.91)
Climb the left-hand groove, finishing somewhat precariously out to the right.

Snake in the Grass 70 feet Very Severe 4b † (28.8.94)
Some suspect rock gives this route a bite. Climb the arête between the left-hand and central grooves direct.

Greenwitch 70 feet Hard Severe 4b † (13.8.91)
Climb the central groove, finishing to the left of the final overhang by some spectacular bridging.

Colin's Grandma 70 feet Very Severe † (28.8.94)
1 45 feet 4b. Twenty feet left of the right-hand groove of *Faff* is a steep wide crack. Climb this until a pull over the top leads to the slabby area beneath the capping overhang of *Faff*.
2 25 feet 4c. Climb up to the overhang and make steep moves left across the hanging wall to reach a grassy groove to finish.

Faff 80 feet Hard Severe 4b † (20.8.94)
Climb the right-hand groove to the large capping roof. Traverse out right to the lip and make an awkward step right around the arête to reach a diagonal crack and some dubious ledges leading to the top.

Pentire Black Zawn

This is at the left-hand side of the next section of sea-cliff to the south, lying below a large vegetated buttress well above sea-level. It can be reached directly from the coast path. As you join the coast path from the Pentire Farm path, turn west, and after a few yards an obvious pinnacle can be seen just above the sea. Go down the grassy slopes to a boulder-strewn platform just above the zawn.

The zawn gives a collection of short, yet highly enjoyable, steep climbs on excellent rock and in fine positions. The routes start at a ledge 20 feet above sea-level, gained by abseil down the east wall to the side of the obvious groove of *The English Way*.

The first three climbs all use the same start and provide exhilarating exposure by traversing over the lip of the sea-cave.

The Rising Dark 80 feet Hard Very Severe † (5.92)
1 40 feet 5a. *Quiet Desperation* pitch 1.
2 40 feet 4b. Traverse left from the belay below an overlap to reach the left-hand crack and follow it to the top.

Quiet Desperation 70 feet Hard Very Severe † (24.6.89)
1 40 feet 5a. From the left end of the ledge, climb an awkward groove; then make a difficult step up the wall on the left (high exposure across the cave lip) to reach a ledge and easier ground. Move left into a yellow bay at the foot of a chimney-crack.
2 30 feet 4c. Climb the chimney-crack to finish.

Camming Round the Mountain 70 feet Hard Very Severe † (5.94)
1 40 feet 5a. *Quiet Desperation* pitch 1.
2 30 feet 4c. Immediately right of the chimney-crack is another crack. Follow this to the top

★Pachyderm Pathway 70 feet Hard Very Severe 5a † (14.8.94)
This takes the fine hanging groove and corner to the left of a prominent grey arête. Step up onto the slab at the start of *The English Way* and traverse delicately left into the right-hand of the two hanging grooves, which has a water-filled finger-jug at its bottom. Climb the groove (awkward if wet) to reach a good ledge at the foot of a steep corner, which gives excellent climbing. Continue up it until a hand-traverse right along an obvious ledge leads to the finishing-platform.

Pigs in Zen 60 feet E3 6a † (15.7.95)
Climb the very obvious grey arête between *Pachyderm Pathway* and *Nipped in the Buddha*. A ruthlessly eliminate approach is necessary to avoid using holds or protection on the latter.

★★Nipped in the Buddha 60 feet Very Severe 4c (5.92)
Divine climbing in a reflective position. To the right of the grey arête is another corner in the upper part of the face. Climb the slab of *The English Way* for 10 feet; then move diagonally left along incut holds to reach the foot of the corner, which is followed with increasing exposure to the top.

One for the Lager Drinkers 50 feet Very Severe 4c (3.9.93)
Between the corner of *Nipped in the Buddha* and the groove of *The English Way* is a subsidiary groove. Climb the slab of *The English Way* for 10 feet and then climb directly up into the groove. Continue to the top.

The English Way 50 feet Hard Severe 4b (30.5.89)
Climb a slab and a prominent V-groove that splits the centre of the wall to broken rock at the top.

Little Black Dress 50 feet E2 5b † (7.95)
Climb the glistening black slabby wall between *The English Way* and *Coal Comfort*.

★**Coal Comfort** 50 feet Hard Very Severe 4c (6.92)
Delicate to start, building to an elegant finish. Start a few feet right of *The English Way*, at a small groove. Climb the groove to reach the slabby wall and continue up to reach an obvious flake leading up into the hanging groove. Make an interesting move into the groove and follow it to the top.

Immediately right is a fine black wall.

★**Brother Chris** 50 feet E3 5c (20.8.94)
A startling wall climb of impeccable quality. Climb up to some good cracks and then step right into the centre of the wall. Make thin moves up the wall and a slim groove to a crozly pocket. The wall steepens here and an intricate and highly enjoyable sequence of moves via hidden holds gives tense, sensational climbing, with limited protection, to reach the finishing-slab.

To the right is an imposing arête.

★**Paranoia Express** 50 feet E2 5b (13.8.94)
Sustained exhilaration. Climb the short wall to reach the arête and continue steeply up it with a slight deviation to protection in a large pocket on the right. The final moves on the arête to reach the finishing-slab are the best.

★**The Midnight Garden** 50 feet E2 5b (3.9.93)
The concave face to the right of the arête gives a minor classic. Start immediately right of the arête. Climb a few feet to a good thread and move right and up to pass the bulge. Continue up the wall using good cracks to reach the overhang. Pass this, using the crack on its left, to a tricky slab finish.

Black Rose 50 feet E3 5c † (7.95)
Climb the wall to the right of *The Midnight Garden*, passing a prominent spike.

Black Power 50 feet E3 5c † (28.8.95)
Climb *Black Rose* to the spike. Follow the crack diagonally rightwards until steep climbing gains the obvious overhang with a flake on its right-hand side. Climb the flake and finish directly up the groove above.

On the seaward face around the arête, and 20 feet to the right, is the prominent diagonal groove and chimney of *Ordinary Men*.

Ordinary Men 70 feet Very Difficult (30.5.89)
A rarity: an easy climb in an impressive situation. Climb the

chimney/groove to the top, where it meets the top of an easy-angled rake. Not over-endowed with protection.

★★**Merchants of Menace** 70 feet E2 5c (13.8.94)
This exquisite bridging test-piece climbs the open, red groove right of *Ordinary Men*. High in the grade. Climb the groove to the overhang. Traverse out left to an arête by some rockfall scars and finish easily up a slabby crack.

A Most Peculiar Practice 130 feet Hard Severe † (24.6.89)
Start 20 feet right of *Ordinary Men*.
1 70 feet 4b. From the foot of the crisp groove, climb diagonally right to a rib. Step right around this to reach a good ledge, ascend a short steep wall to another ledge, and continue diagonally rightwards to reach the easy rake. Drop down this to the base of a prominent open red groove.
2 60 feet 4a. Climb the groove to the top. Not as straightforward as it appears, nor is protection very evident.

The Shield Cliffs

To the right of the easy rake crossed by *A Most Peculiar Practice* is a complex series of cliffs with a wide variety of architecture and standards of climbing, though mostly in the harder grades.

The left-hand section is an impressive steep black wall, The Shield, resembling in miniature The Great Wall. It is half the size of its big brother but is tilted a few degrees beyond vertical. Both its routes offer strenuous and committing test-pieces on excellent rock. Approach as for Pentire Black Zawn, and abseil from the rock buttresses that litter the hillside just to the left (facing out) of the pinnacle to a platform 20 feet above low-tide level (if this is missed, it is easy at low tide to gain it from below). Both routes start from the left-hand end of the platform, beneath a corner forming the right edge of The Shield.

☆☆**Turkish Delight** 70 feet E5 5c † (15.7.95)
Very bold but brilliant. Swing up left onto a ledge below the centre of the headwall, and climb up and leftwards to a flake (nut runner just down and right of a rounded ledge). Make a hard move up to stand on the flake and shuffle to its left-hand side. Attack the flakes above and use pockets to head left towards the arête. The arête is followed with determination to the top.

☆☆☆**The Crusade** 70 feet E5 6a † (1.10.99)
As for *Turkish Delight*, swing up left onto a ledge beneath the smooth headwall and make the initial committing pull up and left. The thin line of sidepulls and pockets above leads directly up the centre of The Shield to a powerful move to reach a small overlap and a rock-up left. More steep, but easier climbing wins the battle.

THE SHIELD CLIFFS
1 Easy Prey E4
2 Hope for Hillebrandt E3
3 Pounding Heart E4
4 Our Stars, Our Sky VS
5 Black Hunter E5
6 Escape Route VD
1
2
3
4
5
5
4
6
THE SHIELD
D.J.S. ~ 2000

To the right of The Shield is a grey-green triangular section of rock set back a little from the surrounding cliffs. Immediately right again the cliff is more broken and red-coloured; it then becomes darker, with a marked overhang at half height. At the right-hand end of the overhang is a prominent downward-pointing nose of rock above a rightward-slanting, black, slaty ramp. This whole section of cliff has a broad pink platform at its base, which is uncovered from half-to-low-tide. To the right of the hanging nose is a gully which leads into the afore-mentioned rake. Further right the cliff becomes more nondescript, gentler in angle, and black, finally ending at a large open corner.

Approach by turning left onto the coast path from Pentire Farm and scrambling down grassy slopes after passing through a gate on the coast path; then turn back north along rock ledges to reach the top of the central gully-system and an abseil descent to the platform.

There is another, red ramp, which rises across the cliff from right to left, starting below the downward-pointing nose. Scramble up the ramp to its left-hand end and belay at the foot of a steep crack.

☆☆**Easy Prey** 100 feet E4 5c † (16.5.99)
Great climbing across the curving wall to the right of The Shield. From the ramp, make committing moves up left to reach good holds and follow these left across the wall to a hard move just before reaching the obvious groove on the left-hand side of the wall. Climb the groove to finish.

☆**Hope for Hillebrandt** 80 feet E3 5c † (16.5.99)
A good climb, taking the crack from the left-hand end of the ramp. A tough start leads to easier climbing and a finish with a final pull over an overhang.

☆☆☆**Pounding Heart** 100 feet E4 6a † (28.7.99)
A stunning route. Above the start of the ramp, and 20 feet left of the downward-pointing nose is a broken groove-line, the first real line of weakness in the overhangs. Climb awkwardly to the overhang over bulges; then make a hard move through the break into the groove above, where good protection can be arranged. Make a glorious but pumpy traverse left across the steep wall to rejoin excellent holds and a crack after 25 feet. Climb the crack to reach easy-angled slabs and cross these, trending right, to belay at the foot of the headwall above. Scramble off to the right.

☆☆**The Black Hunter** 100 feet E5 6b † (1.9.99)
An intricate and spectacular solution to an impressive piece of rock. From the toe of the ramp, climb diagonally rightwards up it towards the downward-pointing nose. Immediately left of the nose, a steep grey-green groove rears up. Pull strenuously into this (jammed wire) to reach a good hold, and continue to the notch above where a scary pull is made to gain the gentle slab above. Step left for a few feet, and reach a peg up to the left and off the line. After clipping it, step back right and make a couple of

very thin moves to gain the sanctuary of a good undercut hold on a block. Pull onto the ramp above; then step back left and wander up the steep little buttress above on huge holds. Continue up slabs to belay at the foot of the headwall. Scramble off to the right.

☆☆**Our Stars, Our Sky** 150 feet Very Severe † (16.5.99)
Start as for the preceding route.
1 50 feet 4b. Climb diagonally rightwards up the ramp, and continue under the downward-pointing nose to reach the easy-angled rock of the central gully. Follow this until a step back left can be made onto a large ledge, which leads back towards the main wall.
2 100 feet 4c. A beautiful pitch. From the left end of the ledge, step left onto the upper wall and cross *The Black Hunter* at the foot of its final steep buttress. Continue traversing leftwards across the wall as holds keep appearing, passing a huge thread in the middle. Cross the final crack of *Pounding Heart* and reach the left edge of the wall. Climb up from here, just right of the arête, to reach easy-angled slabs and climb them to gain a grassy break. Belays are awkward to arrange.

Escape Route 60 feet Very Difficult (7.92)
The line of the abseil descent. Climb the wall to the right of the gully to reach easier-angled rock in the central gully above.

Beach Bum 60 feet Hard Severe 4b (5.8.95)
Start at a good ledge above sea-level, 20 feet right of *Escape Route*, and just left of some grey rockfall scars. Climb awkwardly up a steep overlap, with poor or no protection, until the angle eases. Continue more securely to reach the top of the *Escape Route* gully.

Day Tripper 80 feet Difficult (5.8.95)
Forty feet right of *Escape Route* and 20 feet right of the rockfall scars is a broad, easy-angled groove starting just above sea-level. Climb the groove to a large ledge below an undercut wall. Pull up the wall on the right using a good flake crack, and continue slightly left up pleasant climbing to reach a grassy finishing-platform.

Kamikaze Shrimp 60 feet Difficult (5.8.95)
Well worth doing. Climb the corner at the right-hand end of the black walls. Good holds and protection.

The Big Cheese

A hundred yards right from the last climb, and about half-way towards the red corner of *Touch the Devil*, is a small hidden buttress below a grassy rib jutting out to sea just before reaching some messy, broken zawns. Scramble down grass to the end of the rib; then turn left (facing out) and scramble down over broken ledges to reach a high-tide, level platform. The gently overhanging wall of The Big Cheese is now apparent, the name obvious from the appearance of the rock.

★★★Ocean of Fears 70 feet E2 5a (13.8.96)
Emotional strenuosity, dubious protection, superb position and enjoyable climbing provide another, if somewhat diminutive, potential North Coast classic. There is also a deep-water landing at high tide. Start by crossing a *Kinkyboots*-like gap to reach a good ledge at the foot of the wall. From the left-hand side of the wall, climb steeply up to reach a horizontal slot. Traverse left until the arête is reached and poor runners can be placed. Continue up immediately right of the arête to gain a groove, which leads to a ledge and another groove to finish.

☆Steep Sheep 50 feet Hard Very Severe 5a † (5.8.95)
Graded for the uninitiated into the delights of the North Coast. Step, fall, or climb across the gap to gain the right-hand end of the ledge at the foot of the wall. Climb up on good holds to reach a vague crack and a good rest below the final groove. Finish awkwardly up this to a good stance with awkward belays.

Half Dome Cliff

Some 300 yards to the south-west along the coast a prominent half-dome-shaped buttress can be seen above an impressive red corner. Above the sea-level cliff (The Devil's Cliff) are four smaller buttresses, two of which contain a number of attractive climbs of a less serious disposition yet still with excellent position: Half Dome Buttress at the left-hand end (facing the cliffs), Nondescript Buttress to its right, The Pinnacle to *its* right, and, at the right-hand side, Thursday Buttress.

The Devil's Cliff

Approach the climbs by scrambling down grassy slopes on the south side, then over easy-angled rock. The red corner provides a route of character!

★★Touch the Devil 120 feet E4 6a (30.8.87)
Strenuous but with good protection. Start below the corner. Cross the slab to reach the corner and pull onto the sloping ledge beneath it. Climb the crack to the right of the corner to a peg and then move back left into the corner. Continue up the corner to the overhang at the top and traverse left to a ledge. Pull through the bulge above via the excellent crack to reach the top. (Any pegs in place will be highly suspect.)

A Wok on the Wild Side 80 feet Hard Very Severe † 4c (14.7.90)
Start at the right-hand end of the slab, just above the gully separating the main cliff from the descent route. Climb steeply up the broken corner above, and trend left to reach a ledge. Scramble easily leftwards to reach the final corner. Climb this, taking care of dubious rock; then pull out to the slab on the right and climb up it to finish.

Half Dome Buttress

This has one, major line, a compelling square-cut groove leading to a wide overhanging chimney at its top. It is the natural continuation of *Touch the Devil*.

Silent Screaming 70 feet E1 5a † (16.8.96)
Climb easily up to the start of the groove; then move left up a short slab to the start of the main difficulties. Steep moves up and slightly right lead to a rest on top of a square block. Bridge up into the overhanging chimney section and utilize the right wall and the jamming-crack above to gain safety in the form of a dubious grassy, but easy-angled finish. Belays are awkward to arrange.

Thursday Buttress

The first route takes a broken crack-system just right of a steep gully.

Graceless 60 feet Hard Severe 4b † (8.88)
Start at the left-hand side of the north-facing wall, just right of the obvious chimney, a refugee from the golden age of mountaineering. Climb the crack-system in the wall to reach the top.

Bitter Minnows 80 feet Hard Very Severe 5a † (14.7.90)
Starting at the lowest point of the buttress, scramble over boulders at the foot of the gully until able to traverse right into a hanging groove that leads to the groove-line occupying the centre of the face. Climb the hanging groove carefully; then move left into its continuation and follow it until it fades to a small ledge at the top of a pinnacle. Finish up cracks in the final wall.

Soul Shock 80 feet E2 5b † (12.8.96)
Start at the lowest point of the buttress and climb a steep brutal crack to reach the foot of the prominent hanging groove at the right end of the wall. Continue up the slabby wall to the right of the groove before stepping out right to the arête. Final steep pulls through the overhang at the top of the arête lead to a slabby finish needing care.

Silverfish 90 feet Hard Severe 4b (14.7.88)
[Photo p.288a.] On the front of the buttress is an exciting-looking groove-line. Climb this to its top, progressing carefully over the slab above to reach belays.

On the right-hand side of the buttress lies a broken groove leading to a prominent hanging flake.

Artifice 70 feet Severe 4a † (14.7.88)
Climb the broken groove easily to reach the flake. Pass it by climbing up to the left in an awkward position. *Friends* are useful.

Ramp Buttress

Behind (landward of) Half Dome Cliff and up the grassy slopes lies a small buttress with an easily identified, easy-angled ramp leading diagonally up to the left from the right-hand side of the buttress.

Rampo 60 feet Very Difficult † (14.7.88)
Climb the ramp to its top and make a pull up into the groove above. Continue up this to finish.

Purgatory Buttress

To the right and across a grassy gully lies another buttress with a prominent corner high on the right-hand side of the seaward face (the line of *Sinners*).

Shortcake 25 feet Very Difficult (20.12.88)
The short V-groove in the left wall of the buttress.

Innocents 40 feet Very Difficult † (14.7.88)
Climb the obvious corner in the prominent middle arête of the buttress to reach a large grassy ledge. Continue up the steep crack in the corner at the back of the ledge to reach nut belays.

☆**Sinners** 40 feet E1 5b † (30.8.87)
Although short, this is a good climb on solid rock. A pleasant way to finish off the day. Start below the obvious corner at mid height. Climb the crack to the overlap. Pull over the overlap into the corner and follow this to the top. Large nut belay.

Red Stack Rocks

Directly below Purgatory Buttress is a grassy slope leading to a large broken pinnacle. This marks the top of the routes *Goth* and *Turk*. The section of cliffs below is easily identified from above by the presence of a red-topped sea-stack to the left of the pinnacle as you look out to sea. This area can be reached at low tide and during calm seas by a scramble down the grassy slopes as for *Touch the Devil* but then cutting back left (west) and climbing down a red ramp of rock to reach sea-level boulders in a large, slot-like sea-cave. Continue scrambling around under a huge hanging prow to the next sea-cave, and the lines of *Goth* and *Turk* will become obvious: two grey groove-lines in the upper walls above the cave. Further around, towards the red-topped stack, a large flat platform will be reached, well above sea-level, from which *Safe Haven!?!* starts. This can also be reached by a steep abseil, anchor-points being found in cracks in a small buttress 50 feet south of the aforementioned pinnacle. Scramble on round into the next bay, and a steep and impressive wall is seen, with a broken groove-line at its left-hand end (the line of *Exclusion Zone*) and a deep chimney on its right. There are sea-washed ledges at the foot of the wall.

Eroica (E2/3) Pentire
Climbers: Matt Elphick and Tom Nettleship Photo: David Hope

Black Magic (E5) Pentire
Climber: Ken Palmer Photo: Nick Hanco

Blue Juice 70 feet E5 6a † (13.8.95)
A good route up the wall left of *Goth*. Abseil down *Goth* to a hanging belay at the bottom of the groove, below a left-facing overlap. Climb leftwards around the overlap to gain a ledge on *Goth*. Move diagonally leftwards to a triangular recess; then go rightwards and up the centre of the wall, moving leftwards into the lichened crack near the top.

Goth 110 feet E2 † (7.9.71)
The left-hand groove above the sea-cave, which is reached by climbing the chimney formed by the cave. Start an hour or two after low tide to allow the rock to dry out.
1 60 feet 5b. Follow the chimney to a ledge and continue until the seaward wall eases; climb this to overhangs. Fix a runner and then move down and gain the opposite wall (poor peg). Climb diagonally left with difficulty to good holds, which enable the groove to be gained. Go up for 10 feet to a stance and peg belays.
2 50 feet 5a. Continue up the groove to the roofs; then move left to a crack and follow it to the top.

Turk 110 feet E2 5b (30.4.71)
[Photo rear cover.] The right-hand groove. The crux lacks protection. Climb on slabby rock to a wide crack and follow it to a narrow shelf on the left. Move along this and gain the groove by a delicate move. Climb the groove to a steep finish.

Safe Haven!?! 60 feet Hard Very Severe 5a † (6.8.95)
An escape route from the area! From the platform, scramble up easy rock to a large ledge below a steep wall cut by a quartz band, where poor protection can be arranged. Step right along the ledge and pull up the wall steeply, making an interesting mantelshelf onto the next ledge to gain better handholds on the shelf above. Step up and right onto the slabby ramp and continue up it to the belay platform. Belay on the abseil rope if one has been used.

Exclusion Zone 50 feet Very Severe 4c † (6.8.95)
This takes the hanging groove-line to the right of the westernmost steep wall. Start just right of an overhanging groove. Climb the rightward-slanting diagonal crack towards a blotchy grey and black wall to reach enormous jugs. Follow these back left along the broken crackline until a slabby ramp is gained (as for *Safe Haven!?!*) and follow it to the top.

To the right is an impressive steep wall bounded on its left by a left-facing, hanging groove and on its right by a deep-cut chimney above the sea.

☆☆**Whoops Apocalypse** 80 feet E5 6a (1 pt aid) † (29.7.99)
A startling climb up the wild hanging groove, which gives a great workout for the forearms and a crux that connoisseurs of gritstone jamming will appreciate. Start to the right of *Exclusion Zone*, on sea-level ledges below a deep crack.
Climb the crack to the overhang. Follow it round to the right under the overhang to a good thread; then pull steeply up a short corner to reach an excellent ledge and good *Friend* and nut placements under the main overhang (belay possible). Traverse left under the overhang to gain the steep wall and hanging groove. Go up the groove (peg, rest point) before reaching the bulge. Climb the bulge with difficulty (crux) to reach a welcome thread and rest on the ledge above the bulge. Continue to just below the top, and traverse 10 feet left along a crack to reach the finishing-ledges.

☆**Hiroshima Mon Amour** 110 feet E2 † (6.8.95)
A good outing that tastes the main face but avoids the central challenge.
1 50 feet 5b. Climb *Whoops Apocalypse* to the stance under the main overhang.
2 60 feet 5b. Traverse right from the belay ledge for 10 feet to gain a good ledge and rest below a steep crack. Pull up the crack to reach a large niche and then move more easily up left to a large finishing-platform.

Pentire Point

At the tip of Pentire Point is a gully which leads down past a high cliff to a boulder-cove, with a slab on its left-hand side. In spite of many attempts to find them the exact lines of these climbs have still not been identified by the author. The original descriptions are given below with the appropriate caveat.

Hopener 170 feet Severe † (10.4.71)
An intimidating route for its grade. Start below the lowest point of the slab, on a boulder that is covered at high tide.
1 90 feet. Step onto the slab and move up and left to a corner. Make a committing step onto the right wall and swing up to good holds on the slab. Continue direct until moves right gain a cave stance with thread and nut belays.
2 80 feet. Move back left and go straight up to the top. Nut belays in rocks back from the edge.

Thinisher 150 feet Hard Severe † (8.7.81)
Start right of *Hopener*, at an open corner.
1 80 feet 4b. Climb the corner and continue up the slab to the cave stance of *Hopener*.
2 70 feet 4b. Go up to the white quartz patch right of *Hopener* and then continue to the top.

Butter Hole

OS Ref 908 779

Butter Hole is a small bay in the west flank of the large headland, of which Stepper Point is the northern tip, guarding the southern entrance to Padstow Bay. There is roadside parking at Lellizzick Farm (OS Ref 908 773), from where a way-marked access path leads out to the coast path near the bay. Just beyond the grassy spur to the north is Pepper Hole, an awesome blowhole, deep and vegetated, in the unsavoury depths of which the decaying remains of unfortunate sheep can often be seen socializing with other less readily identifiable garbage. The seaward face of the blowhole is formed by an impressive hanging slab, which has recently succumbed to climbing exploration.

Descent to Butter Hole is by following the cliff edge until a rocky scramble leads down the spur past a nose of rock to ledges at its base. To the north, the ledge-system continues at lowish tides, allowing relatively simple access to Cave Buttress; at high tides the buttress can be reached by a more delicate traverse-line across the wall. To the east of the descent, at the seaward end of the northern side of Butter Hole, there is a series of sharply-defined grey corners and ribs; these have been climbed, though the rock is soft and unpleasant. Further east is Suntrap Slab, south-facing and providing a number of pleasant routes in the low to middle grades; and to the east again is the Hidden Amphitheatre. The Ramp Cliff and the two Butter Hole Slabs lie on the coastline just to the south-west of the bay.

Pepper Hole

☆☆**Mrs Pepper Pot** 180 feet E5 † (30.6.96)

[Photo p.32.b] The first route to breach the overhangs and hanging slab forming the seaward face of Pepper Hole. Two contrasting pitches. Start on the platform just above sea-level on the west side of the face (accessible from Cave Buttress at mid-to-low tide).

1 50 feet 6a. Traverse the slab to an exposed position at the junction with the arch. Place a sling around a spike/flake and, from a very high bridging-position, locate a crucial *Rock 2/3* placement in a short crack above. Swing round onto the hanging nose and traverse left on quartz holds (avoiding a brittle quartz fang) to a small projecting foothold on the cave lip (cams in undercut up left). Move up to an excellent slot below the roof and powerfully undercut the roof-crack rightwards. Layback the continuation crack to regain balance on the slab. Belay ledge 6 feet above.

2 130 feet 5b. Climb the slab, bearing left to a small quartz pancake. Move up right to a prominent flake and good wires (also a good thread in a crystal cluster 15 feet left).Climb right and up to a projecting hold, then direct to another quartz flake and easier ground above. Make a rising traverse leftwards across the hollow white quartz sheet (thread *in situ*) and past a small quartz spike and another thread to a flake and ledge. Finish more easily up the slim groove.

Cave Buttress

The following five routes are found to the left (north) of the cave.

The Weaver 110 feet Hard Very Severe (22.6.96/18.7.96)
This route weaves its way intricately up the groove-line on the left section of Cave Buttress. It involves subtle route-finding, but with good protection if double ropes are skilfully used. Start at the toe of the buttress, one level lower than the start of *Red Parade*, on a flat platform which can be wave-washed at high tide if there is any swell. This is just where the ledges swing landwards and lead to the massive cave and slab of Pepper Hole.
1 30 feet 4b. Step up to a prominent blocky ledge below a groove, but then step left and up before swinging back right into the groove. Exit from this up and left, and move directly up to a pillar and thread belay below the obvious groove.
2 80 feet 4c. Make a few moves into the groove but then swing right across the wall and onto the prow. Climb this to a ledge below an overhang. Step back left into the groove to layback up the groove until it is possible to exit right onto a ledge that has formed where part of the next overhang has 'dropped'. Avoid the groove and overhang by a cheeky rightward foot-traverse, which takes you into an airy position on the face of the buttress. Make delicate moves up and right to pocketed rock, which is climbed up and slightly left to the top of the cliff. Belay 50 feet higher on two stakes.

☆**The Mongfish** 110 feet E3 † (28.7.90)
Contrasting pitches and good scenery. Start 20 feet left of *Red Parade*, below an inverted V-shape (the fish's tail).
1 60 feet 5a/b. Climb up to the apex of the V and move through a small overhang to reach the rightward-rising traverse-line (the fish's backbone). Follow this on large but brittle holds to a junction with *Red Parade*; then swing boldly rightwards to grovel onto a good ledge.
2 50 feet 5c. Climb the very steep crack in the back of the large niche strenuously, but with good jams and protection, to pull over the lip using a large quartz hold. Continue up easier ground to the top. Belay on a rusted stake backed up with wires.

☆☆**Red Parade** 100 feet E1 5b/c † (1.5.85)
A fine, well-protected route up the overhanging crack in the face of the buttress. Climb the crack direct to its top, and then move left to the base of a second, steeper crack, which is followed to a slot. Move right and use good pockets to pass the overhang. The rib on the left leads to the top and an *in-situ* rusted stake (back up with wires).

★**Soweto** 100 feet E4 6a (9.7.89/14.7.89)
Good steep wall-climbing up the edge of the buttress right of *Red Parade*. Quite bold, with some interesting and exciting situations. Start 10 feet right of *Red Parade* and climb up the vague crackline just left of the arête to a niche with a short diagonal crack. Follow a line of good sharp holds up

rightwards to the edge of the buttress and move up precariously into another niche. Make a hard move to exit leftwards to gain jugs, and then go straight up and over the bulge above on good pockets. Continue up less steep rock to the top.

☆**Maggie's Mistake** 100 feet Severe 4a † (19.4.85)
A well-positioned route up the apparently easy-angled slab to the left of the cave. Climb up the left side of the slab to gain the groove and a good spike. Move right across the slab to a crack, which is followed until steeper rock is encountered. Move right, and right again on the narrowing slab above the impending drop; then break right on jams and continue direct to the top, or finish up the slab further right. Belay well back (150 feet of rope needed). (There is a pointless direct start (15.9.96) above the pool to the right.)

Full Term 100 feet Difficult (17.8.85)
Climb the broken rock immediately left of the descent route, linking the grooves to a left-slanting slab with a steeper wall above.

Suntrap Slab

Sally 110 feet Hard Severe 4b (17.2.85)
This takes a line up the left-hand section of the slab, the first 20 feet being awkward and unprotected. Start at a smooth pillar. Climb the right edge of the pillar and move right at its top to a narrow slab. Go up an open groove and continue up the main slab. Various lines are possible to finish on the rocky spur.

☆**Vive la Revolution** 110 feet Severe 4a † (14.7.89)
Very pleasant climbing up the slab between *Sally* and *Ra*. Follow the steep crack through the bulge 15 feet left of the cave of *Ra*; then step left and climb the slab, passing an obvious square-cut groove.

Ra 110 feet Difficult (17.2.85)
A pleasant route. Climb a line up the right-hand edge of the slab, starting in the cave.

☆☆**Little Robert** 70 feet Very Severe 4c † (17.2.85)
A fine little route, on rock of Penwithian reliability, taking the obvious line to the right of the *Ra* cave. Start at the base of a short prominent crack with a niche. Climb strenuously into the niche and continue past a smaller niche to the impending headwall. Traverse right to gain a quartz slab, which is climbed to the top.

Lieve Tina 80 feet Very Difficult (22.6.96)
An easier start from the right to the fine top slab of *Little Robert*. Start 15 feet right of the niche of *Little Robert*, on a slightly higher ledge below a corner. Climb the corner and the slab on the right; then step left onto a slab and go up and left onto the quartz slab of *Little Robert* to finish.

Hidden Amphitheatre

This area is to the right, or east, of Suntrap Slab, but access from the latter is barred by a deep zawn behind the buttress of *Little Robert* and *Lieve Tina*. It is best approached by a 150-foot abseil from two *in-situ* stakes above the buttress of *Crater* to arrive at the east end of the amphitheatre. The floor of the amphitheatre is above high-tide level but it is possible to reach the base of the two most rightward routes only at low tide with a calm sea.

The left end of the amphitheatre is marked by the zawn behind *Little Robert*, the back wall is dominated by a cave, and the right end has two obvious corner-lines, *Crater* and *Moore's the Pity*. From here, a traverse right at sea-level leads to the prominent corner of *The Skiver*.

Climbers' Club Very Ordinary 100 feet Severe (31.3.96)
On the left-hand side of the amphitheatre there is an easy-angled buttress. On the right-hand side of this are an obvious corner and a crack. Climb directly up the crack, using big jugs on the right wall, and then go directly up over bulges, avoiding loose rock at the top.

Ali 90 feet Hard Very Severe 4c † (15.9.96)
Scramble easily up into the cave 15 feet above the platform and belay on its floor, below a groove that goes up to the overhangs. Climb the groove to a resting/bridging-position below the overhang. Step down and make bold moves left until a move up at the left-hand side of the overhang can be made. Climb directly up, using a groove and then a nose on the right. Exit over loose ground to belay stakes on the right.

One for Curly 110 feet E2 5b † (15.9.96)
Start as for *Ali*, and climb the groove to the resting-position. Move right across a short slab and then dynamically up and right to a chimney-like resting-place half-way along the rightward traverses below the overhangs. Move round and down slightly to the right-hand end of the overhangs. Climb straight up from here. At the top, the angle eases and the rock becomes loose. Belay on stakes

Crater 150 feet Very Difficult (31.3.96)
The prominent west-facing corner on the right side of the amphitheatre. Climb steep bubbly rock, past a thread runner, to a ledge right of the corner. Move on steeply up to the base of the corner and on up this to the top of the cliff and belay stakes. Some loose rock at the top.

Moore's the Pity 150 feet Severe 4b (28.4.96)
The shallow south-facing corner with a prominent overhang to the right of *Crater*. Start at the right-hand end of the amphitheatre platform. Climb up the steep wall (good holds, good rock, good protection) to the overhang at the bottom of the open corner. Climb the corner to a ledge, where a traverse left could easily join *Crater*; the arête on the right gives better rock and leads to the top. Belay stakes as for *Crater*.

Toje 150 feet Very Severe 4b † (15.9.96)
The groove at the very right edge of Hidden Amphitheatre and to the right of *Moore's the Pity*. Climb easily up ledges for 10 feet; then steeper climbing up the groove leads to a harder move across the steep wall on the left, made by using a pocket to reach an arête. Step up onto a slab below a steep corner. Climb dynamically up the corner and the short continuation above to reach easier-angled ground. From here, go easily up to belay on the stakes.

To the right of Hidden Amphitheatre is a prominent corner, reached by a low-tide ledge-traverse rightwards from the base of *Moore's the Pity*.

The Skiver 160 feet Very Difficult (18.7.96)
Belay in the base of the obvious corner above a narrow zawn.
1 100 feet. Climb the corner on magnificent rock to a slab at 30 feet, which steepens above to a wall. Climb the crack up the slab and wall until the angle eases and loose rock is encountered. From here, work up and left to the grassy bay.
2 60 feet. A scramble on loose rock. Move left and up across the bay to join the top section of *Crater* and *Moore's the Pity*, and belay on stakes.

The Voice 160 feet Very Severe (18.7.96)
The prominent rightward-leaning crack up the right wall of the corner of *The Skiver*.
1 100 feet 4b. Step right out of the corner to make an off-balance swing to get established in the crack, and climb it until the angle eases. Move straight up the wall to a ledge and then on up to an overlap until the angle eases and some loose rock is encountered. Move left to the belay of *The Skiver*.
2 60 feet. *The Skiver* pitch 2.

To the south, a wall runs towards the cliff-top. The next climb takes a line up the lower, purple-striped wall. Abseil in from stakes.

The Mind Field 180 feet E4 † (20.6.99)
Technically straightforward, but rock and protection require considerable care. Start in the centre of the wall, below a leftward-leaning crackline.
1 60 feet 5a. Climb the crack until able to traverse right to a belay below a flake pinnacle.
2 60 feet 5b. Climb up delicately behind the pinnacle, pull onto the slab above, and continue to a small block (*Friend 1* belay).
3 60 feet 5b. Traverse right from the belay to a V-groove, and climb it to good runners. Now traverse left to finish over blocks.

The horrific wall to the right has also been climbed.

Butter Hole Ramp Cliff

The cliff is 100 yards east of the top of Butter Hole Slab One. There are two *in-situ* stakes that mark the top of a hidden descent ramp. Once located, this ramp gives an easy scramble down and right (facing in) to a vast sea-cave that forms the left-hand side of Butter Hole Slab One.

Foaming Heels 190 feet Severe † (13.9.99)
Very atmospheric with a high tide running. Start at the base of the descent ramp, just below the left wall of the cave, but above the splash zone and well above the high-tide mark.
1 120 feet 4a. Intricate route-finding but easy climbing leads left to just above where the cliff steepens and drops into the sea. A final obvious ledge leads below an overhang; then go up into a scoop, which has a black slab with an overhanging base on its left side. Nut and cam belays in cracks on the left.
2 70 feet 4a. Make a bold swing on big jugs out left onto the slab, which is found to contain a mass of holds and plentiful protection. Climb directly up to finish at grassy rock on the top of the descent ramp.

Butter Hole Slab One

The cliffs to the south of Butter Hole are generally low and easy-angled. However, about 500 yards from the bay is a large slab with a deep corner at its right-hand side. Descent is by abseil from stakes (missing) to a stance in the corner, which can be engulfed in waves. The route is difficult to locate from above.

Soggy Socks 100 feet Very Severe 4b † (15.7.85)
From the belay, move left into the centre of the slab (a drier, alternative stance) and then climb directly up the crack in the slab to the headwall. Step right and climb this direct to belay at the stakes.

Gnome Killer 100 feet Severe 4a (25.7.85)
Climb the deep corner.

Butter Hole Slab Two

A hundred and fifty yards further south and just beyond an incipient zawn is another slabby buttress, rather more broken and with an undercut base, where the abseil is free. Stakes are missing.

★Little Woo 150 feet Difficult (27.9.85)
An enjoyable route of a quality not often associated with this grade on this coast. Start just left of the foot of the abseil descent.
1 70 feet. Climb easily right across slabs by ledges and step across a small zawn/blowhole. Continue up the easy-angled slab to a belay below the overlapping upper slab.
2 80 feet. Step up and right onto the upper slab and traverse easily right

in an exposed position until past the headwall. Finish delicately up the slab above.

★Dark Side of the Zawn 130 feet Very Severe 4b (30.6.88)
Start, as for *Little Woo*. Climb directly up on big jugs to a small smooth slab, which is climbed to jugs at its top to reach an easy leftward-traverse. Swing left from its end to gain the base of the main undercut slab to the left of the buttress. Go up the right side of this, via the corner-crack, to the headwall. Traverse left on good holds above the zawn to reach the left arête, which leads easily to the top.

Gunver Head

OS Ref 894 770

It looks a lot more impressive than it is, with large sweeps of steep though remarkably impermanent rock. Just south of the point are three spectacular stacks which provide the climbing. The quickest approach is from the lane leading to Lellizzick Farm (OS Ref 908 773), but park about half a mile south-west of the farm; from that point, a way-marked access path leads out to the headland. It is possible to scramble down to the right of the waterfall, south of the stacks, from where an interesting low-tide traverse gains ledges immediately opposite. The largest stack has a cairn on the top and was climbed in 1976 by an easy but interesting scramble. The stack with a prominent 15-foot tower on its top gives two, more substantial routes. Low tide is required.

Totem Pole 140 feet Hard Very Severe † (1985)
Start on a sloping ledge at the left-hand side of the seaward face.
1 80 feet 5a. Climb a shallow groove in the smooth wall to reach the left-bounding ridge.
2 30 feet. Continue easily up the ridge to the base of the final tower.
3 30 feet. Climb the tower. The descent is not described by the first ascensionists but those of an enterprising frame of mind sufficient to make the climb will no doubt apply the same enterprise to escape.

Wet Pig 150 feet E1 (1985)
Start as for *Totem Pole*.
1 60 feet 5a. Climb diagonally right to a clean-cut corner leading to the right-bounding arête.
2 60 feet 5b. Climb near to the arête to the base of the final tower. Move right round the base to the final stance of *Totem Pole*.
3 30 feet. *Totem Pole* pitch 3.

Trevone

The loose Marble Cliff (OS Ref 892 764) had one route climbed up its left-hand side in 1975. The only detail remaining is that it was an undeniably unpleasant experience.

Just west of Marble Cliff is The Roundhole (OS Ref 889 763), and on the north side of the headland beyond is an area of excellent rock with some short climbs, reached by a steep fisherman's path down the crest of the headland. Immediately east is an obvious slab, above which two stakes used to reside. Descend by abseil, treating any remaining stakes with caution – i.e., take your own.

Satanic Slab 90 feet Very Severe 4c † (9.12.84)
A worthwhile route on good rock. Start at the seaward end of the ledge at the base of the slab. Climb the slab by the line of least resistance, first on the right, then by moving slightly left before reaching a crack on its right-hand edge. An easy ramp follows to gain the top.

Park Head

OS Ref 841 708

This is the headland to the north of Bedruthan Steps, about one and a half miles from Mawgan Porth beach. The cliff is about 15 minutes walk from The National Trust car-park at Bedruthan Steps. The only route to date is situated on the north side of Park Head. From the crest of the headland a ramp leads down beneath an impending wall. The ramp narrows at one point and can often be greasy. Left of the impending wall is a central, more broken area of cliff, and beyond this there is another wall.

Proctoscopy 135 feet Severe † (9.9.84)
The crack at the back of the central bay. As the name suggests, the rock has a gut-like quality near the top. Start at the base of the crack below high-tide mark. Climb up the steep corner on good holds until the angle eases at 30 feet. Continue up the crack with good protection. An extra rope is needed to reach belays well back and to the right.

Trenance Cliff

OS Ref 847 679

This is a handy crag for those requiring a change from sunbathing and paddling, as it is situated on the north side of Mawgan Porth beach. An obvious 180-foot-high slab rises above a few small boulders. The base is undercut by a series of quartz roofs.

An easy climb, **Alison's Rib** (230 feet Difficult † 3.6.84), takes the rib and slab left of the overhangs in two pitches (stake belays at the top).

Senecio Slab 220 feet Severe 4a † (4.12.83)
A more substantial climb than *Alison's Rib*. Start below the centre of the quartz overhangs.
1 140 feet 4a. Climb to the overhang and surmount it, using good holds above. Traverse up and right to a light-coloured scoop of good rock, and go up this to a grassy bay. Spike and nut belays to the right.
2 80 feet. Climb the slabby rib above to the top.

A technical pitch (30 feet Very Severe 5a) climbs through the widest part of the overhangs, via an open groove and crack, to a junction with an easier route, **The 19th Hole** (220 feet Difficult † 5.3.84), which takes the rib on the right of the slab, gained from the right.

Berryl's Point

OS Ref 842 669

This is just south of Mawgan Porth and is identified by three large rocks just offshore. A ridge runs down to the most southerly of the rocks. At low tide, easy ground just left of the ridge leads down to sea-level. At higher tides, an abseil can be made down the slab on its right. Right of the slab is a wall near where a tunnel goes through the ridge.

Jenny's Jaunt 130 feet Very Severe 4b † (17.4.83)
The easiest line up the wall. Start two-thirds of the way along the wall from the obvious chimney corner, below a small triangular pedestal. Climb directly up the wall on good rock to the left side of the pedestal. From its top, step up and left onto a slab, and then move right to a good crack leading to a ledge at 30 feet. Traverse right for 50 feet; then go up on good holds to another small ledge. Climb directly up using a sharp edge to join the left-trending ramp. Follow this ramp to finish. Belays are a long way back at an old *in-situ* stake (extra rope required).

Rose Street (90 feet Very Difficult † 2.4.83) is the line of the central chimney/crack system, starting to the left of the through-cave and gaining the chimney from the left. An alternative start can be made from the right of the through-cave: **The Fireman's Start** (60 feet Very Difficult 10.10.82); and the ramp at two-thirds height heading up and to the left has been climbed at Hard Severe 4b (2.4.84).

Penhale Camp Area

The cliffs between Penhale Point (OS Ref 756 592) and Ligger Point (OS Ref 757 581) lie on M.o.D. property. An access agreement allows climbing at all times, the text of which will be found on page 15.

The Mine Shaft Cliff

OS Ref 758 591

On the south side of Holywell Bay, exactly where the OS map shows the low-water mark, is a small cove with a 60-foot, north-facing cliff of compact black rock. At the top of the cliff is a hidden mine shaft; next to this is the main belay stake, and there is a second, less secure stake further back to prevent the risk of a pendulum for the second on *Shark's Fin*.

Approach by walking along the beach two hours either side of low tide, or by scrambling down the west side of the cliff. Escape can be made this way when the tide comes in.

There are three 60-foot routes (all 8.6.97) taking, respectively, two prominent corners and a slightly loose crack between them. **Shark's Fin** (Very Severe 4c) climbs the left-hand corner, the crux being at the top. **Crispy Crack** (Hard Very Severe 4c †) is, naturally, the crack. **Desolation** (Severe 4a †) takes the right-hand corner to a ledge before moving left to finish as for *Crispy Crack*.

Island Zawn

OS Ref 758 789

The first zawn to the south of Penhale Point is Island Zawn, and the low headland on its south side is used by fishermen. There are two routes on the slabby south wall of the zawn. These slabs are crossed by a right-to-left-slanting break, which allows access to the slabs at high tide. At low tide, the first route can be approached near sea-level to a good ledge at the foot of the lower, steeper section of the slabs.

Sunny Sunday Stroll 180 feet Severe (29.4.84)
A direct line crosses the break and, if followed correctly, touches grass only near the top. Start at a thin crack above the ledge.
1 30 feet. Climb the crack to a stance on the horizontal break.
2 150 feet. Continue up the easy-angled slab until it steepens. A rib on the left leads up to the fisherman's path at the top.

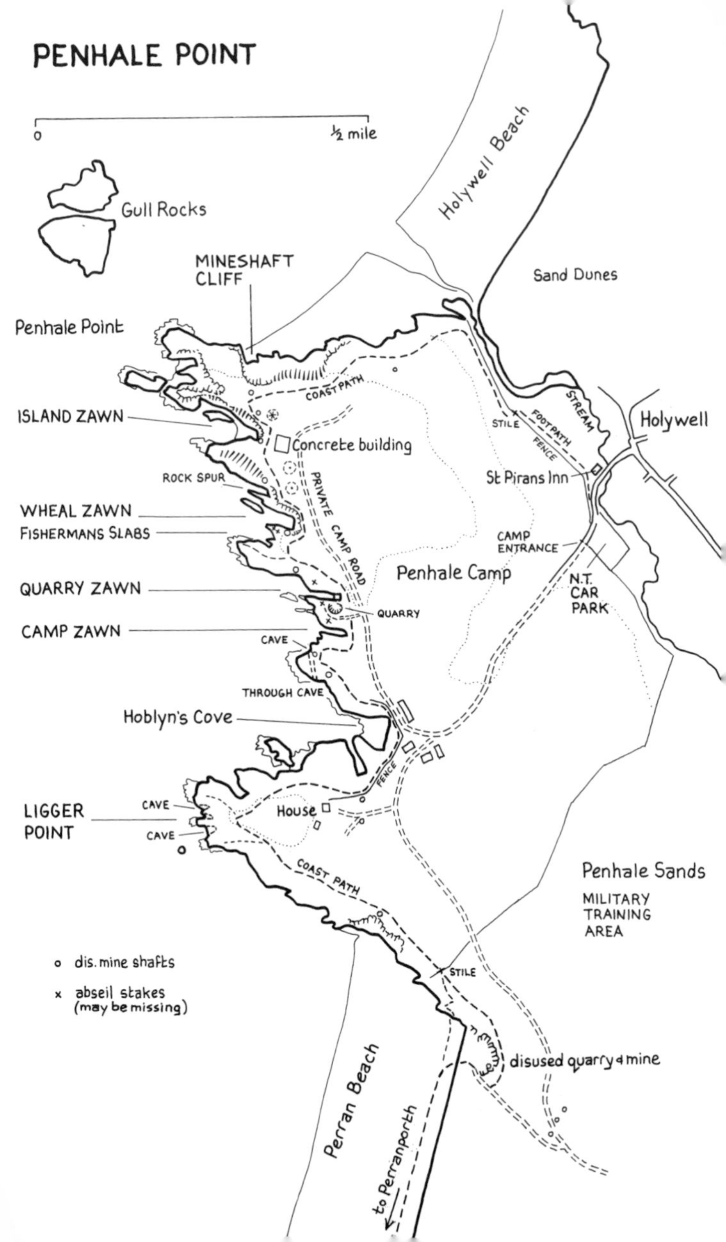

PENHALE POINT
0
½ mile
Gull Rocks
MINESHAFT CLIFF
Penhale Point
Holywell Beach
Sand Dunes
ISLAND ZAWN
COAST PATH
STREAM
STILE
FOOT PATH
FENCE
Holywell
Concrete building
ROCK SPUR
St Pirans Inn
WHEAL ZAWN
FISHERMANS SLABS
PRIVATE CAMP ROAD
CAMP ENTRANCE
Penhale Camp
QUARRY ZAWN
N.T. CAR PARK
QUARRY
CAMP ZAWN
CAVE
THROUGH CAVE
Hoblyn's Cove
FENCE
CAVE
House
LIGGER POINT
CAVE
COAST PATH
Penhale Sands
MILITARY TRAINING AREA
dis. mine shafts
abseil stakes (may be missing)
STILE
disused quarry & mine
Perran Beach
to Perranporth

Unholy Communion 110 feet Hard Severe 4a † (6.7.93)
Not well protected. Start in the minor amphitheatre between *Sunny Sunday Stroll* and *Anna*. Climb delicately up towards the obvious headwall on largish holds. At half height, a rising traverse to the left gains a small ledge. From here, front-point up to a slight bulge of biscuit-like rock and climb over it on large but dubious holds. Stake belay well back and obvious nut placements in the rock behind. (Please replace all holds after use.)

☆**Anna** 90 feet Very Severe 4b † (29.10.85)
Short, but delicate and enjoyable. Start on the diagonal break, below a depression beneath the steeper headwall. Climb up easy slabs to the crack, where the rock steepens and becomes biscuit-textured. Move right and climb the wall to a flake and crack. Go left to finish.

Wheal Zawn

OS Ref 759 587

Wheal Zawn is, in fact, three zawns, the main one of which is the most impressive, being about 250 feet high and readily identified by the mine shaft above its central section. At the right-hand side is an obvious faultline with a 200-foot-high slab to its right which continues to a prominent nose. There is a narrow, subsidiary slab capped by an overhang at the extreme right-hand end before the west-facing nose is reached. There is a series of angle-iron stakes in the small ridge leading to the top of the nose. A 200-foot abseil is made from these stakes – broken at a convenient half-way ledge providing a comfortable change-over – to boulders just below high-water mark beneath the subsidiary slab. In rough seas one can stop on the ledge at the bottom of *Icarus*. Waves permitting, an easy scramble can be made to the base of the nose.

Icarus 190 feet Very Severe † (29.5.84)
This takes the easiest line up the right-hand section of the slabs between the faultline and the subsidiary slab. Start above a short wall below the subsidiary slab, on a ledge below a corner.
1 100 feet 4b. Climb the easy corner for 20 feet to a sharp edge, which is hand-traversed easily left for 10 feet to a series of more difficult moves and the main slab. Climb this without further difficulty to the right to the large ledge passed on descent. Belay on the second ledge, below an obvious crack.
2 90 feet 4a. Climb the crack pleasantly until it ends. Step up and left to grass tufts and a final easy wall. Belay on the abseil stakes.

☆**Crack of Doom** 150 feet Very Severe † (10.6.84)
A good climb taking the right edge of the main slab. Start below the subsidiary slab, at an obvious steep corner. At high tide it is possible to start as for the preceding route and traverse delicately right to the line.
1 50 feet 4c. Climb the corner crack on good jams to belay on the first ledge.

2 100 feet 4b. Ascend directly behind the belay, moving right to the arête at 10 feet. Above, the 'Crack of Doom' gives exposed climbing to the top. Stake belays.

★★**Capital Offence** 130 feet E3 5c (13.7.85)
Originally climbed with a bolt for protection and aid, now unnecessary. Start as for *Crack of Doom*, below the steep corner. Climb the corner for 15 feet; move right to the arête, and then down to a ledge in the groove. Difficult climbing leads past a peg and up and right to zigzag cracks near the right arête. Climb to the top of a corner capped by a roof, and move left to steep grass and the top.

Fisherman's Slabs

These are the slabs on the south side of Wheal Zawn, reached by following the path down the easy rocky spur to large ledges. A calm sea is required for the traverse back east under the slabs from the end of the ledges. There are two short routes.

Failure to Thrive 80 feet Difficult (3.6.84)
A straightforward left-trending line up the slabs near their seaward end. Start below an overhanging nose of rock. Step up left from the belay and make some delicate moves across a white scar to good holds and a crack. Continue left up big steps to finish up a corner. Belays well back.

Sweat Test 50 feet Hard Severe 4b (3.6.84)
Climb the overhanging crack on the west side of the nose.

Quarry Zawn OS Ref 760 585

Generally loose, particularly on the north side, where an unpleasant route, **Tread with Care** (100 feet Very Difficult 22.8.84), takes the obvious left arête. The south side is more slabby, but still generally uninspiring owing to the nature of the rock. Two stakes *in situ* just to seaward of the obvious pinnacles provide the anchors for an abseil to the zawn bed and boulders, which are exposed at high tide. The corner and wall taken by the abseil is the line of **Angus** (130 feet Very Severe 4b † 26.2.84). The wall to its right has also been traversed with unsavoury results.

Camp Zawn OS Ref 761 584

A large zawn which has obvious slabs on its south side and a steeper wall on its north that looks very loose, though the rock is described only as fragile – praise indeed! The simplest descent is by a 250-foot abseil from a wooden path-marker (set in concrete) midway along the south side. There is a convenient grassy ledge half-way down which facilitates the changeover. The abseil ends at a boulder, which should be clear at all states of the tide (the start of *Top Secret*).

On the North Face is a distinctive lighter-coloured wall.

Orca 180 feet E1 † (1.4.84)
A rising leftwards traverse of the wall. Start on the largest of the flat-topped boulders on the bed of the zawn, which is sea-washed.
1 110 feet 5a. Follow the obvious diagonal crack leftwards and then go up to ledges just right of a pillar/block. From the right-hand end of the ledges climb a vertical crack, and move right to the large corner.
2 70 feet 4c. Climb the corner; then move right to the arête, which is followed to finish on the right up a grassy slope. Stake belays *in situ*.

☆**Supercruise** 150 feet Hard Very Severe 5a † (1.4.84)
A fine route taking a faint but distinct crack leading leftwards to a wider crack in the top section of the wall. Start right of the largest flat-topped boulder. Climb the leftward diagonal crack, on quartz holds at first, to enter the wider crack. Continue up this as it widens; then trend left to the top. The belay stakes may need an extension rope.

There are three routes on the south side of the zawn.

Top Secret 250 feet Very Difficult † (1.4.84)
A diagonal line starting from the boulder at the foot of the abseil.
1 130 feet. Make an awkward move onto the wall and go up to a groove, which is climbed to an easy traverse rightwards to a second groove. Climb this to the slabs, and belay at the left end of the large ledge.
2 120 feet. Continue easily up the slab; then traverse right beneath the overhang to climb an open groove on good but biscuit-like rock. Traverse right to *in-situ* stake belays.

Open Secret 250 feet Very Difficult † (1.4.84)
Start below high water, at the most seaward break in the lower wall.
1 130 feet. Climb the obvious crack for 30 feet; then follow the lowest fault easily to the right until beneath a corner with a short steep wall at its base. Climb this, using a thin crack, to a large ledge level with the seaward ridge.
2 120 feet. Climb the arête above the belay to finish over turf. Stake belays.

Crustacean 170 feet Hard Very Severe † (4.84)
A more direct line up the general area of rock shared with the preceding routes. Start 20 feet to the right of the groove of *Open Secret*.
1 100 feet 4c. Climb a thin crack to reach the obvious traverse-line at 20 feet; then move up and left through the bulge to a crack leading to a slab. Climb the slab to the ledge belay of *Top Secret*.
2 70 feet 4a. Climb diagonally left through the overlaps, and then up and left to grass 25 feet beyond. Belay to the path-marker post.

Ligger Point

OS Ref 757 581

A complex little headland, which marks the end of the Penhale climbing area. A fisherman's path descends to the point and a traverse-line leads across the north side into a subsidiary zawn with an obvious corner.

Black Slab 130 feet Very Difficult † (4.84)
Start at a smaller sloping corner with a black slab on its left, half-way to the main corner.
1 65 feet. Climb the corner to a belay in the cave.
2 65 feet. Move left around a nose to a gangway. Finish on its grassy continuation.

Shag Crag

OS Ref 746 541

A small headland of killas opposite the offshore stack of Shag Rock can be reached by following the coastal path east from the top of Cligga Head (15 minutes). The three routes are on the west side of the headland and can be reached by scrambling down the crest to a traverse-line (low tide only) leading back beneath the cliff. There are three distinct sections: a recessed wall, a buttress, and a red wall. At higher tides, the foot of the crag can be reached by an abseil from an obvious block

At the right-hand end of the recessed wall is a corner dividing it from the buttress. A short route, **Poxy Wall** (50 feet Difficult 14.7.83), climbs up and left from the foot of the corner. More substantial is **Alpine Departure** (60 feet Severe 4a † 14.7.83), the corner, finishing at the abseil block.

☆**Fisticuffs** 75 feet Very Severe 4c † (14.7.83)
A good climb, which follows the obvious corner-crack in the left-hand section of the red wall. Solid rock and reliable protection.

The Miners' Cliff

OS Ref 743 538

This is the small but pleasant area of slabs some 400 yards east of The New North Face of Cligga. Many lines are possible at Very Difficult or Severe, based on the slab, which can be gained from the east by traversing at about high-tide level. A major landmark is the prominent and very deep mine fault just to the east of some very easy-angled slabs.

Cligga Head

OS Ref 737 537

A popular cliff which, uniquely for this coast, is composed mainly of granite. Cligga also provides a good selection of shorter routes in the lower grades. It can be reached by taking the B3285 coast road from Perranporth for one and a half miles to the top of a steep hill, where a turning on the right is taken: this leads through a collection of buildings belonging to the Cornwall Gliding Club. Continue on to the main runway – look left, right, forward, backward, and especially upward – and cross it to a rough track, which passes through a devastated landscape of old mine workings and over a small bridge to a quarry on the edge of the cliff-top. Below and to the west is a vast 300-foot scree-chute, bounded by steep rotting cliffs. To the east are more spoil-tips. In between is the main climbing area, which is divided into sections by three natural features. The most conspicuous is The Great Zawn, at the tip of the headland. Eighty yards to the east is The Cleft, and the same distance to the south is The Great Cave. The New North Face extends eastwards from The Cleft. The North Face is between The Cleft and The Great Zawn, whilst The Central Face lies between Cligga Head itself and The Great Cave. Beyond the cave, the West Face, with its frightening earth and boulder cornices, is only too obvious.

The New North Face

This is mainly killas with just a hint of granite. Follow the cliff-top eastwards from The Cleft until it is possible to descend to a platform above the face. There are abseil stakes in place here; they should be used in preference to the original descent, which involved traversing back towards The Cleft for 20 feet to the aptly-named **Grot Gully** (Very Difficult) that was then down-climbed to the foot of the face. A small shelf is sea-washed at high tide.

North Buttress 130 feet Very Difficult † (25.8.84)
This climbs the buttress at the extreme left-hand end of the face, beyond which is an area of cliff with a slabby corner at two-thirds height guarded by steeper walls. Start on a small ledge just right of a rib above an overhanging wall. Climb the slab for 8 feet; then move right across a groove into a chimney/crack. Climb up to a ledge where it begins to open out. Go left to slabs, which are climbed on their left edge to the top.

Lord of the Dance 100 feet Very Severe (16.8.69)
Start at a large tidal platform below the arête 60 feet left of the foot of the abseil descent.
1 50 feet 4b. Climb the arête on holds that are often damp to a ledge at 45 feet. Move left to a tiny belay.
2 50 feet 4c. Climb the steep wall above for 15 feet, then make an ascending traverse left on bad rock to the rib, which leads to the top.

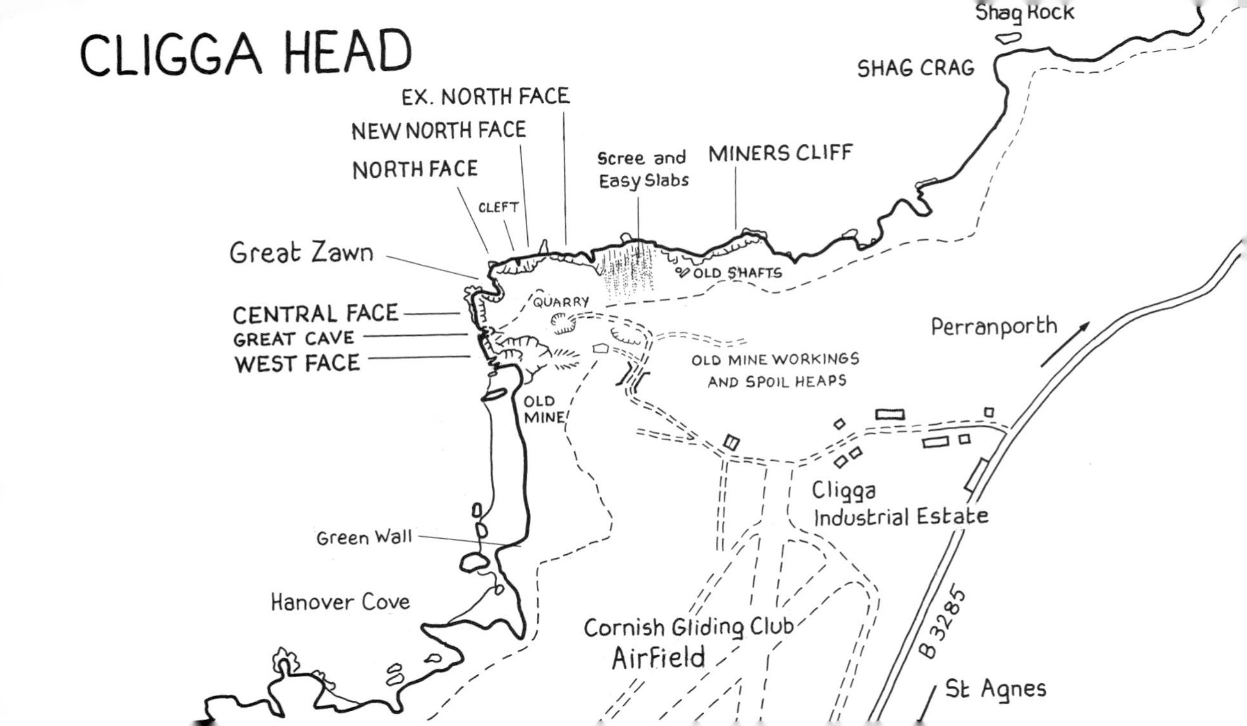
CLIGGA HEAD
Shag Rock
SHAG CRAG
EX. NORTH FACE
NEW NORTH FACE
NORTH FACE
CLEFT
Scree and
Easy Slabs
MINERS CLIFF
Great Zawn
OLD SHAFTS
QUARRY
CENTRAL FACE
GREAT CAVE
WEST FACE
OLD MINE WORKINGS
AND SPOIL HEAPS
Perranporth
OLD
MINE
Cligga
Industrial Estate
Green Wall
Hanover Cove
Cornish Gliding Club
Airfield
B 3285
St Agnes

The Dicer 100 feet Very Severe 4c (20.4.69)
The abseil descent finishes on some sea-washed slabs. Above is a steep chimney with two distinct cracks at its base. Climb the left-hand crack to a long ledge; then step left to a break, which is followed awkwardly to the top.

Ofus 85 feet Severe 4a (19.4.69)
Climb the right-hand crack to exit via the chimney.

Black Veil 120 feet Very Severe 4b (8.9.68)
The wall to the left of The Cleft. Start to the right of *Grot Gully* below a prominent curving veil of rock. Climb easily up the slabs and the short wall above to a ledge. Continue up the veil on thin holds; then step right and take the steep granite groove to finish. Thread belay well back.

The Cleft

The next two routes are both centred on The Cleft and are approached by abseil from awkward belays in the rocks above – a 50-metre rope being needed. Abseil leftwards (facing out) from the best belays into a groove (the top of *Maxwell's Demon*) heading for the east side of The Cleft. Sea-washed sloping ledges are reached.

☆☆**Fear of a Black Planet** 100 feet E2 5b † (19.5.95)
Beautiful, exhilarating climbing. Pendulum leftwards on the abseil rope to good holds about 15 feet left of the mouth of The Cleft (and the very steep crackline taken by the next climb). Climb steadily on good holds, moving slightly right at 50 feet (crux). Continue up a slight groove; then move left a couple of feet to finish up slabbier rock.

☆☆**Maxwell's Demon** 100 feet E5 6b † (25.6.95)
Very strenuous but excellently-protected climbing up a powerful, overhanging crackline. Move left (from the sloping ledges) to enter the initial offwidth crack that is immediately difficult (*Camelot 5 or 4*). Follow this past a face-climbing section leading to a poor rest under the large jutting roof. Pull through with great difficulty to poor finishing-holds on the shelving lip above. Continue up the somewhat easier groove to the top.

Near the northern tip of The Great Zawn is a very conspicuous dyke of rock running diagonally rightwards up the shorter section of the cliff. Descend to seaward (north) of this and traverse back right (facing in) to a spacious ledge below the start of the dyke (15 feet above high-water mark).

☆☆**Fingerin' the Dyke** 100 feet E3 5c † (18.5.95)
A beautiful sequence of moves up the dyke, poorly protected, but on excellent rock and with deep water below! Move up slightly; then traverse right to gain the dyke at the roof. Pull over with difficulty and establish yourself above with even more difficulty. Continue with interest to the top.

The North Face

The granite here is sound and the climbs are worthwhile. Go down the north edge of The Great Zawn, which is awkward in places, to a small pinnacle. Either descend an easy-angled slab and traverse left to a tidal platform (Difficult); or, at the same standard, descend the steep gully below the pinnacle, Gobble Hole Gully, to the same platform. The platform extends beneath the face as far as The Cleft.

Baldy Bane 90 feet Severe 4b (11.8.68)
Start to the right of The Cleft, beneath slabs. Climb to a bay at the foot of a steep slab. Go up the corner on the right, and move awkwardly over a step to a second slab and a short wall, which is turned on the left, to exit at the top of The Cleft.

Stone Table 120 feet Hard Severe 4b (28.7.68)
Start 25 feet right of The Cleft, at a crack splitting the steep wall. Climb the crack to better holds leading up the slab above past a mushroom-shaped bollard on the left (stance possible). Surmount the short wall above on the left and continue direct to the top.

C Land Super 120 feet Very Severe 4c (4.8.68)
In the centre of the face is a prominent overhanging nose, and to its left a broad square-cut chimney. Climb up to the nose and move left into the chimney. Climb the slab at its back and exit on the right. Finish up the left-hand crack above.

★**Dreamboat Annie** 130 feet Hard Very Severe (1.4.78)
A fine route, starting as for *C Land Super*.
1 65 feet 5a. Climb up to the nose; then traverse right with difficulty to the arête. Continue traversing for 20 feet to the groove (of *Bronco*).
2 65 feet 4c. Climb the groove for 15 feet, break left onto the wall, and continue up a shallow groove to the top on slightly brittle rock.

Bronco 120 feet Very Difficult (4.8.68)
Start right of the overhanging nose, in the corner formed by the nose and the large slab. Climb the corner to an overhang. Step right along the ledge and surmount the large projecting block to reach the top.

Toad in the Hole 100 feet Very Severe 5a (10.77)
Start as for *Shades of Nod* at a small pinnacle. Climb the slab; then move left and go up the impending wall to a shelf. Traverse right to a groove, which is followed to the top.

Shades of Nod 100 feet Very Difficult (25.8.68)
Start at a small pinnacle below the large slab right of the nose. Climb directly up the slab and the wall above by a groove on the right. Finish up a shallow sloping chimney.

The Orange-Throated Gronk 100 feet Severe 4b (20.4.69)
Start at the right-hand end of the slab, below an orange niche. Move up into the niche and exit on the right. Step left and finish direct on steep rock but good holds.

Gail's Waist 80 feet Hard Severe (4.6.83)
Start 15 feet right of the orange niche, on a small ledge.
1 40 feet 4c. Climb direct for 8 feet to good holds; then traverse left to gain the niche at its right-hand edge.
2 40 feet 4b. Leave the scoop via an obvious crack in the back and continue to a small chimney, which leads to the top. A better finish is to step left at a small black band of rock to another, gently-overlapping chimney; climb this past some loose rock to the top.

The Viking 90 feet Severe 4a (28.7.68)
Left of the descent gully the wall is split by an obvious fault, which is climbed to a slab on the right. Go up to a corner at the top of the slab and finish either by traversing right or by taking the left wall on fragile holds.

The Central Face

This is the area of cliff extending south from The Great Zawn. A fisherman's path descends, steeply, the south edge of the zawn.

★★**Queen Jane** 130 feet Difficult (20.4.69)
A pleasant route, having the atmosphere of typical zawn climbing without the more usual difficulties. Start to the left of the bottom of the path, at a depression between the cliff and the headland rock. From just above high-water mark, traverse left into the zawn to a narrow slab, which is climbed on good holds to a roof. Turn this on the left and finish up the long slab above.

An easier route, **Reflections of Inot** (100 feet Difficult 6.10.68), climbs the rock to the left of the path via an orange-coloured ledge formed by a block, and finishes up the wall on the left. To the right of the path are two short easy routes, **Clint's Route** (70 feet Difficult 17.8.68), taking a short gully, and **Dingo** (60 feet Moderate), up a series of steps and an obvious vein.

Right again are three large slabs and a smaller one sloping from left to right.

Second Choice 60 feet Difficult (10.8.68)
The left-hand slab.

Discretion 60 feet Severe (10.8.68)
The second slab: dubious rock.

★**The Masterdon** 120 feet Very Difficult (28.7.68)
Climb the third and largest slab centrally past a bollard; then step left into a groove, which is followed to the top on rock which requires a little caution.

Two Fair Maidens 120 feet Very Difficult (28.7.68)
Right of the previous route is a crack, which is followed to the bollard. Climb direct on poor rock to the top or, better, finish up the groove on the left.

Cobblers 120 feet Severe (28.7.68)
Start at a black spike below a sentry-box. Climb up to the left-hand corner of the sentry-box. Exit right and continue past a block to finish on very doubtful rock.

The West Face

There is one short route in the black zawn at the south end of the face. Follow the footpath down into the cove, where there are several mine-workings and natural caves. The zawn can be reached through the last of these, or by a low-tide traverse and a 15-foot climb.

★**Season of the Witch** 60 feet Very Severe 5a (24.8.68)
A good little route takes the only fault in the sloping right wall of the zawn. Place a peg below harder moves that lead to a ledge; then finish up the steep groove on the left.

Green Slab

There is one route on the bright green (copper-stained) slab on the next headland, 500 yards to the south of The West Face of Cligga Head. **Green Slime Crime** (200 feet Hard Severe † 9.86) starts at the right-hand side of the green stain up a line of slabby holds, which lead after 50 feet to loose, easier-angled rock. Continue straight up on steeper, more vegetated rock until a rising traverse left at 100 feet leads to a large gully with a prominent mine adit near the top. Loose, poorly protected, and not recommended – the description is 'for the record only'.

Carn Gowla

OS Ref 698 512

The stretch of coastline between Newdowns and Tubby's Head, one mile west of St Agnes, forms one of Cornwall's premier climbing areas. Unfortunately, apart for the three-star line of *Mercury*, it has dropped out of fashion in recent years. This is due to the erroneous perception many have as a result of numerous epic tales of escapes from various routes, high seas, suspect rock, and adrenalin-inducing abseils. For the adventurous, however, there is no better venue in Cornwall and much scope remains for exploration. Carn Gowla itself is the promontory at the junction of Teflon Slab with the Baptist Cliff.

From St Agnes, follow the minor coast road to the south towards Hell's Mouth across the seaward slopes of the prominent St Agnes Beacon. A turning on the

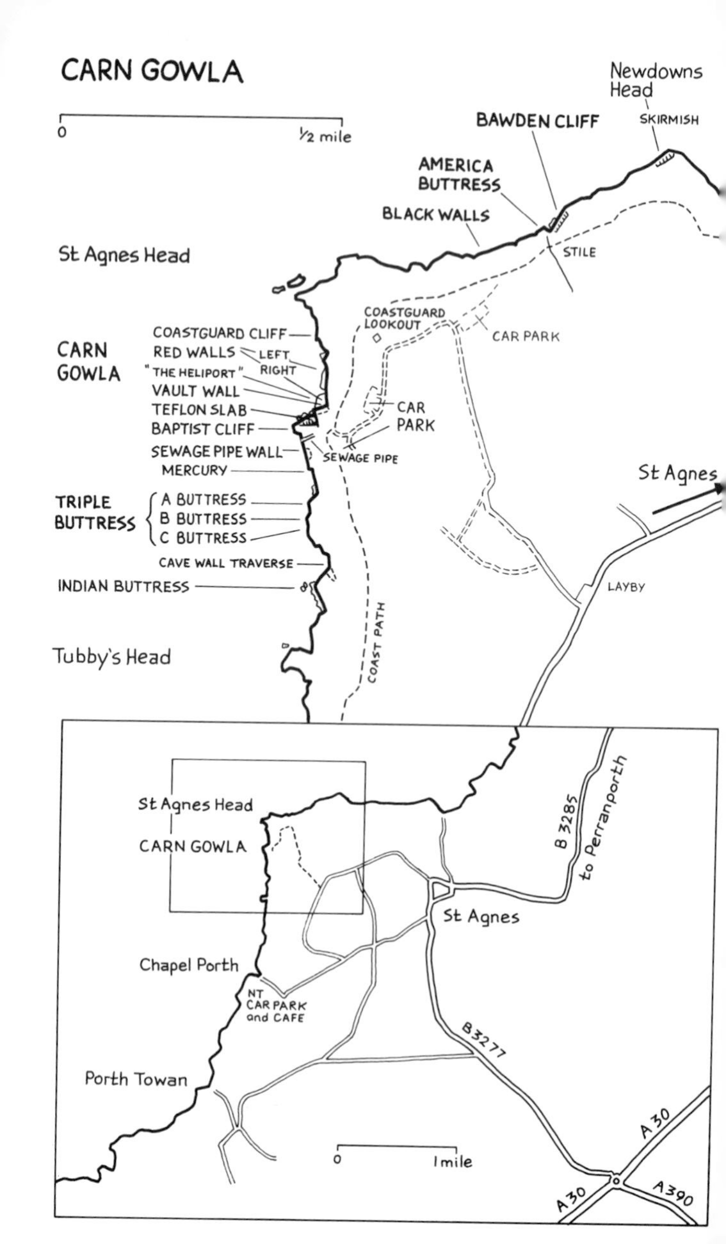
CARN GOWLA
0
½ mile
Newdowns Head
SKIRMISH
BAWDEN CLIFF
AMERICA BUTTRESS
BLACK WALLS
St Agnes Head
STILE
COASTGUARD LOOKOUT
CAR PARK
CARN GOWLA
COASTGUARD CLIFF
RED WALLS
LEFT
RIGHT
"THE HELIPORT"
VAULT WALL
TEFLON SLAB
BAPTIST CLIFF
CAR PARK
SEWAGE PIPE WALL
SEWAGE PIPE
MERCURY
St Agnes
TRIPLE BUTTRESS
A BUTTRESS
B BUTTRESS
C BUTTRESS
CAVE WALL TRAVERSE
INDIAN BUTTRESS
LAYBY
COAST PATH
Tubby's Head
St Agnes Head
CARN GOWLA
B 3285
to Perranporth
St Agnes
Chapel Porth
NT CAR PARK and CAFE
B3277
Porth Towan
A30
0
1 mile
A30
A390

right is reached after approximately a mile, and a minor road leads across to parking-areas near the Coastguard Station. St Agnes Head lies directly beneath the Lookout post and makes a good viewpoint for identifying the Red Walls and the Vault Walls immediately to the south. Four hundred yards to the east and identified by a stone wall on its crest is the summit of America Buttress. The same distance to the south is a conspicuous rusty ventilation pipe, which is situated at the top of the descents to Red Walls, Teflon Slab, and the Mercury Area.

Each section of the complex of cliffs here has its own distinctive character, owing to the differing geology and structures of the rock. These provide a variety of interesting and unusual climbs, the nature of which can take some getting used to. The rock is remarkably solid and, particularly in the lower regions of the cliffs, it can be very compact, with protection thus being somewhat sparse. The warnings concerning *in-situ* gear are undoubtedly merited, as many pegs are at least twenty years old and should be treated with the greatest caution. Some of the abseil stakes are also well past their sell-by date, the original ones above Black Walls, for example, having completely disintegrated. The most convenient descents are by abseil, but there are alternative climbing or scrambling approaches for those with little enthusiasm for adrenalin rushes. Some abseil points may require back-up ropes to outcrops well back from the cliff edge. The pessimistic might well justify carrying jumars or prusik loops; also, the rock near sea-level quickly becomes treacherous when wet, Teflon Slab being notorious in this respect.

Half-way between Bawden Cliff and Newdowns Head are two isolated climbs on the easternmost of two large slabs characterized by deep corners on their right-hand sides (facing in). Access to *The Skirmish* is by abseil down the left side to half-tide ledges below the undercut base of the easternmost slab.

The Skirmish 160 feet Hard Very Severe † (2.4.78)
Start beneath the large sloping roof to the left of a blunt pillar adjoining the slab.
1 50 feet 4a. Traverse diagonally right across the back of the overhung bay to reach the pillar and a stance at the base of the slab.
2 110 feet 5a. Go up to a niche (peg removed), and then trend leftwards beneath an overlap to finish on a narrow ledge. Peg belays removed. Walk off to the left.

A few yards west of the top of *The Skirmish* is a grassy hollow. The following route lies on the next buttress to the west of this hollow and is approached by descending a rake westwards from the top of the buttress to reach an adit. An abseil down the seaward slab leads to the base of the cliff.

War without Tears 70 feet E2 5b † (10.98)
Start below the left-hand side of the hanging slab, below a small overhang. Surmount the overhang and follow the corner above to the left of the slab until it is possible to step straight onto the slab itself. Move a few feet right; then climb directly to the top.

Bawden Cliff and America Buttress

The chief merit of Bawden Cliff is the grandstand view its summit provides of one of the most formidable crags in the West Country, the America Buttress: a huge overhanging prow above a smooth slanting slab, beneath which sharp ribs and half-hidden dark corners plunge steeply into the sea. Devotees of Bosigran's Great Zawn with its infamous crevasse will relish the commitment of the original approach. Even the easier alternative of the abseil has a distinct 'edge of the world' feel to it.

Bawden Cliff, an area of dark-coloured slabs, ends abruptly at its right-hand side in an evil cleft above a narrow zawn. It contains one route, which shares the first and easiest part of the *America* approach. Scramble easily down the left (east) rim of the slabs to a broad ledge 50 feet above sloping terraces that extend for some distance beneath the cliff. Climb down (Very Difficult) or rope down to these, and traverse right until the narrow zawn prevents further progress.

Ratcliffe Highway 240 feet Hard Severe (16.9.72)
An exploratory route of some character, the intrinsic qualities of which are withered by its glowering neighbour. Start a few feet left of the cleft.
1 100 feet 4b. Climb the wall, on large holds at first, taking the easiest line diagonally left to reach an obvious bay. Poor belays.
2 140 feet 4b. Go up easily to a large sloping ledge at 75 feet. Move diagonally left up the lichenous slab to a groove. Climb this to thread belays in a rabbit warren.

To continue to the foot of *America* requires a combination of the tide at its lowest and the sea at its calmest. Lasso a spike on the far side of the cleft and swing across before descending to half-exposed boulders. Boots and trousers may need to be removed before crossing these to a sloping, tidal ledge at the foot of the buttress. From the landing-ledge of the rope-move starts a poor route up the rock above, **Beresford** (350 feet Hard Very Severe † 9.78): climb to the top in three pitches.

The alternative abseil approach is made from a series of iron stakes on the crest of the buttress, using joined ropes, to the ledge forming the first stance of *America*, or further if sea and tide permit.

★★★**America** 330 feet E4 (16.6.73)
A superlative route which provides continuously sustained and serious climbing, though lowish in its grade. The upper reaches are very exposed. The rock is sound throughout but protection on the lower pitches is sparse, and in any but the driest of conditions the central slab can become a major obstacle. Start beneath the blunt rib forming the left edge of the lower wall.
1 90 feet 5b. Climb to a ledge beneath a short groove (stance possible if the sea threatens). Continue up more easily; then trend right to the edge of the slab (poor peg). Step right and climb up to the obvious niche. Move

AMERICA BUTTRESS
1 America E4
2 Guernica E6
3 Ku Klux Klan E6
4 Mausoleum E3
5 Escapist Direct E2
6 Running on Empty E4
7 Motion Sickness E3
8 Excellent Wall E2
9 Deceleration Lane VS
10 Reality Bypass E4
abseil approaches
D.J.S. ~ 2000

right again and follow the wide crack above to a comfortable stance on top of a flake. Peg belays.
2 140 feet 5b. Climb easily to where the slab steepens and becomes smooth. Move left to the edge, which is followed to a blank section. Use holds on the right to reach a dubious flake. Regain the arête and continue to an easing of the angle and good peg cracks in the upper wall.
3 100 feet 5c. Climb the obvious groove and enter another above. Climb up for a few feet and then traverse right on flat holds to a steep groove. Follow this past the remains of a large bird's nest, and move left onto an arête. Steep, strenuous climbing leads to a ledge, above which is a thin crack leading to the top. Stake and hawthorn belays.
Direct Finish E5 6b (1989). Climb the grooves, as for pitch 3, and continue directly up and through the roof to rejoin the original at the thin crack.

☆**1492** 120 feet E6 † (5.7.92)
An audacious venture up the hostile overhanging territory between *America* and *Guernica*. The situations on the upper pitch are particularly exposed. Start from the last stance of *America* and accustom yourself to the sight of an awesome hanging flake crack to the right.
1 40 feet 6b. Gain the leaning wall below the flake crack (poor peg). Small flakes lead up the crack; thereafter, power-laybacking propels you past a hanging block into the niche of *America* (after its traverse right). Good belays.
2 80 feet 6b. Follow *America* to the hands-on-ledge position immediately above its crux. Launch boldly rightwards onto the lip of the roof that forms the great jutting prow of the buttress. Continue for 20 feet past two pegs, 6b moves, and the fear threshold to a tricky exit into a small niche at the top.

★★**Guernica** 350 feet E6 (16.5.82/4.87)
A formidable companion to *America*. A very serious lead on which small wires provide marginal protection. The final pitches take the impending wall to the right of the top pitch of *America*. Start as for *America*, at low tide, beneath the blunt rib forming the left edge of the wall.
1 90 feet 5b. *America* pitch 1.
2 120 feet 5b/c. Climb easily, bearing right, to reach the corner formed by the junction of the central slab with the wall above. Climb the slab just left of the corner and continue for 25 feet to belay at an obvious vertical crack formed by a huge block.
3 80 feet 6a. Move up left for 15 feet; then climb the wall above to a large flat handhold. Traverse right to gain a large block on the lip of an overhang. Climb the wall above into a leftward-slanting groove and, at its top (peg), break right to a point where it is almost possible to rest (peg). Make a series of committing moves up and left to some flakes on the impending wall; then a sensational hand-traverse rightwards gains a large ledge.
4 60 feet 5b. Climb steeply from the left end of the ledge to a bay which

may contain a nest. Traverse left and move left past the next overhang into a short corner, which leads to the top. Belay well back on the left.

☆☆**Ku Klux Klan** 100 feet E6 6a/b † (4.89)
This takes the top half of the huge obvious arête left of *Mausoleum*. Start as for the top pitch of *Mausoleum*. Poorly protected on the arête (two pegs removed). Follow *Mausoleum* until an obvious 30-foot traverse to the left gains the arête at some spikes and stuck-on blocks. Follow the arête to a niche and pull out (crux) to a thread. Continue up the arête to a huge ledge and finish to the right.

★★**Mausoleum** 280 feet E3 (29.4.73)
A brilliant route, the outstanding feature of which is the compelling right-angled corner forming its top pitch. Unfortunately, this takes a certain amount of water seepage and needs a spell of good weather to come into condition. This also means that vegetation flourishes. The grade is E2 if the abseil approach down the final corner is used to avoid pitches 1 and 2. Start from the right-hand side of the sloping tidal ledge, right of the blunt rib of *America* at a chimney. This area is liable to be more wave-swept, being lower than the *America* start.
1 100 feet 5a. Climb the chimney and the leftward-slanting groove above to a peg belay on the slab. Very serious because of its situation and seepage.
2 80 feet. Make a leftward-rising traverse to peg belays beneath the obvious corner.
3 100 feet 5b. Climb the corner strenuously to a ledge, then on better holds to where the crack widens beneath a roof. Gain a ledge on the left and pull over the bulge on good holds. Continue to the top.

Escapist Direct 160 feet E2 (1 pt aid) † (4.73/26.8.73)
The second pitch, though easier than its neighbours, should not be underestimated. Start beyond *Mausoleum*, below a corner-crack (often below sea-level as well).
1 80 feet 5b. A nasty damp pitch. Climb the corner with increasing difficulty to a peg below the overhangs, which is used to gain holds on the right arête. Swing right onto easier rock and continue to a stance below the shallow corner at the lower, right-hand end of a ramp.
2 80 feet 5a. Climb the shallow corner above to easy finishing-slabs.

The following routes lie on the west flank of America Buttress, to the left (looking out to the sea) of the corner of *Escapist Direct*, and just to the right (facing out) of the huge corner where The Black Walls meet America Buttress. They are reached by an abseil.

Just below the top of America Buttress, in a bracken-filled hollow and to the left of the corner, is a large black hanging slab. The slab is reached by the abseil (nut and cam anchors in the outcrop above) down a short corner above its centre. This corner is not visible from the top of The Black Walls but is easily located from above. By extending the rope, the abseil may be continued over the left-hand end of the slab, down an overhanging wall to ledges above the high-tide level, just to the right of a large red pillar. All the following routes start from the left-hand edge of the ledges and are reached by traversing left from here.

Running on Empty 110 feet E4 † (15.9.96)
1 50 feet 4c. Traverse left for 20 feet; then move boldly up and left to a stance on a hanging slab below an overhang. Belays include a crucial *Friend* 2 in a pocket.
2 60 feet 6a. Surmount the overhang using steep and intricate moves; then follow the groove and arête to the top.

☆**Motion Sickness** 110 feet E3 5c † (10.98)
A harder companion to *Excellent Wall*, following a parallel line up the black wall 10 feet to the right of *Running on Empty*.

Excellent Wall 140 feet E2 5b † (10.98)
Traverse around the base of the pillar; then climb the groove on its left to the overhang. Climb straight over this and the wall above, and continue directly to the top of the crag.

☆☆☆**Deceleration Lane** 110 feet Very Severe † (14.9.96)
An excellent find, taking the corner where the pillar abuts the face on its right-hand side.
1 80 feet 4b. Climb the pillar, starting up the corner on its right-hand side, to reach a steep crack at its top. Move rightwards over easier ground; then climb the left-hand of two grooves to belay close to the base of the black slab.
2 30 feet. There are several different options for gaining the cliff-top, including the short corner above the centre of the slab.

The Black Walls

The Black Walls, hidden, and for a long time untouched except for the prime line of *Supernatural*, have experienced recent exploration. They extend westwards from America Buttress for some 200 yards from the huge black corner to the right of *Deceleration Lane*. The start of *Reality Bypass* can be reached by abseil from stakes (not in place) about a hundred yards west of America Buttress, at the right-hand end of the bracken-filled hollow where the vegetation changes to heather. Further left is another grassy hollow where stakes *should* be found for the abseil to the bottom of *Supernatural*, though they may not be in place; if they are they will need careful checking for corrosion. (Using a combination of ropes, it is possible to get additional belays well back on some small outcrops.) The stunning prow at the top of *Pierrot le Fou* can be seen from here, thus identifying this descent.

To the left of *Supernatural* is a wall taken by *Just Natural* and by *Natrel Plus*, bounded by an arête on its left-hand side. To the left of the arête is a large wall with tiered overhangs. The start of the first route can be reached by scrambling leftwards from the base of *Supernatural* at low tide and in quiet seas, or by the first abseil mentioned above to reach the left edge of the wall.

☆☆**Reality Bypass** 200 feet E4 † (4.8.96)
An exciting route following a logical rising traverse-line through the overhangs. At the left-hand side of the wall is a green chimney which narrows to a steep crack.
1 50 feet 5b. Follow the chimney and crack for 50 feet to a hanging belay in the crack below the level of the first roof.
2 90 feet 5c. Move right around the rib into a corner below the roof, traverse 15 feet right to the base of an overhung groove, and reach the slab above with difficulty (poor peg removed). Continue rightwards until a higher slab and corner can be gained; then move up and right to good cam placements below an overlap. Climb the overlap and move up rightwards into the corner above, taking care with a loose block. Move right to belay on the arête.
3 60 feet 5a. Skip up the wall just to the right of the arête. Stake belay in place.

Natrel Plus 130 feet E3 6a † (30.7.95)
Start from the belay of *Supernatural*, and traverse left with difficulty to the base of a crack. Climb the crack and move into a shallow groove on the right when the crack fades out. Move over an overlap to a good ledge, and climb the wall above with care.

★**Just Natural** 130 feet E2 5b (6.9.86)
Delicate and absorbing climbing. Start from the belay ledge of *Supernatural*. Make a couple of moves up *Supernatural* and step left to gain the thin crack running up the black wall immediately to the left. Climb this crack until it fades by some small ledges at the changeover from black rock to red. Trend up and slightly right to pass a small overlap using crystal-filled holds, and continue up over the final ledges with care to belay on the abseil rope.

★**Supernatural** 130 feet Very Severe 4b (4.73)
A secluded and very good little route. Abseil down a good crack in a smooth wall to a ledge some way above the sea, and then climb the crack all the way back up again.

☆☆☆**Pierrot le Fou** 130 feet E5 6a † (30.7.95)
[Photo p.288b.] The stunning hanging prow doesn't disappoint. Belay in the crack of *A Sackful of Clowns*, 40 feet below the top and level with a horizontal weakness stretching leftwards. Follow the weakness past a peg, and continue boldly in the same line (high poor peg) to a large ledge on the prow. Sustained technical climbing (with good protection in a crack to the left) leads up the left arête past a peg and a short crack. Take care with the loose finishing-blocks.

Some 40 feet right of the hanging prow is a superb black corner. Abseil down the corner from two tubular scaffold pipes and, usually, some knackered pegs to belay at small ledges above the sea at the base of the corner.

★★★**A Sackful of Clowns** 130 feet E1 5b (20.9.87)
[Photo p.288b.] Perfect rock, perfect position, perfect protection, and a dramatic arena. What more could one ask? Low in the grade. Climb the first steep section from the belay ledges to reach a good ledge and the widening crack. Continue jamming and bridging up the corner, passing left of the final overhang. Belay on the abseil rope.

Coastguard Cliff and Left-Hand Red Walls

Although the Red Walls present a continuous expanse of rock, a large cave/zawn in the centre effectively divides them into two sections with different approaches. From the Coastguard Station, follow the obvious path down towards St Agnes Head, and then bear south down easy shelving slabs until a ledge-system is reached which can be followed towards a 70-foot-high subsidiary buttress – Coastguard Cliff. These ledges fade just north of the buttress and a few tricky moves are required to gain the platform at its base. At low tide, easy scrambling at sea-level avoids this hiatus. Right of Coastguard Cliff, further ledges and shelves lead into a dark tidal zawn capped by overhanging rotten-looking cliffs, beyond which is the conspicuous pinnacle beneath the left arête of the Red Walls. A convenient terrace well above the reach of even the meanest of waves leads beneath the generally undercut base of this section of the cliff until it comes to an abrupt halt at the central cave. The steep entry shared by *Chicken Flesh* and *Ruby* is found at this point. Elsewhere the routes take crack-systems or lines of weakness up the slabby wall above. At high tides, an abseil can be made from small outcrops at the top of the grassy slope. Joined 50-metre ropes are required.

Coastguard Cliff

This diminutive buttress contains one minor gem, the strenuous offwidth corner of *Desire*. To the left of the platform, beneath the seaward face, is an area of slabs and slanting corners.

Crystal 70 feet Very Severe 4c (8.7.84)
Start towards the left-hand side of the crag and climb a ramp into a niche. Move up; then go out right to finish up an exposed slab.

Sluice 75 feet Hard Very Severe 5a (10.83)
Start beneath the right-hand edge of the seaward face of the buttress. Climb a short wall and the arête above to a big ledge. Move left over an unstable roof to the slab above, which is climbed to the top.

★★**Desire** 50 feet E2 5b (11.83)
The uncompromising, overhanging corner-crack immediately right of the seaward face is climbed to its large capping roof. Step left to the arête and

Silverfish (HS) Pentire
Climbers: Ian Parnell and James Cornwell Photo: David Hope

Pierrot le Fou (E5 ~ first ascent) Carn Gowla
Climbers: Ian Parnell and Kath Pike Photo: Jim Cheshire
Unknown climbers on *A Sackful of Clowns* (E1) beyond

finish more easily up a crack on the right.

Left-Hand Red Walls

Above the pinnacle the left arête provides a convenient exit and, once its position is established, a reasonable entry.

Yellow Arête 80 feet Severe 4a (6.83)
Start just right of the arête and climb leftwards just above an overlap to reach it. Continue in the same line to a grassy finish.

Weighout 90 feet Very Severe 4c (7.85)
Start 15 feet right of the pinnacle. Pull over the overhang and follow a thin crack leftwards; then cross an overlap on the right and finish just right of the arête.

The Final Cut 100 feet E1 5b (9.83)
Start 5 feet right of a fierce overhanging groove. Climb up to and over the overhang, leftwards then back right, and continue up the centre of a narrow slab to a diagonal overlap. Move rightwards across this and go up to a ledge. Climb over the overhang behind, and then leftwards up the slab to an earthy cave. Finish on the left at good belays.

★**Nowhere Man** 125 feet E2 5b (18.9.78)
A good route. Start at the foot of a leaning wall, directly beneath a crackline 40 feet above. Climb steeply up and left to a good ledge. Go up, and then head right for the base of the crack by a series of delicate moves. Follow the crack, which is sustained, to reach an earthy cave. Finish on the left.

☆☆**Barren Lands** 150 feet E6 6a/b † (21.6.92)
This takes the smooth and bald exposure of slab to the right of *Nowhere Man* on an intricate, sustained, and run-out line: a fall from the crux could prove traumatic; however, the rock is excellent. Start below the middle of the impending, stratified wall some 25 feet right of *Nowhere Man*.
From a short overhung groove, pull up left (poor peg removed) and then go back right to good holds in the red rock over the lip of the small roof. Pull up onto the slab (crucial *Friend* 2) and step up to reach the base of a hairline, rightward-slanting, diagonal crack (thread – wire needed). Follow the crack thinly rightwards to its end and then traverse back leftwards past an *in-situ* thread to a pocketed crackline in the middle of the slab (crucial *Friend 2, Rock 4*). Move tenuously upwards and very boldly, slightly rightwards, to a sloping hold and good peg just above. Move up again; then trend diagonally left to the shallow cave and exit of *Nowhere Man*.

The next three routes share an entry which is both strenuous and intimidating. At the far end of the platform, just before it disappears into the void of the cavern, is an overhung rib at the right-hand end of an impending stratified wall, the only real line hereabouts.

Carn Gowla
Coastguard Cliff and Red Walls

x abseil point

Coastguard Cliff

1	Crystal	VS
2	Sluice	HVS
3	Desire	E2

Left-Hand Red Walls

4	Yellow Arête	S
5	Weighout	VS
6	The Final Cut	E1
7	Nowhere Man	E2
8	Broadside	E3
9	Ruby	E3
10	Chicken Flesh	E3

Right-Hand Red Walls

11	Gravity's Rainbow	E2
12	Rotwand	HVS
13	Downward Bound	HVS
14	Happy Hunting Ground	HVS
15	Here and Now	HVS
16	Dark Lady	E3

Broadside 190 feet E3 (3.6.76)
Start below the rib.
1 70 feet 5b. Climb rightwards onto the rib, move up steeply to a resting-ledge on the left, and continue leftwards into a large depression with poor belays. The first decent protection arrives at 30 feet.
2 120 feet 4c. Go easily to the apex of the depression and swing right to a good hold. Continue up the crack and the open slab above.

★**Ruby** 140 feet E3 5b (30.12.73)
A good open face climb after a serious start. Climb *Broadside* to the resting-ledge, and then the thin crack above with difficulty to easier ground at a left-slanting faultline, which is followed for 40 feet to vegetation. Move right and climb the open face above to the top with well-spaced protection. Pull up one rope to enable blocks well back to be used as a belay.

★**Chicken Flesh** 210 feet E3 (3.6.73)
The best and most serious of the trio, taking a diagonal line up the exposed wall above the cave. Preplace a belay rope from the small outcrop above the finish.
1 100 feet 5b. As for the preceding two routes, attain the resting-ledge. Strenuous, well-protected climbing leads to a slab, which is climbed directly to a stance 15 feet left of the left-hand of two depressions in the wall to the right. Belay on wires and cams.
2 110 feet 5a. A potentially serious pitch, on which the need for care when placing protection and handling the rock must be emphasized. Many small wires needed. Traverse right to the first depression. Continue up its right arête until moves rightward gain a smaller depression. Leave this by a thin crack, which leads diagonally right to a sandy ledge. Two finishes are possible: either move right to a V-groove and protection, climb the rib of the groove, and move left at the top with great care (serious); or move left along the ledge (belay possible to avoid rope-drag) and finish leftwards over grassy rock.

Right-Hand Red Walls, Vault Wall, Teflon Slab

Three distinct areas, which share a common abseil approach and little else. Four hundred yards south of the Coastguard Station the track ends at a parking-area next to a small quarry and the ventilation pipe. Below, a series of broken, rocky ridges and towers rise above steep grass and scree slopes. The highest of these overlooks the top of the aptly named Teflon Slab. It is possible to descend the grass below this ridge to the seaward end of the slab, from where climbing at Very Difficult standard (or abseiling from good medium and large nut anchors) leads down the arête to broken ledge-systems beneath. The original and certainly more atmospheric descent is to follow the edge of the cliff (Demerara Wall) northwards from the quarry via terraces and grass, until a tiny and very exposed platform with good medium or large hex anchors is reached. Further back-ups can be found 30 feet up the slope but an extra rope would be needed. A 45-metre rope will reach the lower part of the left-hand bounding corner of Teflon Slab The abseil is free for most of its length, and from its foot an easy scramble leads to a large boulder-strewn platform beneath the Vault and Right-Hand Red Walls, known as the Heliport, terminating at the large central cave/zawn. This can be crossed at very low tides and calm seas.

When the rock is dry the Teflon Slab provides a number of easier pleasant routes which can be used as escapes if necessary. However, when wet the compact rock becomes lethally slippery and the abseil rope would then provide the only means of salvation.

Right-Hand Red Wall

To the right of the cave the red walls become higher and are split by a series of vague grooves and corners. A number of slanting overhangs are distributed across the lower half of the cliff.

☆☆**The Magic Wand** 180 feet E5 † (6.7.92)
Exquisite climbing up the undercut left-hand side of the *Rotwand* slab. Situations are superb and the rock is perfect, but the protection tends to be well spaced on the slab. Start 20 feet right of the sea-cave and 10 feet left of *Gravity's Rainbow*, diagonally down right of an impressive leaning groove.
1 100 feet 6a. Make a committing diagonal traverse, but on positive holds, leftwards into the foot of the groove (peg missing). Force the groove, and at its top exit left (*in-situ* thread) onto the foot of the slab. Follow a horizontal crack leftwards across the lip of the sea-cave for 20 feet. Tiptoe boldly straight up the slab on a line of reasonable footholds to reach a small jagged ledge and spike runner (crucial *Friends 1* and 2½ above). Move left for 10 feet and then follow pockets directly to a rightward-slanting crack and a ledge that leads to the *Rotwand* stance.
2 80 feet 5a/b. Climb right and up, as for *Gravity's Rainbow*, to the slanting roof (*Friend* 2½). Pull over the centre of the roof on jugs, and follow a thin crackline to join and finish up *Gravity's Rainbow*.

★**Gravity's Rainbow** 180 feet E2 (9.78)
Start just to the right of the cave/zawn beneath a small overhang at 12 feet.
1 90 feet 5c. Climb to the overhang; then make a blind swing to the left and continue in a direct line up the open face to a stance and peg belays on the half-height horizontal fault (as for *Rotwand*).
2 90 feet 5b. Traverse right (crucial *Friend* 3) and move up to the right-hand end of the slanting roof. Pull over leftwards using a flake and climb the slab to the top (cams). Peg and nut belays well back.

★**Rotwand** 190 feet Hard Very Severe (18.8.72)
A good open face climb. Start 15 feet right of the zawn at a steep narrow wall with overhangs to its right.
1 110 feet 4c. Climb the steep wall, and step left at the overlap to reach

a ledge above. Continue up the face on the left on good holds and head for a ledge on the faultline beneath a diagonal overlap. Peg belays.
2 80 feet 4c. Move up to the overlap and cross it to the left to a good crack, which is followed to a small ledge. Step right and climb the short red wall to a solid finish.

Downward Bound 220 feet Hard Very Severe (27.5.78)
A natural line but unfortunately loose in its upper section. Start as for *Rotwand*.
1 120 feet 4c. Climb the short wall until a tricky move to bypass the roof leads to a ledge in the corner/groove above. Follow the open groove to a large ledge. Peg belay 10 feet left by a large flake.
2 100 feet. Climb the flake crack and move left to regain the groove, which is followed past several loose sections. Finish up the broken wall on the left, using friable holds.

★**Happy Hunting Ground** 300 feet Hard Very Severe (2.6.73)
A good, long climb, low in the grade but with sparse protection in places.
1 100 feet 4c. Starting as for *Rotwand*, climb rightwards up a leaning wall to reach shallow grooves leading to turf ledges beneath a darker-coloured groove under an overhang.
2 90 feet 5a. Step up onto the right edge of the groove and climb the wall diagonally right to a large grassy ledge. Climb either side of a sharp flake and follow the crack above to a ledge. Move left to belays beneath the black slab.
3 110 feet 4a. Climb the slab near its right edge and finish up the open groove.

Here and Now 185 feet Hard Very Severe (29.6.78)
Start 30 feet right of the zawn at a groove to the right of a leaning corner.
1 65 feet 5a. Climb up to an overlap; then follow the groove above to the large triangular overhang. Traverse left beneath the roof to reach better holds and a belay in the groove of *Happy Hunting Ground*.
2 120 feet 5a. Take a direct line up the slab above, on earthy rock and with very little protection.

Near the right-hand side of the Red Walls, and before they merge with the steeper rock of The Vault, is a long slanting line of weakness which always oozes moisture and green slime. To the right is an obvious groove just left of the junction with Vault Wall.

Dark Lady 250 feet E3 † (6.73)
The original was a good natural line until the start fell off leaving a loose, very hard pitch that has not been reclimbed. The route described utilizes the *Spectre* start, which is much harder than anything above. Start just left of an overhanging groove at a leaning wall.
1 50 feet 6a. Make a dynamic series of moves up the leaning wall until a move right gains better holds. Climb up to a slab, which is crossed

leftwards to the overhangs. Go up the left side of these to poor belays at the foot of a groove.
2 60 feet 4c. Climb the groove to a stance below the huge overhangs. Peg belay.
3 70 feet 5a. Move up the groove for a few feet; then use the crack on the right to reach another, bigger crack on the left, which ends at a slab. Climb the slab to a stance at a huge flake.
4 70 feet 4c. Continue up the slab for another 30 feet and then move onto the left-retaining wall. Traverse left using holds beneath a roof. Pull over at a large flake and finish up the wall and groove above.

A girdle of the central and right-hand section of the Red Walls was completed in 1974 but never described in detail. It starts as for *Ruby* and *Chicken Flesh*, then ascends diagonally right above the cave to the stance of *Rotwand*. From here the traverse continues more or less horizontally across the wall to reach the penultimate stance of *Dark Lady*. Up to this point the grade is probably E1, though after the *Ruby* entry difficulties are not sustained but protection is poor. An independent start from the left-hand end of the Red Walls and a finish up *Midnight Rambler* would complete a very exciting expedition at E1 to E2 standard.

The Vault Wall

This shadowed, north-facing wall consists of a series of large roofs and smooth slabs. In its centre is a pea-pod gash, the line of *The Vault*, right of which the impending lines of *Killing Time* and *Halcyon Days* overlook the Teflon Slab. Unfortunately, the wall, despite its macho appearance, is incontinent and, unless there has been a prolonged spell of fine weather, is streaked by numerous areas of seepage.

★★Midnight Rambler 290 feet E2 (30.6.78)
A fine route when dry but very unhealthy otherwise. Start at the base of a smooth corner at the junction of the Red and Vault Walls.
1 30 feet 5b. Climb the corner to a belay in the larger corner where the angle eases.
2 80 feet 4c. Continue up the corner to a point where the rock deteriorates. Step left onto the slabby wall and follow a crack diagonally left to the stance at the end of the second pitch of *Dark Lady*, beneath the main overhang.
3 90 feet 5a. Climb the short chimney above the stance; then move right onto the lip of the overhang. Traverse right (not for agoraphobics) for about 30 feet until the slab narrows and then ends abruptly at a bulge. Climb the bulge on good holds to reach the large slab above (dangerous if at all wet). Continue up a crack, which provides dubious peg belays below a quartz bulge.
4 90 feet. Surmount the bulge and finish up the slab above.

★★★The Tomb 250 feet E2 (1974)
A superb route, which threads its way through the impressive roofs of The Vault Wall via a series of hanging slabs. A grade or two higher if the peg in pitch 2 is missing or unserviceable. Dry conditions are essential. Start at a rightward-leaning ramp above a spring surrounded by bright green moss.
1 70 feet 4c. Climb the ramp to a groove, step up, and then go leftwards to the end of the overhang above. Move up to a belay on the slab 10 feet above the roof.
2 60 feet 5b. Climb the slab rightwards in a superb position to its top right-hand corner and a poor peg. Surmount the overlap on the right; then go up to a ledge and a flake belay.
3 120 feet 4c. Cross into the corner (of *The Vault*), move up a few feet, and step out right onto a small hanging slab, which is followed rightwards to a large flake. Climb this to a ledge and move right to a thin crack leading to easier-angled slabs. Continue rightwards to belay at the abseil point.

☆☆Rise Above 150 feet E4 6a † (17.7.94)
A belay rope can be fixed from the finish of *Midnight Rambler*. Climb *The Vault* for 15 feet and gain the large hanging slab. Follow the bottom edge to a slot and continue straight up to gain the arête. Cross *The Tomb* (peg) and go up to a large dusty ledge. Take the exposed hanging slabs (two pegs) to a rightwards exit, joining the finishing-slab of *Midnight Rambler*.

★The Vault 250 feet E1 (29.4.73)
The central gash in the wall. A powerful line which is usually dripping and dank. Start on the Teflon Slab at the foot of a steep crack leading up to the main pod.
1 130 feet 5a. Climb the crack to reach the groove, which is followed to an overhang. Surmount this and move left along a crack to reach the ledge and flake belay shared with *The Tomb*.
2 120 feet 4c. Climb to a niche in the left wall. Move left and go up just right of a rib to gain slabby rock where the pod closes. Climb the rib above past a good crack on the right and finish up the clean rock above. Block belay.

☆☆☆Saviourblade 180 feet E5 6a † (17.7.94)
A sensational and hard line. Start 20 feet up and right of *The Vault*, below the leftward-leaning slab. Climb the entry slab to jugs in shattered rock. Follow the narrowing slab (hidden peg) until a dramatic swing left gains the arête. Go up this on smaller holds and then into a niche for a rest. Regain the arête and climb it past a peg and a *Hex* 8 placement. Exit on the right to a small-wire belay on the traverse of *The Tomb* (pitch 3). Finish up this.

☆☆Wolfstone 170 feet E6 6b † (16.7.94)
Follow the slab of *Saviourblade* for 20 feet; then bear right along a flake to a good ledge beneath the radical hanging dyke (four pegs) until massive

Carn Gowla

Vault Wall and Teflon Slab

16	Dark Lady	E3
17	Midnight Rambler	E2
18	The Tomb	E2
19	The Vault	E1
20	Killing Time	E2
21	Halcyon Days	E3
22	Bridge of Sighs	E5
23	Demerara	VS
24	Last Exit to St Agnes	VS
25	Black Night	HVS
26	Taming of the Shrew	S

x abseil/belay point

The Heliport

Teflon Slab

Baptist Cliff

jugs on the right can be gained (thread runner). Pull onto the black arête, move up, and then step left across the prominent, bottomless, pod-like groove to reach a belay on the large flake of *The Tomb* (pitch 3). Finish up this.

☆**Where's Heinz?** 160 feet E4 6a † (16.7.94)
Rewarding, reasonably protected, and tremendously positioned. It follows the right-to-left sandwiched red slab. Start 70 feet up and right of *The Vault*, at a rounded rib forming the right-hand edge of a stratified wall. Climb the rib to a recess at the start of the red slab. Follow this leftwards, and thinly, up to large pocket-holds above a bulge (thread runner). Traverse leftwards, then diagonally leftwards along the (now black) slab to join *Wolfstone* at the exposed step across the groove. Move up to the flake belay and finish up *The Tomb*.

Eternity and a Spacious Grave 140 feet E5 6a (16.7.94)
Serious. Start at a short quartz corner 40 feet left of *Halcyon Days*. Climb the left wall of the corner; then go up to a peg at 30 feet. Traverse left to a talc block and pull straight up to hidden holds and a traverse left around a large hanging block. Go straight up to join the left-hand groove, which joins the top slab of *The Tomb*.

The next three routes are all serious propositions owing to the lack of reliable protection. They take lines based on the arête forming the junction between Vault Wall and the left retaining wall of Teflon Slab.

Killing Time 130 feet E2 5a (21.7.78)
Start to the left of the arête, below two disconnected red-sided grooves. Climb the leaning wall on good holds to a groove and continue boldly to its top. Move up and right to a ledge on the arête. Climb the arête until it is possible to go left into the second groove and again move right at its top to regain the arête, which is followed to the abseil point.

★★**Halcyon Days** 130 feet E3 5b (23.7.78)
Excellent climbing, but protection on the arête is appalling. At the upper limit of the grade. Start just to the right of the arête and make a series of hard, bold moves up and left to reach a small slab on the rib. Continue up to a small ledge on the left; then move right beneath an overlap until it is possible to surmount it and gain a ramp on the right. Finish up the crack above and bear left to the abseil point.

Bridge of Sighs 125 feet E5 5c (8.79)
Again, there is very little protection, and friable quartz holds may lead to further destruction of brain cells – if nothing else. Climb the wall between the arête and a flake on small holds until a difficult move enables the welcome haven of the flake to be reached. Continue up until life becomes worrying once again and difficult moves must be made past a friable hand-jam to gain the ramp. Easier climbing leads to the top.

☆**Bitter Sweet** 120 feet E3 5b † (16.7.94)
Climb the thin crack and slab just left of *Demerara* past a hollow flake to the right-hand side of the central overlap. Move up right across the ramp and continue directly through the upper slab past two small overlaps to the abseil point.

★**Demerara** 140 feet Very Severe 4c (1974)
A pleasantly-situated route up the middle of the left-retaining wall of Teflon Slab. It has positive holds and reasonably solid rock and could be climbed in the wet. From the arête, climb the corner of the slab (as for *Last Exit to St Agnes*) to a groove on the left after 20 feet. Climb the groove to a ledge, move left on to the face, and go up to a ramp-line. Follow this leftwards and finish at the abseil point.

Teflon Slab

Large, black, and of comparatively easy angle. The routes here are very pleasant when the sun shines, but quite the opposite when wet.

Last Exit to St Agnes 270 feet Very Severe (13.10.79)
This follows the left corner of the slab. Start at its base.
1 140 feet 4b. Climb the corner and the overlap above; then traverse right to the groove formed by the left edge of the slab. Poor stance.
2 130 feet 4b. Move round the overlap and continue to a quartz wall. Climb this until the angle eases and continue to the final roof, which is avoided on the right. Scramble to the top.

★**Black Night** 260 feet Hard Very Severe (19.5.84)
The most substantial route on the slab. The second pitch is particularly good and, though the difficulties are not great, the climbing is sustained and the protection barely adequate. Start at low tide, beneath the short wall at the base of the slab, 15 feet right of the obvious initial corner of *Last Exit to St Agnes*.
1 150 feet 4b. Climb a slippery slab to a tiny corner at 10 feet. Move right over the overlap and continue rightwards to a fault. Follow this easily for 20 feet; then move right up the delicate slab to a belay beneath the overlap.
2 110 feet 5a. Move right; then go over the overlap and climb up and right to a loose crack (the only runners on the pitch). Traverse 10 feet left and climb the bulge on pocket-holds. Finish up the cleaned slab above.

Tempest 300 feet Hard Severe (1973)
The slab is split by a central crackline. This is followed in two long pitches. Loose and undistinguished – pegs should be carried.

Taming of the Shrew 160 feet Severe (6.70)
From the right-hand side of the slab, climb to a quartz pocket; then go up to a corner and short wall. Continue to a rusted peg, move right, and finish with care to the left of a large block on the skyline.

The Baptist Cliff

Hidden round the corner from Teflon Slab is a compact area of steep cliff littered with overhangs and vertical corners. It is severely tide-affected, and here also a period of dry weather is required for maximum enjoyment. Unfortunately, the best place for identifying the routes is about 100 yards offshore, but a wave-washed sloping shelf does allow a certain perspective to be obtained.

There are two descents. The simplest, particularly on a first visit, is by the rocky spur immediately below the rusty ventilation pipe, which eventually becomes grassy as it nears the top of Teflon Slab. Follow the slopes down and left to a large outcrop on the cliff edge. There are two boulders beside the bluff 30 feet back from the edge, which provide good anchors for abseiling down the orange wall above the start of *The Baptist*. If 50-metre ropes are not used a spare rope is needed. Care should be taken near the top with the numerous sharp-edged flakes. The last section of the abseil is free, and if the tide is in this could result in complicated manoeuvres to avoid a swim. The rope can be moved 10 feet or so to the left (facing out) and should then reach dryish land. Alternatively, the old sewage pipe can be followed down the scree slopes; bear right near the bottom and aim for a large conspicuous thread on the seaward edge of a bluff of rock on the cliff edge. Use this as an abseil point, or continue down and to the left (south) over a series of earthy ledges to the top of a steep rake slanting down the face, which is descended on large holds (exposed – Very Difficult) to a sloping platform running back right to the tidal shelf beneath the centre of the cliff.

Near the seaward point is a deep sea-cave, right of which is a sizeable colony of overhangs, large and small. Right again is the conspicuous tapering groove of *Diabolist* with its distinctive, pale-coloured left wall. This is bounded by a rib, beyond which is an orange wall with a thin, diagonal left-to-right crack at its base near a shallow cave – the start of *The Baptist*. Further on, a series of corners and steep ribs ends at a blunt arête before the cliff begins to lose height close to the exit/entry route. The platform becomes increasingly tidal at its northern end.

★★**Towards the Light** 110 feet E3 6a (6.7.92)
Fine climbing in tantalizing positions on the sandwiched slabs of the left-hand side of the cliff. Start from a raised ledge next to a short black cleft cutting into the base of the left-hand end of the cliff; accessible at low-to-mid tide, or even higher with settled seas. Descend from Teflon Slab to gain the stance.
Move up the cleft and step right onto a ledge on the edge of a smooth black slab. Traverse rightwards across the slab, and step down onto a small ledge on its right-hand arête overhanging the sea-cave. Go straight over the improbable bulge above on comforting holds to get established on a left-slanting, sandwiched wall. Climb diagonally left, and then go up to a short groove through the next bulge. Make bold moves straight up

Carn Gowla
The Baptist Cliff

	Route	Grade
1	Aprez-Vous	E1
2	The Awakening	E3
3	The Haze	E5
4	Diabolist	E1
5	The Baptist	E2
6	Elixir	E3
7	Continental Retreat	E2
8	Nativity	HVS
9	Soma	HVS
10	alternative descent	VD

onto the upper *Aprez-Vous* slab and follow this in reverse up its steep groove on the left to the good nut belays on Teflon Slab.

The next fully-described route is a girdle of The Baptist Cliff at half height. However, a higher and parallel line, finishing up the last few moves of *Diabolist*, has been reported without detail: **The Seafront** (E1 5a 1996).

★★Aprez-Vous 250 feet E1 (6.8.74)
A superb expedition in dramatic surroundings. Start at a peg belay at the point where the climbing descent of the seaward edge of Teflon Slab commences.
1 80 feet 5b. Descend steeply to the right for 30 feet to the lower line of overhangs. Move right around the edge and traverse the steep slab on small holds to a very small ledge. Peg and nut belays.
2 70 feet 5a. Traverse right with the cave below and overhangs above to make a sensational swing across an overhanging corner on large holds. Continue traversing right on very steep rock until the angle eases. Follow a line across the orange-tinted slab to a poor belay in the corner of *Diabolist*.
3 100 feet 5a. Traverse right for 20 feet to a point just before the niche on *The Baptist*. Zigzag through the roof directly above to reach another steep orange slab below an obvious diagonal roof. Follow the line of the roof to the top. Belay well back.

Two impressively-situated routes take the steep area of rock between the sea-cave and *Diabolist*. A bolt was placed on each, but these may have deteriorated or disappeared and are believed not to be necessary.

★The Awakening 210 feet E3 (29.4.85)
A good climb which takes a challenging line right of the cave on surprisingly good holds. Start 25 feet left of *Diabolist*, at the foot of a slab containing a small V-groove. Low tide is necessary.
1 90 feet 5c. Climb the groove to a small ledge on its right (belay possible if chased by the sea). Continue up the slab on the left to reach a steep wall. Traverse left across the wall, step down, and move left around the overlap to an overhanging corner and a peg. Keep traversing across the wall to a slab (peg), and continue left to a small stance.
2 120 feet 5b. Climb the groove above, then a short wall to an overhang (peg), crossing *Aprez-Vous*, and traverse right to another roof. Pull over onto a slab and climb directly to the top. Belay at the abseil block.

★★The Haze 180 feet E5 (30.4.85)
A remarkable route which forces its way over six or seven separate overhangs. Start as for *The Awakening*, at low tide, below a slab with a short V-groove.
1 100 feet 6a. Climb the groove to a ledge and then go straight up to the roof. Swing up and right on to a constricted slab. Climb this past a drilled peg to two small roofs. From a large hold on the right below another roof, swing up and out to yet more overhangs, which are climbed

until a traverse left can be made across a slab that is merely steep to belays on the left.
2 80 feet 6a. Traverse back right for 10 feet to an undercling beneath an overhang. Climb this and then the slab above. Belay on the abseil rope or the blocks above.

★Frankly... 140 feet E4 6b (4.7.92)
The left-hand arête of *Diabolist*. A bouldery start, though with good wire protection, leads to an enjoyable and tamer romp up the crackline above. Boulder straight up the impending arête until good holds lead over a bulge and onto easier-angled rock. Climb easily to the *Aprez-Vous* traverse and surmount the bulge directly above to gain a crack-system in the steep slab to the left of *Diabolist*. Follow the crack, which eventually merges with *Diabolist* at its exit.

★★Diabolist 130 feet E1 5c (28.6.72)
The obvious corner right of the cave, one of Carn Gowla's more enjoyable offerings, which after a strenuous start provides interesting climbing, always well protected and on solid rock. Start at lowish tide beneath the smooth corner, which is climbed with increasing difficulty to the first roof. After this is surmounted, better holds appear in time for the second and larger roof. Finish up the groove above and belay as for *The Haze*.

☆Welcome, to the Human Race 150 feet E5 6a † (21.6.92)
A highly exacting climb that attempts to pursue a central line up the beckoning orange wall above the start of *The Baptist*. The climbing is strenuous, and the protection very marginal in places, though there is quite a lot of it to place. The pegs are in poor condition. Go up the first 10 feet of *The Baptist* and then break diagonally leftwards to a projecting jug (*Friend 1*). Make a hard pull into a shallow groove (peg) and, from a further peg on the right, go up left over a bulge to big but weak pockets (thread runner *in situ*). Move left, using high finger-pockets, into an open groove (good wires on the left) and climb it to a junction with *The Baptist*. Finish up the rightward-slanting crack in the slab, as for *The Baptist*.

★★The Baptist 150 feet E2 5c (10.6.72)
A difficult and bold entry is followed by open face-climbing. Start in the obvious shallow cave/niche 60 feet right of the corner of *Diabolist*. Climb the lower of two diagonal cracks in the smooth left wall with difficulty to reach an obvious pocket. Move left into an obvious short smooth groove and break out of this onto the slab above, which is followed more easily to a niche on the right. Climb out on good holds and move right to an orange slab. Finish up a rightward-slanting crack in the slab. Nut belays.

★Elixir 200 feet E3 (4.81)
This route takes a wandering line up the highest part of the cliff and is both technical and strenuous. Start in the niche/cave as for *The Baptist*.
1 140 feet 5c. Go up and left across the niche and pull out onto the

Carn Gowla

The Sewage Pipe Cliffs and The Mercury Area

The Sewage Pipe Cliffs

1	Black Knight	HVS
2	Silver Dollar	HVS
3	Castaway	E1
4	Crystal Voyage	E1
5	Alpha-Beta	HVS
6	Magic Fly	E2
7	Life on Mars	E1

The Mercury Area

8	The Mercury Connection	HVS
9	Quicksilver	HVS
10	Mercury	E2
11	Andromeda Strain	E5
12	Terra Nova	HVS

x abseil point

steep left wall. Follow the upper diagonal crack to the left until it is possible to pull rightwards over the bulge to a resting-place. Step right and climb over the overhang; then continue up the wall above and trend rightwards around the edge to belay in the large corner of *Nativity*.
2 60 feet 5b. Move back leftwards to the edge on poor rock and climb to the top.

★**Continental Retreat** 150 feet E2 5b (18.8.78)
Exhilarating wall-climbing up the face left of the corner of *Nativity*. Start half-way between the shallow cave and the base of the corner. Climb up for 15 feet; then make a rising traverse right to join *Nativity*. Go back left above the initial overhangs for 10 feet and continue straight up to reach the steep slab above the top roof. Move diagonally left until beneath the roof (peg removed); then step right and surmount the overhang direct to reach the upper slab. Trend slightly left, then back right to finish.

Nativity 110 feet Hard Very Severe 5a (10.6.72)
The steep right-hand corner. The rock in parts is typical Gowla biscuit. Large cams or nuts essential. Start at the base of the corner. Climb the steep wall to reach the corner, which is followed to a pleasantly-exposed exit on the right. Belay well back.

Soma 90 feet Hard Very Severe (30.7.78)
To the right of the corner, the wall, though lower, is very steep and has a distinctive juggy appearance. Start at a left-leaning groove on the left-hand side of an overhanging buttress.
1 50 feet 5a. Surmount two small overhangs to gain the groove, which is followed until a move right on large holds is made to reach a good stance.
2 40 feet 4b. Climb the steep wall above and then a crack to the top. Good block belay 40 feet above (possible abseil anchor).

The Sewage Pipe Cliffs

An unfortunate name for an impressive sweep of rock, which is the cliff extending southwards from The Baptist Cliff as far as the great arching corner of *Mercury*.

It uses the same entry routes as The Baptist Cliff to reach the sloping platform. From here, traverse easily on a system of ledges just above high-tide mark, but beware of bright green seaweed and waves bearing names. Initially, the ledges lead beneath a vile dripping corner with the narrow dark face of *Black Knight* immediately to its right. Right again, the cliff gradually increases in height and is characterized by a vast ramp in its upper section and a shallow arched cave in the centre. *Silver Dollar* and *Crystal Voyage* take surprisingly amenable lines on either side of this cave. To the right, further ledges and platforms eventually peter out tantalizingly close to *Mercury*'s left-bounding arête. However, this short blank section can be crossed by *The Mercury Connection*, a subtle and excellent traverse, possible at high tide in calm seas, providing a very worthwhile approach to *Mercury*.

An alternative descent can be made by abseiling 250 feet down *Silver Dollar* from good nut and cam anchors in the outcrop above. This descent finishes just left of centre of the cave, and the rope is then well placed for a belay at the finish of *Silver Dollar*.

All in all, this area is a great place to climb and should appeal to many, as it is covered in huge holds. The first route takes the general area of rock beneath the old discharge pipe.

Black Knight 280 feet Hard Very Severe (27.8.78)
Start 150 feet along the sea-level traverse, at a short corner below a narrow black wall.
1 80 feet 5a. Climb 20 feet up the corner; then step onto the wall and go over the bulge on good holds. Carry on up to a small ledge on the left beneath a small overhang. Move round left and up to a larger ledge with various belays.
2 80 feet 5a. Climb the right-trending crack to a wide horizontal crack. Continue past this to the right-hand end of a long, narrow foot-ledge. From its left end, climb up to a ledge beneath a bulge (peg belays).
3 120 feet 4c. Move a few feet left; then go back right over a large grass tussock and continue diagonally left to the top, or follow a vegetated groove up and slightly right. Belay well back.

★**Silver Dollar** 260 feet Hard Very Severe (23.8.78)
A very good route taking an obvious line just left of the shallow arched cave. Start beneath the corner formed by the left edge of the cave.
1 100 feet 5a. Climb over greasy ledges into the corner and step up and left at a good spike to gain the steep slab, which is climbed on good holds at first to a shallow groove slanting rightwards. Step right onto steeper rock and pull strenuously over a ragged bulge. Follow the line up the groove until a short traverse left gains a niche and nut belays (peg removed).
2 130 feet 4c. Traverse back right and go up past a peg to a large quartz patch (The Silver Dollar), which is semi-detached and sounds hollow but is covered in large holds. From its top, step left to a weakness and left again to a ledge on the slab above. Continue up the slab to reach a right-slanting crack and smaller areas of quartz (The Silver Dimes). These lead to block overhangs and a small cave. Move up left onto a gently inclined slab with grass warts on it. Use peg (removed), thread, nut, and any other belays that you can engineer.
3 30 feet. Escape left or right via the easiest line to reach steep grass, and belay well back or on the abseil rope.

☆**Castaway** 250 feet E1 † (1980)
Another fine route, which starts as for *Silver Dollar* and then traverses airily into the centre of the wall above the cave.
1 110 feet 5a. Follow *Silver Dollar* as far as the ragged bulge; then traverse right on the lip of the roof to a safe niche in a fine position (nut belays).

2 110 feet 5a. Continue traversing right for 30 feet to reach a shallow, open groove. Climb the groove, and then the wall above on good but spaced holds to a junction with *Crystal Voyage* and *Silver Dollar* at the overhangs and small cave. Surmount the roof on the left to reach a small stance.
3 30 feet. *Silver Dollar* pitch 3.

★★**Crystal Voyage** 290 feet E1 (28.8.78)
An immaculate first pitch, steep and technical, leading to a second on large holds reminiscent of the more eccentric sections of Gogarth's Red Wall, where a carefree approach cannot be recommended. Start in the centre of the cave, below an obvious right-slanting slab.
1 80 feet 5a. Climb the slab, easily at first, to the capping roof and an antediluvian peg (*Friend 3½* placement). Traverse steeply right and move up to gain a wide vertical band of quartz, which is followed, passing a fine collection of dog-tooth crystals, for 20 feet until level with the lip of a smaller subsidiary roof. Traverse horizontally left above the roof to a stance on a foot-ledge in a sensational position. Peg (removed) and micro-wire belays requiring ingenuity.
2 150 feet 4c. A jug-pulling feast. Climb straight up above the stance using a prominent quartz jug; then trend leftwards on steep rock and large, sharp holds past various threads (hanging stance possible). Continue in a direct line; then move right to exit at the top end of the huge ramp. Multiple belays.
3 60 feet. Climb the slabby wall above the ramp – effectively its continuation. (This gives better rock and a quicker arrival at grassy ledges and belays in an outcrop than the original line, which joined *Silver Dollar*.)

Alpha-Beta 260 feet Hard Very Severe (26.8.78)
Start as for *Crystal Voyage*.
1 110 feet 5a. Climb rightwards to the roof, traverse rightwards past a peg, and climb up into a crystal-lined crack, which is followed to a large ledge just below its top.
2 150 feet 4c. Climb slightly left onto the wall above the belay. Climb towards the V-notch in the skyline, which turns into a groove, exit right, and go straight up over loose mixed terrain. (This pitch can be avoided by traversing the obvious line of weakness leftwards to a hanging stance at the threads on pitch 2 of *Crystal Voyage*.)

The following routes all have excellent first pitches on compact rock, after which life becomes more exciting on the infamous Gowla biscuits above the vast broken rake.

Crash Landing 250 feet E2 (28.8.78)
Start on the second small platform beyond the cave, beneath an impending wall left of an obvious groove.
1 120 feet 5b. Climb up to the wall and 6 feet up it before moving slightly left to step-like ledges above. Traverse right for a few moves; then

go up to a rusting peg below the overhang and a junction with *Magic Fly*. Continue rightwards for 15 feet and go up to a roof. Difficult moves on sidepulls allow the blank-looking wall above to be reached (peg below the roof removed). Climb the wall on excellent finger-jugs to a small sloping stance on a huge ramp.
2 130 feet 4a. *Life on Mars* pitch 2.

★Magic Fly 260 feet E2 (26.8.78)
The first pitch is excellent. Start 30 feet right of the cave, below a short, prominent groove.
1 110 5c. Climb up into and up the groove; at its top, continue up the steep wall, passing a peg, to the small roof. Climb up and right to a good jamming-crack, which leads to the stance of *Alpha-Beta* on the large ledge.
2 150 feet 4c. *Alpha-Beta* pitch 2.

Life on Mars 250 feet E1 (27.8.78)
Start as for *Magic Fly*.
1 120 feet 5b. Step onto the wall and climb rightwards to a vague sentry-box. Exit from this and climb the wall to the first of two overlaps, traverse left, and pull over the roof; then move back right and climb up the quartz wall to a stance just below the huge ramp.
2 130 feet 4a. Above the ramp is a scarred wall of large holes giving enormous holds. Climb this, and then yellow, lichen-covered rock to the right of the vegetation to a ledge beneath a small roof. Avoid this roof on its right and continue to an overlap, which is climbed at its narrowest point to a vague groove leading to the top.

★The Mercury Connection 120 feet Hard Very Severe 5a (8.79)
An excellent way of reaching *Mercury* for those averse to long abseils. Start at the far end of the ledge-system running beneath The Sewage Pipe Cliff and traverse rightwards for 70 feet. Descend to grooves on the arête and follow these down until it is possible to swing around the rib to the platform in the base of the corner of *Mercury*.

The Mercury Area

The magnificent sculpted corner taken by *Mercury* is one of the North Coast's most dramatic features. Hidden from above, it dominates the view as you look north from the top of the neighbouring Triple Buttress. The lonely triangular platform at its base is the starting-point for three routes and can be reached by traversing in from The Sewage Pipe Cliff by *The Mercury Connection*.

The most popular approach is by abseil. This was once a spectacular and potentially lethal affair straight over the razor-sharp lip of *Mercury*'s capping roof, but there is a much safer alternative. From the old discharge pipe, follow the cliff edge south for 50 yards as far as an obvious grassy defile. Low outcrops on its left-hand side (facing in) provide a good tape thread and various other anchors. Two joined ropes will reach the base of the cliff, effectively going down the line of *Quicksilver*, to the left of the left-bounding arête of the *Mercury* groove. Ensure that the rope does not snag on any loose edges. If all goes to plan the knot changeover will take place at a system of ledges at half height. *Mercury* is immediately right and a careful swing around the arête into space will bring the target platform into view. If this is hidden by waves there is a ledge 40 feet up the groove which provides a satisfactory stance.

It is advisable to preplace an extra rope to belay at the top of *Mercury* and *Andromeda Strain*. The anchor point for this is 70 feet higher up the grassy slopes where there is a good thread below an outcrop identified by a small cairn.

Quicksilver 260 feet Hard Very Severe (28.8.78)
Mercury's poor relation, which has acquired that route's unwanted original finishing-pitches. Start as for *Mercury*, on the platform at the base of the corner.
1 140 feet 5a. Move left to the arête, which is followed with a slight detour to the left after a few feet to an easing of the angle and a groove. This leads past a good spike to poorer rock and a stance on the break to the left of the first belay of *Mercury*.
2 80 feet 4b. Climb the slabby face above on highly dubious rock to a ledge at the point where it becomes lichenous. Peg and nut belays.
3 40 feet 4b. If the abseil rope is handy, grab it and run. If not, move diagonally right until the rock fades and the grass begins in earnest. Belay well back.

★★★**Mercury** 290 feet E2 (1974/1979)
A superb line with two highly distinctive pitches. Start at the platform in the base of the corner.
1 140 feet 5a. Climb the corner-crack on good holds to a ledge and thread at 40 feet (stance possible). Continue up the obvious wide crack, easily at first, until it steepens (large hex or *Friend* 4). More difficult and bolder climbing leads to a large jammed flake. Move right to better holds in a crack leading to a commodious ledge on the left wall of the corner. Escape is now possible at this point by taking the finishing-pitches of *Quicksilver* (*Mercury*'s original finish).
2 150 feet 5b. This pitch varies in difficulty depending on the amount of seepage in the middle section. Follow the sustained but well-protected corner above the stance until it curves right to form a subsidiary roof. Harder moves lead round this. Traverse immediately right on small sloping holds to cross the slab, stepping down where it steepens, to reach easier ground at a reddish pillar of more compact rock. Move up to foot-ledges beneath two pegs of dubious merit. Continue direct for 15 feet; then move right to an obvious break in the capping overhang. Above is a vague ragged groove of large but brittle holds, which leads more easily to the top and the preplaced belay rope.
Variation
2a 150 feet 5b. Follow the corner to the subsidiary roof. After moving

round this continue up the looser continuation groove (rather than traversing right) past a fixed sling of doubtful age to reach unstable terrain under the large roof. Traverse right for 10 feet to a precarious stance, praying that the belay rope is correctly positioned.

☆☆**Dead Run Down** 240 feet E5 † (4.89/3.10.92)
A predictably distressing voyage up the left side of the *Andromeda Strain* slab. The second pitch is the crux and brandishes two substantial runouts. However, the rock is good throughout and, as with *Andromeda Strain*, escape onto *Mercury* at the half-height ledge is possible. Start as for *Mercury*.
1 90 feet 5c. From the ledge, climb up and rightwards to a bulge at 12 feet. Now, either traverse rightwards to the foot of the orange groove (as for *Andromeda Strain* to this point) and swing left into an open grey groove; or stretch diagonally leftwards across the bulge to enter the grey groove more directly. Follow the groove fairly steadily past an undercut flake, and continue up the broad rib above to the half-height ledge and nut belays of *Andromeda Strain* on the right.
2 150 feet 5c. From 10 feet left of the belay, bear leftwards to an expanding flake (thin tape) some 15 feet right of the *Mercury* corner; then trend back rightwards up a ramp to a sloping ledge (good peg, *Friend 1* placement). Now climb warily up the slab, aiming for a second (also good) peg in a slight groove above a thin, leftward-facing flake-line. Again, run it out, trending very slightly right at a bulge; then step left to the top of the *Mercury* Variation corner (and runners!) and finish as for that route.

★★**Andromeda Strain** 270 feet E5 (26.6.77)
An outstanding but extremely serious route. Protection on both pitches is appalling and although difficulties are nowhere excessive they are continuous, making this one of the boldest leads of its day in the South West. Start as for *Mercury*, on the platform at the base of the corner.
1 120 feet 5c. Traverse right, rising slightly at first, to a series of small ledges beneath a shallow open groove of orange rock. A small wire placement can be found on the left. Move up to a large hold; then traverse left into a bay beneath a small roof. Turn this on its left and climb direct to nut belays on the sloping half-way ledge.
2 150 feet 5c. Climb up, trending right for 25 feet, to a small downward-pointing flake. Move right; then climb direct up a shallow groove (vital wire runner) to a long narrow ledge. Go leftwards up the steep slab on small holds to an overlap, which is surmounted on the left. Step right and continue to another roof, which is also passed on the left. Traverse right on its lip and move up to a rib of compact reddish rock which leads, after a few feet, to small foot-ledges and two dubious pegs (junction with *Mercury*). Climb direct for 15 feet towards the capping roof, and then move right to a break, which is followed through the overhangs to finish up the easier ragged groove above to the preplaced rope belay.

Right of *Andromeda Strain* the cliff, though still extensive, degenerates into steep vegetation and crumbling rock. One route picks a way up this.

Terra Nova 240 feet Hard Very Severe † (25.8.78)
Forty feet right of the *Mercury* corner is a large boulder separated from the cliff by a narrow trench. Make a 250-foot abseil directly onto the boulder.
1 50 feet 5a. Climb boldly up the wall past a spike masquerading as a runner to reach easier ground. Poor peg and nut belay on the left. Better alternatives may exist on a ledge to the right.
2 80 feet 4b. Head towards a vague groove slanting left. Follow this and exit right to a small stance and peg belays.
3 110 feet 4b. Climb up to a groove, which trends right and leads to the top. Peg and nut belays.

Triple Buttress

This is the prominent headland about 150 yards south of the sewage pipe. It consists of three separate buttresses diminishing in height from north to south and referred to as A, B, and C Buttresses. On the north face of A Buttress is a conspicuous roof above a large easy-angled slab bounded on its landward side by a deep narrow cleft. *Bohemian* takes the roof direct and the corner above. Hidden beyond the seaward arête is another large corner taken by *McVitie*. This has another rib on its right-hand side which defines the left end of B Buttress, which is characterized by a series of rough grooves and sharp overhangs. A ramp slants down its southern edge on the landward side of another deep cleft which almost separates C Buttress from the main cliff. The seaward face of this buttress is an impressive, smooth, pink wall upon which a few sharp-edged flakes appear to have been cemented. To the south the cliff becomes slabbier and more broken and ends at the deep corner/groove-line taken by *Daydream*.

A Buttress

Descent for the first four routes is by abseil, from a metal stake and block anchors, down the obvious corner and roof of *Bohemian*. This is free below the roof, and the razor-like construction of the lip of the overhang has already created one near heart-attack and potential death from the severance of several rope strands. Therefore, progress should be maintained by a delicate and somewhat surreptitious slide down the rope rather than by an extravagant emulation of commando-style bouncing if a happy landing is to be achieved on the smooth, easy-angled slab below.

★**Bohemian** 150 feet E2 5b (31.8.78)
The prominent roof and corner on the north-west face of the buttress. Start at the lower right-hand end of the slab on a good ledge. Climb the slab easily to an enormous block below an overhanging section. Traverse left to a pillar that almost reaches the corner-crack above the roof. Go up its right-hand side to a resting-position, suitable for hunchbacks, and a peg. Pull steeply out on good holds to gain the corner, which is followed more easily, in a fine position, until a traverse right can be made to the block belays and spike of the abseil point.

Carn Gowla
Triple Buttress

A Buttress

1	Bohemian	E2
2	The Arête	HVS
3	Blue Meany	HVS
x	abseil point	

B Buttress

4	McVitie	VS
5	Hard Tack	HVS
6	Fourth Dimension	HVS
7	Wageslave	HVS
8	Starbound	HVS
9	Journey to Ixtlan	HVS

C Buttress

10	Looking for a Rainbow	S
11	Rainbow Games	
12	Four for Texas	E2
13	Sundance	HS
14	Daydream	HVS
15	Nightride	S

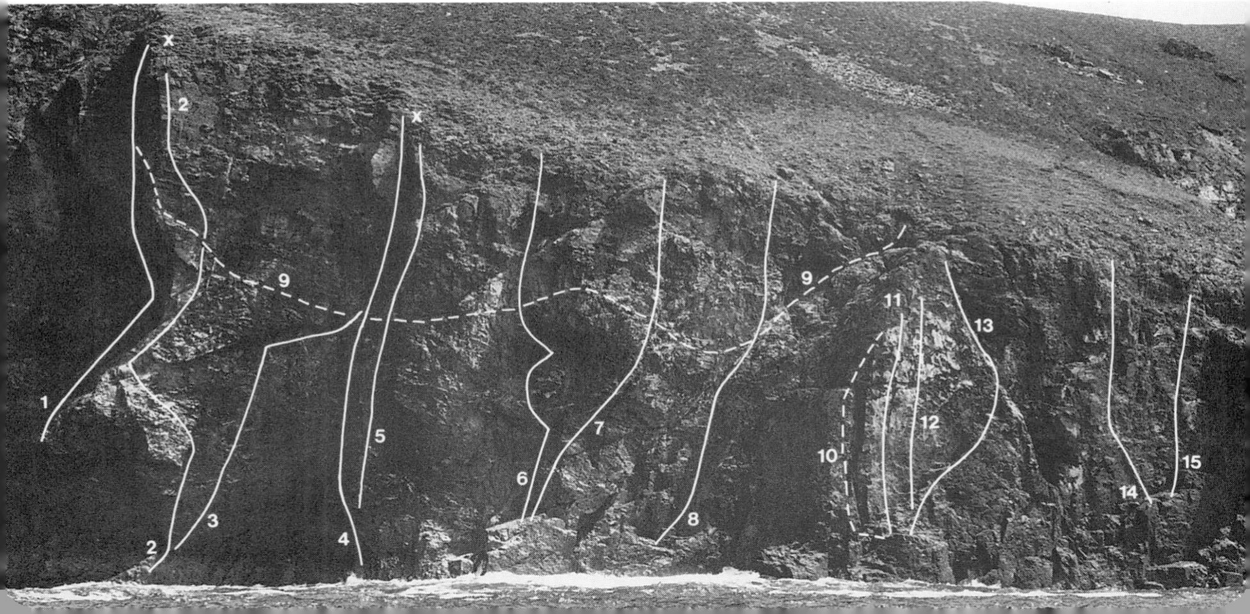

Euthanasia 80 feet E1 5b (24.8.78)
The overhang and wall above the huge block. Start on the slab below the centre of the overhang, beneath the block. Climb the right-hand side of the block and the crack above to the roof. Pull over into the crack (peg) splitting the wall above. Finish up this.

★**The Arête** 165 feet Hard Very Severe (24.8.78)
The right-hand arête of the north-west face. Start as for *Bohemian*.
1 100 feet 4c. Follow the arête, easily at first, until it begins to overhang, and then move right onto the wall.
2 65 feet. Climb the right edge of the slab and move right onto the wall on the right-hand side of the tower. Climb this wall until level with a red section of rock on the left, cross it, and move upwards on the arête. Climb just left of the edge to the top.

Blue Meany 180 feet Hard Very Severe (24.8.78)
An obvious traverse-line across the left wall of the groove of *McVitie*, which divides A and B Buttresses. Start as for *The Arête*.
1 130 feet 4c. Climb the arête to the roof and move right to a steep groove. Climb the groove and on up to the continuous line of roofs. Follow these horizontally rightwards into the corner of *McVitie* and belay on a small ledge.
2 50 feet 4b. Climb the corner-crack to the top.

B Buttress

There are two possible descents. The first is to abseil down the corner of *McVitie*, which is the junction of A and B Buttresses. This is difficult to identify from above, but becomes obvious if the cliff edge is followed as close as is comfortable from the top of A Buttress. A short, easy, but exposed crack is descended to a ledge and good nut placements above the line of the groove. A 130-foot abseil down the right wall of the corner (facing in) leads to a series of ledges above high-tide mark and right of a deep cleft at the base of the corner. This point can also be reached by descending an easy-angled ramp on the landward side of the narrow zawn separating B and C Buttresses. Where it steepens, abseil to ledges which lead across various corners and ribs for 60 feet to the cleft beneath *McVitie*.

McVitie 160 feet Very Severe (18.10.77)
The groove between A and B Buttresses. A good line, but the holds on the second pitch have a digestive-like texture and may crumble. Start on the ledges below and to the right of the corner.
1 90 feet 4c. Climb the right wall via a crack to reach a ramp leading left into the corner. Go up for a few feet to a small ledge and spike belays on the right.
2 70 feet 4b. Follow the steep corner on large but sometimes dubious holds to a ledge and belays 10 feet below the top. Easy climbing remains.

Hard Tack 150 feet Hard Very Severe 4c † (12.12.85)
The right wall of the groove, with thinner holds than *McVitie* but a lot more solid. Start as for *McVitie*. Climb the crack to the ramp but then break right onto the wall. Climb this on good but spaced holds to reach a corner. Climb the corner and step left at its top to the final belay of *McVitie*.

★**Fourth Dimension** 130 feet Hard Very Severe (1.9.78)
The seaward face of B Buttress is a steep wall, broken by horizontal bands. A prominent feature is a short groove leading to the left-hand end of the main overhang in the middle of the face. A fine climb with good protection. Start on the ledges below the groove.
1 80 feet 4c. Climb the initial groove and the short wall to a bulge at 25 feet. Climb over the bulge on its left and then go diagonally right on good holds to the main overhang. Traverse left to reach another, steeper groove and pull out right at its top to a constricted stance in a niche. Rope-drag on the rough rock can be a problem on this pitch.
2 50 feet 4b. Exit rightwards from the niche and go up on good holds to easier ground. Belays on the grass slope above are more apparent than real. It is better to continue to the rope's end and dig in.

Wageslave 155 feet Hard Very Severe (1.9.78)
Bold and steep but the holds are good. Start as for *Fourth Dimension*, on the ledge below the short groove.
1 95 feet 4c. From the right-hand end of the ledge, step right around the rib onto a steep black wall, which is climbed trending right to a faint, rightward-leaning groove. Climb the groove to gain the exposed arête. Move right to a good thread and nut belays.
2 60 feet 4b. Climb up and right past a good crack and surmount the bulge at its weakest point to gain a small ledge. Take the prominent corner on the left to the top. Peg (removed) and nut belays on top of the obvious block.

Starbound 125 feet Hard Very Severe (2.9.78)
The first pitch is sustained and well protected, the second is its antithesis. Start at the right-hand end of the ledge of *Wageslave* and jump or climb across a deep chimney/crack. Move right to another ledge at the base of a prominent slanting groove.
1 75 feet 4c. Climb the groove to a quartz bulge; then move right and onto easier ground. Spike and nut belays are found where the ramp flattens to a ledge.
2 50 feet 4c. Above the belay is a steep reddish wall. From its right-hand end, climb straight to the top. Nut belays on a large quartz block.

★★**Journey to Ixtlan** 410 feet Hard Very Severe (2.9.78)
An excellent route which takes a high traverse-line across B and A Buttresses, safely above the reach of the waves. The climbing is sustained, steep, and exposed, but the holds are usually accommodating. Start on the cliff-top above the easy-angled ramp on the landward side of the cleft

between B and C Buttresses.
1 70 feet. Wander down the ramp easily until it steepens below a good ledge (nut belays).
2 70 feet 4c. Continue down for a further 15 feet; then move left onto the wall. Climb diagonally leftwards to a small ledge level with the belay. Move up, and carry on traversing left on steep rock to the arête and around it to an exposed stance on its far side (peg and nut belays).
3 70 feet 4c. Descend slightly, and traverse across two groove-lines into a corner. Move across this and descend slightly diagonally left to the arête. Nut and spike belays.
4 120 feet 4c. Traverse left into the large corner of *McVitie* and continue left across the wall, rising slightly. More exposed moves lead to yet another arête, which is climbed for 20 feet to a block higher up (peg belays removed).
5 80 feet 4c. Climb the arête and move left to reach a diagonal line, which is followed across the wall. Climb steeply until just short of the corner and finish up the left-hand side of the block (as for *Bohemian*). Block and metal-spike belays.

C Buttress

The tip of C Buttress is the small headland projecting from the south side of the Triple Buttress area. Approach by abseiling down the impressive, pink, seaward wall taken by *Rainbow Games* and *Four for Texas*. A good ledge is reached just above high-tide level. The first four routes start from this ledge, but the others require a traverse rightwards along more ledges.

★**Looking for a Rainbow** 110 feet Severe 4a (27.5.90)
A colourful little find. Traverse left from the foot of the pink wall to a good-looking chimney/groove. Climb this to reach a large platform. From here, climb up a short, steep wall on the right and continue easily to finish at the top of the buttress.

★★★**Rainbow Games** 100 feet E2 5b (27.5.90)
[Photo p.336d.] A fantastic pot of gold. Good technical interest in a stunning position. Climb the thin crack running up the pink wall 10 feet left of *Four for Texas* before moving left into a better crack. Continue up this direct and follow its indefinite continuation (peg) to reach the top.

★★**Four for Texas** 90 feet E2 5b (20.9.87)
[Photo p.336c.] An exhilaration of exposure matched only by the hugeness of its holds. Irresistible. Start at the right-hand side of the abseil ledges, at the foot of a thin crack. Climb the crack on small holds until good holds and a thread are reached. Continue up the wall on a central line using holds that grow and grow. Heavy climbers tread delicately.

★**Sundance** 90 feet Hard Severe 4a (2.9.78)
A pleasant route. Start at the right-hand end of the abseil ledge. Climb the

black slab, to the right of the impending abseil wall, until it narrows to form a rib. Follow the rib to its junction with a large vein of quartz running up to the left. Make a series of steeper moves up the vein to a notch and continue to the top.

Daydream 90 feet Hard Very Severe 5a (19.7.78)
Start on the ledges to the right of the abseil descent and just left of an obvious short corner. Climb the wall to a narrow ledge. From its left-hand end, go directly up to another ledge 10 feet higher. Follow the crack above, passing a third ledge, to a groove leading to the top. Spike belays well back.

Nightride 90 feet Severe 4a (19.9.78)
Start below the obvious short corner. Climb the wall above the corner to reach the slab, which is ascended to a finish up a groove.

The Song of the Shirt 120 feet Hard Severe 4b (27.5.90)
Rambling but very pleasant. Start as for *Nightride*. Climb down and to the south to reach the top of sea-washed rock; then traverse right onto the centre of the face of the buttress. Climb directly up, starting by a short crack, then by countless jugs.

South C Walls

On the south side of C Buttress is a series of walls, south-facing, easily approachable, and non-tidal, and of generally good-quality rock (i.e., a good deal less gripping than most of Carn Gowla). There are two prominent cracks, the left-hand of which is taken by *Chimney Route* and the right-hand by *Crackline*, both of which are left of a central gully, *Fine Line*. Approach by scrambling down the easy terraces below the prominent red wall immediately south of the walls and following a break back right (facing out) to reach a gully at an old adit. Scramble down to the platform at the foot of the walls.

Sideline 40 feet Very Difficult † (6.7.96)
A poor route. Traverse left from the base of *Saline* until easier ground allows scrambling to the top.

☆**Saline** 60 feet Hard Very Severe 5a † (6.7.96)
To the left of the left-hand crack (*Chimney Route*) is an arête. Climb the obvious crack in its right wall; then use a good hold to pull onto the arête to a huge hold. Climb the arête on its left-hand side to reach ledges.

Chimney Route 50 feet Severe 4a (29.5.83)
The original route of the area climbs the left-hand crack.

☆☆**Crackline** 40 feet Hard Severe 4b † (6.7.96)
Climb the right-hand of the two prominent cracks.

Feline 50 feet Very Severe 4b † (27.6.96)
Climb the red ramp a few feet right of *Crackline*.

☆**Fine Line** 70 feet Difficult † (27.7.96)
Climb the gully in the centre of the wall.

☆**Bee Line** 70 feet Hard Very Severe 5b † (6.7.96)
To the right of *Fine Line* is an obvious groove. Start at the left-hand end of a platform, at a crack. Gain the groove and climb it to a steep wall above. Step left and climb the wall direct.

Bubble Trouble 60 feet Hard Very Severe 5a † (27.7.96)
From the right-hand end of the platform, climb directly to the top.

Cave Wall Area

The approach to the adit is described above under South C Walls.

Absolutely Adit 140 feet E1 5a † (6.7.96)
A more-or-less direct route starting from the right-hand side of the adit at the start of *Cave Wall Traverse*. Protection is poor. Climb the rib and slab above until the angle steepens. Step left and climb the red wall for a few feet. Move right below an overhang, gain a groove, and continue to the top. Some ingenuity will be required to reach the adequate belays.

★**Cave Wall Traverse** 210 feet Hard Severe (19.3.78)
An isolated climb with one excellent pitch. Start at the adit.
1 100 feet 4a. Move right onto the reddish wall and follow the obvious, often wet traverse-line, which descends slightly to an exposed stance on top of a pillar on the edge of the face.
2 50 feet 4b. Climb the wall above the pillar, trending right to a slanting overlap. Use a series of holds on the lip of the vast sea-cave to gain a comfortable ledge.
3 60 feet. Go straight up above the belay to mixed ground.

Indian Buttress

Further south is a bay with two large caves, the southernmost of these being a high, vertical slit. To its right is a narrow black slab with a line of overhangs low down, and immediately right of this is a higher, steeper, black wall facing north, split in its centre by a prominent chimney/crack. Some 20 feet offshore from the west face of the buttress is an entertaining sea-stack known as The Little Big Horn.

Three climbs take the black slab, which is reached by a carefully-arranged abseil from the broken rocks above. At sea-level there is a clean, grey, washed ledge.

Counting Coup 100 feet Severe 4a (16.7.88)
From the grey ledge climb diagonally left up the slab to reach a black groove. Climb this by a good crack for 20 feet to a platform; then pick an arbitrary way up the easy rock above to the top.

Blackfoot Trots 100 feet Very Severe 4c † (16.7.88)
Directly above the grey ledge is a crack leading to and passing through a roof. The difficulty and interest lie in the roof, which provides a lot of entertainment for the second. Climb up to the roof and then pull through it to reach the platform above. Continue easily to the top.

★**The Hairy Men from the East** 110 feet Difficult (16.7.88)
An impressive situation for an easy climb. The experience is well worthwhile. From the grey ledge, climb diagonally right to reach a crack and groove. Follow the groove to the top.

To the left of the central chimney/crack are two fine climbs up the steep walls of the north face of the buttress. Their starts are reached by abseil, or by descending *Spirit* and crossing the foot of the chimney to reach small ledges.

☆**Crescenda** 120 feet E2 5c † (6.93)
The cracks in the left wall of *Alex of Gowla*. Start at the base of the corner of *Alex of Gowla*. Climb the corner for a short way until a large quartz-filled pocket allows a move left onto the overhanging wall. Climb through a small roof to a good ledge. The distinctive crack with an undercut start leads to the top.

★★**Alex of Gowla** 120 feet E1 5b (19.6.88)
An immaculate corner climb. Reach the bottom by abseiling down the corner at the left-hand side of the face. Alternatively, traverse left from the right-hand end of the ledges to reach a stance with a spike and thread belay. Climb the corner to reach the large capping overhang. Traverse right across the steep wall to gain the upper groove, and follow this to the top.

★★**Indian Country** 120 feet E2 5b (19.6.88)
From the left-hand end of the ledges, climb an obvious steep corner-crack for 40 feet; then continue up to a line of overhangs (peg). Traverse right and slightly down to bridge across a gap below a crack. Follow a series of slabby grooves that trend slightly left to reach easier ground and multiple belays.

At the western end of the buttress is a friendly hollow for belaying, setting up abseils, lunching and general procrastination, and sunning oneself. The following routes start and/or finish hereabouts.

Spirit 50 feet Moderate (19.6.88)
More useful as an easy way down. To the right of the central chimney crack is a series of stepped grooves. Start at the foot of the face below a central

overhanging crack. Climb diagonally up and left around an arête to reach the stepped grooves. Continue up these to the top.

☆☆**Touch the Earth** 75 feet Very Severe 4b † (19.6.88)
Delightful steep face-climbing. Abseil down the seaward arête to reach ledges at sea-level. Step up the arête; then traverse left onto the face and continue up and left to reach an obvious groove. Climb the groove, step left at its top, and continue up the steep wall and cracks above to reach the belay area.

Shaman 60 feet Severe 4a † (19.6.88)
Start at the foot of the arête as for *Touch the Earth*. Climb the arête directly, steeply at first, then taking care of suspect rock in the upper section.

Tipi 50 feet Very Difficult (19.6.88)
Start as for *Touch the Earth* and climb the easy-angled slab to the right of the arête to reach the obvious V-groove. Climb this to the top.

Red Cloud 40 feet Severe † (9.9.95)
Climb the fine thin crack in the arête right of *Tipi*. Very sharp holds and good protection; short but sweet.

Ghost Dance 50 feet Hard Severe † (9.9.95)
A ramp leads down rightwards from the slab of *Tipi* to the belay ledge of *How the West Was Won*. Cross the top of the ramp to reach a bulging left-facing groove and climb this on interesting rock.

The Little Big Horn

Offshore to the west is the stack of The Little Big Horn.

★**How the West Was Won** Severe (19.6.88)
An absolute must for the jaded rock-jock. A classical approach is essential for this 'mixed' climb with its unusual ambience. Abseil into the gap between the buttress and the stack. A belay can be taken on a small, rounded ledge just below high-tide level, but it is simpler to swim across to the intervening rocky stump while still attached to the end of the abseil rope for safety. From the stump, jump, step, or fall across the gap (or into the sea) to gain the stack. Ascend to its summit by the central groove-system in the landward face. Jumar or Tyrolean back to shore. Perfect for a sun-filled, blue-sky day.

Yellow Hair 50 feet Difficult (19.6.88)
Traverse around the seaward face of The Little Big Horn to reach the foot of the north arête and climb it to the top.

Tubby's Head

South of Indian Buttress and before Tubby's Head itself is reached, a steep wall can be seen, marked by two orange patches of rockfall scar. One route takes this wall.

Kansas City 100 feet Hard Very Severe 5a † (21.2.88)
Start from the good ledge at the foot of the wall. Step up to another ledge and move left to the crackline. Follow the crackline to a hard pull rightwards at the top. Continue up steep earth at the top of the wall, using the abseil rope to reach a stake belay.

The coastline between Tubby's Head and Chapel Porth consists of a long section of steep cliffs with desperate-looking finishing-slopes of earth, grass, and gravel. There is tremendous potential here for the insanely adventurous.

Chapel Porth

OS Ref 697 496

There is an impressive amount of cliff here but a less impressive amount of rock. The south-side cliffs appear to have many good lines, but the finishes leave a lot to be desired. The same is true of the north side where two climbs have been done, but the visitor is more likely to be enticed into the area by the legendary *croque-monsieurs* served at the laid-back Chapel Porth café.

About 200 yards along the beach is a blatant, steep, square-cut corner, *Toby's Corner*. The first route is located on a multi-coloured wall below and about 100 yards north of Wheal Coates, the prominent mine on the coast path. Access is by scrambling down to fishermen's ledges just north of the cliff and traversing back south 50 yards along ledges accessible except within two hours of high tide. It is possible to walk along the sandy beach from Chapel Porth at very low tide.

Wheal Coates Wall 120 feet E2 † (24.6.95)
The climb takes an obvious diagonal line from left to right. Start at the left side of the wall, in a corner.
1 40 feet 5a. Climb steeply up and right to gain an overhung ledge. Surmount the overhang above to belay on a large ledge at the foot of a ramp.
2 80 feet 5a. Climb fascinatingly-coloured rock diagonally right for 40 feet; then continue straight up to the crumbling corner above, which leads to a very loose exit (two pegs). A serious pitch.

Toby's Corner 40 feet Hard Very Severe 4c † (6.8.96)
Climb the corner. The crux lies in persuading enough holds to stay on long enough to negotiate the finishing bulge. A good line!

Further along and around a little promontory is a fine large cave, bounded on the right by an easy slab, itself bounded by a bottomless corner.

Chapel Porth Eliminate 50 feet Very Severe 4b † (6.8.96)
Climb the slab direct into the corner. Move left a few feet above the lip of the cave to make an exposed mantelshelf onto a good ledge. Finish up 'Weetabix'.

Hell's Mouth

OS Ref 605 430

A popular tourist attraction, much favoured by the suicidal as this steep rotten cliff is only a few yards walk from the road. For the real enthusiast, a quick turn of the wheel and a sharp stab of the accelerator makes for a spectacular finish. The rock scenery is very impressive and will repay further inspection from sea-level. From the car-park, walk west for 300 yards to a promontory with a dip in its crest. Descend to the right of the crest via a faint path leading directly down steep grass to sloping rock ledges. Traverse back east to an obvious sea-level crag across a boulder-filled cave, which is sea-washed at high tide. The crag faces the afternoon sun and, although there is some loose rock on the surface, this should clear after a few ascents.

Psychosis 90 feet Very Difficult † (1.83)
Traverse left to a ramp-line, which is followed diagonally left to the top of the crag.

★**Paranoia** 90 feet E3 5b (28.3.83)
The obvious, striking crackline in the centre of the face. Start at the foot of the chimney, which is climbed to a traverse-line across the lip of the overhang (*Friend* 3 and 3½). Climb the groove above to a lone flake. Make a hard move past this and move onto the left arête. Climb the final overhang and finish easily up a friable groove.

The coast from Hell's Mouth to Fishing Cove (OS Ref 596 429) has been traversed, giving an exciting expedition, and starting with a frightening abseil descent down the suicide line from the fenceposts. Loose rock, grass, and incoming tides all enhance the enjoyment.

First Ascents

No details for:	**Daylight, Dingo, Edge of the West, Grot Gully, In Marion's Eyes, Keep Left, The Ridge of Khazad-Dum, Tide's In, Vaudeville Jazz Pooftah**
1898	**Scrattling Crack** T Longstaff *Years ahead of its time and still a classic. 'I then tied myself onto the rope and made the ascent. It is easier than coming down; there are holds all the way, and the only awkwardness comes about a third of the way up; here where the holds are shallowest, the cliff wall comes inconveniently close, and one feels that it is trying to push one out of them. But the difficulty is slight and after perhaps 15 or 20 feet everything is simple and straightforward once again. With a man to control the rope at the top, the whole route, both up and down, is completely safe; but a leader climbing unsupported as Lawder did, cannot afford to make a mistake. Though technically not hard, the exposure of the leader over a length of 120 feet caused Lawder to classify the ascent, in rock-climbing parlance as "easy very difficult".' (C H Archer, on the second known ascent in the mid 50s)*
c.1930	**North Ridge, Troy** R Bere
1957	**Vicarage Tower** K M Lawder, E C Pyatt *The first accurate description of a Culm route.*
1957	**Horn of Plenty** K M Lawder, E C Pyatt
1957	**Hawker's Slab** K M Lawder, E C Pyatt
1959 Sept 27	**The Cleaver** T W Patey, V N Stevenson
1959 Sept 27	**The Needle** T W Patey
1959	**Consolation** (Bear Rock) K M Lawder, E C Pyatt
1959	**Wreckers' Slab** T W Patey, J Deacon (AL), K M Lawder *A notable achievement.*
1959	**Smugglers' Slab** T W Patey, J Deacon (AL), K M Lawder
1959	**The Nose** T W Patey
1959	**Quarterdeck** V N Stevenson, T W Patey
1961	**Barely Possible, Hatchway and Rigging** R Lewis, D Finlayson
1961	**Mainsail, Gangway** D Finlayson, R Lewis *The former was a bold effort.*
1962	**Bubbly** K M Lawder, E C Pyatt
1963	**South Pier** J Davies, J Whitehead
1968 July 20	**Argonaut** P R Littlejohn, J D Fowler *Littlejohn's first Culm route.*
1968 July 28	**The Masterdon, Two Fair Maidens, Cobblers, Stone Table, The Viking** W A Carver, P H Stanier *Cligga Head rediscovered.*
1968 Aug 4	**Bronco, C Land Super** W A Carver, D Brown
1968 Aug 10	**Discretion, Second Choice** D Brown, J Atherton
1968 Aug 11	**Baldy Bane** D Brown, J Atherton
1968 Aug 17	**Clint's Route** W A Carver, R Powell

1968 Aug 24 **Season of the Witch** W A Carver, P H Stanier
1968 Aug 25 **Shades of Nod** W A Carver, P H Stanier
1968 Sept 8 **Black Veil** W A Carver, P H Stanier
1968 Oct 6 **Reflections of Inot** D Brown, P H Stanier
1968 **Moonshot** P H Biven, J D Fowler, P R Littlejohn
Seventy years after Longstaff, a companion route for Scrattling Crack arrives. So called because it was the day of the first orbit of the moon by a manned spacecraft, which the climbers watched on Fowler's portable television while sitting on top of the cliff.
1969 April 19 **Ofus** W A Carver, P H Stanier
1969 April 20 **Queen Jane** P H Stanier, W A Carver
That rarity: a quality North Coast easy route!
1969 April 20 **The Orange-Throated Gronk** W A Carver, P H Stanier
1969 April 20 **Resurrection** P R Littlejohn, S B Jones
Littlejohn ignoring the obvious at Baggy.
1969 April 20 **The Dicer** W A Carver, P H Stanier
1969 April **Loose Woman** W Chevrest, I F Duckworth
The discovery of Blackchurch. With aid; led free in September 1974 by K Darbyshire.
1969 Aug 16 **Lord of the Dance** P H Stanier, W A Carver (AL)
1969 Sept 5 **Surfer's Slab** N Gough, I Maxwell
1969 Sept 6 **Skull and Crossbones** N Gough, D Bland
1969 Sept 7 **Shivering Chimney** N Gough, D Bland
1969 Oct 8 **Urizen** A C Willmott, M C Spring, D Edwards
The North London Mountaineering Club Roadshow arrives at Baggy Point.
1969 Oct 12 **The Concrete Rose** A C Willmott, M C Spring, D Edwards
1969 Oct 13 **Pink Void** A C Willmott, M C Spring
Originally climbed with a hard start from below the centre of the slab, and subsequently approached direct at Very Severe standard. A large rockfall obliterated the former and made the latter much harder.
1969 Oct 18 **Twinkletoes** B Wintringham, M Wintringham, A D Baker, D Johnston
1969 Oct 19 **Heart of the Sun** A C Willmott, M C Spring (AL)
Climbed as an aid route; free climbed in February 1977 by A Strapcans and C King (AL). It then shared the now obliterated original start to Pink Void; the start described was climbed by C King and N Gifford in April 1977.
1969 Oct 19 **In Her Eyes, The Bridge of Khazad-Dum** D Godfrey, G Croft
1969 Oct 19 **Kinkyboots** D Johnston, B Wintringham (AL)
Direct Start climbed on 26 October 1969 by B Wintringham (solo).
1969 Oct 26 **Sexilegs** B Wintringham, M Wintringham
With a point of aid, soon eliminated.
1969 Oct 26 **The Narrow Way** A C Willmott, M C Spring
1969 Nov 1 **G-String** B Wintringham, M Wintringham
1969 Nov 1 **Smile** (Baggy Point) D Edwards, D Godfrey
1969 Nov 1 **Double Overhang** D Edwards, D Godfrey (both solo)
1969 Nov 2 **White Noise** D Godfrey, D Edwards

1969 Nov 2 **Bike** A C Willmott, M C Spring
Named after a decaying bicycle frame half-way up. Bike Direct *and* Tandem *were climbed by M Fowler in 1980.*
1969 Nov 15 **Midnight Cowboy** B Wintringham, M Wintringham
1969 Nov 23 **Pickpocket** B Wintringham, M Wintringham
1969 Nov 30 **Grand Vizier's Garden Party** A C Willmott, M C Spring
1970 Jan 31 **Lost Horizon** B Wintringham, M Wintringham
One point of aid, soon eliminated.
1970 Feb 1 **The Straight and Narrow** B Wintringham, M Wintringham
1970 Feb 8 **Rite of Spring** P R Littlejohn, P Biven, A Chadwick, J Hammond
The Devon faithful rediscover Blackchurch.
1970 Feb 14 **Ben, Marion** B Wintringham, M Wintringham
1970 Feb 28 **Renata** D Johnston, M Wintringham
1970 Feb 28 **Peeping Tom** B Wintringham, A D Baker
1970 March 1 **Shangri-La** B Wintringham, M Wintringham, A D Baker, D Johnston
Baggy Point's most popular route.
1970 March 14 **The Scythe** B Wintringham
1970 March 15 **Doors of Perception** B Wintringham, J Browne
Originally gained from Twinkletoes. Direct Start *climbed with aid in January 1970 by A D Baker and N Helliwell: climbed free on 22 July 1976 by C King and N Gifford.*
1970 March 27 **The Great Beast** A D Baker, D Edwards (AL)
The line described was climbed by M Morrison and M Fowler (AL) on 18th September 1977. The original easier line came in from the right.
1970 March 27 **Sting** A D Baker, D Edwards
1970 March 28 **Satisfaction** N Helliwell, D Johnston
1970 March 28 **Fools Rush In** B Wintringham, M Wintringham
Aid was used to leave Urizen*: climbed free in 1972 by N Lockwood and P Jenkinson.*
1970 March 28 **Svenja** D Johnston, N Helliwell
1970 March 28 **Egg** P R Littlejohn, G Skerratt
The variation pitch was climbed by M Fowler and M Morrison on 18 September 1977.
1970 March 29 **Multiplater** D Edwards, A D Baker
Mad dogs and Englishmen – but who was the dog?
1970 March 29 **The Pox** B Wintringham, M Wintringham
1970 March 30 **The Archtempter** P R Littlejohn, G Skerrat
The first major route on the shale! 'The raw material was crude, but by the lengthy refinement process of gardening an excellent rock-climb was produced.'
1970 June **Taming of the Shrew** T Newberry, P Jose
Minor route but a major discovery.
1970 Aug 3 **Nudy Rudy** C Robson, D McVean
1970 Aug 4 **Corner Route** P H Stanier, D Cawley
1970 Sept 11 **Astronomy Domine** D Johnston, C Johnston
1970 Sept 12 **Blind Faith** D Johnston, C Johnston
1970 Dec **Bonk** J Hammond, K Darbyshire
1971 Feb 7 **Hatchet** P R Littlejohn, M Chambers

1971 Feb	**Stone Man, Pooh Corner, Heffalump Trap** K Darbyshire, M Gray
1971 April 3	**The Smile** (Lower Sharpnose) P R Littlejohn, S B Jones *'Feels big for its size.'*
1971 April 10	**Chouinard's Yard 1** and **2** D Johnston, A D Baker
1971 April 10	**Hopener** C A Morton, K Darbyshire
1971 April 11	**Long Rock Eliminate** D Johnston, A D Baker
1971 April 11	**Spare Rib** D Johnston, M Johnston
1971 April 11	**Eroica** P R Littlejohn, C A Morton *A superb discovery. Two preplaced pegs were used for aid; one was eliminated by E R Hart and D Hope in August 1973, and the route was finally climbed free by P Livesey and J Lawrence in 1975.*
1971 April 16	**Trailblazer** P R Littlejohn, K Darbyshire *Pointing the way to Il Duce.*
1971 April 17	**Ahab** P R Littlejohn, K Darbyshire
1971 April 17	**Decumanus** P R Littlejohn, S B Jones
1971 April 30	**Turk** I F Duckworth, P R Littlejohn (AL)
1971 April 30	**Lunakhod** K Darbyshire, P R Littlejohn
1971 April	**Clawtrack** P R Littlejohn, K Darbyshire
1971 June 11	**The Almighty** S B Jones, P R Littlejohn (AL), K Goodman
1971 June	**Xanthoria** K Darbyshire, J Darbyshire
1971 Sept 7	**Goth** P R Littlejohn, K Goodman
1971 Sept 11	**Cirrus Minor** A McFarlane, S Chadwick (AL)
1971 Sept	**Jolly Roger** K Darbyshire, S L Titt
1971 Oct 26	**Caprice** P R Littlejohn, S B Jones *The Direct Start was climbed on 2 January 1983; climbers unknown.*
1972 April 23	**Il Duce** P R Littlejohn, K Darbyshire *An epic ascent, using one point of aid. 'We stared pop-eyed at one of the most awe-inspiring lines we had ever seen.' Climbed free in 1980 by T Jones and R J Hughes.*
1972 April 25	**Darkinbad the Brightdayler** P R Littlejohn, I F Duckworth *A major breakthrough, despite five points of aid. 'While this action departs from the purest traditions of a first ascent, in this case I believe it to have been in the best interests of the climb. No one could be gladder than I to emerge from the dark'n bad lower walls to a finish touched by the last rays of the sun.' Climbed free in 1976 by R Fawcett and P Gomersall with some variation in line.*
1972 April	**Right-Hand Eliminate** D Johnston, J Zangwill
1972 April	**Shortera** A D Baker, A Randall
1972 June 10	**Nativity** P R Littlejohn, D Hardy
1972 June 10	**The Baptist** P R Littlejohn
1972 June 28	**Diabolist** P R Littlejohn, K Darbyshire
1972 Aug 18	**Rotwand** P R Littlejohn, S B Jones
1972 Aug 27	**Uphill** P R Littlejohn *One point of aid was used. Climbed free by M Fowler in 1980.*
1972 Aug 27	**Mascon** P R Littlejohn, H Clarke *The Bolder Boulder variation was climbed by C Nicholson and N White on 6 March 1983;* Village Idiot *by Nicholson with A Morley in June 1983.*

1972 Sept 8 **Houdini** K Darbyshire, H Clarke
1972 Sept 8 **The Break** P R Littlejohn (solo)
1972 Sept 9 **Dark Comedy** K Darbyshire, P R Littlejohn (AL), H Clarke
1972 Sept 16 **Ratcliffe Highway** W A Carver, P H Stanier
The road to America.
1972 Sept **Jo** R Linford, S Chadwick
1972 Dec 2 **The Plank** K Darbyshire, A Randall
1973 Feb 4 **Magical Staircase** T Colter, S Chadwick
1973 Feb 18 **Solid Air** S Chadwick
1973 April 7 **Dulcima** P R Littlejohn, K Darbyshire
1973 April 7 **Blunt End** F E R Cannings, W Hurford
1973 April 7 **Sparrow** K Darbyshire, P R Littlejohn
1973 April 7 **Alpine Groyne** J Cleare, P H Biven (AL) and Alpine Club party
1973 April 29 **The Vault** P R Littlejohn, K Darbyshire
1973 April 29 **The Mausoleum** K Darbyshire, P R Littlejohn (AL)
'A reverential ascent.'
1973 April **Escapist** H Clarke, K Darbyshire
Direct Start by P R Littlejohn and K Darbyshire on 26 August 1973.
1973 April **Supernatural** K Darbyshire, H Clarke, P R Littlejohn
A superb find, with a descent out of all proportion to its size.
1973 May 6 **Hassle, Westerlation** K Darbyshire, H Clarke
1973 June 2 **Happy Hunting Ground** P R Littlejohn, K Darbyshire
1973 June 3 **Chicken Flesh** P R Littlejohn, K Darbyshire (VL)
1973 June **Dark Lady** P R Littlejohn, K Darbyshire
1973 July 16 **America** P R Littlejohn, K Darbyshire
The last of the Atlantic coast big four. 'Hypertense and committed we pull on damp trousers and damp PAs after crossing the boulders in the nick of time.'
'I'm on a lichenous knife-edge trying to fathom a blank section. Raindrops clinch it; the arête soars dramatically over an abyss filled with sea noise...'
The direct finish climbed by R Warke in 1989.
1973 Sept 15 **Fever, The Obelisk, Udolpho, Trebarwith to Backways Cove Coastal Traverse** P R Littlejohn, K Darbyshire
Thus completing a gentle day out for the pair.
1973 Sept **Savage God** P R Littlejohn, K Darbyshire
'Connoisseurs of the harder South Stack routes will find Savage God no less demanding and satisfying.'
Savage God Direct by F Ramsay in June 1993.
1973 Oct 27 **Carbonek** K Darbyshire, P R Littlejohn
1973 Dec 30 **Ruby** P R Littlejohn, K Darbyshire
The end of a year's campaign which added a new dimension to Cornish climbing.
1973 **Tempest** P Biven, A N Other
1974 March 20 **Undercracker** P R Littlejohn, P Tower, P W Thexton
Done in mistake for Twinkletoes.
1974 April 27 **Bandstand** J Kingston, J Jones, C Phoenix, K J Wilson
No prizes for guessing the conductor.
1974 April **Needle Direct** I Peters, A Clarke
1974 May 20 **The Sexton** K Darbyshire, D Garner
Literally excavated.

1974 May 20 **Sacré Coeur** P R Littlejohn, H Clarke
The Direct Finish was climbed by P Twomey and P Saunders on 27 November 1988.

1974 Aug 6 **Aprez-Vous** R Perriment, D Gough
A local team take charge on this local crag.

1974 Aug 14 **The Verger** K Darbyshire, P Buttrick
After an all-night party which left other team members unconscious.

1974 Aug **Prayermat** D Hope, E R Hart (AL)
Climbed to avoid the walk back through the undergrowth; a couple of hours were spent regretting the decision! Relimbed and named by M Fowler in March 1976 – the first stirrings of interest in 'loose living'?

1974 Oct 25 **Earth Rim Roamer** P R Littlejohn, S B Jones
Not destined for longevity, it probably had only three ascents before it collapsed.

1974 **Crimtyphon** K Darbyshire, D Garner
The best in Darbyshire's meteoric development of the shale cliffs. The Every Rose Has Its Thorn *finish climbed by T Greenhalgh and T Glass in 1991.*

1974 **Father Christmas's Nightmare, Sugar Magnolia, Notre Dame, Barabbas** K Darbyshire, D Garner

1974 **Tydomin** K Darbyshire, A Clark

1974 **Fruichon, Wharf Rat, Berlin** K Darbyshire, D Garner, H Clarke

1974 **Corinth** P R Littlejohn, K Darbyshire

1974 **Pipsqueak** H Clarke, A Clark

1974 **Ironside** K Darbyshire, A Clark, I Peters

1974 **Menachurch Wall** K Darbyshire, P Buttrick

1974 **Mercury** P R Littlejohn, S B Jones
A magnificent route with a complicated evolution. The original finished up what is now Quicksilver. *The finish described was climbed as part of* The Mercury Connection *in August 1979. The groove in its entirety was completed by M Fowler and M Hunt in October 1979.*

1974 **The Tomb** R Perriment, R Broomhead
A superb find.

1974 **Snakebite** K Darbyshire, H Clarke

1974 **Back to Grand Falls, Demerara, The Shrink** K Darbyshire, D Garner
One point of aid on the last, soon eliminated.

1975 Jan **Caravanserai** K Darbyshire, A Clark

1975 Feb **The Entertainer** K Darbyshire, I Peters

1975 Feb **Chicago** P R Littlejohn, D Garner

1975 April **Sita, Honeypot** M Pettifer, N Tritton

1975 April **Last Leviathan, Cobra** P Livesey, J Lawrence
Was he going for the hanging groove? Both in the course of a clean-up Cornwall campaign.

1975 Sept **Yorkshire Pud** A Evans

1975 Oct 18 **Loosera** R Harrison, J Fivesdale
The Pinch of Salt variation was climbed by S Lewis and G Lewis on 12 April 1980.
1975 Oct 23 **Wee Beastie** I Fletcher, J Fivesdale
1975 Oct 26 **Antichrist** P R Littlejohn, D Garner, P Buttrick
1975 Nov **Lightfingers** I Peters, P Buttrick
1975 Nov **Trident** J Fowler, C Gibson, I Peters, P Buttrick
Direct Start climbed by B R E Wilkinson and M A Grapes on 6 June 1993.
1976 May 16 **Terrapin** P R Littlejohn, P Buttrick, D Garner
The left-hand variant was climbed on 4 September 1976 by B Wintringham.
1976 June 3 **Broadside** A Strapcans, C King
1976 June **Crab Slab** D Hope, S Hope, V Thomas, A Mills
1976 June **Thin Lion, Playing with the Boys** V Thomas, D Hope
1976 June **Great Mills** A Mills (solo)
1976 June **Culm-de-sac** D Hope, S Hope
1976 Aug 5 **The Flame** I Peters, P Buttrick
1976 Aug 5 **Britannia** J Fowler, C Gibson
1976 Sept 5 **Soft Touch** B Wintringham, M Wintringham, A D Baker
One point of aid – a Baggy test-piece. Climbed free by A Sharp.
1976 Sept 5 **The Great Gig in the Sky** R Harrison, D Marshall
1976 Sept 15 **Freddie** I Bentley, N Tritton
1977 March 5 **Mozambique** I Peters, P Buttrick
1977 March 20 **Silk** P Buttrick, P Freeman (AL)
1977 March 20 **White Sabbath** I Peters, P Buttrick (AL)
1977 April 2 **Gog, Magog** I Peters, P Buttrick
1977 June 26 **Lotus, Andromeda Strain** P R Littlejohn, I Peters
Top pitch only of the latter; the first pitch had been climbed some years before by P R Littlejohn and K Darbyshire.
1977 Aug 20 **Rindstone** P R Littlejohn, C King
1977 Aug **Dynamo Hum** (Menachurch Point) C Gibson, R McCabe
1977 Aug **Aphrodite** J Fowler, C Gibson
1977 Sept 3 **The Go Between, Blowin' Free** A Sharp, S Lewis, G Lewis
1977 Sept 30 **Stopford** M Morrison, M Fowler
1977 Oct 8 **Summerhouse** M Fowler, M Morrison, M Quantrell
1977 Oct 18 **McVitie** I Peters, P Buttrick (AL)
1977 Oct **Toad in the Hole** P O'Sullivan, D Ball
A subdued start for a prolific campaigner.
1978 Jan 7 **The Heathen** M Fowler, M Morrison (AL), J Maund
1978 March 19 **Cave Wall Traverse** I Peters, P Buttrick (AL)
1978 April 1 **Dreamboat Annie** J Maund, M Dunning
1978 April 2 **The Skirmish** I Peters, P Buttrick
1978 May 26 **Vagabond** M Fowler, M Morrison
Variation pitch: F Ramsay and D Smith on 10 June 1990.
1978 May 27 **Sick Rose** P R Littlejohn, C King
1978 May 27 **Downward Bound** R Perriment, C George (AL)
1978 May **Over My Head** R Harrison, P O'Sullivan
1978 June 29 **Here and Now** R Perriment, C Owen
1978 June 30 **Midnight Rambler** S Harry, A Tobin
An important contribution by another team of Gowla habitués.

1978 July 19 **Daydream** S Harry, R Perriment
1978 July 21 **Killing Time** A Tobin, S Harry
1978 July 23 **Halcyon Days** S Harry, A Tobin
1978 July 30 **Soma** C Owen, R Perriment
1978 Aug 9 **Godspell** P Whillance, D Armstrong
The Culm's hardest route to that date.
1978 Aug 18 **Continental Retreat** R Perriment, D Marvin
1978 Aug 23 **Silver Dollar** R Edwards, P Renouf
The arrival of Edwards adds a sense of urgency to Gowla development.
1978 Aug 24 **The Arête, Blue Meany** R Edwards, P Renouf
1978 Aug 24 **Euthanasia** R Edwards
1978 Aug 25 **Terra Nova** A Tobin, S Harry
1978 Aug 26 **Magic Fly, Alpha-Beta** R Edwards, P Renouf
1978 Aug 27 **Black Knight, Life on Mars** A Tobin, S Harry
1978 Aug 28 **Crash Landing, Quicksilver** A Tobin, S Harry
The upper pitches of Quicksilver were Mercury's originals from 1974.
1978 Aug 28 **Crystal Voyage** R Edwards, P Renouf
The Sewage Pipe Cliff comes of age.
1978 Aug 31 **Bohemian** R Perriment, C Owen
1978 Sept 1 **Fourth Dimension** C Owen, R Perriment
1978 Sept 1 **Wageslave** R Perriment, C Owen
1978 Sept 2 **Journey to Ixtlan** R Perriment, C Owen
1978 Sept 2 **Starbound** C Owen, R Perriment
1978 Sept 2 **Sundance** (Carn Gowla) S Harry, R Perriment
1978 Sept 18 **Nowhere Man** R Perriment, S Harry
1978 Sept 19 **Night Ride** R Perriment, S Harry
1978 Sept **Gravity's Rainbow** S Harry, R Perriment
1978 Sept **Beresford** M Fowler, M Morrison
1978 Oct 1 **Blunderbuss** M Fowler, M Morrison
1978 Oct 10 **Eric Pode's Route** P O'Sullivan, D Sargeant, C Woodhead
1978 Oct 21 **Pilgrim** M Fowler, J English
1978 Dec 9 **The Wager** I Peters, P Buttrick (AL)
Direct finish by P O'Sullivan, 1984.
1978 **Come Back Canute** M Brown, J Whiffin, P Jane
1978 **Sleepy Toes** M Brown, A Wilcox
1979 Jan 21 **Dream Lover** P O'Sullivan, B Rossiter
1979 April 8 **The Wine Dark Sea** P O'Sullivan, W Taylor
1979 April 14 **Bumpers, Celsius** P O'Sullivan, B Adams, J Maund
1979 April 15 **Spring Surprise** P O'Sullivan, H Cain
1979 April 28 **Tourist Trap** P O'Sullivan, R Mear
1979 April 28 **Sea Breeze** R Mear, P O'Sullivan
1979 April 29 **Reverie of Bone** P O'Sullivan, R Mear
1979 April 29 **Föhn** R Mear, P O'Sullivan
1979 May 5 **Private World** M Fowler, M Morrison
An apt name for a new concept on the North Coast.
After an eventful repeat ascent with C Alston, I Parnell comments: 'I was finding things even more worrying than usual having dropped one of my shoes from pitch 3 into the sea. Through the gathering darkness I looked back at Clark trying not to weight the

pathetic belay. We were both thinking the same thing: if I couldn't pass this next section of 5c mud and talc we were in really big trouble...'

1979 May 12 **Gladiator** A Brazier, J Colwell
Pitch 1 only; pitch 2 was climbed on 22 September 1979 by G Gibson and J Walker.

1979 May 13 **Half-Mast** I Peters (solo)
1979 May **Briny Walk** P O'Sullivan, B Adams, J Maund
1979 May **Stuffed Badger** P O'Sullivan, B Adams, H Cain
1979 May **Blisterin' Barnacle** P O'Sullivan, B Adams
The easier routes at Dyer's Lookout may have have been climbed before.

1979 June 23 **The Blacksmith** M Fowler, S Fenwick
1979 June 23 **The Arête** (Baggy Point) M Fowler (solo)
1979 June 30 **The Sceptred Race, Atlantean** P O'Sullivan, D Sargeant
1979 July 3 **Matchless** I Peters, P Freeman
An excellent reward for heavy excavations.

1979 July 6 **Bantam** I Peters, A Clark, S Cardy
1979 July 6 **Starfire** S Cardy, A Davy
1979 July 6 **Nippy Norman** A Davy, S Cardy
1979 July 7 **Breakaway** M Fowler, M Morrison
The ultimate shale horror. The lower pitches had been climbed by K Darbyshire some years earlier. The second ascent by F Ramsay and D Thomas was made even more 'interesting' by the latter's migraine attack on the crux pitch.

1979 July 14 **Tsunami** P O'Sullivan, N Crowhurst, D Sargeant
1979 July 14 **Ripple** D Sargeant, N Crowhurst
1979 July 15 **Dominator** I Peters, A Clark, P Freeman
1979 July 22 **Les Invalides** P O'Sullivan, C Woodhead
1979 July 24 **Intensive Care** P O'Sullivan, D Ball
1979 Aug 9 **Dreadlock Holiday** P Whillance, R Parker
1979 Aug 24 **Salt Lake City** I Peters, D Gregan
1979 Aug **Bridge of Sighs** A Tobin, S Harry
1979 Aug **The Mercury Connection** R Edwards and party
1979 Sept 7 **Tactical Retreat** P O'Sullivan, I Peters
Exmansworthy discovered.

1979 Sept 9 **Second Sight** P O'Sullivan, I Peters (AL), D Sargeant
1979 Sept 22 **Cool Canute** C Nicholson, A Gallagher
1979 Sept 26 **Slip Sliding Away** B R E Wilkinson, A Gallagher (AL)
The name refers to the original start.

1979 Oct 2 **The Tourist** M Fowler, M Morrison
1979 Oct 6 **Ye Olde Scrote** S Lewis, G Lewis
1979 Oct 13 **Last Exit to St Agnes** A Bond, R Gookey
1979 Oct 14 **Permafrost** G Gibson, P Wilson
1979 Oct 14 **Sheet Whitening** G Gibson, P Wilson (AL)
1979 Oct 17 **Nomad** R Perriment, P O'Sullivan
1979 Oct 18 **Shadow Walker** P O'Sullivan, R Perriment
The bes tof the early but now defunct routes at Exmansworthy was gained from Tactical Retreat and climbed with two aid points. Climbed free with the Direct Start by P O'Sullivan and R Pawsey in 1980. The Superdirect Start climbed by M Fowler in 1982.

1979 Nov 18 **Slip It In Quick** S Bell, D Carroll
1979 **Bags' Corner** M Fowler (solo)
1979 **Crumbs..., The Plumed Serpent** P O'Sullivan, B Adams
1979 **No Sweat** Unknown
1970s **Wicks' Folly** Unknown
1980 Jan 5 **Popadom, Rock-Pool Crack, Shivering Timbers, Walking on the Moon** C Nicholson, A Gallagher
1980 Jan 5 **Dresden** P O'Sullivan, R Mear (AL)
1980 Jan 6 **Cat Burglar** P O'Sullivan, R Mear
1980 March 12 **Hand Job** P O'Sullivan, R Croft
1980 March 15 **Half-Life** P O'Sullivan, C Gibson
1980 April 12 **Danzig** A Brazier, M Corbett
1980 April 26 **Coast of Triumphs** G Gibson, D Beetlestone
The crux, and thus the point, of this route was climbed much earlier as a variation to Pickpocket.
1980 April 27 **Noir et Blanc** G Gibson, D Beetlestone
1980 April 27 **Carriatid** P O'Sullivan, C Griffiths
1980 April 29 **The Shrine** M Fowler, S Fenwick
1980 April 29 **Chien Lunatique** P O'Sullivan, R Croft
1980 April 29 **Sheepdog Trials in Babylon** P O'Sullivan, C Griffiths, R Croft
1980 May 3 **Ratcatcher** P Thompson, C Gibson
1980 May 3 **Nasty Little Bags of Poison** C Gibson, P Thompson
1980 May 4 **Formation Flying** P O'Sullivan, R Turnbull
1980 May 4 **Cul-de-sac** P Thompson, R Pawsey
1980 May 10 **Muffin Man** M Fowler, J Godding
1980 May 11 **King Arthur's Crack** M Fowler, J Godding
The Direct Finish was climbed in April 1990; climbers unknown.
1980 June **Umbra Crack** M Fowler, P O'Sullivan
1980 July 8 **Don't Bring Harry, Drift** G Gibson (solo)
1980 July 8 **Speed and Distance** G Gibson, D Beetlestone
1980 July 27 **Out of the Blue** K Marsden, A March
1980 Sept 6 **Serpico** I Peters, A Clark, S Cardy
1980 Oct **Cornflake Crack** S Monks
1980 **Castaway** R Perriment, A Tobin
1981 March 20 **Snapping Bubblies** R Hughes, L McGinley
1981 April 14 **Multiple Fractures** J de Rohan, A McConnachie
1981 April 16 **Sundance** (Baggy Point) D Viggers, M Borland
1981 April 25 **Last Laugh** S Bell, R Perriment
1981 April **Steppin' Razor** R Croft, H Cain
1981 April **Dark Attraction** E Cleasby, R Matheson
1981 April **Watergate** A Phizacklea, E Cleasby
1981 April **Elixir** E Cleasby, R Matheson (AL)
1981 April **Sea Thrift, Sunstorm** E Cleasby, R Matheson (AL), M Lynch
The start described for Sea Thrift *was climbed in December 1985 by D Hillebrandt.*
1981 May 6 **Angola** M Corbett, D Jacobs
1981 May 7 **Shamrock, Clover** M Corbett, D Jacobs
1981 May 9 **Decadent Days** M Corbett, A Brazier

1981 May 15 **Flight Path** K Jones, R Hughes, S Downes
Started at 5.30 p.m. The last pitch was climbed in the dark, illuminated by flashes from the lighthouse.
1981 May 30 **In Memoriam** M Fowler, M Morrison (AL)
1981 June 28 **Oiseaux** B R E Wilkinson, L Petherick
1981 June 28 **Crazy Streak** I Peters, G A Jenkin
1981 June **Pulses Unreal** A Grondowski, S Findlay
1981 June **Dislocation Dance** S Findlay, A Grondowski
1981 July 4 **The Snake** B Woodley, A Morely, B R E Wilkinson
1981 July 8 **Thinisher** D Thomas, N Hancock
1981 July 11 **Jamaican Dub** P O'Sullivan, P Bingham, J Thompson
Direct Start climbed by I Parnell and A Forbes on 29 September 1990.
1981 July 12 **Rasta Collie** P O'Sullivan, P Bingham, J Thompson
1981 July 12 **Astrodyne** M Fowler, M Morrison (AL)
1981 July 20 **Titmould Incorporated** B R E Wilkinson, J Stewart
1981 July **The Lemming** R Perriment, A N Other
1981 Aug 1 **Choreographic Variant** P O'Sullivan, P Bingham, J Thompson
1981 Aug 2 **Tigger** I Peters, A Clark
1981 Aug 7 **The Outlaw** M Corbett, A Brazier
A worthy companion to Cat Burglar.
1981 Dec 27 **Polar Airstream** M Dunning, A Dunning
1982 April 10 **Seal Appeal** M Fowler, M Morrison (AL)
1982 April 10 **Under Pressure** (Lye Rock) M Fowler, M Morrison
1982 April 17 **Bird Brain** M Fowler, M Smith
No Brain *variation: M J Crocker and I Parnell on 6 July 1997.*
1982 April 20 **Macho Duck** P O'Sullivan, R Swinden, R Croft
1982 April 20 **One in Every Port** R Swinden, P O'Sullivan, R Croft
1982 April 20 **Naughty Sneaky** P O'Sullivan, R Swinden
1982 April 23 **Sukharita** D Gregan, J Bell
1982 April **Goats** A Cunningham, C Rees-Jones
1982 April **Yellow Submarine, Shark's Fin Soup** C Rees-Jones, A Cunningham
1982 May 9 **Earth Rim Roamer II** P R Littlejohn, C Gibson
Climbed on sight, in terror. A very impressive replacement for Earth Rim Roamer I.
1982 May 16 **Guernica** P R Littlejohn, H Clarke
A formidable undertaking, even with one point of aid. Both first and second ascents (the latter by M Fowler) involved gear-stripping falls onto seconds. Littlejohn eliminated the aid point in April 1987.
1982 June **Illiteracy** C Cooke, M Pennington
1982 July 3 **King's Arête** A Meyers, M Fowler (AL)
The Republican Start *was climbed in 1997; climbers unknown.*
1982 July 3 **Short Rock Eliminate** C Rees-Jones, A Cunningham
1982 July 30 **Not Blisterin' Barnacle** D Garrett, H Sharp
1982 July **Gumbo, Interalp's Yard** A Cunningham, C Rees-Jones
1982 Aug 6 **Elephantitis** M Fowler, M Lynden (AL), S Lewis
Second ascent by F Ramsay, roped solo.
1982 Sept 11 **Three Slab Pebble** J Bebb, N Hancock, A Grieve (AL)

1982 Sept	**Slipstream I** C Nicholson, B R E Wilkinson
1982 Oct 11	**Dance on a Volcano** C Nicholson, B R E Wilkinson
1982 Oct	**Two Pints to Capel** N Hancock, D Thomas, A Grieve
1982 Oct	**Crocus Cat** A Grieve, D Thomas, J Bebb, N Hancock
1982 Oct	**Parsley Pig** D Thomas, A Grieve
1982 Dec	**Cold Comfort** R Croft, I Peters
1982 Dec	**Starkadder, Lounge Lizard** I Peters, R Croft
1982	**Bulging Speedeye Wall, Jazz Discharge Party Hat** M Miller, R Jones, I Hamilton
1982	**Visage** G A Jenkin, K Marsden (AL)
1982	**Freedom** C Nicholson, R Thorns *With a point of aid; eliminated by I Parnell and J Cheshire on 15 July 1994.*
1982	**Tears for Fears** C Nicholson, R Thorns
1982	**The Wall** C Nicholson, B R E Wilkinson
1982	**Culmination** C Nicholson, A N Other
1982	**Nose Decay** M Miller, R Jones
1982	**Angle Grinder** C Nicholson
1982	**Culm Dancing** (Exmansworthy) P Whillance
1982	**The Smirk** Unknown
1983 Jan 14	**The Wick** M Corbett, A Brazier, S Briggs
1983 Jan 16	**Avon Calling** M Corbett, D Critchley, A Brazier
1983 Jan 16	**Local Hero** D Critchley, A Brazier, M Corbett
1983 Jan	**Foul Brood, Big Business** I Peters, R Croft Big Business *originally climbed the whitish corner and then traversed left on a high line. The start as described climbed by P O'Sullivan and P Haworth in May 1983.*
1983 Jan	**White Rasta** R Croft, I Peters
1983 Jan	**Psychosis** J Hooper
1983 March 6	**Weekend Millionaires** C Nicholson, N White
1983 March 6	**Port, Starboard** Unknown
1983 April 2	**Rude Nude** M Fowler, P Watts, C Jones
1983 April 2	**Rose Street** D Hillebrandt, B Thomas (AL) The Fireman's Start *had been climbed previously, on 10 October 1982, by Hillebrandt with H Morris.*
1983 April 10	**Prevarication** P O'Sullivan, M Dunning
1983 April 16	**Kneewrecker Chimney** C Rees, M Davies
1983 April 16	**Sundare** D Garrett, T Williams, F Boissondale
1983 April 17	**Jenny's Jaunt** D Hillebrandt, B Thomas
1983 April 17	**Ocean Rendezvous** P O'Sullivan, D Brooke, I Peters
1983 April 17	**Zinc Silhouette** I Peters, P O'Sullivan
1983 May 28	**Paranoia** J Hooper
1983 May 29	**Chimney Route** D Hillebrandt
1983 June 4	**Gail's Waist** D Furness, A Dicks
1983 June 30	**Eraser Blade** P Bull, A Winfield
1983 June	**Yellow Arête** J Hooper
1983 June	**Challenger** C Nicholson, B R E Wilkinson
1983 June	**Broken English** P O'Sullivan, S Cooper
1983 July 12	**New Boots and Panties** M Fowler, A N Other
1983 July 14	**Poxy Wall** D Hillebrandt (solo)
1983 July 14	**Alpine Departure** M Doyle (solo)

1983 July 14 **Fisticuffs** M Doyle, D Hillebrandt
1983 July 16 **Leprosy** S Bell, R Perriment
1983 July **Lead Boots** P O'Sullivan, S Deeming, S Cooper
1983 July **Baha** P O'Sullivan, I Thomas, S Deeming
1983 Aug **Siren's Cry** R Harrison
Climbed in mistake for Last Leviathan. *A notable route from an infrequent visitor.*
1983 Sept **The Final Cut** J Hooper, M Doyle
1983 Oct 25 **Summer Wine** I Peters, P Buttrick
1983 Oct **Sluice** J Hooper, J Francom, R Whybra
1983 Nov 13 **Slipstream II, Subsultus** D Kerr, P Moulam
1983 Nov 13 **Fowl Play Fowler** P Moulam, D Kerr
1983 Nov **Crucial Bunny** P O'Sullivan, I Thomas, M Doyle
1983 Nov **Desire** M Doyle, J Hooper
1983 Dec 4 **Senecio Slab** D Hillebrandt, I Morris
1983 Dec **Hussle** I Peters, D Sargeant
1983 **Coitionary Tales** P Bull, K Williamson
1983 **Cool Moon** N White
1983 **Affluence of Incahol** Unknown
1984 Feb 26 **Angus** D Hillebrandt, A Cole
1984 March 5 **The 19th Hole** D Hillebrandt, I Morris, A Cole
Direct Finish by D Hillebrandt and I Morris on 25 April 1984.
1984 April 1 **Orca** J Hooper, M Doyle (AL)
1984 April 1 **Supercruise** M Doyle, J Hooper
1984 April 1 **Top Secret** R Cope, D Hillebrandt (AL)
1984 April 1 **Open Secret** D Hillebrandt, R Cope (AL)
1984 April 7 **Rising Moisture** M Fowler, S Fenwick (AL), P Watts
1984 April 13 **Haile Selassie** I Peters, P O'Sullivan
1984 April 14 **Little and Large** M Fowler, C Watts (AL)
1984 April 20 **Slippery Mhic** M Fowler, A Saunders
1984 April 20 **Reefer Madness** P O'Sullivan, D Sargeant
1984 April 21 **Bloodbath** A Saunders, M Fowler (AL)
1984 April 28 **Wolf Solent** I Peters, R Croft
1984 April 29 **Sunny Sunday Stroll** A Cole, D Hillebrandt (AL)
1984 April **Black Slab, Crustacean** R Cope, P O'Sullivan
1984 April **Private Enterprise** P O'Sullivan, I Thomas, D Ball
1984 May 5 **Making Plans for Nigel** M Fowler, C Jones, P Watts
1984 May 12 **Dog Burglar** M Fowler, A Saunders
1984 May 19 **Cool, Culm and Collected** C Nicholson, M Minky, N White
1984 May 19 **Black Night** Unknown
1984 May 27 **Thief of Baghdad, Sinbad** P O'Sullivan, I Peters, K Tole
1984 May 27 **Sheik of Araby** I Peters, P O'Sullivan, K Tole
1984 May 29 **Icarus** (Penhale) D Hillebrandt, A Cole
1984 May 31 **Machineries of Joy** C Jones, W Porter
1984 May **Gardener's Delight** I Day, A N Other
1984 June 2 **Cockney Disorder** M Fowler, C Watts
1984 June 3 **Sunday, Bloody Sunday, Stormy Weather** P O'Sullivan, K Tole
1984 June 3 **Alison's Rib, Failure to Thrive, Sweat Test** D Hillebrandt, A Gillams
1984 June 10 **Crack of Doom** M Doyle, D Hillebrandt (AL)

1984 June 16	**Cuchulain** I Thomas, P O'Sullivan
1984 June 23	**Pressure Drop** P O'Sullivan, M Doyle, I Thomas
1984 June 23	**Finn McCool** P O'Sullivan, I Thomas, M Doyle
1984 July 7	**Dirty Dick** P O'Sullivan, M Doyle
1984 July 8	**Crystal** J Hooper, J Francom
1984 July 15	**World's Weird Wall** P O'Sullivan, M Doyle (AL)
1984 July 19	**Bradworthy 5** I Peters, P O'Sullivan
1984 July 23	**Nautilus, Nemo** P O'Sullivan, G Lloyd
1984 Aug 16	**A Tonic for the Troops, Diamond Smiles** C Nicholson, N White *A bold line up* The Smile *wall.*
1984 Aug 17	**West South West** P O'Sullivan, M Dunning
1984 Aug 18	**The Red O** P O'Sullivan, A Glanville
1984 Aug 19	**Red Tape** P O'Sullivan, A Glanville
1984 Aug 22	**Tread with Care** D Ferguson, D Hillebrandt
1984 Aug 25	**North Buttress** D Hillebrandt, R Piper, D Ferguson
1984 Aug	**Red Carnation** B Rossiter, P O'Sullivan
1984 Sept 9	**Protoscopy** D Hillebrandt, M Doyle
1984 Sept 24	**Gun Money** P O'Sullivan, A Pearson
1984 Nov 4	**Mortal Coil** P O'Sullivan, M Dunning
1984 Nov 25	**Up the Ante** P O'Sullivan, M Dunning
1984 Dec 9	**Satanic Slab** D Hillebrandt, J Lucas
1984	**The Beast** (Compass Point) A Bedland (solo)
1985 Jan 4	**Box of Delights** P O'Sullivan, M Dunning
1985 Jan 13	**Pandora** P O'Sullivan, M Dunning, D Sargeant
1985 Feb 3	**Little Dribbler** P O'Sullivan, M Dunning, R Cope
1985 Feb 3	**Wellington's Stand** R Cope, M Dunning, P O'Sullivan
1985 Feb 3	**Cuboid** P O'Sullivan, M Dunning
1985 Feb 17	**Sally, Ra, Little Robert** D Hillebrandt, J Lucas
1985 March 8	**Iron Fist** P O'Sullivan, T Fryer
1985 March 30	**Detroit** A Watt, I Peters, P O'Sullivan
1985 April 6	**Frog Abuse, Fisting Groove** M Fowler, P Watts
1985 April 8	**Silver Lining** P R Littlejohn, M Burgoyne
1985 April 10	**Easter Risings** P O'Sullivan, R Cope
1985 April 10	**The Curate's Egg** I Peters, A Clark
1985 April 14	**Joker Man** P Baker
1985 April 14	**Gonad** M Davies (solo)
1985 April 19	**Maggie's Mistake** D Hillebrandt, J Lucas *The variation start was climbed on 15 September 1996; climbers unknown.*
1985 April 20	**Arabesque** P O'Sullivan, A Watt
1985 April 29	**The Awakening** R Edwards, M Edwards
1985 April 30	**The Haze** M Edwards, R Edwards *A profitable return to Carn Gowla.*
1985 May 1	**Red Parade** M Doyle, D Hillebrandt *A fine climb in unlikely surroundings.*
1985 June 1	**Last of the Big Nuts** N Hancock, J Wilson
1985 June 10	**Steam Power** I Peters, P O'Sullivan (AL)
1985 June 10	**Zanussi** I Peters, P O'Sullivan *The appliance of science!*
1985 June 16	**Fallen Angel** P Bull, N Tetley (AL)

The Entertainer (E3) Compass Point
Climber: Frank Ramsay Photo: Dave Turnbull

Streamline (E4 ~ first ascent), Speke's Mill Mouth
Climber: Simon Young Photo: Andy Grieve

Four for Texas (E2 ~ first ascent) Carn Gowla
Climber: Tony Penning   Photo: David Hope

Rainbow Games (E2) Carn Gowla
Climber: Kath Pyke Photo: Ian Parnell

1985 July 13 **Capital Offence** M Doyle, P O'Sullivan
... being the placement of a bolt used for protection and aid. It is now climbed without, but the first free ascent has not been recorded.

1985 July 13 **Dynamo Hum** (Doyden) M Fowler, S Fenwick, A Sawyer

1985 July 13 **Illegal Alien** M Fowler, S Fenwick
Pitch 1 variation climbed by M J Crocker and D Henderson on 8 April 1995.

1985 July 15 **Soggy Socks** I Peters, D Hillebrandt

1985 July 25 **Gnome Killer** D Hillebrandt, J Lucas

1985 July **Weighout** J Hooper, M Doyle

1985 Aug 1 **Ghecko Blaster** P Bull, M Lee

1985 Aug 17 **Full Term** D Hillebrandt

1985 August **Hot, Sweet, and Sticky** H Tingle, A N Other

1985 Sept 13 **Front Loader** P O'Sullivan, D Sargeant

1985 Sept 27 **Little Woo** D Hillebrandt, I Morris

1985 Sept 28 **Poker Face** C Nicholson, I Peters

1985 Oct 28 **Stiff Upper Lip** P O'Sullivan, D Ball

1985 Oct 29 **Anna** D Hillebrandt

1985 Nov 22 **Hadrian** P O'Sullivan, R Cope, J Barber

1985 Nov 24 **AWOL, Groundfall** P O'Sullivan, R Cope

1985 Dec 6 **Frostbite** I Peters, J Barber (AL)

1985 Dec 9 **Feint** D Thomas (solo)

1985 Dec 9 **Margin** S Young, D Thomas

1985 Dec 9 **Ruled** D Thomas, S Young

1985 Dec 12 **Hard Tack** I Peters, R Perriment

1985 Dec 31 **Master of Deceit** I Peters, K Hosie, P Buttrick

1985 **Totem Pole** M Fowler, P Bingham

1985 **Wet Pig** B Craig, S Fenwick, P Bingham
Named after a failed Tyrolean on the return.

1985 **Inferno** P Bull, N Tetley
Baggy's friction tested. One point of aid, eliminated by C Nicholson in 1986.

1986 Jan 26 **Visco-City** I Peters, A N Other

1986 Jan **Javelin** P O'Sullivan and party

1986 March 26 **The French Connection** D Hillebrandt, N Seguier

1986 March 27 **Gabion** J Barber, P O'Sullivan

1986 March 27 **Tetrapod** J Barber, P O'Sullivan

1986 March 28 **Archie Andrews** P O'Sullivan, J Barber

1986 March 29 **In Memoriam** (Vicarage Cliff) D Hillebrandt, C Stripp

1986 March 30 **Tombstone** C Stripp, D Hillebrandt

1986 April 3 **Parallel Flow** J Barber, P O'Sullivan, S Bell

1986 April 6 **Gambit, Endgame, Zugzwang** K Hosie, I Peters (VL)
Pitch 1 of Endgame had been climbed some years earlier by R Turnbull, R Swinden, and R Croft. The two rest-points on Zugzwang were soon eliminated by S Cardy.

1986 April 12 **Spoils of War** S Bell, P O'Sullivan
A much-eyed line at Lower Sharpnose.

1986 April 24 **Break On Through** P R Littlejohn, P Amphlett
The old protagonist returns. A breakthrough in Culm Coast standards.

1986 April 26 **Flying Circus** I Peters, K Hosie
1986 April 26 **Claire** D Hillebrandt, C Stripp
1986 May 15 **Sigmoidoscopy** D Hillebrandt, B Rowe
They should be ashamed of themselves!
1986 May 15 **Fay** P R Littlejohn, M Hardwick
1986 May 15 **Crooked Mile** M Hardwick, P R Littlejohn
1986 May 16 **Twilight Zone, Pacemaker** P R Littlejohn, M Hardwick
A superb haul finally takes Lower Sharpnose into the 80s.
1986 May 17 **Exit Route** Unknown
1986 May **Under Pressure** (Damehole Point) P O'Sullivan, A Watt
1986 July 6 **Seal Clubbing** B Davison, R Jones, A Smith
1986 July 19 **Open Day** P O'Sullivan, P Parsons
1986 Aug 24 **Micro Non Entity** A Grieve, K Palmer
1986 Sept 4 **The Promenade** D Thomas (solo)
1986 Sept 5 **Embers** D Thomas
1986 Sept 6 **Just Natural** E R Hart, D Hope, I Peters
1986 Sept 9 **Contraband, The Last Lap** D Thomas, D Hubbard
1986 Sept 9 **Clipper** D Thomas (solo)
1986 Sept 27 **Alice** D Hillebrandt, C Stripp
1986 Sept 28 **Widowmaker** I Peters, D Hillebrandt
1986 Sept **Green Slime Crime** D Sargeant, K Bailey
1986 Oct 12 **Through the Looking-Glass** (Pentire) T Penning, D Hope
A long-awaited solution to Pentire's hanging groove.
1986 Oct 12 **Twilight** T Penning, R W Lanchbury
1986 Oct **The Rook** P O'Sullivan, K Hosie (AL)
1986 Nov **Ripsnorter** P O'Sullivan, J Barber
1986 **Chouinard's Back Yard** Unknown
1987 Jan 15 **Salute to the Admiral** D Hillebrandt, J O'Neill
Climbed soon after Admiral Lawder's death as a memorial. Cornwall's first recorded ice-climb!
1987 Feb 22 **Duty Free** I Peters, J Barber
1987 Feb 22 **Bootleggers** J Barber, I Peters
1987 March 9 **Alaska** I Peters, D Hillebrandt
1987 March 9 **The Dimpsy** D Hillebrandt, I Peters
1987 April 22 **Early Ming, Ning Nong** C Nicholson, M Courtier
1987 April 26 **Paschendaele** P O'Sullivan, K Hosie
Pitch 3 variation climbed by M Fowler in May 1991.
1987 April 26 **CJW Arête, Tom's Route** D Hillebrandt, D Waind, J Squire
1987 May 4 **American Express** C Nicholson, M Courtier
1987 May 4 **Cold Snap, Grypt-Up Phynne** N White, C Alston
1987 May 5 **Nirex** P O'Sullivan, N Crowhurst
1987 May 6 **Hotpoint** P O'Sullivan, P Telford, J Barber, E Primeau
1987 May 14 **Blackthorn Winter** C Nicholson, M Courtier
1987 May 17 **Coronary Country** S Monks, J Wilkinson
Initially graded E7 (the area's first), it gained a reputation for defeating visitors intent on making the second ascent. It has now settled at hard E6, but continues to prove a very tricky on-sight lead.
1987 May 18 **The Devonian** S Monks, J Wilkinson
1987 May 27 **Black Magic** (Pentire) S Monks, J Wilkinson
1987 May 28 **Culm Dancing** (Lower Sharpnose) S Monks, J Wilkinson

1987 May 31 **Dangerous Driver** G Butler, N Hancock
1987 May 31 **The Suicidal Optimist** N Hancock, G Butler
1987 May **Triton** D Hillebrandt, D Waind
Created from the remains of an earlier route, Neptune. *The Direct Start by B R E Wilkinson and M A Grapes on 6 June 1993.*
1987 June 20 **Somewhere over the Rainbow** P O'Sullivan
1987 June **Sea Green** R Harrison, K Marsden
1987 June **Magnox** P O'Sullivan, N Crowhurst
1987 July 5 **Chase the Dragon** P O'Sullivan, P Telford
1987 July 12 **Rant** P O'Sullivan, N Crowhurst
1987 July **Mustard, Urco's Revenge** R Harrison, D Carter
1987 Aug 15 **The Butterfly Boy** B R E Wilkinson, J Gregory
1987 Aug 23 **Wafer Phynne, Wraith** N White, C Alston
1987 Aug 23 **Misery Goat** C Alston, N White
When the Goat Comes In *climbed by C Waddy, M Silcocks, J Bull in April 1988.*
1987 Aug 30 **Touch the Devil** T Penning
1987 Aug 30 **Sinners** T Penning, R W Lanchbury
1987 Aug 31 **Robert of Pentire** T Penning, P Cresswell, R W Lanchbury
1987 Aug 31 **Reflections** T Penning, P Cresswell
1987 Aug 31 **Propeller** B R E Wilkinson, I Day
1987 Sept 20 **Four for Texas** T Penning, R W Lanchbury, P Creswell, D Hope
1987 Sept 20 **A Sackful of Clowns** D Hope, T Penning, R W Lanchbury, P Cresswell
A little exploration turns up two more hidden gems for Gowla's crown.
1988 Feb 21 **Culm to Mother** N White
1988 Feb 21 **Help Save the Rhino** B Aikman, N White
1988 Feb 21 **Finesse, Small Plate McGinty** C Waddy, A Gostick
1988 Feb 21 **Kansas City** T Penning, R W Lanchbury
1988 May 21 **Play It Straight** P R Littlejohn
1988 May 22 **Solace** P R Littlejohn (solo)
The variation start climbed by E Heslam and B R E Wilkinson on 7 July 1989.
1988 June 19 **Spirit, Tipi, Yellow Hair** D Hope
1988 June 19 **How the West Was Won** T Penning, D Hope
1988 June 19 **Shaman** D Hope, R W Lanchbury, P Cresswell
1988 June 19 **Touch the Earth** D Hope, R W Lanchbury
1988 June 19 **Alex of Gowla** T Penning, R W Lanchbury, P Cresswell, D Hope
1988 June 19 **Indian Country** T Penning, P Cresswell, D Hope
1988 June 30 **Dark Side of the Zawn** D Hillebrandt, D Waind
1988 June **Your Funeral, My Trial** C Waddy, E Stone
1988 July 14 **Artifice, Innocents, Rampo, Silverfish** D Hope, D Hillebrandt
1988 July 16 **Blackfoot Trots** D Hope
1988 July 16 **Counting Coup, The Hairy Men from the East** D Hope, A Milburn
1988 Aug **Graceless** D Hope, D Hillebrandt, D Waind
1988 Sept 14 **Rectory Tearooms** D Hillebrandt, K Atkinson
1988 Oct 1 **Touch and Go** D Carroll, D Viggers
1988 Oct 2 **The Oldest Swingers in Town** D Viggers, D Carroll (AL)

1988 Oct 13 **Choss and Chips** D Hillebrandt, D Waind, K Atkinson
1988 Oct 23 **Romping Robert** D Hillebrandt, K Atkinson, D Waind
1988 Nov 3 **Shady Pete** D Hillebrandt (solo)
1988 Dec 20 **Shortcake** D Hope, J Cornwell
1988 Dec **Hearts and Minds** F Ramsay, N White
1988 **Dry Stone Wall** C Waddy, F Ramsay
The Magic Carpet Finish climbed by N Jenkins and J Jordan on 9 May 1994.
1988 **Helsinki** C Waddy
1988 **Lord Lucan is Missing** J Wyatt, AN Other
1989 April 13 **Duff Hunch** D Hillebrandt (solo)
1989 April 13 **Two Williams' Wall** D Hillebrandt, D Waind
1989 April 22 **Set the Controls** D Carroll, D Viggers
1989 April **Ku Klux Klan** C Waddy, R Rogers
1989 April **Pete's Route** P Bull, C Alston
1989 May 14 **Piran P** D Hillebrandt, K Atkinson, K Muncie
1989 May 21 **Israel Gow** D Hannigan, D Hillebrandt (AL)
1989 May 30 **Lucky Streak** P Bull, C Alston
1989 May 30 **Ordinary Man, The English Way** D Hope, J Cornwell
1989 May 31 **Azrael** N White, D Pegg
1989 May **A Handful of Rust, The Monk's Satanic Verses** M Edwards, R Edwards
The latter an outsandingly technical and bold lead, still unrepeated.
1989 June 4 **Smugglers and Rockpools** D Hillebrandt, A Moore, K Atkinson
1989 June 24 **A Most Peculiar Practice, Quiet Desperation** D Hope, J Cornwell, A Camm
1989 July 1 **Rock-a-Bye-Baby, The Somme** E Heslam, B R E Wilkinson
The latter on sight in wet conditions.
1989 July 1 **Tiger's Eye** B R E Wilkinson, E Heslam
1989 July 8 **Down to a Sunless Sea** D Carroll, D Viggers
Controversial use (at the time) of seven pegs in one pitch, but a quality route nevertheless.
1989 July 9 **Haile Dubious** D Viggers, D Carroll
1989 July 9 **Soweto** J Biddle, C Flood
With one point of aid; climbed free by J Biddle five days later.
1989 July 14 **Vive la Revolution** J Biddle (solo)
1989 July 20 **Mary's Journey** D Hillebrandt, P Austin
1989 July 20 **Surface Tension** D Thomas, N White
1989 July 22 **The Pastafarian** D Viggers, D Carroll
1989 July 23 **Darkness Visible, Knight's Move** E Heslam, G Williams
The former on sight in wet conditions.
1989 July 23 **Sacred River** D Carroll, D Viggers
1989 July 24 **The Culmination** D Thomas, N White
1989 July 24 **The Earthsea Trilogy Part 1** N White, D Thomas
Two powerful routes in one day by an on-form team.
1989 July 30 **Consolation** (Kellan Head)**, Deliverance, The Bishop** E Heslam, C Thomas
Consolation *with one point of aid. Climbed free on 14 April 1995 by M J Crocker and R Chappell.*

1989 Aug 14 **Must Be Mental, Why Me Mum?** P Matthews
1989 Aug 23 **Consenting Adults, Katabatic** D Carroll, D Viggers
1989 Aug **Creeping Flesh** K Palmer, P Saunders
The Great Slab (Smoothlands) breached, opening the way for further developments.
1989 Aug **Divergent Thinking** E Heslam, B R E Wilkinson
1989 Aug **Ironbeak** B Rowe, K Bater, A N Other
1989 Sept 7 **Belly Board, Malibu, Pat** D Hillebrandt, K Atkinson
1989 Sept **The Mighty Quin** E Heslam, C Thomas
1989 Nov 26 **Gizmo** B R E Wilkinson, E Heslam
1989 Nov 26 **Lifeline** E Heslam
1989 Nov 29 **Sunstruck** B R E Wilkinson, P A Wilcox
1989 Dec 27 **Harpoon** B R E Wilkinson, P A Wilcox
1989 Dec 28 **Sol** B R E Wilkinson, P A Wilcox
1989 **Dogsbody** C Waddy
1989 **Tales of Don Juan** P Bull
1989 **Hobson's Choice** A Evans
1990 Jan 11 **Cyclops, Minotaur** B R E Wilkinson, P A Wilcox
1990 March 9 **Volupte** B R E Wilkinson, P A Wilcox
1990 March 17 **Sensual Seas** B R E Wilkinson, P A Wilcox
1990 April 4 **Blackwater Down, Virgo** B R E Wilkinson, P A Wilcox
1990 April 28 **Joi de Vivre** B R E Wilkinson, P A Wilcox
1990 April 29 **Where There's a Will** D N Turnbull, A Donson
Climbed in mistake for Private World. *It was even reported in the French magazine* Vertical, *but still awaits a first French ascent!*
1990 April 30 **Hellbound** K Palmer, A Grieve (AL)
The scene of three 50-foot falls onto RPs during an attempted second ascent by A Donson.
1990 May 12 **Titanic Nights** B R E Wilkinson, P A Wilcox
1990 May 27 **Looking for a Rainbow, Rainbow Games, The Song of the Shirt** D Hope, A Camm
1990 June 9 **Travelling Man** F Ramsay, D Smith (AL)
1990 June **The Strangest Secret** D N Turnbull, F Ramsay
1990 July 14 **A Wok on the Wild Side, Bitter Minnows** D Hope, J Cornwell
1990 July 28 **The Mongfish** J Biddle, J Williams
1990 Aug 11 **Psycho-soma** B R E Wilkinson, P A Wilcox
1990 Aug 12 **Athabasca Falls** M J Crocker
1990 Sept 1 **Haunted by Hoodoos** M J Crocker, R Thomas
1990 Sept 17 **Spanking Colonel** M Corbett, D Hillebrandt
1990 Sept 22 **Black Dog** B Rowe, D Hillebrandt, M Corbett
1990 Sept 22 **Rockhound** M Corbett, B Rowe, D Hillebrandt
1990 Sept 30 **Bulldyke** G Forward, M Corbett
1990 Oct 7 **Lazy Dawg** B Rowe, D Hillebrandt, B R E Wilkinson
1990 Oct 9 **The Snuffler** M Whitaker, R Howard
1990 Oct 12 **Compass-tures Green** C Rees
1990 Oct 12 **Persistent Pup** D Hillebrandt, B Rowe
1990 Oct 13 **Over the Moon** M Corbett, G Forward
Corbett begins the Cow and Calf offensive, and gives the crag a new lease of life.
1990 Oct 14 **Tormented Tendon** J O'Neil, J Dyer

1990 Oct 20 **Howling at the Moon** J Matthias, G Forward, M Corbett
1990 Oct 22 **Boiling Mercury, Pearl Necklace** M Corbett, G Forward
1990 Oct 24 **Elisa Johanna** M Corbett, G Forward, J Matthias
1990 Oct **Dr Bollox** G Forward, J Potokar, M Corbett
1990 Nov 3 **Lord Bafta** F Ramsay, D Smith (AL)
1990 Nov 4 **Luminarc** B R E Wilkinson, P A Wilcox
1990 Nov 18 **Dog Day Afternoon** B Rowe, D Hillebrandt
1990 Nov 25 **Jizz** G Forward, M Corbett
1990 Nov 25 **Stalking Horse** M Corbett, G Forward
1990 Dec 2 **Avalon** B R E Wilkinson, P A Wilcox
1990 Dec 23 **Dinner with the Creggs** D Hillebrandt, K Atkinson
The Creggs are a local family of folk legend who lived in a cave near Clovelly and ate passing travellers.
1991 Jan 13 **Desert Storm** M Corbett, G Forward
1991 May 4 **Lunartic** M Corbett, G Forward
1991 May 25 **Slave to the Rhythm** A Grieve, L Earnshaw
1991 May 27 **The Flying Finn** C Alston, P Bull
1991 May **Candyman** D Ryden, M Faucher
1991 May **Nanda's Delight** M Fowler, M Lasota
1991 June 12 **Bird Ban** D Carroll, D Viggers
1991 June 14 **Bugsy** D N Turnbull, H Hooper, C Rees
A seminal route, showing what could be done on The Black Wall. Second ascent solo by I Parnell.
1991 June 15 **Abandon Hope...** D N Turnbull, C Rees
The longest roof on the North Coast.
1991 June 26 **Pit Bull** D Ryden, J Hunt
1991 July 26 **Waisted Youth** P Cooper, A Weare
1991 July **The Naked God** F Ramsay, R Swift
1991 Aug 1 **Up Yours** A Weare, P Cooper
1991 Aug 4 **Another Nervous Breakdown, Beneath Black Waters** M J Crocker
1991 Aug 13 **Greenwitch, Groove of Illusions** D Hope, J Cornwell
1991 Aug 14 **Heaven in Your Eyes** Jon Bowden, Joe Bowden
1991 Aug 17 **Compass Mentis** C Rees, A Grieve
1991 Aug 18 **Take My Breath Away** Joe Bowden, Jon Bowden
1991 Aug 26 **Destination Unknown** D Hillebrandt, Joe Bowden, Jon Bowden
1991 Aug **Mountain Biker** C Rees
1991 Sept 3 **Second Coming** L Earnshaw, A Grieve
The logical and better approach to the Easter Risings *slab.*
1991 Sept 3 **The Kiss** C Rees, A Grieve
1991 Sept 4 **Tunnel Vision** A Grieve, L Earnshaw
1991 Sept 8 **A Groove Full of Mirrors** M J Crocker, G A Jenkin
1991 Sept 21 **Fantasy Land** D Smith, J Tidmus
1991 Oct 6 **Floodland** M Lee, A Forbes
1991 Oct 13 **The Flight of the Laden Swallow** S Hawken, C Carpenter
1991 Oct **Mini Moose's Turnip Poem** D Ryden (roped solo)
1991 **Boj Wolb** T Greenhalgh (solo)
1991 **Crutch Upon Crutch** T Greenhalgh, D Haydock
1991 **Samantha** T Greenhalgh, K Bungee
1992 Feb 5 **Sailing the Seas of Cheese** P Twomey, J Hunt, I Parnell

1992 April 4 **Elend, Little Lambs, Silence of the Lambs** D Hillebrandt, K Siemund
1992 April 4 **Pale Fire, Ragamuffin** I Parnell, J Winby
1992 April 4 **Rock-Pool Slab** Unknown
1992 April 12 **What Goes Up** A Forbes, K Siemund
1992 May 4 **Hellhound on My Trail** P Twomey, J Hunt
1992 May 17 **Ocean Colour Dream** M J Crocker
1992 May 17 **Faschisti, Isle of Avalon** M J Crocker, P O'Sullivan
A drained O'Sullivan was later heard to exclaim 'After all these years, I'd like to know who gave him my telephone number'.
1992 May 17 **Kermit** M Kemball, L Bartrop
1992 May 20 **Eeyore** C Alston, D Hanson
1992 May 24 **Bert** M Kemball, C Calow
1992 May 24 **Elmo** M Kemball, C Calow, W McKee
1992 May 24 **Ernie** C Calow, M Kemball
1992 May 24 **Snuffelupagus** A Dorey, R Johnston
1992 May **The Rising Dark, Nipped in the Buddha** D Hope, A Camm
1992 June 21 **Barren Lands, Welcome to the Human Race** M J Crocker, J Harwood
1992 June **Coal Comfort** D Hope, J Cornwell
1992 July 4 **Frankly...** M J Crocker, F Ramsay
1992 July 5 **Polymorphous Pervert** B Rowe, D Hillebrandt
1992 July 5 **Spacewalker** D Hillebrandt, B Rowe
1992 July 5 **1492, Towards the Light** M J Crocker, F Ramsay
'To this day, this is the most exposed position I have landed myself in, on British rock.'
1992 July 6 **The Magic Wand** M J Crocker, F Ramsay (AL)
1992 July 12 **Arterial Bypass** D Carroll, D Viggers, B Watson
1992 July 19 **Dyer Need** S Mooney (solo)
1992 July 19 **Easy Culm, Easy Go** S Mooney, P Rigby
1992 July 19 **Languishing Limpet** S Mooney, R Wych, P Rigby
1992 July 25 **Kalahari Black** M J Crocker, J Harwood
A bold and serious testament to Crocker's drive and commitment. 'As if the route wasn't serious enough, spray from a moderate sea kept wetting the foot of the wall. Eventually we just went for it.'
1992 July **Escape Route** D Hillebrandt
1992 Aug 2 **Deimos** S Mooney, R Bloxham, B Voss
1992 Aug 2 **Gullible Too** S Mooney, B Voss, R Bloxham
1992 Aug 2 **Mind-Melt, Smoothtalkin'** M J Crocker, J Harwood
1992 Aug 16 **Zinfandel** B R E Wilkinson, M A Grapes
1992 Sept 20 **Atom Head** B R E Wilkinson, M A Grapes
1992 Sept 26 **Pilot Hotel** C Griffiths, D Hillebrandt
1992 Oct 3 **Dead Run Down** M J Crocker, F Ramsay
Pitch 2. Pitch 1 had been climbed by C Waddy and R Rogers in April 1989 (in mistake for Andromeda Strain).
1992 Oct 4 **Spotted Dick** B R E Wilkinson, M A Grapes
1992 Oct 4 **Last Testament** M J Crocker, A Tallant, G A Jenkin
Attempted earlier by I Parnell, who fell off the last move of the crux. The lightning reactions of his belayer, P Twomey, just prevented a ground fall from 50 feet.

1992 Oct 11 **Fitzharber** R Bloxham, S Mooney
1992 Oct 31 **'My Word Is My Bond'** J Potokar, D Hillebrandt, S Berry
1992 **Turbid Legacy** L Bartrop, L Bannister
1993 April 25 **The Ghost of Belle Aire** M J Crocker
The spiritual inhabitant of the Ramsay's house in Barnstaple. The first ascensionist and his wife were paid a visit by the ghost the night before while staying there.
1993 May 2 **Bolivian Consummation** D Hillebrandt, C Riggs
1993 May 2 **Medusa, The Trials of Isosceles** B R E Wilkinson, M A Grapes
1993 June 6 **Kalashnikov** B R E Wilkinson, M A Grapes
1993 June 13 **kLINGON kULTURE-sHOK** B R E Wilkinson, M A Grapes
Author and editor clashed over the application of guidebook 'house-style'; an uneasy compromise was reached!
1993 June 25 **Full Tilt** A Grieve
1993 June **Crescenda** M Raine, M Crayton
1993 July 6 **Unholy Communion** Unknown
Nick, Paul, and Eric did not risk confession (of their true identity).
1993 July 11 **La Bella Negra** B R E Wilkinson, M A Grapes
Wilkinson (re)discovers the Lynstone fins.
1993 July 17 **Holdrush** B R E Wilkinson, M A Grapes
1993 July **Bronte** J Dyer, J O'Neil
1993 Aug 15 **Big Sea Swimmer** D Scott-Maxwell (solo)
1993 Aug 15 **Up the Damehole** C Rees, D Scott-Maxwell, G Butler, P Dearden
1993 Aug 22 **Black Dog Bite, Obsidian Rose** B R E Wilkinson, M A Grapes
1993 Sept 3 **One for the Lager Drinkers** B Bigger, J Warren
1993 Sept 3 **The Midnight Garden** D Hope, J Cornwell
1993 Sept 11 **Bronco Belayer** S Hawken, A Grieve
1993 Sept 17 **Both Ends Burning** A Grieve, L Earnshaw
1993 Sept 25 **Mad Mags' Parasol** B R E Wilkinson, M A Grapes
1993 Sept 26 **Avoiding the Touch** S Hawken, L Earnshaw
1993 Oct 2 **Kicking Over the Traces** B R E Wilkinson, M A Grapes
1993 Oct 10 **Out of Season** D Scott-Maxwell, P Robertson
1993 Oct 24 **Millennium** B R E Wilkinson, M A Grapes
1993 Oct 31 **South Face of the Horn** B R E Wilkinson, M A Grapes
1993 Nov 19 **Frats in a Rage** B Rowe, D Hillebrandt
1993 Nov 27 **Green's Goolies** I Ross, D Hillebrandt
1993 Nov 27 **Time Critical Injury** D Hillebrandt, I Ross
1993 Nov 28 **Kleptomaniac** B R E Wilkinson, M A Grapes
1993 **Barefoot Lee's** L Bartrop (solo)
1993 **Sun, Sea, Sand** B R E Wilkinson, M A Grapes
One or more of these routes had probably been climbed before, but they were led and named in 1993 for inclusion in the guide.
1994 Jan 16 **Cancer Crack** M Rescorle, S Hawken
1994 Jan 16 **Heaven and Hell** S Hawken, L Earnshaw (AL)
Hawken proves that Cornakey and the spirit of adventure are not forgotten.
1994 Jan 16 **Till Dreaming's Done** B R E Wilkinson, M A Grapes
1994 Feb **Two Birds, One Stone** I Parnell, J Cheshire

1994 Feb **Fafnir** J Cheshire, I Parnell
1994 March 13 **Bison Bison** D Hillebrandt, R Knight
1994 April 10 **Heart By-Pass** D Henderson, P Wright
A classic natural 'line' discovered on an over-developed wall.
1994 April 30 **Absence** D Hillebrandt, I Ross
1994 May 1 **Sunscape** D Henderson
1994 May 22 **Blood Brothers, Flying Blind** B R E Wilkinson, G F Hollyman
The Cracking Up *finish to the latter climbed by M J Crocker (solo) on 7 April 1996.*
1994 May **Camming Round the Mountain** A Camm, D Hope
1994 June 16 **Shaken Not Stirred** D Hillebrandt, M Scholl, I Maddock, I Ross
1994 June 26 **Murphy's Nightmare** I Ross, D Hillebrandt, I Maddock
1994 June **Vickers** K Hosie, P O'Sullivan
1994 July 1 **Emmental Arête** I Parnell, D Henderson, A Sheahy
1994 July 3 **Culming Apart** A Moore, D Hillebrandt
1994 July 15 **The Right to Silence, Dark Angel** I Parnell, J Cheshire
After the former and the FFA of Freedom, *a quick drive from Northcott Mouth to Baggy saw Parnell abseiling down Cheesegrater Cliff with a saw and a length of two-by-two dangling from his harness in order to fashion the correct-sized wooden wedge (now gone) for the initial off-width.*
1994 July 16 **Wolfstone** M J Crocker, I Parnell
1994 July 16 **Where's Heinz?** M J Crocker, I Parnell
Where were H Zak and his camera when they were needed?
1994 July 16 **Eternity and a Spacious Grave** I Parnell, M J Crocker
1994 July 16 **Bitter Sweet** I Parnell, M J Crocker
1994 July 17 **Rise Above** I Parnell, M J Crocker
1994 July 17 **Saviourblade** M J Crocker, I Parnell
1994 July 18 **Bare Necessities** S Hawken, A Grieve
1994 July 18 **Gypsy Queen, One Stood against Many** M J Crocker, I Parnell
1994 July 18 **Wicked Gravity** I Parnell, M J Crocker
1994 July 23 **Flaky Pastry** M Jones, R Baker
1994 July 23 **Malefactor** P Twomey, I Parnell
1994 July 23 **Slice of Life** I Parnell, P Twomey
1994 July 24 **Big Black** I Parnell, P Twomey
1994 July 24 **Fortune Faces the Brave** P Twomey, I Parnell
Following in Turnbull's footsteps, Parnell and Twomey lay siege to The Black Wall. *After the pegs had been removed by a local activity centre, Parnell soloed both the above two routes. An audacious effort and major achievement.*
1994 July 30 **Knights of the Intriguing Niche, Overkeel, Pengenna Pie, Seadogger** M J Crocker, F Ramsay
1994 July 31 **The Big Sheep** F Ramsay, C Alston
1994 July 31 **Frank's Corner, Frank's Crack** F Ramsay, M J Crocker
1994 July 31 **Astroslide, Chancelot, Legend Has It** M J Crocker, D Sargeant
1994 July **Reunion** D Scott-Maxwell, G Butler, N Hancock
1994 Aug 4 **The Needle Tree** P Twomey, I Parnell

1994 Aug 4 **The Ungrateful Seconds** I Parnell, D Henderson, P Twomey
1994 Aug 5 **Oceans** P Twomey, D Henderson, I Parnell
1994 Aug 6 **Malawi, Zambia** M Wilson, S Wilson
1994 Aug 8 **Booby Prize** A Grieve
1994 Aug 8 **The Concrete Trampoline** D Ryden, J Cheshire
1994 Aug 13 **Merchants of Menace, Paranoia Express** D Hope, T Cruise
1994 Aug 14 **Pachyderm Pathway** D Hope, T Cruise
1994 Aug 20 **Brother Chris** D Hope, A Rai, T Nettleship
1994 Aug 20 **Faff** T Nettleship, A Rai, D Hope
1994 Aug 21 **The Joseph Bell, Warrior Mouse** D Hope, A Rai, T Nettleship
1994 Aug 28 **Colin's Grandma** T Nettleship, P Hitchin
1994 Aug 28 **Snake in the Grass** M Elphick, T Nettleship, P Newson, P Hitchin, D Hope
1994 Sept 25 **Satin** B R E Wilkinson, M A Grapes
1994 Oct 9 **Grapejuice Cocktail** B R E Wilkinson, M A Grapes
1994 **Electric Lemonade** W Morland, A Gipps
1994 **Give Us a Break** B R E Wilkinson, M A Grapes
1994 **Night Maer** P Twomey, I Parnell
1994 **Tha' Wer' 'Ard** W Morland, A Cunningham
1994 **Tha' Wer' Easy** W Morland, A Gipps, A Cunningham
1994 **Maxland Armadillo** A Ashley, B Marmer, M Williams
1994 **Savage Poodle** M Williams, A Ashley, B Marmer
1995 Feb 23 **Mine's a Point** S Hawken, A Grieve
1995 April 8 **Fanny Calder** S Atkinson, A Quennell
1995 April 8 **Yogic Flyer** D Henderson, M J Crocker
1995 April 8 **Wilting** M J Crocker, D Henderson
Climbed in mistake for Visage. 'By the time I realized my error I was hopelessly committed above hopeless gear!'
1995 April 9 **Kellan Arête** M J Crocker, D Henderson
1995 April 14 **Living Time Warp** M J Crocker, R Chappell
1995 April 14 **Kellan Corner** M J Crocker, R Chappell
1995 April 15 **Kellanesis** M J Crocker
1995 May 8 **Madame Sixtoes** B R E Wilkinson, M A Grapes
1995 May 13 **Back to the Old Ways** D N Turnbull, D Scott-Maxwell
1995 May 18 **Out to Lunch** D Hillebrandt, A Moore
1995 May 18 **Fingerin' the Dyke** N Hancock (solo)
1995 May 19 **Fear of a Black Planet** N Hancock (solo)
1995 May 22 **Bill the Bollock-Biter** D Hillebrandt, I Ross, M Scholl
1995 May 22 **de Genieter** M Scholl, I Ross, D Hillebrandt
1995 May 22 **Wall of Holes** D Hillebrandt, M Scholl, I Ross
1995 June 24 **Wheal Coates Wall** D Scott-Maxwell, N Hancock
1995 June 25 **Maxwell's Dream** N Hancock, D Scott-Maxwell
1995 July 1 **North Coast Fever** D N Turnbull, D Scott-Maxwell
1995 July 2 **Bend Over Backways** D Scott-Maxwell, D N Turnbull
1995 July 15 **Pigs in Zen, Turkish Delight** P Twomey, P Bull
1995 July 23 **Basketball with the President** N Hancock, M Wintroath
1995 July 29 **Reborn Man** P Twomey, D Thomas
1995 July 30 **Natrel Plus** J Cheshire, I Parnell

1995 July 30 **Pierrot le Fou** I Parnell, K Pyke
The rediscovery of The Black Walls proved fruitful.
1995 July **Little Black Dress** I Parnell, A Sheahy
1995 July **Black Rose** I Parnell, J Cheshire, D Ryden
1995 Aug 5 **Beach Bum, Day Tripper, Steep Sheep** D Hope, J Cornwell
1995 Aug 5 **Kamikaze Shrimp** D Hope
1995 Aug 6 **Exclusion Zone, Hiroshima Mon Amour, Safe Haven!?!** D Hope, J Cornwell
Fifty year anniversary of the dropping of the Bomb.
1995 Aug 6 **Death on a Stick, Hawaiian Pipeline** P Twomey, C Alston
1995 Aug 13 **Blue Juice** P Twomey, I Parnell
1995 Aug 13 **The Teardrop Explodes** S Hawken (solo)
1995 Aug 28 **Black Power** D Ryden, J Cheshire
1995 Sept 9 **Red Cloud, Ghost Dance** M Whitaker, P Cocks
1995 Sept 16 **Baffler** M Fowler, M Morrison
An overdue return of the Shale Guru to the coast.
1995 Sept 16 **Slugs on Jugs** S Sustad, S Yates (AL)
1995 Sept 16 **The Urge** M Fowler, M Morrison (AL)
1995 Sept 16 **Chossy Chimney** S Sustad, S Yates
1995 Sept 17 **Forces of Nature** M Fowler, M Morrison
Fowler resurfaces on Culm with a typically adventurous offering.
1995 Sept 17 **Raiders of the Lost Bark** S Yates, S Sustad
1995 Oct 10 **Borderline** S Hawken, A Grieve
Subsequently soloed by I Parnell thinking it was a first ascent.
1995 Nov 3 **Turmoil** D Hillebrandt, I Ross
1995 **Absence of Inselbergs** B Rowe, A Reynolds
1995 **Sundance** (Maer Cliff) N Hancock (solo)
1995 **Twilight Waters** I Parnell, C Alston, J Cheshire
1995 **Basketball with the President** Unknown
1996 Feb 3 **Bird's Nest Crack** D Ryden, J Cheshire
1996 March 2 **Moluscicide** D Ryden, J Cheshire
1996 March 9 **Never Too Slate** D Ryden, J Cheshire, A Forbes
1996 March 31 **Climbers' Club Very Ordinary** M Kemball, D Hillebrandt
1996 March 31 **Crater** D Hillebrandt, T Filmore, M Kemball
1996 April 6 **The Ex-man Cometh** M J Crocker, J Harwood
The most sustained full rope-length on Culm, and one of Britain's most challenging slab routes.
1996 April 7 **Carboverdrive, Left for Dead, Sprain Stop Play, Strip-Teaze, Sugar Puff Power, Training for The Eiger** M J Crocker
1996 April 8 **Brainchild** S Hawken, A Grieve
1996 April 21 **Lowlife, Swaying in the Wind** M J Crocker
1996 April 27 **Aimless, More than a Match** M J Crocker (roped solo)
1996 April 28 **A Dying Art, Crazy Paving, Hippodrome** M J Crocker (solo)
1996 April 28 **Moore's the Pity** D Hillebrandt, I Ross
1996 May 11 **A Scream Edgeways, Peardrop, Surrealands** M J Crocker (roped solo)
1996 May 12 **En Famille, Forthright, Homo Erectus, Qui-3, Straightjacket** M J Crocker

1996 June 22 **The Weaver** D Hillebrandt, M Scholl
Pitch 2 was climbed on 18.7.96.
1996 June 22 **Lieve Tina** M Scholl, D Hillebrandt
1996 June 30 **Mrs Pepper Pot** D N Turnbull, C Jones, M Carnall
1996 July 6 **Absolutely Adit, Bee Line, Crackline, Saline, Sideline** J Cheshire, D Ryden (VL)
The second named after an unpleasant apian incident nearby.
1996 July 18 **The Skiver, The Voice** D Hillebrandt, M Scholl
1996 July 20 **Jerusalem** D Scott-Maxwell, D N Turnbull
Another 'Henna Horror' type escapade up a daunting precipice.
1996 July 27 **Feline** J Cheshire, J Goode
1996 July 27 **Fine Line** D Ryden (solo)
1996 July 27 **Bubble Trouble** D Ryden, J Cheshire
1996 July **Bodysnatchers, The Name Doesn't Matter** S Young
1996 July **Bloodbeak** Unknown
1996 Aug 4 **Reality Bypass** D Ryden, J Cheshire (AL)
1996 Aug 6 **Toby's Corner** T Parkins, M Thompson
1996 Aug 6 **Chapel Porth Eliminate** M Thompson, T Parkins
1996 Aug 12 **Soul Shock** D Hope, G Catcheside
1996 Aug 13 **Ocean of Fears** D Hope, G Catcheside
1996 Aug 16 **Silent Screaming** D Hope, G Catcheside
1996 Sept 5 **Through the Looking-Glass** (Baggy Point) N Hancock, L Earnshaw (unroped)
1996 Sept 14 **Deceleration Lane** J Cheshire, D Ryden
1996 Sept 15 **Running on Empty** D Ryden, J Cheshire
1996 Sept 15 **Ali** M Kemball, D Hillebrandt
1996 Sept 15 **One for Curly** M Kemball, D Hillebrandt
1996 Sept 15 **Toje** D Hillebrandt, M Kemball
1996 Nov 16 **It'll End in Smears** A Grieve, J Putnam
1996 **Half a Point** I Parnell, C Alston
1996 **The Seafront** J Cheshire, K Pike (AL)
1997 March 8 **Stag Night Fright** D Scott-Maxwell, P Dearden, J Tidmus
A fightening, loose, and prickly adventure on the first ascensionist's stag night.
1997 March **Warts** B Rowe
1997 April **Poodle Power** D Ryden, M Lee
1997 May 26 **Penny for the Guy** A Grieve
1997 June 8 **Crispy Crack** K Pattinson, K Long, D Hillebrandt
1997 June 8 **Desolation** D Hillebrandt, K Long, K Pattinson
1997 June 8 **Shark's Fin** K Long, K Pattinson, D Hillebrandt
1997 June 15 **The Stunted Razor Snout** S Young
1997 June 15 **Streamline** Unknown
1997 June 18 **Ed** S Young
1997 June 28 **Hold-up** T Gavin, A Grieve
1997 July 5 **A Weekend on Mars, Pathfinder** M J Crocker, I Parnell
1997 July 6 **Rick, Kill** M J Crocker (solo)
1997 July 6 **Open Claw** M J Crocker, I Parnell
1997 July **Probing Phobia** L Bartrop, M Vigg, J Sehti
1997 Sept **Living with Looneys** B Rowe, A Grieve
1997 Sept **Mighty Wurlitzer** A Grieve, B Rowe
1997 Sept **The Flying Limpet** J Lloyd, A Grieve

1997 Nov 23 **More Tea, Vicar?** D Hillebrandt, B Rowe (AL)
1997 Nov 23 **The Bitch from the Bush** K Pattinson, K Long (AL)
1998 Feb 18 **Dutch Departure** B Rowe
1998 Feb 28 **Chapman's Sister, Who's Chapman?** M Kemball, R Galley
1998 Feb 28 **Was Chapman a Fat Boy?** R Galley, M Kemball
1998 June 14 **Schwarzchild** J Cowen
1998 July 19 **The Enchanted Cabbage Garden** D Hillebrandt, B Rowe
1998 Aug 3 **Dyer Straits** I Vickers
Another 'last great problem' succumbs to top-rope practice and an inspired lead.
1998 Aug 22 **O'Sullivan's Conundrum** M J Crocker (roped solo)
1998 Aug 23 **Cry of Love** J Lloyd, B Rowe
1998 Sept 20 **Midst of a Trauma** B Rowe, J Lloyd
1998 Oct **War without Tears** D Ryden, I Parnell
1998 Oct **Excellent Wall, Motion Sickness** I Parnell, D Ryden
1999 Jan 10 **The Coffins Wait for Betty Trembelow** B Rowe, D Hillebrandt
Sloo Slabs discovered by the peripatetic Dr Hillebrandt.
1999 Mar 14 **Concrete Karma** D Ryden, R Weigel
1999 May 1 **Molly's 29-Hour Party** C McGibbon
1999 May 11 **Foxman and Robin's Zawn Duel** L Bartrop, R Galley
1999 May 16 **Easy Prey, Hope for Hillebrandt** T Penning, J Boosey
1999 May 16 **Our Stars, Our Sky** D Hope, T Dunn, D Hillebrandt
1999 May 27 **Bent Sixpence** D Hillebrandt, A Moore
1999 June 15 **Ik Heb, Witch's Slide** D Hillebrandt, A Moore
1999 June 17 **Dark Night** S Young
1999 June 20 **The Mind Field** T Penning, J Boosey
'James, we've got a classic VS here.' Experience is a great teacher!
1999 June **After Dark, Angry Cockroaches, Mexican Blackbird** S Young
1999 July 3 **Kirsten's Last Climb** D Hillebrandt, A Partington
1999 July 7 **Longevity** A Comber, M Stephens
1999 July 14 **Inch In, Inch Out** L Bartrop, N Carter
1999 July 20 **Canard** S Young
1999 July 22 **Visit to the Quack Doctor** S Young
1999 July 23 **Water off a Duck's Back** N Dill
1999 July 26 **Diamondback** S Young, T Galvin, J Nichols
1999 July 28 **Whoops Apocalypse, Pounding Heart** T Penning, D Hope
The latter named in memory of Chris Pound.
1999 July **Exceptionally Smooth Bit Underside** L Bartrop, M Kemball
1999 July **The Incredible Hulk** S Young (solo)
1999 Sept 1 **The Black Hunter** T Penning, D Hope
1999 Sept 13 **Foaming Heels** D Hillebrandt, A Partington
1999 Sept 26 **Mother's Ruin** C Alston, B R E Wilkinson
1999 Oct 1 **The Crusade** I Parnell, D Ryden
Finally, after four attempts spread over five years.
1999 Oct 17 **Kung Fu Kecks** C Alston, B R E Wilkinson
Alston shows Wilkinson that you need a little more than a pair of fancy oriental trousers to cut the mustard at Lower Sharpnose.

Index

Addendum

The following route description was received after the book had been typeset.

Lye Rock

Echo Wall 285 feet Extremely Severe (1 pt aid) † (14.5.88)
An excellent adventurous route up the main wall of Lye Rock. Start at the left side of the boulders below the cliff, beneath a prominent, left-facing flake crack at 40 feet.
1 80 feet 4c. Climb the steepening slab and ear-shaped flake to a stance on top.
2 60 feet 5a. From the right-hand end of the ledge, a short overhanging wall leads to a quartz hand-traverse line. Follow this rightwards for 15 feet to a shallow corner, which leads to a ledge in the middle of the wall. Belay at the right-hand end.
3 75 feet 5b. Climb just right of the faultline above, and move into it at 30 feet. Traverse out right under a very dubious large block, and move 20 feet right to a short corner, which leads to an excellent ledge beneath the final overhangs.
4 70 feet 5c. Move 15 feet left along an obvious ramp-line and climb an overhanging, tenuous, right-trending weakness to the left end of the huge overhangs above the stance (peg to rest). Move right onto the slab above the overhangs, and follow the crack in the left-bounding corner to the top.
FA M Fowler, J Lincoln

New Climbs